James William Gilbart

The History, Principles, and Practice of Banking

Vol. 1

James William Gilbart

The History, Principles, and Practice of Banking
Vol. 1

ISBN/EAN: 9783743407923

Manufactured in Europe, USA, Canada, Australia, Japa

Cover: Foto ©ninafisch / pixelio.de

Manufactured and distributed by brebook publishing software (www.brebook.com)

James William Gilbart

The History, Principles, and Practice of Banking

STANDARD WORKS PUBLISHED BY

New Edition [1880], with a Supplement of upwards of 4600 New Words and Meanings.

WEBSTER'S DICTIONARY
OF THE ENGLISH LANGUAGE.

NOTE.—*The only authorized Editions of this Dictionary are those here described: no others published in England contain the Derivations and Etymological Notes of Dr. Mahn, who devoted several years to this portion of the Work.* See page 4.

WEBSTER'S GUINEA DICTIONARY

OF THE ENGLISH LANGUAGE. Thoroughly revised and improved by CHAUNCEY A. GOODRICH, D.D., LL.D., and NOAH PORTER, D.D., of Yale College.

The peculiar features of this volume, which render it perhaps the most useful Dictionary for general reference extant, as it is undoubtedly one of the cheapest books ever published, are as follows:—

1. **Completeness.**—It contains 114,000 words—more by 10,000 than any other Dictionary; and these are, for the most part, unusual or technical terms, for the explanation of which a Dictionary is most wanted.

2. **Accuracy of Definition.**—In this department the labours of Dr. Webster were most valuable, in correcting the faulty and redundant definitions of Dr. Johnson, which had previously been almost universally adopted. In the present edition all the definitions have been carefully and methodically analysed by W. G. Webster, Esq., the Rev. Chauncey Goodrich, Prof. Lyman, Prof. Whitney, and Prof. Gilman, with the assistance and under the superintendence of Prof. Goodrich.

3. **Scientific and Technical Terms.**—In order to secure the utmost completeness and accuracy of definition, this department has been subdivided among eminent Scholars and Experts, including Prof. Dana, Prof. Lyman, &c.

4. **Etymology.**—The eminent philologist, Dr. C. F. MAHN, has devoted five years to perfecting this department.

5. **The Orthography** is based as far as possible on Fixed Principles. *In all cases of doubt an alternative spelling is given.*

6. **Pronunciation.**—This has been entrusted to Mr. W. G. WEBSTER and Mr. WHEELER, assisted by other scholars. The pronunciation of each word is indicated by typographical signs, which are explained by reference to a KEY *printed at the bottom of each page.*

7. **The Illustrative Citations.**—No labour has been spared to embody such quotations from standard authors as may throw light on the definitions, or possess any special interest of thought or language.

8. **The Synonyms.**—These are subjoined to the words to which they belong, and are very complete.

9. **The Illustrations**, which exceed 3000, are inserted, not for the sake of ornament, but to elucidate the meaning of words which cannot be satisfactorily explained without pictorial aid.

The Volume contains 1628 pages, more than 3000 Illustrations, and is sold for One Guinea. It will be found, on comparison, to be one of the cheapest Volumes ever issued. Cloth, 21s.; half-bound in calf, 30s.; calf or half-russia, 31s. 6d.; russia, £2.

To be obtained through all Booksellers.

GEORGE BELL & SONS.

New Edition, with a New Biographical Supplement of upwards of 9700 Names.

WEBSTER'S COMPLETE DICTIONARY

OF THE ENGLISH LANGUAGE, AND GENERAL BOOK OF LITERARY REFERENCE. With 3000 Illustrations. Thoroughly revised and improved by CHAUNCEY A. GOODRICH, D.D., LL.D., and NOAH PORTER, D.D., of Yale College.

In One Volume, Quarto, strongly bound in cloth, 1919 pages, price £1 11s. 6d.; half-calf, £2; calf or half-russia, £2 2s.; russia, £2 10s.

Besides the matter comprised in the WEBSTER'S GUINEA DICTIONARY, this volume contains the following Appendices, which will show that no pains have been spared to make it a complete Literary Reference-book:—

A Brief History of the English Language. By Professor JAMES HADLEY. This Work shows the Philological Relations of the English Language, and traces the progress and influence of the causes which have brought it to its present condition.

Principles of Pronunciation. By Professor GOODRICH and W. A. WHEELER, M.A. Including a Synopsis of Words differently pronounced by different authorities.

A Short Treatise on Orthography, By ARTHUR W. WRIGHT. Including a Complete List of Words that are spelt in two or more ways.

An Explanatory and Pronouncing Vocabulary of the Names of Noted Fictitious Persons and Places, &c. By W. A. WHEELER, M.A. This Work includes not only persons and places noted in Fiction, whether narrative, poetical, or dramatic, but Mythological and Mythical names, names referring to the Angelology and Demonology of various races, and those found in the romance writers; Pseudonyms, Nick-names of eminent persons and parties, &c., &c. In fact, it is best described as explaining every name which is not strictly historical. A reference is given to the originator of each name, and where the origin is unknown a quotation is given to some well-known writer in which the word occurs.

This valuable Work may also be had separately, post 8vo., &c.

A Pronouncing Vocabulary of Scripture Proper Names. By W. A. WHEELER, M.A. Including a List of the Variations that occur in the Douay version of the Bible.

A Pronouncing Vocabulary of Greek and Latin Proper Names. By Professor THACHER, of Yale College.

An Etymological Vocabulary of Modern Geographical Names. By the Rev. C. H. WHEELER. Containing:—L A List of Prefixes, Terminations, and Formative Syllables in various Languages, with their meaning and derivation; II. A brief List of Geographical Names (not explained by the foregoing List), with their derivation and signification, all doubtful and obscure derivations being excluded.

Pronouncing Vocabularies of Modern Geographical and Biographical Names. By J. THOMAS, M.D.

A Pronouncing Vocabulary of Common English Christian Names, with their derivations, signification, and diminutives (or nick-names), and their equivalents in several other languages.

A Dictionary of Quotations. Selected and translated by WILLIAM G. WEBSTER. Containing all Words, Phrases, Proverbs, and Colloquial Expressions from the Greek, Latin, and Modern Foreign Languages, which are frequently met with in literature and conversation.

A New Biographical Dictionary of upwards 9700 Names of Noted Persons, Ancient and Modern, including many now living—giving the Name, Pronunciation, Nationality, Profession, and Date of Birth and Death.

A List of Abbreviations, Contractions, and Arbitrary Signs used in Writing and Printing.

A Classified Selection of Pictorial Illustrations (70 pages). With references to the text.

"The cheapest Dictionary ever published, as it is confessedly one of the best. The introduction of small woodcut illustrations of technical and scientific terms adds greatly to the utility of the Dictionary."—*Churchman.*

To be obtained through all Booksellers.

STANDARD WORKS PUBLISHED BY

WEBSTER'S DICTIONARY.

From the QUARTERLY REVIEW, *Oct.* 1873.

"Seventy years passed before JOHNSON was followed by Webster, an American writer, who faced the task of the English Dictionary with a full appreciation of its requirements, leading to better practical results." . . . .

"His laborious comparison of twenty languages, though never published, bore fruit in his own mind, and his training placed him both in knowledge and judgment far in advance of Johnson as a philologist. Webster's 'American Dictionary of the English Language' was published in 1828, and of course appeared at once in England, where successive re-editing *has as yet kept it in the highest place as a practical Dictionary.*"

"The acceptance of an American Dictionary in England has itself had immense effect in keeping up the community of speech, to break which would be a grievous harm, not to English-speaking nations alone, but to mankind. The result of this has been that the common Dictionary must suit both sides of the Atlantic." . . . .

"The good average business-like character of Webster's Dictionary, both in style and matter, made it as distinctly suited as Johnson's was distinctly unsuited to be expanded and re-edited by other hands. Professor Goodrich's edition of 1847 is not much more than enlarged and amended, but other revisions since have so much novelty of plan as to be described as distinct works." . . . .

"The American revised Webster's Dictionary of 1864, published in America and England, is of an altogether higher order than these last [The London Imperial and Student's]. It bears on its title-page the names of Drs. Goodrich and Porter, but inasmuch as its especial improvement is in the etymological department, the care of which was committed to Dr. MAHN, of Berlin, we prefer to describe it in short as the Webster-Mahn Dictionary. Many other literary men, among them Professors Whitney and Dana, aided in the task of compilation and revision. On consideration it seems that the editors and contributors have gone far toward improving Webster to the utmost that he will bear improvement. The *vocabulary has become almost complete,* as regards usual words, *while the definitions keep throughout to Webster's simple careful style,* and the derivations are assigned with the aid of good modern authorities."

"On the whole, the Webster-Mahn Dictionary as it stands, is most respectable, and **CERTAINLY THE BEST PRACTICAL ENGLISH DICTIONARY EXTANT.**"

LONDON: GEORGE BELL & SONS, YORK STREET, COVENT GARDEN.

GEORGE BELL & SONS.

SPECIAL DICTIONARIES AND WORKS OF REFERENCE.

Dr. Richardson's Philological Dictionary of the ENGLISH LANGUAGE. Combining Explanation with Etymology, and copiously illustrated by Quotations from the Best Authorities. *New Edition*, with a Supplement containing additional Words and further Illustrations. In 2 vols. 4to. £4 14s. 6d. Half-bound in Russia, £5 15s. 6d. Russia, £6 12s.

The *Words*, with those of the same family, are traced to their origin. The *Explanations* are deduced from the primitive meaning through the various usages. The *Quotations* are arranged chronologically, from the earliest period to the present time.

The Supplement separately. 4to. 12s.

An 8vo. edition, without the Quotations, 15s. Half-russia, 20s. Russia, 24s.

Synonyms and Antonyms of the English Language. Collected and Contrasted. By the late Ven. C. J. SMITH, M.A. Post 8vo. 5s.

Synonyms Discriminated. A Catalogue of Synonymous Words in the English Language, with their various Shades of Meaning, &c. Illustrated by Quotations from Standard Writers. By the late Ven. C. J. SMITH, M.A. Demy 8vo. 16s.

A Biographical Dictionary. By THOMPSON COOPER, F.S.A., Editor of "Men of the Time," and Joint Editor of "Athenæ Cantabrigienses." 1 vol. 8vo. 12s.

This volume is not a mere repetition of the contents of previous works, but embodies the results of many years' laborious research in rare publications and unpublished documents. Any note of omission which may be sent to the Publishers will be duly considered.

"It is an important original contribution to the literature of its class by a painstaking scholar.... It seems in every way admirable, and fully to justify the claims on its behalf put forth by its editor."—*British Quarterly Review.*

"The mass of information which it contains, especially as regards a number of authors more or less obscure, is simply astonishing."—*Spectator.*

"Comprises in 1210 pages, printed very closely in double columns, an enormous amount of information."—*Examiner.*

"Mr. Cooper takes credit to himself, and is, we think, justified in doing so, for the great care bestowed upon the work to insure accuracy as to facts and dates; and he is right perhaps in saying that his dictionary is the most comprehensive work of its kind in the English language."—*Pall Mall Gazette.*

A Biographical and Critical Dictionary of Painters and Engravers. With a List of Ciphers, Monograms, and Marks. By MICHAEL BRYAN. *Enlarged Edition, thoroughly revised.* [*In the press.*]

A Supplement of Recent and Living Painters. By HENRY OTTLEY. 12s.

The Cottage Gardener's Dictionary. With a Supplement, containing all the new plants and varieties to the year 1869. Edited by GEORGE W. JOHNSON. Post 8vo. Cloth. 6s. 6d.

LONDON: GEORGE BELL & SONS, YORK STREET, COVENT GARDEN

STANDARD WORKS PUBLISHED BY

THE ALDINE SERIES OF THE BRITISH POETS.
CHEAP EDITION.

In Fifty-two Volumes, Bound in Cloth, at Eighteenpence each Volume.

Akenside, with Memoir by the Rev. A. Dyce, and additional Letters. 1s. 6d.

Beattie, with Memoir by the Rev. A. Dyce. 1s. 6d.

Burns, with Memoir by Sir Harris Nicolas, and additional Copyright Pieces. 3 vols. 4s. 6d.

Butler, with Memoir by the Rev. J. Mitford. 2 vols. 3s.

Chaucer, edited by R. Morris, with Memoir by Sir Harris Nicolas. 6 vols. 9s.

Churchill, Tooke's Edition, revised, with Memoir, by James Hannay. 2 vols. 3s.

Collins, edited, with Memoir, by W. Moy Thomas. 1s. 6d.

Cowper, including his Translations. Edited, with Memoir, and Additional Copyright Pieces, by John Bruce, F.S.A. 3 vols. 4s. 6d.

Dryden, with Memoir by the Rev. R. Hooper, F.S.A. Carefully revised. 5 vols. 7s. 6d.

Falconer, with Memoir by the Rev. J. Mitford. 1s. 6d.

Goldsmith, with Memoir by the Rev. J. Mitford. Revised. 1s. 6d.

Gray, with Notes and Memoir by the Rev. John Mitford. 1s. 6d.

Kirke White, with Memoir by Sir H. Nicolas, and additional Notes. Carefully revised. 1s. 6d.

Milton, with Memoir by the Rev. J. Mitford. 3 vols. 4s. 6d.

Parnell, with Memoir by the Rev. J. Mitford. 1s. 6d.

Pope, with Memoir by the Rev. A. Dyce. 3 vols. 4s. 6d.

Prior, with Memoir by the Rev. J. Mitford. 2 vols. 3s.

Shakespeare, with Memoir by the Rev. A. Dyce. 1s. 6d.

Spenser, edited, with Memoir, by J. Payne Collier. 5 vols. 7s. 6d.

Surrey, edited, with Memoir, by James Yeowell. 1s. 6d.

Swift, with Memoir by the Rev. J. Mitford. 3 vols. 4s. 6d.

Thomson, with Memoir by Sir H. Nicolas. Annotated by Peter Cunningham, F.S.A., and additional Poems carefully revised. 2 vols. 3s.

Wyatt, edited, with Memoir, by James Yeowell. 1s. 6d.

Young, with Memoir by the Rev. J. Mitford, and additional Poems. 2 vols. 3s.

Complete sets may be obtained, bound in half-morocco. £9 9s.

N.B.—Copies of the Fine Paper Edition, with Portraits, may still be had, price 5s. per volume (except Collins, 2s. 6d.).

LONDON: GEORGE BELL & SONS, YORK STREET, COVENT GARDEN.

THE ALDINE EDITION OF THE BRITISH POETS.

SUPPLEMENTARY SERIES.

THE fifty-two volumes which have hitherto formed the well-known Aldine Series, embody the works of nearly all the more popular English poetical writers, whether lyric, epic, or satiric, up to the end of the eighteenth century. But since that time the wonderful fertility of English literature has produced many writers equal, and in some cases far superior, to the majority of their predecessors; and the widely augmented roll of acknowledged English poets now contains many names not represented in the series of "Aldine Poets."

With a view of providing for this want, and of making a series which has long held a high place in public estimation a more adequate representation of the whole body of English poetry, the Publishers have determined to issue a second series, which will contain some of the older poets, and the works of recent writers, so far as may be practicable by arrangement with the representatives of the poets whose works are still copyright.

One volume, or more, at a time will be issued at short intervals; they will be uniform in binding and style with the last fine-paper edition of the Aldine Poets, in fcap. 8vo. size, printed at the Chiswick Press. Price 5s. per volume.

Each volume will be edited with notes where necessary for elucidation of the text; a memoir will be prefixed, and a portrait, where an authentic one is accessible.

The following are already published:—

THE POEMS OF WILLIAM BLAKE. With Memoir by W. M. Rossetti, and portrait by Jeens.

THE POEMS OF SAMUEL ROGERS. With Memoir by Edward Bell, and portrait by Jeens.

THE POEMS OF THOMAS CHATTERTON. 2 vols. Edited by the Rev. W. Skeat, with Memoir by Edward Bell.

THE POEMS OF SIR WALTER RALEIGH, SIR HUGH COTTON, and Selections from other Courtly Poets. With Introduction by the Rev. Dr. Hannah, and portrait of Sir W. Raleigh.

THE POEMS OF THOMAS CAMPBELL. With Memoir by W. Allingham, and portrait by Jeens.

THE POEMS OF GEORGE HERBERT. (Complete Edition.) With Memoir by the Rev. A. B. Grosart, and portrait.

THE POEMS OF JOHN KEATS. With Memoir by Lord Houghton, and portrait by Jeens.

LONDON: GEORGE BELL & SONS, YORK STREET, COVENT GARDEN.

STANDARD WORKS PUBLISHED BY

In Ten Volumes, price 2s. 6d. each; in half-morocco, £2 10s. the set.

CHEAP ALDINE EDITION OF
SHAKESPEARE'S DRAMATIC WORKS.

EDITED BY S. W. SINGER.

Uniform with the Cheap Edition of the Aldine Poets.

' THE formation of numerous Shakespeare Reading Societies has created a demand for a cheap portable edition, with LEGIBLE TYPE, that shall provide a sound text with such notes as may help to elucidate the meaning and assist in the better understanding of the author. The Publishers therefore determined to reprint Mr. Singer's well-known Edition, published in 10 vols., small 8vo., for some time out of print, and issue it in a cheap form, uniform with the well-known Aldine Edition of British Poets.

CONTENTS.

Vol. I. The Life of Shakespeare. The Tempest. The Two Gentlemen of Verona. The Merry Wives of Windsor. Measure for Measure.

Vol. II. Comedy of Errors. Much Ado about Nothing. Love's Labour Lost. Midsummer Night's Dream. Merchant of Venice.

Vol. III. As You Like It. Taming of the Shrew. All's Well that Ends Well. Twelfth Night, or What You Will.

Vol. IV. Winter's Tale. Pericles. King John. King Richard II.

Vol. V. King Henry IV., Parts I. and II. King Henry V.

Vol. VI. King Henry VI., Parts I. II. and III. King Richard III.

Vol. VII. King Henry VIII. Troilus and Cressida. Coriolanus.

Vol. VIII. Titus Andronicus. Romeo and Juliet. Timon of Athens. Julius Cæsar.

Vol. IX. Macbeth. Hamlet. King Lear.

Vol. X. Othello. Antony and Cleopatra. Cymbeline.

Uniform with the above, price 2s. 6d; in half-morocco, 5s.

CRITICAL ESSAYS ON THE PLAYS OF SHAKESPEARE,

BY WILLIAM WATKISS LLOYD;

Giving a succinct account of the origin and source of each play, where ascertainable and careful criticisms on the subject-matter of each.

A few copies of this Work have been printed to range with the fine-paper Edition of the Aldine Poets. The price for the Eleven Volumes (not sold separately) is £2 15s.

LONDON: GEORGE BELL & SONS, YORK STREET, COVENT GARDEN.

GEORGE BELL & SONS.

POCKET VOLUMES.

A Series of Select Works of Favourite Authors, adapted for general reading, moderate in price, compact and elegant in form, and executed in a style fitting them to be permanently preserved. Imperial 32mo., cloth.

Gatty's Parables from Nature. 2 vols. 5s.
Captain Marryat's Masterman Ready. 2s. 6d.
Lamb's Elia. Eliana and Last Essay with Memoir, by BARRY CORNWALL. 2 vols. 5s.
Bacon's Essays. 2s. 6d.
Burns's Poems. 3s.
——— Songs. 3s.
Coleridge's Poems. 3s.
C. Dibdin's Sea-Songs and Ballads. And others. 3s.
Midshipman, The. Autobiographical Sketches of his own early Career, by Captain BASIL HALL, R.N., F.R.S. 3s. 6d.
Lieutenant and Commander. By Captain BASIL HALL, R.N., F.R.S. 3s. 6d.
George Herbert's Poems. 2s. 6d.
——— Remains. 2s.

——— Works. 3s. 6d.
The Sketch Book. By WASHINGTON IRVING. 3s. 6d.
Tales of a Traveller. By WASHINGTON IRVING. 3s. 6d.
Charles Lamb's Tales from Shakspeare. 3s.
Longfellow's Evangeline and Voices, Sea-side, and Poems on Slavery. 3s.
Milton's Paradise Lost. 3s.
——— Regained, & other Poems. 3s.
Robin Hood Ballads. 3s.
Southey's Life of Nelson. 3s.
Walton's Complete Angler. Portraits and Illustrations. 3s.
——— Lives of Donne, Wotton, Hooker, &c. 3s. 6d.
White's Natural History of Selborne. 3s. 6d.

Shakspeare's Plays & Poems. KEIGHTLEY's Edition. 13 Vols. in cloth case, 21s.

ELZEVIR SERIES.

Small fcap. 8vo.

These Volumes are issued under the general title of "ELZEVIR SERIES," to distinguish them from other collections. This general title has been adopted to indicate the spirit in which they are prepared; that is to say, with the greatest possible accuracy as regards text, and the highest degree of beauty that can be attained in the workmanship.
They are printed at the Chiswick Press, on fine paper, with wide margins, and issued in a neat cloth binding.

Longfellow's Evangeline, Voices, Sea-side and Fire-side. 4s. 6d. With Portrait.
——— Hiawatha, and The Golden Legend. 4s. 6d.
——— Wayside Inn, Miles Standish, Spanish Student. 4s. 6d.
Burns's Poetical Works. 4s. 6d. With Portrait.
——— Songs and Ballads. 4s. 6d.
These Editions contain all the copyright pieces published in the Aldine Edition.
Cowper's Poetical Works. 2 vols., each 4s. 6d. With Portrait.
Coleridge's Poems. 4s. 6d. With Portrait.

Irving's Sketch Book. 5s. With Portrait.
——— Tales of a Traveller. 5s.
Milton's Paradise Lost. 4s. 6d. With Portrait.
——— Regained. 4s. 6d.
Shakspeare's Plays and Poems. Carefully edited by THOMAS KEIGHTLEY. In seven volumes. 5s. each.
Southey's Life of Nelson. 4s. 6d. With Portrait of NELSON.
Walton's Angler. 4s. 6d. With a Frontispiece.
——— Lives of Donne, Hooker, Herbert, &c. 5s. With Portrait.

LONDON: GEORGE BELL & SONS, YORK STREET, COVENT GARDEN.

STANDARD WORKS PUBLISHED BY

HISTORY AND TRAVELS.

Rome and the Campagna. A Historical and Topographical Description of the Site, Buildings, and Neighbourhood of ancient Rome. By the Rev. ROBERT BURN, late Fellow and Tutor of Trinity College, Cambridge. With eighty engravings by JEWITT, and numerous Maps and Plans, and an Appendix, bringing the Work down to 1876. Demy 4to. £3 3s.

Ancient Athens; its History, Topography, and Remains. By THOMAS HENRY DYER, LL.D., Author of "The History of the Kings of Rome." Super-royal 8vo. Illustrated, cloth. £1 5s.

The History of the Kings of Rome. By Dr. T. H. DYER, Author of the "History of the City of Rome;" "Pompeii: its History, Antiquities," &c., with a Prefatory Dissertation on the Sources and Evidence of Early Roman History. 8vo. 16s.

Modern Europe, from the Fall of Constantinople in 1453. By THOMAS HENRY DYER, LL.D. Second Edition, Revised and Continued. In 5 vols. £2 12s. 6d.

The Decline of the Roman Republic. By the late GEORGE LONG, M.A., Editor of "Cæsar's Commentaries," "Cicero's Orations," &c. 8vo.
Vol. I. From the Destruction of Carthage to the End of the Jugurthine War. 14s.
Vol. II. To the Death of Sertorius. 14s.
Vol. III. Including the third Mithridatic War, the Catiline Conspiracy, and the Consulship of C. Julius Cæsar. 14s.
Vol. IV. History of Cæsar's Gallic Campaigns and of contemporaneous events. 14s.
Vol. V. From the Invasion of Italy by Julius Cæsar to his Death. 14s.

A History of England during the Early and Middle AGES. By C. H. PEARSON, M.A., Fellow of Oriel College, Oxford, and late Lecturer in History at Trinity College, Cambridge. Second Edition, revised and enlarged. 8vo. Vol. I. to the Death of Cœur de Lion. 16s. Vol. II. to the Death of Edward I. 14s.

Historical Maps of England. By C. H. PEARSON, M.A. Folio. Second Edition, revised. 31s. 6d.
An Atlas containing Five Maps of England at different periods during the Early and Middle Ages.

The Footsteps of our Lord and His Apostles in PALESTINE, SYRIA, GREECE, AND ITALY. By W. H. BARTLETT. Seventh Edition, with numerous Engravings. In one 4to. volume. Handsomely bound in walnut, 18s. Cloth gilt, 10s. 6d.

Forty Days in the Desert on the Track of the ISRAELITES; or, a Journey from Cairo to Mount Sinai and Petra. By W. H. BARTLETT. 4to. With 25 Steel Engravings. Handsome walnut binding, 18s. Cloth gilt, 10s. 6d.

The Nile Boat; or, Glimpses in the Land of Egypt. By W. H. BARTLETT. New Edition, with 33 Steel Engravings. 4to. Walnut, 18s. Cloth gilt, 10s. 6d.

The Desert of the Exodus. Journeys on Foot in the Wilderness of the Forty Years' Wanderings, undertaken in connection with the Ordnance Survey of Sinai and the Palestine Exploration Fund. By E. H. PALMER, M.A., Lord Almoner's Professor of Arabic and Fellow of St. John's College, Cambridge, Member of the Asiatic Society, and of the Société de Paris. With Maps, and numerous Illustrations from Photographs and Drawings taken on the spot by the Sinai Survey Expedition and C. F. TYRWHITT DRAKE. 2 vols. 8vo. 28s.

LONDON: GEORGE BELL & SONS, YORK STREET, COVENT GARDEN.

STANDARD WORKS.

Corpus Poetarum Latinorum. Edited by E. WALKER. One thick vol. 8vo. Cloth, 18s.

'Containing:—Catullus, Lucretius, Virgilius, Tibullus, Propertius, Ovidius, Horatius, Phaedrus, Lucanus, Persius, Juvenalis, Martialis, Sulpicia, Statius, Silius Italicus, Valerius Flaccus, Calpurnius Siculus, Ausonius, and Claudianus.

Cruden's Concordance to the Old and New Testament, or an Alphabetical and Classified Index to the Holy Bible; specially adapted for Sunday School Teachers, containing nearly 54,000 references. Thoroughly revised and condensed by G. H. HANNAY. Fcap. 2s.

Perowne (Canon). The Book of Psalms. A New Translation, with Introductions and Notes, Critical and Explanatory. By the Very Rev. J. J. STEWART PEROWNE, Dean of Peterborough. 8vo. Vol. I., Fourth Edition, 18s.; Vol. II., Fourth Edition. 16s.

——— ABRIDGED EDITION for Schools. Third Edition. Crown 8vo. 10s. 6d.

Adams (Dr. E.). The Elements of the English Language. By ERNEST ADAMS, Ph.D. Fifteenth Edition. Post 8vo. 4s. 6d.

Whewell (Dr.). Elements of Morality, including Polity. By W. WHEWELL, D.D., formerly Master of Trinity College, Cambridge. Fourth Edition. In 1 vol. 8vo. 15s.

Gilbart (J. W.). The Principles and Practice of BANKING. By the late J. W. GILBART. New Edition, revised (1871). 8vo. 16s.

BIOGRAPHIES BY THE LATE SIR ARTHUR HELPS, K.C.B.

The Life of Hernando Cortes, and the Conquest of MEXICO. Dedicated to Thomas Carlyle. 2 vols. Crown 8vo. 15s.

The Life of Christopher Columbus, the Discoverer of AMERICA. Fourth Edition. Crown 8vo. 6s.

The Life of Pizarro. With Some Account of his Associates in the Conquest of Peru. Second Edition. Crown 8vo. 6s.

The Life of Las Casas, the Apostle of the Indies. Second Edition. Crown 8vo. 6s.

The Life and Epistles of St. Paul. By THOMAS LEWIN, Esq., M.A., F.S.A., Trinity College, Oxford, Barrister-at-Law, Author of "Fasti Sacri," "Siege of Jerusalem," "Caesar's Invasion," "Treatise on Trusts," &c. With upwards of 350 Illustrations finely engraved on Wood, Maps, Plans, &c. Fourth Edition. In 2 vols. demy 4to. £2 2s.

"This is one of those works which demand from critics and from the public, before attempting to estimate its merits in detail, an unqualified tribute of admiration. The first glance tells us that the book is one on which the leisure of a busy lifetime and the whole resources of an enthusiastic author have been lavished without stint. . . . This work is a kind of British Museum for this period and subject in small compass. It is a series of galleries of statues, gems, coins, documents, letters, books, and relics, through which the reader may wander at leisure, and which he may animate with his own musings and reflections. It must be remembered throughout that this delightful and instructive collection is the result of the devotion of a lifetime, and deserves as much honour and recognition as many a museum or picture-gallery which has preserved its donor's name for generations."—*Times.*

LONDON: GEORGE BELL & SONS, YORK STREET, COVENT GARDEN.

STANDARD WORKS PUBLISHED BY

ILLUSTRATED OR POPULAR EDITIONS OF STANDARD WORKS.

Dante's Divine Comedy. Translated by the Rev. HENRY FRANCIS CARY. With all the Author's Copyright Emendations. Post 8vo. 3s. 6d.

Shakespeare. Shakespeare's Plays and Poems. With Notes and Life by CHARLES KNIGHT, and 40 engravings on wood by HARVEY. Royal 8vo. Cloth. 10s. 6d.

Fielding. Works of Henry Fielding, complete. With Memoir of the Author by THOMAS ROSCOE, and 20 Plates by GEORGE CRUIKSHANK. Medium 8vo. 14s.

Fielding. The Novels separately. With Memoir by THOMAS ROSCOE, and Plates by GEORGE CRUIKSHANK. Medium 8vo. 7s. 6d.

Swift. Works of Jonathan Swift, D.D. Containing interesting and valuable passages not hitherto published. With Memoir of the Author by THOMAS ROSCOE. 2 vols. Medium 8vo. 24s.

Smollett. Miscellaneous Works of Tobias Smollett. Complete in 1 vol. With Memoir of the Author by THOMAS ROSCOE. 21 Plates by GEORGE CRUIKSHANK. Medium 8vo. 14s.

Lamb. The Works of Charles Lamb. With a Memoir by Sir THOMAS NOON TALFOURD. Imp. 8vo. 10s. 6d.

Goldsmith's Poems. Illustrated. 16mo. 2s. 6d.

Wordsworth's White Doe of Rylstone; or, the Fate of THE NORTONS. Illustrated. 16mo. 3s. 6d.

Longfellow's Poetical Works. With nearly 250 Illustrations by BIRKET FOSTER, TENNIEL, GODWIN, THOMAS, &c. In 1 vol. 21s.

Longfellow's Evangeline. Illustrated. 16mo. 3s. 6d.

Longfellow's Wayside Inn. Illustrated. 16mo. 3s. 6d.

Washington Irving's Sketch-Book. (The Artist's Edition.) Illustrated with a Portrait of the Author on Steel, and 200 Exquisite Wood-Engravings from the Pencils of the most celebrated American Artists. Crown 4to. 21s.

Adelaide Anne Procter's Legends and Lyrics. The Illustrated Edition. With Additional Poems, and an Introduction by CHARLES DICKENS, a Portrait by JEENS, and 20 Illustrations by Eminent Artists, and a short Memoir by Mrs. EWING. Fcap. 4to. Ornamental cloth. 21s.

Mrs. Gatty's Parables from Nature. A Handsomely Illustrated Edition; with Notes on the Natural History, and numerous Full-page Illustrations by the most eminent Artists of the present day. *New complete edition, with Short Memoir by J. H. EWING.* Fcap. 4to. 21s.

The Book of Gems. Selections from the British POETS. Illustrated with upwards of 150 Steel Engravings. Edited by S. C. HALL. 3 vols. Handsomely bound in walnut. 21s. each.
　　FIRST SERIES—CHAUCER TO DRYDEN.
　　SECOND SERIES—SWIFT TO BURNS.
　　THIRD SERIES—WORDSWORTH TO TENNYSON.

LONDON: GEORGE BELL & SONS, YORK STREET, COVENT GARDEN.

BOOKS FOR THE YOUNG.

CAPTAIN MARRYAT'S BOOKS FOR BOYS.

Poor Jack. With Sixteen Illustrations after Designs by CLARKSON STANFIELD, R.A. Twenty-second Edition. Post 8vo., 3s. 6d. Gilt, 4s. 6d.

—— Cheap Edition. 1s.

The Mission; or, Scenes in Africa. With Illustrations by JOHN GILBERT. Post 8vo., 3s. 6d. Gilt, 4s. 6d.

The Settlers in Canada. With Illustrations by GILBERT and DALZIEL. Post 8vo., 3s. 6d. Gilt, 4s. 6d.

The Privateers Man. Adventures by Sea and Land IN CIVIL AND SAVAGE LIFE, ONE HUNDRED YEARS AGO. Illustrated with Eight Steel Engravings. Post 8vo., 3s. 6d. Gilt, 4s. 6d.

Masterman Ready; or, the Wreck of the Pacific. Embellished with Ninety-three Engravings on Wood. Post 8vo., 3s. 6d. Gilt, 4s. 6d.

—— Cheap Edition. 1s.

The Pirate and Three Cutters. Illustrated with Eight Steel Engravings from Drawings by CLARKSON STANFIELD, R.A. With a Memoir of the Author. Post 8vo., 3s. 6d. Gilt, 4s. 6d.

A Boy's Locker. A Smaller Edition of the above Tales, in 12 volumes, enclosed in a compact cloth box. 21s.

Hans Christian Andersen's Tales for Children. With Forty-eight Full-page Illustrations by Wehnert, and Fifty-seven Small Engravings on Wood by W. THOMAS. A new Edition. Very handsomely bound. 6s.

Hans Christian Andersen's Fairy Tales and Sketches. Translated by C. C. PEACHEY, H. WARD, A. PLESNER, &c. With 104 Illustrations by OTTO SPECKTER and others. 6s.

This volume contains several tales that are in no other Edition published in this country, and with the above volume it forms the most complete English Edition.

Mrs. Alfred Gatty's Presentation Box for Young PEOPLE. Containing "Parables from Nature," "Aunt Judy's Tales," and other Popular Books, 9 volumes in all, beautifully printed, neatly bound, and enclosed in a cloth box. 31s. 6d. Any single volume at 3s. 6d.

Anecdotes of Dogs. By EDWARD JESSE. With Illustrations. Post 8vo. Cloth. 5s. With Thirty-four Steel Engravings after COOPER, LANDSEER, &c. 7s. 6d.

The Natural History of Selborne. By GILBERT WHITE. Edited by JESSE. Illustrated with Forty Engravings. Post 8vo. 5s.; or with the Plates Coloured, 7s. 6d.

A Poetry Book for Schools. Illustrated with Thirty-seven highly-finished Engravings by C. W. COPE, R.A., HELMSLEY, PALMER, SKILL. THOMAS, and H. WEIR. Crown 8vo. 1s.

Select Parables from Nature. By Mrs. GATTY. For the Use of Schools. Fcap. 1s.

Besides being reprinted in America, selections from Mrs. Gatty's Parables have been translated and published in the German, French, Italian, Russian, Danish, and Swedish languages.

LONDON: GEORGE BELL & SONS, YORK STREET COVENT GARDEN.

SOWERBY'S ENGLISH BOTANY:

Containing a Description and Life-size coloured Drawing of every British Plant. Edited and brought up to the Present Standard of Scientific Knowledge by T. BOSWELL (formerly SYME), LL.D. F.L.S., &c. With Popular Descriptions of the Uses, History, and Traditions of each Plant, by Mrs. LANKESTER, Author of "Wild Flowers Worth Notice," "The British Ferns," &c. The Figures by J. E. SOWERBY, JAMES SOWERBY, F.L.S., J. DE. C. SOWERBY, F.L.S., and J. W. SALTER, A.L.S. In Eleven Volumes, super-royal 8vo.; or in 83 Parts, 5s. each.

"Under the editorship of T. Boswell Syme, F.L.S., assisted by Mrs. Lankester, 'Sowerby's English Botany,' when finished, will be exhaustive of the subject, and worthy of the branch of science it illustrates. . . . In turning over the charmingly executed hand-coloured plates of British plants which encumber these volumes with riches, the reader cannot help being struck with the beauty of many of the humblest flowering weeds we tread on with careless step. We cannot dwell upon many of the individuals grouped in the splendid bouquet of flowers presented in these pages, and it will be sufficient to state that the work is pledged to contain a figure of every wild flower indigenous to these isles."—*Times.*

"Will be the most complete Flora of Great Britain ever brought out. This great work will find a place wherever botanical science is cultivated, and the study of our native plants, with all their fascinating associations, held dear."—*Athenæum.*

"A clear, bold, distinctive type enables the reader to take in at a glance the arrangement and divisions of every page. And Mrs. Lankester has added to the technical description by the editor an extremely interesting popular sketch, which follows in smaller type. The English, French, and German popular names are given, and, wherever that delicate and difficult step is at all practicable, their derivation also. Medical properties, superstitions, and fancies, and poetic tributes and illusions, follow. In short there is nothing more left to be desired."—*Guardian.*

"Without question, this is the standard work on Botany, and indispensable to every botanist. . . . The plates are most accurate and beautiful, and the entire work cannot be too strongly recommended to all who are interested in botany."—*Illustrated News.*

Sold separately, prices as follows:—

	Bound cloth.			Half morocco.			Morocco elegant.		
	£	s.	d.	£	s.	d.	£	s.	d.
Vol. I. (Seven Parts)	1	18	0	2	2	0	2	8	6
II. ditto	1	18	0	2	2	0	2	8	6
III. (Eight Parts)	2	3	0	2	7	0	2	13	6
IV. (Nine Parts)	2	8	0	2	12	0	2	18	6
V. (Eight Parts)	2	3	0	2	7	0	2	13	6
VI. (Seven Parts)	1	18	0	2	2	0	2	8	6
VII. ditto	1	18	0	2	2	0	2	8	6
VIII. (Ten Parts)	2	13	0	2	17	0	3	3	6
IX. (Seven Parts)	1	18	0	2	2	0	2	8	6
X. ditto	1	18	0	2	2	0	2	8	6
XI. (Six Parts)	1	18	0	1	17	0	2	3	6

Or, the Eleven Volumes, 22*l.* 8*s.* in cloth; 24*l.* 12*s.* in half-morocco; and 28*l.* 3*s.* 6*d.* whole morocco.

A Supplementary Volume, containing ferns and other cryptogams, with an Index to the whole work, is in preparation by Professor BOSWELL (formerly SYME).

LONDON: GEORGE BELL & SONS, YORK STREET, COVENT GARDEN.

GEORGE BELL & SONS.

LIBRARY OF NATURAL HISTORY.

"Each volume is elegantly printed in royal 8vo., and illustrated with a very large number of well-executed engravings, printed in colours. . . . They form a complete library of reference on the several subjects to which they are devoted, and nothing more complete in their way has lately appeared."—*The Bookseller.*

BREE'S BIRDS OF EUROPE AND THEIR EGGS, not observed in the British Isles. With 252 beautifully coloured Plates. Five vols. 5*l.* 5*s.*

COUCH'S HISTORY OF THE FISHES OF THE BRITISH ISLANDS. With 252 carefully coloured Plates. Four vols. 4*l.* 4*s.*

GATTY'S (MRS. ALFRED) BRITISH SEAWEEDS. Numerous coloured Illustrations. Two vols. 2*l.* 10*s.*

HIBBERD'S (SHIRLEY) NEW AND RARE BEAUTIFUL-LEAVED PLANTS. With 64 coloured Full-page Illustrations. Executed expressly for this work. One vol. 1*l.* 5*s.*

LOWE'S NATURAL HISTORY OF BRITISH AND EXOTIC FERNS. With 479 finely coloured Plates. Eight vols. 6*l.* 6*s.*

LOWE'S OUR NATIVE FERNS. Illustrated with 79 coloured Plates and 900 Wood Engravings. Two vols. 2*l.* 2*s.*

LOWE'S NATURAL HISTORY OF NEW AND RARE FERNS. Containing Species and Varieties not included in "Ferns, British and Exotic." 72 coloured Plates and Woodcuts. One vol. 1*l.* 1*s.*

LOWE'S NATURAL HISTORY OF BRITISH GRASSES. With 74 finely coloured Plates. One vol. 1*l.* 1*s.*

LOWE'S BEAUTIFUL-LEAVED PLANTS: being a description of the most beautiful-leaved Plants in cultivation in this country. With 60 coloured Illustrations. One vol. 1*l.* 1*s.*

MAUNDS' BOTANIC GARDEN. New Edition. Edited by J. C. NIVEN, Curator of the Botanic Gardens, Hull. With 250 coloured Plates, giving 1247 figures. Six vols. 12*l.* 12*s.*

MORRIS' HISTORY OF BRITISH BIRDS. With 360 finely coloured Engravings. Six vols. 6*l.* 6*s.*

MORRIS' NESTS AND EGGS OF BRITISH BIRDS. With 223 beautifully coloured Engravings. Three vols. 3*l.* 3*s.*

MORRIS' BRITISH BUTTERFLIES. With 71 beautifully coloured Plates. One vol. 1*l.* 1*s.*

MORRIS' BRITISH MOTHS. With coloured Illustrations of nearly 2000 specimens. Four vols. 6*l.* 6*s.*

TRIPP'S BRITISH MOSSES. With 39 coloured Plates, containing a figure of each species. Two vols. 2*l.* 10*s.*

WOOSTER'S ALPINE PLANTS. First Series. With 54 coloured Plates. 25*s.*

WOOSTER'S ALPINE PLANTS. Second Series. With 54 coloured Plates. 25*s.*

LONDON: GEORGE BELL & SONS, YORK STREET, COVENT GARDEN.

STANDARD WORKS

PUBLISHED BY

GEORGE BELL & SONS.

₊ *For List of* BOHN'S LIBRARIES *see the end of the Volume.*

THE HISTORY,

PRINCIPLES, AND PRACTICE

OF

BANKING.

BY THE LATE

J. W. GILBART, F.R.S.,

FORMERLY DIRECTOR AND GENERAL MANAGER OF THE LONDON AND
WESTMINSTER BANK.

NEW EDITION, REVISED TO THE PRESENT DATE,

By A. S. MICHIE,

DEPUTY MANAGER OF THE ROYAL BANK OF SCOTLAND,
LONDON.

VOL. I.

LONDON: GEORGE BELL AND SONS,
YORK STREET, COVENT GARDEN.
1882.

[*The right of translation is reserved.*]

CHISWICK PRESS:—CHARLES WHITTINGHAM AND CO. TOOKS COURT,
CHANCERY LANE.

CONTENTS OF THE FIRST VOLUME.

SECTION	PAGE
I. The Origin and Progress of Banking	1
II. The Rise of Banking in England	13
III. The History of the Bank of England	30
IV. The London Bankers	103
V. Country Banks	105
VI. Joint-Stock Banks	114
VII. Branch Banks	121
VIII. Banks of Deposit	127
IX. Banks of Remittance	136
X. Banks of Circulation	143
XI. Banks of Discount	157
XII. Cash Credit Banks	185
XIII. Loan Banks	192
XIV. Savings Banks	199
XV. The Nature of Banking	210
XVI. The Utility of Banking	213
XVII. Banking Terms	224
XVIII. The General Administration of a Bank	232
XIX. The Administration of a Bank with Regard to Proceedings on Bills of Exchange	258
XX. The Administration of a Bank with Regard to the Employment of its Surplus Funds	291
XXI. The Administration of a Bank during Seasons of Pressure	309
XXII. The Administration of a Bank under the Act of 1844	326
XXIII. The Administration of the Banking Department of the Bank of England	365
XXIV. The Administration of Joint-Stock Banks, with an Inquiry into the Causes of their Failures	397

PREFACE.

OF the numerous writings of the late Mr. Gilbart none are so well known or so deservedly popular as his "History and Principles of Banking" and his "Practical Treatise on Banking."

Ten years ago, with the view of bringing them within the reach of a wider circle of readers, these works were combined in one volume, and the cost was materially lessened. And with the view of still further carrying out that object, the present edition has been prepared in a form, and at a cost, which it is hoped will make it easily accessible to all.

These works, having been originally published nearly fifty years ago, when joint-stock banking was almost in its infancy, necessarily contained much matter, which, although interesting and instructive at the time, is now quite obsolete. Much, therefore, which appeared in previous editions has been struck out of the present issue, but great care has at the same time been taken to delete nothing of any historical interest, or that bears directly or indirectly on any pending question.

Besides the various excisions alluded to, the sections on the "Moral and Religious Duties of Banking Companies," and "Ten Minutes' Advice about keeping a Banker," have been struck out bodily—the first, on the ground that the subject trenches somewhat on the domain of each individual's personal moral responsibilities, and is scarcely adapted to a work of this kind; and the second, on the ground that at this period of time such advice is wholly superfluous.

But if much has been taken out, much also has been put in, and, it is hoped, many improvements made otherwise.

Of the new matter introduced, the section on the London Clearing House may be mentioned. In addition to the inherent interest of the subject to the general reader, the Editor has introduced it in the hope that the description of the clearing which he has been able to give, will be sufficiently plain to enable such towns as are not at present so provided, to organize such an institution for themselves.

Of the new matter also, the accounts of the recent crises, and of the recent banking legislation, may be mentioned. Considerable space has been devoted to the first-named subject, and this, the Editor thinks, is justified by the fact, that the failure of the City of Glasgow Bank was an event of unparalleled and national importance, and deserves in a work of this kind something more than a passing notice. Prominence has also been given to Sir Stafford Northcote's Banking Act of 1879, and to the events and discussions leading up to and flowing from it. In connection with the latter, the recent discussion between the three senior Scotch banks and the Treasury has been somewhat detailed. This has been done with the view of putting before the banking world in a more permanent form than the passing notice of the daily or weekly journals, some material for coming to a conclusion respecting the general question of the paper currency of the country. It is not unlikely that this subject will by-and-by be taken up by the Government of the day, and an attempt made to settle it on the lines foreshadowed in the Treasury minutes.

Many changes in the form of much of the old matter will, it is hoped, be regarded as an improvement. Instead of pages of paragraphs in chronological form of the various changes in the capital, dividends, and rates of discount of the Bank of England, all such information has been tabulated in the present edition—a form which will be found much less irksome to read, and much more convenient for reference. A table has also been added of the average bank rate for each year from 1826 downwards.

In the preparation of this edition, the Editor, in all he has expunged, and added, and altered, has kept steadily in view that the Publishers' desire is to bring it chiefly within the reach of the rising generation of bankers; and while, no doubt, it will prove most useful to them, he feels sure that from Mr. Gilbart's knowledge of his subject, his prescience and sagacity, his works may be studied with great advantage even by the oldest and most experienced.

It only remains for the Editor to acknowledge with much sincerity his deep obligations to his numerous friends who have so ungrudgingly given him the benefit of their advice and assistance. When all have been so kind it would be invidious to mention names, but to each and all he now returns his most grateful thanks.

A. S. M.

BIOGRAPHICAL NOTICE OF THE AUTHOR.

JAMES WILLIAM GILBART, though of Cornish descent, was born in London, March 21, 1794. The name of Gilbart is said to be peculiar to Cornwall; Gilbert is common to several other counties.

In the year 1813, when nineteen years of age, he entered, as junior clerk, a London bank, there remaining until the panic of December, 1825, when that establishment, and several others, were compelled to stop payment—the bank in which Mr. Gilbart had been engaged, paying all its creditors in full, with interest, a few months afterwards, though it did not resume business. He was for several years during this period a member of a debating society called the "Athenian," of which the Right Hon. M. T. Baines, Edward Baines, Esq., M.P., Edwin Chadwick, Esq., C.B., Baron Channell, and several gentlemen afterwards at the Bar, were also members. He was subsequently a member of the "Union Society"—a debating club formed in 1825, by Mr. John Stuart Mill, and of which Lord Macaulay was a member. About this time Mr. Gilbart assisted in the formation of the City of London Literary and Scientific Institution, the first of the kind designed for the education of the middle classes, and in furtherance of the views entertained by him he became a liberal contributor to the popular periodicals issued at a price within the reach of all.

Consequent upon the stoppage of the bank alluded to, Mr. Gilbart accepted the place of cashier to a large firm in Birmingham; but the occupation being distasteful to him, he resigned it.

In the beginning of 1827 he returned to London, and published his first book on Banking—"A Practical Treatise on Banking; containing an Account of the London and Country Banks, a view of the Joint-stock Banks of Scotland and Ireland, with a Summary of the Evidence delivered before the Parliamentary Committees, relative to the Suppression of Notes under Five Pounds in those Countries." A few months after the publication of this work, Mr. Gilbart was appointed Manager of the Provincial Bank of Ireland, and opened a branch at Kilkenny.

In 1829 he was promoted to the managership of a larger branch at Waterford.

There, as at Kilkenny, Mr. Gilbart published in the local papers various articles on Banking, with the object of circulating a correct knowledge of the system introduced; and associating himself with several gentlemen of influence, he established the Waterford Literary and Scientific Institution, on the plan of the Institution in the City of London, already referred to; besides which he found time to give a series of lectures on subjects so varied and extensive, that those who knew how industriously and indefatigably he applied himself to his daily duties, were at a loss to imagine how he could find opportunities to acquire such knowledge. He delivered ten lectures during the first session of the society. Of these, five were upon "Ancient Commerce," comprising the commerce of Egypt,

Greece, Rome, Tyre, and Carthage, and that of the ancients with the East Indies. The subjects of the remaining five were, "The Philosophy of Language," "The Means of Preserving the Sight," "The Agriculture of the West of England," "Scientific Terms," and "The Commerce of Waterford." While he was thus engaged, his professional labours were signally successful, and his reputation for prudence, intelligence, and ability becoming known in London, he received an invitation which induced him to leave Ireland, and settle in the metropolis. It was in 1833 that a Committee was formed for the establishment of the first Joint-stock bank in London. Almost the first consideration of the Committee was to seek an efficient manager. Without having any personal knowledge whatever of Mr. Gilbart, and guided entirely by his reputation in Ireland, in union probably with that derived from his writings, they made him an offer to become their manager. Having received another invitation from a similar establishment then in the course of formation, Mr. Gilbart came to London, and, after an interview with both parties, engaged with the London and Westminster Bank, on the 10th of October, 1833—signing the first letters of allotment of shares on the following day. Mr. Gilbart's antecedents were well calculated to qualify him for this appointment. He had been thirteen years in a London bank, by which he had acquired a perfect knowledge of banking, being, moreover, favourably known as an author on the subject; besides which he had for six years and a half fulfilled the onerous duties of manager in a Joint-stock bank—a young establishment which had to contend against popular ignorance and a chartered rival—which two opponents, a new bank in London, founded on similar principles, would probably have to encounter. The London and Westminster Bank was opened March 10, 1834.

As the General Manager from the commencement of the bank, Mr. Gilbart had to withstand the violent opposition of interested and influential bodies which met its rise and early progress. He had to conquer the apathy and distrust of the public, and to contend against law proceedings, injunctions, adverse bills in parliament, and other formidable difficulties. All were successfully overcome, and at length he had the satisfaction of seeing the bank to a remarkable extent prosper. Year by year it increased in importance, until it became one of the largest and richest Joint-stock banks in the kingdom. An excellently-written history of the undertaking was produced by Mr. Gilbart in 1847, which was printed for private circulation.

About two years after the opening of the bank, a spirit of general speculation arose which became directed towards the establishment of Joint-stock banks throughout the country. It being thought that some of these new banks might appoint the London and Westminster Bank to be their agent, Mr. Gilbart assisted in the formation of several.

To secure the right to attend their meetings, he took shares, and urged upon all the shareholders and directors the advantage of connecting their business relations in London with London Joint-stock banks. The London and Westminster Bank thus obtained a large and valuable country connection.

In this year the directors, under the advice of Mr. Gilbart, opened several branches in London.

In June, 1837, Mr. Gilbart was examined as a witness before the Committee of the House of Commons upon Joint-stock banks.

This Committee was appointed "to inquire into the operation of the Acts permitting the establishment of Joint-stock banks in England and Ireland, under certain restrictions, and the expediency of making any amendment in the provisions of those Acts." The Committee had made a hostile report in 1836, but this session they resolved only to report evidence. In the course of the same year the Bank of England obtained an injunction against the London and Westminster, prohibiting their accepting any bills drawn at less than six months after date. It was supposed that this decision would be fatal to the connection of the country banks, but it was not so. When in Ireland, Mr. Gilbart had seen bills drawn by the Bank of Ireland upon the Bank of England, "without acceptance," and it occurred to him that the country establishments might draw upon the London and Westminster Bank in the same manner. With the sanction of his directors, he visited all the country banks, and made the suggestion. It was universally adopted, and consequently the London and Westminster Bank lost none of its connections.

The "Association of Joint-stock Banks" was formed in the latter part of 1838, and all such establishments in England, Wales, and Ireland, were invited to attend a public meeting in London. This meeting appointed from their number a Committee "to communicate with the Government, and to promote the passing of such laws as might be beneficial to Joint-stock banks."

This Committee was styled "The Committee of Deputies," and those members who resided in London were authorized to act, in ordinary matters, on behalf of the whole Committee. Mr. P. M. Stewart, M.P., a Director of the London and Westminster Bank, was Chairman; Mr. Oliver Vile, the Manager of the Westminster Branch of the London and Westminster Bank, was the Honorary Secretary, and the circulars to the banks and the correspondence were written chiefly by Mr. Gilbart.

The Chancellor of the Exchequer at that time was Mr. Spring Rice (Lord Monteagle), who had been a Director of the Provincial Bank of Ireland during the time that Mr. Gilbart was Manager, and the Government being thus readily accessible on banking questions, several important improvements in the laws respecting Joint-stock banks were passed on the suggestion of the Chancellor of the Exchequer. In consequence of the pressure of 1839, a Select Committee of the House of Commons was appointed in 1840, "To inquire into the effects produced on the circulation of the country by the various Banking establishments issuing notes payable on demand." Mr. Vincent Stuckey, of Bristol, and Mr. Gilbart, represented, by request, the English Joint-stock banks, and received the thanks of those companies for the manner in which they had given their evidence.

In 1844, Sir Robert Peel passed his Bill, renewing the Charter of the Bank of England, and regulating other banks; by this enactment, the London and Westminster, and other similar banks, acquired the power of suing and being sued by their public officer, and to accept bills at less than six months after date.

Another pressure on the money market occurred in 1847, when both houses appointed a Committee of Inquiry, the chief question being—" Whether the pressure of 1847 was produced in whole or in part by the Act of 1844?" To this Mr. Gilbart gave an answer in the fifth edition of his "Practical Treatise" published in 1849, a work dedicated to the then Chancellor of the Exchequer, a sixth edition following in 1859.

A prize of £100 was offered by Mr. Gilbart in January, 1851, for the best essay "On the Adaptation of Recent Inventions collected at the Great Exhibition of 1851, to the purposes of Practical Banking." The prize was gained by Mr. Granville Sharp, of Norwich. In 1854, the object for which Mr. Gilbart had frequently contended, viz., the admission of the Joint-stock banks into the clearing-house, was attained. In 1859, he published his "Logic of Banking."

In the course of the same year, the Directors of the Bank, in acknowledgment of his long and eminent services, passed a resolution to allow him to retire at the close of the year, with a pension of £1,500 per annum; and on their recommendation, he was appointed an extra director in anticipation of the next vacancy.

Mr. Gilbart received further gratifying tokens of the estimation in which he was held.

Prior to his departure from Waterford, the Members of the Literary and Scientific Institution requested him to sit for his portrait to be placed in the Lecture-room,—complimentary resolutions passed being accompanied by a letter from the President.

In the year 1846, a service of plate was presented to him by the Joint-stock banks, in acknowledgment of his exertions in favour of Joint-stock banking.

On the 10th of March, 1860, a testimonial of plate was presented to him by the officers of the London and Westminster Bank on his retirement from the office of General Manager, an address accompanying it.

Mr. Gilbart was a Fellow of the Royal Society, a life member of several literary and scientific associations, and a Member of the Statistical Society, to which he contributed various valuable papers.

He died on the 8th day of August, 1863, in the 69th year of his age.

THE HISTORY, PRINCIPLES, AND PRACTICE OF BANKING.

SECTION I.

THE ORIGIN AND PROGRESS OF BANKING.

AN eminent historian observes, that "it is a cruel mortification, in searching for what is instructive in the history of past times, to find that the exploits of conquerors who have desolated the earth, and the freaks of tyrants who have rendered nations unhappy, are recorded with minute and often disgusting accuracy, while the discovery of useful arts, and the progress of the most beneficial branches of commerce are passed over in silence, and suffered to sink into oblivion."[1] This remark is strictly applicable to the origin and progress of banking. We have but little information as to what kind of banks existed in the earlier ages, or on what system they conducted their business. As most of the nations of antiquity subsisted chiefly on agriculture, they probably had little occasion for banks; for it is only in commercial countries that these institutions have attained to any high

[1] Robertson's Historical Disquisition on India, page 46.

degree of prosperity. And as even the commercial nations of antiquity were unacquainted with joint-stock companies, or commercial corporations, and had not discovered the use of paper-money or bills of exchange, the business of a banker, even among them, must have been somewhat different from that of a banker of the present day. The merchants of those early times employed as money, gold and silver bullion; and received it and paid it away by weight. It is probable that the merchants would require that the precious metals they received should be of a certain degree of fineness. We read of Abraham[1] weighing unto Ephron 400 shekels of silver, *current money with the merchant*—a phrase which implies that the money current with the merchant was different from that in ordinary use.

After bullion was superseded by coin, and each nation had a coin of its own, the merchants would necessarily in the course of their business receive coins belonging to different nations, and hence would be applied to by strangers who wished to exchange their own money for the money of the country in which they sojourned. This would take place more particularly in those oriental countries whose inhabitants were accustomed in certain seasons to meet together for the celebration of public festivals. We read in the New Testament[2] of money-changers who had tables in the Temple of Jerusalem. It is probable they attended for the purpose of giving Jewish money in exchange for those various coins which persons coming from the neighbouring countries might have brought with them. Whether the business of money-changing was carried on as a separate employment, or united with the general business of a merchant, we are not informed; but it is stated, that the exchangers allowed interest for money

---

[1] Genesis xxiii. 16.   [2] Matthew xxi. 12.

lodged in their hands. "Thou wicked and slothful servant, thou oughtest to have put my money to the exchangers, and then at my coming I should have received mine own with usury."[1] From the circumstance of their allowing interest on money, we may infer that they also lent money on interest; otherwise they would have had no use for the money they borrowed. This scanty information forms the whole of our knowledge respecting the mode of banking practised by the ancient Babylonian, Egyptian, and Jewish nations.

With respect to the bankers of Greece we have more ample details.

In Greece the first banks were the temples.

"The wealth and growing estimation of Delphi had also another source, of which information remains only so far as to assure us of the fact with far less explanation of circumstances than for its importance might be desired. In the general insecurity of property in the early ages, and especially in Greece, it was highly desirable to convert all that could be spared from immediate use into that which might more easily be removed from approaching danger. With this view, by a compact understood among men, the precious metals appear to have obtained their early estimation. Gold, then, and silver, having acquired their certain value as signs of wealth, a deposit secure against the dangers continually threatening, not individuals only, but every town and state in Greece, would be a great object of the wealthy. Such security offered nowhere in equal amount as in those temples, which belong not to any single state, but were respected by the common religion of the nation. The priesthood, not likely to refuse the charge, would have a large interest in acquiring the reputation of fidelity to it. Thus Delphi appears to have become the great

[1] Matthew xxv. 27.

bank of Greece, perhaps before Homer, in whose time its riches seem to have been already proverbial. Such then was found the value of this institution, that when the Dorian conquerors drove so large a part of the Greek nation into exile, the fugitives who acquired new settlements in Asia, established there their own national bank in the manner of that of their former country, recommending it to the protection of the same divinity. The Temple of Apollo, at Branchidæ, became the great depository of the wealth of Ionia."[1]

Afterwards the temple of Olympia, like that at Delphi, became an advantageous repository for treasure. But although the temples discharged one of the offices of banks, by being places of security, yet as they did not grant interest on the money deposited, they did not supersede banks of deposit established by private individuals. At Athens, especially, banking was a flourishing trade.

"The greater part of the Athenians employ their money in trade, but they are not permitted to lend it for any place but Athens. They receive an interest for the use of it which is not fixed by the laws, but stipulated in a contract, deposited either in the hands of a banker or some friend to both parties. If, for instance, a voyage is to be made to the Cymmerian Bosphorus, the instrument specifies the time of the departure of the vessel, the kind of commodities with which she is to be freighted, the sale which is to be made of them in the Bosphorus, and the merchandise which she is to bring back to Athens; and as the duration of the voyage is uncertain, some agree that their money shall not be payable till the return of the vessel, while others, more timid, and contented with a less profit, require that it shall be repaid at the Bosphorus immediately after the sale of the goods carried out; in which case they either themselves repair to the place where

[1] Mitford's History of Greece, vol. i. page 193.

they are to receive it, or send thither some person in whom they can confide, and whom they empower to act for them.

"The lender has his security, either on the merchandise or the goods of the borrower; but as the dangers of the sea are in part risked by the former, and the profit of the latter may be very considerable, the interest of money thus lent may rise as high as thirty per cent., more or less, according to the length and hazards of the voyage.

"The usury of which I have spoken is known by the name of maritime; that called landed is more oppressive, and no less variable.

"Those who, without risking the dangers of the sea, wish to derive profit from their money, lend it to bankers at the rate of twelve per cent. per annum, or rather one per cent. for every new moon. But as the laws of Solon do not prohibit those who have money from demanding the most extravagant interest for it, some persons receive more than sixteen per cent., and others, especially among the lower classes of people, exact every day the quarter of the principal. These extortions are not concealed, and cannot be punished, except by the public opinion, which condemns, but does not sufficiently despise those who are guilty of them.

"Commerce increases the circulation of wealth, and this circulation has given birth to the occupation of bankers, which facilitates it still more. A person who is about to make a voyage, or who fears to keep by him too great a sum of money, lodges it in the hands of these bankers, sometimes only as a trust, and without requiring any interest, and sometimes on condition of sharing with them the profit it shall produce. They advance money to generals who go to take on them the command of armies, or other individuals who stand in need of their assistance.

"In the greater part of bargains made by them, no witness is required; they content themselves with entering in a register that such a person has deposited in their hands such a sum, which they must repay to such another, if the former should happen to die. It would sometimes be very difficult to prove that they have received a sum of money, were they to deny it; but if they should expose themselves to such a charge more than once, they would lose the confidence of the public, on which depends their success in the business in which they are engaged.

"By employing the money deposited in their hands, and lending it at a greater interest than they are to pay for it, they amass riches which gain them friends, whose protection they purchase by assiduous services. But all is lost when, unable to call in their money, they are incapable of fulfilling their engagements. They are then obliged to conceal themselves, and can only escape the severity of justice by surrendering all their remaining property to their creditors.

"Those who wish to exchange foreign moneys apply to the bankers, who by different means, as the touchstone and the balance, examine whether they are not adulterated or deficient in weight."[1]

In a treatise published by Xenophon, upon the Athenian revenue, we meet with the first suggestion for the establishment of a joint-stock bank.

"A very remarkable project, which seems to have been original with Xenophon, next occurs—the establishment of a bank by subscription, open to all the Athenian people. The interest of money, it appears, was enormous at Athens, an unavoidable consequence of the wretched insecurity of person and property. Throughout modern Europe, land

[1] See Travels of Anacharsis in Greece, by the Abbé Barthelemy, and the authorities there referred to.

is, of all property, esteemed the safest source of income; but in Greece it was held that the surest return was from money lent at interest. For in the multiplied division of Greece into small republics with very narrow territories, the produce of land was continually liable to be carried off or destroyed by an invading enemy, but a moneyed fortune, according to Xenophon's observation, was safe within the city walls. In proportion, then, to the interest of money, and the insecurity of all things, the profits of trade will always be high, and thus numbers would be induced to borrow, even at a high interest. Xenophon therefore proposed, by lending from the public stock, and encouraging commercial adventure by just regulations, to raise a great revenue, and, by the same means, instead of oppressing to enrich individuals. As a corollary, then, to his project, when the amount of the subscription or its profits might allow, he proposed to improve the ports of Athens, to form wharves and docks, to erect halls, exchanges, warehouses, market-houses, and inns, for all which tolls and rents should be paid; and to build ships to be let to merchants. Thus, while numbers of individuals were encouraged and enabled to employ themselves for their private benefits, the whole Athenian people would become one great banking company, from whose profits every member, it was expected, would derive at least an easy livelihood." [1]

At Rome, the bankers were called *Argentarii*, *Mensarii*, *Numularii*, or *Collybistæ*. The banking-houses or banks were called *Tabernæ Argentariæ*, or *Mensæ Numulariæ*. Some of these bankers were appointed by the government to receive the taxes, others carried on business on their own account. Their mode of transacting business was somewhat similar to that which is in use in modern times.

[1] Mitford's History of Greece, vol. iv. page 22.

Into these houses the State, or men of wealth, caused their revenues to be paid, and they settled their accounts with their creditors by giving a draft or cheque on the bank. If the creditor also had an account at the same bank, the account was settled by an order to make the transfer of so much money from one name to another. To assign over money or to pay money by a draft, was called *perscribere*, and *rescribere;* the assignment or draft was called *attributio*. These bankers, too, were money-changers. They also lent money on interest, and allowed a lower rate of interest on money deposited in their hands. In a country where commerce was looked upon with contempt, banking could not be deemed very respectable. Among most of the ancient agricultural nations there was a prejudice against the taking of interest for the loan of money. Hence the private bankers at Rome were sometimes held in disrepute, though those whom the government had established as public cashiers, or receivers-general, as we may term them, held so exalted a rank that some of them became consuls.[1]

The Romans had also loan banks, from which the poor citizens received loans without paying interest. We are told that the confiscated property of criminals was converted into a fund by Augustus Cæsar, and that from this fund sums of money were lent without interest to those citizens who could pledge value to double the amount. The same system was pursued by Tiberius. He advanced a large capital, which was lent for a term of two or three years to those who could give landed security to double the value of the loan. Alexander Severus reduced the market-rate of interest by lending sums of money at a low rate, and by advancing money to poor citizens to purchase lands, and agreeing to receive payment from the produce.

[1] See Beckmann's History of Inventions, vol. ii. p. 5 (Bohn's Stand. Lib.).

After commerce and the arts had revived in Italy, the business of banking was resumed. The word bank is derived from the Italian word *Banco*, a *bench*—the Jews in Lombardy having benches in the market-place for the exchange of money and bills.[1] When a banker failed, his bench was broken by the populace; and from this circumstance we have our word *bankrupt*. Though the States of Venice and Genoa made the most rapid advances in commerce, and established public banks, yet the department of banking appears to have fallen more particularly into the hands of the Florentines. "As the Florentines did not," like the Venetians and the Genoese, "possess any commodious seaport, their active exertions were directed chiefly towards the improvement of their manufactures and domestic industry. About the beginning of the fourteenth century, the Florentine manufacturers of various kinds, particularly those of silk and woollen cloth, appear, from the enumeration of a well-informed historian, to have been very considerable. The connections which they formed in different parts of Europe, by furnishing them with the productions of their own industry, led them to engage in another branch of trade, that of banking. In this they soon became so eminent, that the money transactions of almost every kingdom in Europe passed through their

---

[1] This is the commonly received derivation. A more accurate explanation of the use of the word is that which makes it synonymous with the Italian *Monte* (Latin, *Mons*), a mound, heap, or bank. Thus the Italian *Monte di Pietà* and the French *Mont de Piété* signify "A Charity Bank." Bacon and Evelyn use the word in the same sense. Bacon says, "Let it be no *Bank* or common stock, but every man be master of his own money." Evelyn, adverting to the *Monte di Pietà* at Padua, writes, "There is a continual *bank* of money to assist the poor." Blackstone also: "At Florence, in 1344, government owed £60,000, and being unable to pay it, formed the principal into an aggregate sum called, metaphorically, a *Mount* or *Bank*."—(Vol. i.)

hands, and in many of them they were entrusted with the collection and administration of the public revenues. In consequence of the activity and success with which they conducted their manufactures and money transactions—the former always attended with certain though moderate profit, the latter lucrative in a high degree, at a period when neither the interest of money nor the premium on bills of exchange were settled with accuracy—Florence became one of the first cities in Christendom, and some of its citizens extremely opulent."[1] Cosmo di Medici was reckoned the most wealthy merchant ever known in Europe, and in a treaty whereby Louis XI. engaged to pay Edward IV. fifty thousand crowns annually, it was expressly stipulated that the king of France should engage the partners of the Bank of Medici to become bound for the faithful and regular performance of this agreement on the part of himself and his heirs.[2]

Although the business of banking has probably always been carried on by private individuals before it has been carried on by a public company, yet most countries have found it useful to establish a public or national bank. Some of these banks have been founded for the purpose of facilitating commerce, others to serve the government.

The most ancient bank was that of Venice. It is supposed to have been established in 1157.[3] The State being involved in debt, through a long and severe war, the public creditors were formed into a corporation, with peculiar privileges, and the debts were allowed to be transferred from one name to another, much in the same way as our public funds, or the stock of our public banks. It was made a particular regulation that all payments of wholesale

[1] Robertson's Disquisition on India, page 113.
[2] Macpherson's History of Commerce, vol. i. page 698.
[3] Anderson's History of Commerce, vol. i. page 156.

merchandise, and bills of exchange, should be in bank money; and that all debtors and creditors should be obliged, the one to carry their money to the bank, the other to receive their payments in banco, so that payments were made by a simple transfer of stock from one account to the other. This bank may be deemed a wonder for the twelfth century, but requiring much alteration to adapt it to the modes and manners of the nineteenth.[1]

So early as the year 1349 the business of banking was carried on by the drapers of Barcelona, who were probably the most wealthy class of merchants in that city. But by an ordinance of the king of Arragon, they were not allowed to commence this branch of trade until they had first given sufficient security. In the year 1401 a public bank was established by the magistrates, and the city funds were responsible for the money placed in the bank. They exchanged money, received deposits, and discounted bills of exchange, both for the citizens and for foreigners.[2]

The bank of Genoa was established in 1407. This bank, like that of Venice, owed its origin to the debts of the State. Considerable confusion had arisen from the multitude of loans which the republic had contracted with its citizens. These various loans were now formed into one total amount, and made the capital of the bank. This bank was called the Chamber of St. George, and its management was entrusted to eight directors, elected by the proprietors

---

[1] See Montefiore's Commercial Dictionary, Article *Bank*. It was not until 1587 that the Bank of Venice became a bank in the modern sense of the word. The extensive foreign trade of the city brought thither coins of all countries, and in every state of wear. To remedy the loss and inconvenience thus caused, the merchants were ordered to bring their coins to the bank, where they were weighed, the merchants receiving notes, promising to pay the bearer on demand bullion of the proper or standard fineness, equal to the value of the coins paid in.

[2] Macpherson's History of Commerce, vol. i. pp. 540, 612.

of the stock. As a security for the debt, the State made over to the bank several cities and territories, among which were the port of Caffa and the little kingdom of Corsica.

The Bank of Amsterdam was founded in the year 1609. It was occasioned by the vast quantity of worn and clipped coins then in circulation, in consequence of which the value of the currency was reduced above nine per cent. below that of good money fresh from the mint. The bank received these deficient coins at nearly their intrinsic value, and made all its issues in coin of the standard weight and fineness. At the same time a law was made that all foreign bills of exchange should be paid in bank money. This law raised the value of bills on Holland in foreign countries, and compelled every merchant to keep an account at the bank, in order that he might at all times have legal money to pay his foreign bills. The premium (called the Agio) on bank money was regulated by the market price of gold, and was subject to considerable fluctuations. To prevent the gambling to which these fluctuations gave rise, the bank at length determined to sell bank money for currency at five per cent. agio, and to buy it again at four per cent. From this and other sources of profit the bank is supposed to have gained a considerable revenue. It was the entire property of the city of Amsterdam, and was placed under the direction of four burgomasters, who were changed every year.[1]

The Bank of Amsterdam was the model on which were formed most of the European banks now in existence; but they have varied very considerably from each other, according to the circumstances of the respective countries in which they have been established.

---

[1] Adam Smith's Wealth of Nations, vol. ii. p. 220. Edition 1812.

SECTION II.

THE RISE OF BANKING IN ENGLAND.

THE exchanging of money; the lending of money; the borrowing of money; the transmitting of money, are the four principal branches of the business of modern banking, and in most countries they seem to have taken their rise in the order in which they are here named.

MONEY-CHANGING.

For several centuries the only coin current in England was made of silver, and the highest denomination was the silver penny. This coin contained about half as much silver as one of our sixpences. There were also silver halfpence and silver farthings, and frequently the silver pennies were cut into halves and quarters to serve the purpose of half-pence and farthings, until laws were made to prohibit the practice. Copper was not coined in England until the year 1609, and then the small leaden tokens previously issued by private individuals were suppressed.

Gold was first coined in England in 1257, but soon went out of circulation, and did not enter permanently into currency until 1344, when Edward III. issued gold nobles, half nobles, and farthing nobles; the noble to pass for 6s. 8d., the half noble for 3s. 4d., and the farthing noble for 1s. 8d. This coinage seems to have given rise to the office of Royal Exchanger.

"It was not so easy a matter in the times we are now

considering to exchange gold and silver coins for each other as it is at present, and, therefore, Edward III. and several of his successors took this office into their own hands, to prevent private extortion as well as for their own advantage, and they performed it by appointing certain persons, furnished with a competent quantity of gold and silver coins, in London and other towns, to be the only exchangers of money, at the following rate:—When these royal exchangers gave silver coins for a parcel of gold nobles, for example, they gave one silver penny less for each noble than its current value, and when they gave gold nobles for silver coins they took one penny more, or 6s. 9d. for each noble, by which, in every transaction, they made a profit of $1\frac{1}{5}$th per cent. These royal exchangers had also the exclusive privilege of giving the current coins of the kingdom in exchange for foreign coins, to accommodate merchant-strangers, and of purchasing light money for the use of the mint. As several laws were made against exporting English coin, the king's exchangers, at the several seaports, furnished merchants and others who were going beyond seas with the coins of the countries to which they were going, in exchange for English money, according to a table which hung up in their office for public inspection. By these various operations they made considerable profits, of which the king had a certain share. The house in which the royal exchanger of any town kept his office was called the *Exchange*, from which it is probable the public structures where merchants meet for transacting business derive their name."[1]

This institution continued until the middle of the reign of Henry VIII., when it fell into disuse. It was re-established in 1627, by Charles I., who then issued the following proclamation:—

[1] Henry's History of England, vol. viii. page 347.

"Whereas the exchange of all manner of gold and silver current in moneys or otherwise, as the buying, selling, and exchanging of all manner of bullion, in species of foreign coins, billets, ingots, &c., fine, refined, or allayed howsoever, being fit for our mint, hath ever been and ought to be our sole right, as part of our prerogative, royal and ancient revenue, wherein none of our subjects of whatever trade or quality soever, ought at all, without any special licence, to intermeddle, the same being prohibited by divers Acts of Parliament and Proclamations, both ancient and modern. And whereas ourself and divers of our royal predecessors have, for some time past, tolerated a promiscuous kind of liberty to all, but especially to some of the mystery and trade of goldsmiths in London and elsewhere, not only to make the said exchanges, but to buy and sell all manner of bullion, and from thence some of them have grown to that licentiousness, that they have for divers years presumed, for their private gain, to sort and weigh all sorts of money current within our realm, to the end to cull out the old and new moneys, which, either by not wearing or by any other accident, are weightier than the rest, which weightiest moneys have not only been molten down for the making of plate, &c., but even traded in and sold to merchant-strangers, &c., who have exported the same, whereby the consumption of coins has been greatly occasioned, as also the raising of the silver even of our own moneys to a rate above what they are truly current for, by reason whereof no silver can be brought up to our mint but to the loss of the bringers, &c.—For the reforming of all which abuses we have, by the advice of our Privy Council, determined to assume our said right, for our own profit and the good of the realm, and for this end we do now appoint Henry Earl of Holland and his deputies, to have the office of our changes, exchanges, and out-changes whatsoever, in England, Wales, and Ireland.—And we do hereby strictly charge and command that no goldsmith nor other person whatsoever, other than the said Earl of Holland, do presume to change, &c."[1]

As this measure occasioned some dissatisfaction, the king authorized, in the following year, the publication of a pamphlet, entitled "Cambium Regis, or the Office of his Majesty's Exchanger Royal." In this pamphlet it was attempted to be shown:—

"That the prerogative of exchange of bullion for coin has always been a flower of the Crown, of which instances are quoted from the time of King Henry I. downwards. That King John farmed out that office for no smaller a sum than five thousand marks—that the place or office where the exchange was made in his reign was near St. Paul's Cathedral in London, and gave name to the street still called the Old 'Change—that in succeeding reigns there were several other places for those exchanges besides London—that this method continued to Henry the Eighth's time, who suffered his coin to be so far debased that no regular exchange could be made—that the same confusion made way for the London goldsmiths to leave off their proper trade of *goldsmithrie*, *i.e.*, the working and selling of new gold and silver plate, and manufacture, the sole intents of all their charters, and to turn exchangers of plate and foreign coins for our English coins, although they had no right to buy any gold or silver for any other purpose than for their manufacture aforesaid, neither had any other person but those substituted by the Crown a right to buy the same. The king, therefore, has now resumed this office, not merely to keep up his right so to do, but likewise to prevent those trafficking goldsmiths from culling and sorting all the heavy coin, and selling the same to the mint of Holland,

---

[1] Anderson's History of Commerce, vol. ii. page 324.

which gained greatly thereby, or else by melting those heavy coins down for making of plate, witness the pieces of thirteenpence-halfpenny, old shillings of Queen Elizabeth, ninepenny and fourpenny-halfpenny pieces, which, being weighty moneys, none of them were now to be met with, whereby they have raised the price of silver to twopence per ounce above the value of the mint, which thereby has stood still ever since the eleventh of King James—that for above thirty years past it has been the usual practice of those exchanging goldsmiths to make their servants run every morning from shop to shop to buy up all weighty coins for the mints of Holland and the East countries, whereby the king's mint has stood still."

Not only the Goldsmiths' Company of London, but the lord mayor, court of aldermen, and common council, petitioned against the revival of the office of the Royal Exchanger. They were not, however, successful; and on a second application of the Goldsmiths' Company, the king told them "to trouble him no farther, since his right to the office was undoubtedly clear." After the death of Charles I. this office was not continued, and the business of money-changing fell again into the hands of the goldsmiths. Their shops were situated chiefly on the south row of Cheapside, and extended from the street called the Old 'Change unto Bucklersbury.[1]

MONEY-LENDING.

That part of the business of banking which consists in the lending of money lay, during the Middle Ages, under severe restraints. The taking of interest for the loan of money was deemed sinful, and stigmatized with the name of usury. This opinion appears to be wholly unwarranted,

---

[1] See Maitland's History of London, page 826.

either by the principles of natural equity or the enactments of the Mosaic law. "The taking of interest from Israelites was forbidden by Moses; not, however, as if he absolutely and in all cases condemned the practice, for he expressly permitted interest to be taken from strangers, but out of favour to the poorer classes of the people. The farther we go back towards the origin of nations, the poorer do we commonly find them, and the more strangers to commerce; and where this is the case, people borrow, not with a view to profit, but from poverty, and in order to procure the necessaries of life; and there it must be, no doubt, a great hardship to give back more than has been got. The taking of interest from *strangers*, Moses has not only nowhere forbidden, but even expressly authorized. Hence it is clear that he does by no means represent interest as in itself sinful and unjust. Any such prohibition of interest in our age and country would, without doubt, be unjust towards lenders, and destructive to trade of every description. Among all the remnants of ancient laws, it would be difficult to find one which, in the present state of society, it would be more foolish and hurtful to revive and enforce. It would only suit a State so constituted as was that of the Israelites by Moses."[1] The taking of interest for the loan of money was first prohibited in England by Edward the Confessor. This law, however, appears to have become obsolete; for, in a council held at Westminster, in the year 1126, usury was prohibited only to the clergy, who, in case they practised it, were to be degraded; and in another Council, held twelve years afterwards, it was decreed that, "such of the clergy as were usurers and hunters after sordid gain, and for the public employments of the laity, ought to be degraded." The earliest mention we find in

---

[1] See Michaelis's Commentaries on the Laws of Moses, vol. ii. pp. 324, to 342.

English history, of a certain yearly allowance for the usury or interest of money, is in the year 1199, the tenth and last year of Richard I. In this case the rate of interest was 10 per cent. This appears to have been the ordinary or market-rate of interest from that period until the time of Henry VIII., but there are many instances on record of a much higher rate of interest being taken, especially by the Jews and the Lombards, who, in those times, were the principal money-lenders. The exorbitant interest taken by them is supposed by eminent writers to have been the effect of the prohibition of usury.

The Jews, who were previously famous in foreign countries for their "egregious cunning in trade and in the practice of brokerage," arrived in England about the time of the Conquest, and soon became remarkable for wealth and usury. "The prejudices of the age," says Hume, "had made the lending of money on interest pass by the invidious name of usury; yet the necessity of the practice had still continued it, and the greater part of that kind of dealing fell everywhere into the hands of the Jews, who, being already infamous on account of their religion, had no honour to lose, and were apt to exercise a profession odious in itself by every kind of rigour, and even sometimes by rapine and extortion. The industry and frugality of this people had put them in possession of all the ready money, which the idleness and profusion common to the English with the European nations enabled them to lend at exorbitant and unequal interest."[1] Henry III. prohibited the Jews taking more than twopence a week for every 20s. they lent to the scholars at Oxford.[2] This is after the rate of £43 6s. 8d. per cent. per annum. Peter of Blois, Archdeacon of Bath, writes thus to his friend the Bishop of Ely: "I am dragged

---

[1] Hume's History of England, chap. 10.
[2] Henry's History of England, vol. vi. page 280.

to Canterbury to be crucified by the perfidious Jews amongst their other debtors, whom they ruin and torment with usury. The same sufferings await me also at London, if you do not mercifully interpose for my deliverance. I beseech you, therefore, O most Rev. Father and most loving friend, to become bound to Samson the Jew for £6 which I owe him, and thereby deliver me from that cross."[1] The wealth and the rapacity of the Jews occasioned the most cruel proceedings against them on the part of both the populace and the Government. These persecutions terminated by their expulsion from England in the year 1290. They were not readmitted until the time of Oliver Cromwell. On this occasion the Protector summoned an assembly to debate two questions: 1st, whether it were lawful to tolerate the Jews; and 2nd, if it were, on what conditions? The assembly consisted of two judges, seven citizens of London, among whom were the lord mayor and the sheriffs, and fourteen divines. The judges considered toleration merely as a point of *law*, and declared they knew of no law against it, and that if it were thought useful to the State, they would advise it. The citizens viewed it in a *commercial* light, and they were divided in their opinions about its utility. Both these, however, despatched the matter briefly; but the divines violently opposed it by text after text for four whole days. Cromwell was at length so weary that he told them he had hoped they would have thrown some light on the subject to direct his conscience, but, on the contrary, they had rendered it more obscure and doubtful than before; that he desired, therefore, no more of their reasonings, but lest he should do anything rashly, he begged a share in their prayers.

Previous to the expulsion of the Jews, the Lombards had settled in England, and they soon became as great

[1] Henry's History of England, vol. vi. page 280.

usurers as the Jews themselves. By *Lombards* were generally understood Italian merchants from the four republics of Genoa, Lucca, Florence, and Venice. The foreign commerce of those times was usually carried on by companies of merchants who, on payment of certain duties, were invested by the Government with a monopoly of the trade to those countries of which they were natives, and they also possessed peculiar privileges. "As the Lombards engrossed the trade of every kingdom in which they settled, they soon became masters of its cash. Money, of course, was in their hands not only a sign of the value of their commodities, but became an object of commerce itself. They dealt largely as bankers. In an ordinance, A.D. 1295, we find them styled *mercatores* and *campsores*. They carried on this, as well as other branches of their commerce, with somewhat of that rapacious spirit which is natural to monopolizers who are not restrained by the competition of rivals: an opinion which prevailed in the Middle Ages was, however, in some measure the cause of their exorbitant demands, and may be pleaded in apology for them. Commerce cannot be carried on with advantage, unless the persons who lend a sum are allowed a certain premium for the use of their money, as a compensation for the risk which they run in permitting another to traffic with their stock. This premium is fixed by law in all commercial countries, and is called the legal interest of money. But the Fathers of the Church absurdly applied the prohibitions of usury in Scripture to the payment of legal interest, and condemned it as a sin. The schoolmen, misled by Aristotle, whose sentiments they followed, implicitly and without examination adopted the same error and enforced it. Thus the Lombards found themselves engaged in a traffic which was deemed criminal and odious. They were liable to punishment if detected. They were not satisfied, therefore, with that moderate premium which they might have claimed, if their trade had been open and authorized by law. They exacted a sum proportional to the danger and infamy of a discovery. Accordingly we find it was usual for them to demand twenty per cent. for the use of money in the thirteenth century. About the beginning of that century the Countess of Flanders was obliged to borrow money in order to pay her husband's ransom. She procured the sum requisite, either from Italian merchants or from Jews. The lowest interest which she paid to them was above twenty per cent., and some of them exacted near thirty. In the fourteenth century, A.D. 1311, Philip IV. fixed the interest which might be legally exacted in the fairs of Champagne at twenty per cent. The interest of money in Arragon was somewhat lower. James I., A.D. 1242, fixed it by law at eighteen per cent. As late as the year 1490, it appears that the interest of money in Piacenza was at the rate of forty per cent. This is the more extraordinary, because at that time the commerce of the Italian States was become considerable. It appears from Lud. Guicciardini that Charles V. had fixed the rate of interest in his dominions in the Low Countries at twelve per cent., and at the time when he wrote, about the year 1560, it was not uncommon to exact more than that sum. He complains of this as exorbitant, and points out its bad effects both on agriculture and commerce. This high interest on money is alone a proof that the profits on commerce were exorbitant. The Lombards were also established in England in the thirteenth century, and a considerable street in the city of London still bears their name. They enjoyed great privileges, and carried on an extensive commerce, particularly as bankers."[1]

[1] Robertson's History of Charles V., vol. i. page 257.

The English monarchs frequently borrowed money of the Lombards, as well as of other public bodies and of private individuals. The companies of foreign merchants made advances of money, which were repaid by the duties on their merchandise. The oldest and wealthiest of these companies, the Steel-Yard Company, was a kind of bank to our kings, whenever they wanted money on any sudden emergency, but the company was sure to be well paid in the end for such assistance.[1]

In the year 1546 the taking of interest for money was made legal in England, and the rate was fixed at ten per cent. This Act was repealed in the year 1552, but it was re-enacted in 1571. The legal rate of interest was reduced to eight per cent. in 1624, and to six per cent. in 1651. In the year 1714 it was reduced to five per cent. After the taking of interest was sanctioned by law, the term USURY, which was previously applied to interest in general, became limited, to denote a rate of interest higher than that which the law allowed.

MONEY BORROWING.

That part of the business of banking which consists in the borrowing of money, with a view of lending it again at a higher rate of interest, does not appear to have been carried on by bankers until the year 1645, when a new era occurred in the history of banking. The goldsmiths, who were previously only money-changers, now became also money-lenders. They became also money-borrowers, and allowed interest on the sums they borrowed. They were agents for receiving rents. They lent money to the king on the security of the taxes. The receipts

---

[1] Anderson's History of Commerce, vol. ii. page 192.

they issued for the money lodged at their houses circulated from hand to hand, and were known by the name of "goldsmiths' notes." These may be considered as the first kind of bank notes issued in England. The following account of these banking goldsmiths is taken chiefly from Anderson's "History of Commerce."[1]

When our merchants became enriched by commerce, they wished for a place of security in which they might deposit their wealth. Hence they usually sent their money to the mint in the Tower of London, which became a sort of bank. The merchants left their money here when they had no occasion for it, and drew it out as they wanted it. But in 1640, King Charles I. took possession of £200,000 of the merchants' money that had been lodged in the mint,[2] and from that period the merchants kept their money in their own houses, under the care of their servants and apprentices. On the breaking out of the civil war between Charles I. and the Parliament, it became very customary for the apprentices to rob their masters, and then run away and join the army. As the merchants could now place no confidence either in the public authorities or in their own servants, they were under the necessity of employing bankers.

These bankers were the goldsmiths. Previous to this period, the business of the goldsmiths was similar to what it is in our own time. They bought and sold plate and foreign coins; they procured gold to be coined at the mint, and supplied refiners, plate-makers, and others with the precious metals. To deal in gold and silver bullion to any large extent, implies the possession of considerable wealth; and as all the money in the country then consisted of gold and silver coin, it was natural enough that

---

[1] Vol. ii. page 402.
[2] This money was in no long time repaid.

the goldsmiths should become the bankers of those who had money for which they had no immediate use.

An account of the bankers of those days is related in a curious pamphlet, published in the year 1676, and entitled, "The mystery of the new-fashioned Goldsmiths or Bankers discovered." The author observes that:—

"This new banking business soon grew very considerable. It happened," says he, "in those times of civil commotion, that the Parliament, out of plates and old coins brought into the mint, coined seven millions into half-crowns; and there being no mills then in use at the mint, this new money was of a very unequal weight, sometimes twopence and threepence difference in an ounce, and most of it was, it seems, heavier than it ought to have been in proportion to the value in foreign parts. Of this the goldsmiths made naturally the advantage usual in such cases, by picking out or culling the heaviest, and melting them down and exporting them.

"Moreover, such merchants' servants as still kept their masters' running cash, had fallen into a way of clandestinely lending the same to the goldsmiths at fourpence per cent. per diem, who, by these and such-like means, were enabled to lend out great quantities of cash to necessitous merchants and others, weekly or monthly, at high interest, and also began to discount the merchants' bills at the like or higher interest.

"Much about the same time, the goldsmiths (or new-fashioned bankers) began to receive the rents of gentlemen's estates remitted to town, and to allow them and others who put cash in their hands some interest for it, if it remained but a single month in their hands, or even a lesser time. This was a great allurement for people to put money into their hands, which would bear interest till the day they wanted it; and they could also draw it out by one hundred pounds or fifty pounds, &c., at a time, as they wanted it, with infinitely less trouble than if they had lent it out on either real or personal security.

"The consequence was, that it quickly brought a great quantity of cash into their hands, so that the chief or greatest of them were now enabled to supply Cromwell with money in advance, on the revenues, as his occasion required, upon great advantages to themselves.

"After the Restoration, King Charles II. being in want of money, the bankers took ten per cent. of him barefacedly and by private contracts; on many bills, orders, tallies, and debts of that king, they got twenty, sometimes thirty per cent., to the great dishonour of the government.

"This great gain induced the goldsmiths more and more to become lenders to the king, to anticipate all the revenue, to take every grant of Parliament into pawn as soon as it was given; also to outvie each other in buying and taking to pawn bills, orders, and tallies, so that in effect all the revenue passed through their hands."

The "new-fashioned bankers" were also attacked by Sir Josiah Child, in his "New Discourse of Trade," in the following terms:—

"And principally this seeming scarcity of money proceeds from the trade of bankering, which obstructs circulation, advanceth usury, and renders it so easy, that most men, as soon as they can make up a sum of from £50 to £100, send it in to the goldsmith, which doth and will occasion, while it lasts, that fatal pressing necessity for money visible throughout the whole kingdom, both to prince and people.

"A seventh accidental reason why land doth not sell at present at the rate it naturally should in proportion to the legal interest, is that innovated practice of *bankers* in London, which hath more effects attending it than most I have conversed with have yet observed; but I shall here take notice of that only which is to my present purpose, viz. :—

"The gentlemen that are bankers, having a large interest from his Majesty for what they advance upon his Majesty's revenue, can afford to give the full legal interest to all persons that put money into their hands, though for never so short or long a time, which makes the trade of usury so easy and hitherto safe, that few, after having found the sweetness of this lazy way of improvement (being by continuance and success grown to fancy themselves secure in it), can be led (there being neither ease nor profit to invite them) to lay out their money in land, though at fifteen years' purchase; whereas before this way of private banking came up, men that had money were forced often times to let it lie dead by them until they could meet with securities to their minds, and if the like necessity were now of money lying dead, the loss of use for the dead time being deducted from the profit of six per cent. (*communibus annis*) would in effect take off £1 per cent. per annum of the profit of usury, and consequently incline men more to purchase lands, because the difference between usury and purchasing would not, in point of profit, be so great as now it is, this new invention of cashiering having, in my opinion, clearly bettered the usurer's trade one or two per cent. per annum. And that this way of leaving money with goldsmiths hath had the aforesaid effect, seems evident to me from the scarcity it makes of money in the country; for the trade of bankers being only in London, doth very much drain the ready money from all other parts of the kingdom." [1]

In the year 1667 occurred the first RUN of which we have any account in the history of banking. The business of the

[1] See page 56.

new-fashioned bankers had increased so fast, and they had become so numerous, that their trade was supposed to be at its height in this year; when, during the time that a treaty of peace was under consideration, the Dutch fleet sailed up the Thames, blew up the fort of Sheerness, set fire to Chatham, and burned four ships of the line. This disaster occasioned great alarm in London, particularly among those who had money in their bankers' hands, as it was imagined that the king would not be able to repay the bankers the money they had lent him. To quiet the fears of the people, the king issued a proclamation, declaring that the payments to the bankers should be made at the Exchequer the same as usual.

In 1672, five years afterwards, a much greater calamity befell the bankers: for King Charles II. shut up the Exchequer, and would not pay the bankers either the principal or the interest of the money which he had borrowed. The amount then due by the king was £1,328,526, which he had borrowed of the bankers at eight per cent., and which he never repaid.

The mode in which the bankers transacted their loans with the king was this: as soon as the parliament had voted to the king certain sums of money out of particular taxes, the bankers advanced at once the money voted by the parliament, and were repaid in weekly payments at the Exchequer as the taxes were received. The mode of making the repayments and the rate of interest were agreed upon at the time of making the loan.

The shutting up of the Exchequer occasioned great distress among all classes of the people. Persons not in trade had then no way of employing their money with advantage but by placing it out at interest in the hands of a banker. Hence, not merchants only, but widows, orphans, and others, became suddenly deprived of the whole of their property. They came in crowds to the bankers, but could obtain neither the principal nor the interest of the money they had deposited. The clamour became so great, that the king granted a patent to pay six per cent. interest out of his hereditary excise; but he never paid the principal. But, about forty years afterwards, the parliament made arrangements by which the debt was assumed to be discharged.[1]

The business of banking remained entirely in the hands of the new-fashioned bankers until the establishment of the Bank of England, in the year 1694.

TRANSMISSION OF MONEY.

The transmission of money was in ancient times effected by sending a messenger with the coin. During the Middle Ages, it was accomplished by means of bills of exchange, which were purchased by merchants. Ultimately, a class of persons carried on this kind of traffic, and purchased or sold bills to suit the convenience of parties who wished to deal with them. The pecuniary transactions of independent nations are still adjusted in the same way. But the transmission of money from one part of the country to another part, is more frequently effected upon the principle of transfers, without the passing of any bill. I have explained this mode of operation in my " Practical Treatise on Banking."

---

[1] That is, it still forms part of the National Debt. The creditors never received a farthing.

SECTION III.

THE HISTORY OF THE BANK OF ENGLAND.

THE Bank of England was first projected by Dr. Hugh Chamberlain, but the plan actually adopted was proposed by Mr. William Paterson. The object was to raise money for the use of the Government. After the scheme had received the sanction of the ministry, it was brought before the parliament. Here it underwent a long and violent discussion. One party expatiated upon the national advantages that would accrue from such a measure; they said it would rescue the nation out of the hands of extortioners and usurers, lower interest, raise the value of land, revive and establish public credit, extend the circulation, consequently improve commerce, facilitate the annual supplies, and connect the people more closely with the government. The opposition party affirmed that it would become a monopoly, and engross the whole money of the kingdom; that as it must infallibly be subservient to government views, it might be employed for the worst purposes of arbitrary power; that instead of assisting, it would weaken commerce, by tempting people to withdraw their money from trade and employ it in stock-jobbing; that it would produce a swarm of brokers and jobbers to prey upon their fellow creatures, encourage fraud and gambling, and thus corrupt the morals of the nation.[1] Notwithstanding these objections, the Act passed both

---

[1] See Smollett's History of England, chap. iv.

houses of parliament, and received the royal assent. The following observations upon the establishment of the Bank of England are taken from Bishop Burnet's " History of his own Times :"—

" Some thought a bank would grow to be a monopoly, all the money in England would come into their hands, and they would, in a few years, become masters of the wealth and stock of the nation; but those that were for it argued that the credit it would have must increase trade, and the circulation of money, at least in bank notes. It was visible that all the enemies of the government set themselves against it with such a vehemence of zeal that this alone convinced all people that they saw the strength that our affairs would receive from it. I had heard the Dutch often reckon up the great advantages they had from their banks; and they concluded that as long as England continued jealous of the government, a bank could never be settled among us, nor gain credit enough to support itself; and upon that, they judged that the superiority in trade must still lie on their side.

" The advantages the king and all concerned in tallies had from the bank was soon so sensibly felt that all people saw into the secret reasons that made the enemies of the constitution set themselves with so much earnestness against it."

The Act of Parliament by which the bank was established, is entitled, " An Act for granting to their Majesties several duties upon tonnage of ships and vessels, and upon beer, ale, and other liquors, for securing certain recompenses and advantages in the said Act mentioned, to such persons as shall voluntarily advance the sum of fifteen hundred thousand pounds towards carrying on the war with France." After a variety of enactments relative to the " duties upon tonnage of ships and vessels, and upon beer, ale, and other liquors," the Act authorizes the raising of £1,200,000 by voluntary subscription, the subscribers to be formed into a corporation, and be styled "The Governor and Company of the Bank of England." The sum of £300,000 was also to be raised by subscription, and the contributors to receive instead annuities for one, two, or three lives. Towards the £1,200,000 no one person was to subscribe more than £10,000 before the first day of July next ensuing, nor at any time more than £20,000. The corporation were to lend their whole capital to government, for which they were to receive interest at the rate of eight per cent. per annum, and £4,000 per annum for management; being £100,000 per annum in the whole. The corporation were not allowed to borrow or owe more than the amount of their capital, and if they did so the individual members became liable to the creditors in proportion to the amount of their stock. The corporation were not to trade in any "goods, wares, or merchandise whatsoever;" but they were allowed to deal in bills of exchange, gold or silver bullion, and to sell any goods, wares, or merchandise upon which they had advanced money, and which had not been redeemed within three months after the time agreed upon.

The whole subscription having been filled in ten days, a charter was issued on the 27th day of July, 1694.

The charter declares—

"That the management and government of the corporation be committed to the governor, deputy-governor, and twenty-four directors, who shall be elected between the 25th day of March and the 25th day of April each year, from among the members of the company duly qualified.

"That no dividend shall at any time be made by the said governor and company, save only out of the interest, profit, or produce arising out of the said capital, stock, or fund, or by such dealing as is allowed by Act of Parliament.

"They must be natural born subjects of England, or naturalized subjects; they shall have in their own name and for their own use, severally, viz., the governor at least £4,000, the deputy-governor £3,000, and each director £2,000, of the capital stock of the said corporation.

"That thirteen or more of the said governors or directors (of which the governor or deputy-governor shall be always one), shall constitute a court of directors for the management of the affairs of the company, and for the appointment of all agents and servants which may be necessary, paying them such salaries as they may consider reasonable.

"Every elector must have, in his own name and for his own use, £500 or more, capital stock, and can only give one vote; he must, if required by any member present, take the oath of stock, or the declaration of stock if it be one of those people called Quakers.

"Four general courts to be held in every year, in the months of September, December, April, and July. A general court may be summoned at any time, upon the requisition of nine proprietors duly qualified as electors.

"The majority of electors in general courts have the power to make and constitute by-laws and ordinances for the government of the corporation, provided that such by-laws and ordinances be not repugnant to the laws of the kingdom, and be conformed and approved, according to the statutes in such case made and provided."

The above charter, which was originally granted for ten years only, was subject to various renewals. A chronological account of these, together with an account of the various additions to the capital, and of other incidents in the history of the Bank, will be found in the following pages.

1697. Bank notes were from fifteen to twenty per cent. discount. During the re-coinage in 1696, the bank had issued its notes in exchange for the clipped and deficient coin previously in circulation, and it was not able to procure from the mint a sufficient quantity of the new coins to discharge the notes presented to it for payment. This compelled the bank to make two calls of twenty per cent. each upon its stockholders. It paid some of its notes by bills, bearing interest at six per cent. The bank also advertised, that while the silver was re-coining, " such as think it fit, for their convenience, to keep an account in a book with the bank, may transfer any sum under five pounds from his own to another man's account."

Exchequer tallies and orders for payment having, in 1696, been at a discount of forty, fifty, and sixty per cent., and bank notes at a discount of twenty per cent., the bank was empowered to receive subscriptions for the enlargement of its stock; four-fifths in tallies and orders, and the remaining one-fifth in bank notes. The sum subscribed was £1,001,171 10s., which, with the original capital of £1,200,000, raised the capital to the sum of £2,201,171 10s.

The bank charter was extended or renewed until the expiration of twelve months' notice, to be given after the first day of August, 1710, and until payment by the public to the bank of the demands therein specified; being an extension or renewal for five years (8 and 9 William III. c. 20). It was also enacted, "that the common capital and principal stock, and also the real fund of the governor and company, or any profit or produce to be made thereof, should be exempted from any rates, taxes, assessments, or impositions whatever, during the continuance of the bank;" and that the forgery of the company's seal, or of any of its notes or bills, should be felony without benefit of clergy.

1707. The subscription of £1,001,171 10*s*., raised in the year 1697, was restored. This reduced the bank capital to the original sum of £1,200,000.

1708. The bank charter was extended or renewed until the expiration of twelve months' notice, to be given after the first day of August, 1732, and until payment by the public to the bank of the demands therein specified; being an extension or renewal of the said charter for twenty years (7 Anne, c. 7). By this Act it is provided, "That during the continuance of the said corporation of the Governor and Company of the Bank of England, it shall not be lawful for any body politic or corporate whatsoever, created or to be created (other than the said Governor and Company of the Bank of England), or for any other persons whatsoever, united or to be united in covenants or partnership, *exceeding the number of six persons*, in that part of Great Britain called England, to borrow, owe, or take up any sum or sums of money on their bills or notes, payable at demand, or at a less time than six months from the borrowing thereof."

1709. In this year there was a new subscription of £1,001,171 10*s*., another of £2,201,171 10*s*., and a call upon the proprietors of fifteen per cent., £656,204 1*s*. 9*d*.; altogether making the total capital of the bank, £5,058,547 1*s*. 9*d*. This increase of capital became necessary, from the bank having in the preceding year lent the government £400,000 without interest, and agreed to cancel one million and a half exchequer bills in its possession, amounting, with interest, to £1,775,027 17*s*. 10½*d*.

1710. A further call of £501,448 12*s*. 11*d*., which increased the bank capital to £5,559,995 14*s*. 8*d*.

1713. The bank charter was extended or renewed until the expiration of twelve months' notice, to be given after the first day of August, 1742, and until payment by the public to the bank of the demands therein specified; being an extension or renewal of the said charter for ten years (12 Anne, Stat. I. c. ii.). In consideration of receiving this privilege, the bank undertook to circulate £1,200,000 in exchequer bills. In this year the legal rate of interest was reduced from six to five per cent.

1717. The bank cancelled £2,000,000 exchequer bills, and received interest from the government at five per cent. on the amount.

1718. Subscriptions for government loans were first received at the bank. From this period the government have found it more convenient to employ the bank as their agents in all operations of this nature, than to transact them at the treasury or the exchequer. The bank, becoming by degrees more closely connected with the government, began to make advances of money in anticipation of the land and malt taxes, and upon exchequer bills and other securities.

1720. THE SOUTH SEA BUBBLE commenced April 7.

"The directors opened their books for a subscription of one million, at the rate of £300 for every £100 capital. Persons of all ranks crowded to the house in such a manner, that the first subscriptions exceeded two millions of original stock. In a few days this stock advanced to £340, and the subscriptions were sold for double the price of the first payment. The infatuation prevailed till the 8th day of September, when the stock began to fall. Then did some of the adventurers awake from their delirium. The number of the sellers daily increased. On the 29th day of the month, the stock had sunk to one hundred and fifty. Several eminent goldsmiths and bankers, who had lent great sums upon it, were obliged to stop payment and abscond. The ebb of this portentous tide was so violent, that it bore down everything in its way, and an infinite number of families were overwhelmed with ruin; public credit sustained a terrible shock; the nation was thrown into a dangerous ferment; and nothing was heard but the ravings of grief and despair. Some principal members of the ministry were deeply concerned in these fraudulent transactions. When they saw the price of stock sinking daily, they employed all their influence with the bank to support the credit of the South Sea Company. That corporation agreed, though with reluctance, to subscribe into the stock of the South Sea Company, valued at £400 per cent., £3,500,000, which the company was to repay to the bank on Lady-day and Michaelmas of the ensuing year. This transaction was managed by Mr. Robert Walpole, who with his own hand wrote the minute of agreement, afterwards known by the name of the Bank Contract. Books were opened at the bank to take in a subscription for the support of public credit, and considerable sums of money were brought in. By this expedient the stock was raised at first, and those who contrived it seized the opportunity to realize. But the bankruptcy of goldsmiths and the sword-blade company, from the fall of South Sea stock, occasioned such a run upon the bank, that the money was paid away faster than it could be received from the subscription. Then the South Sea stock sunk again, and the directors of the bank, finding themselves in danger of being involved in the company's ruin, renounced the agreement; which, indeed, they were under no obligation to perform, for it was drawn up in such a manner as to be no more than the rough draft of a subsequent agreement, without due form, penalty, or clause of obligation."[1]

The directors of the South Sea Company took legal advice, with a view to compel the bank to perform its contract; but the matter was arranged through the inter-

[1] Smollett.

vention of the government, who remitted to the South Sea Company two millions sterling as a compensation for the non-performance of the bank contract.

1721. By the 8th Geo. I. c. 21, the South Sea Company were authorized to sell £200,000 per annum, government annuities; and corporations purchasing the same at twenty-six years' purchase were allowed to add the amount to their capital stock. The bank purchased the whole of this £200,000 per annum, at twenty years' purchase, making £4,000,000.

1722. The bank capital increased £3,400,000 by a new subscription. This made the amount of capital £8,959,995 14s. 8d.

1726. The stock called three per cents. 1726, was created this year by the means of a lottery.

1727. The bank advanced to government, £1,750,000 upon the coal and culm duties, at four per cent. interest (1 Geo. II. c. 8).

1728. The bank advanced to government, £1,250,000 upon the lottery, at four per cent. (2 Geo. II. c. 8).

1732. Thursday, 3rd of August, about one o'clock, the governor, sub-governor, and several of the directors of the bank, came to see the first stone laid of their new building, in Threadneedle Street; and after they had viewed the stone, on which his Majesty's and their several names were engraved, the same was covered with a plate of lead, and that, with the base of a pillar.

1734. Thursday, 5th of June. The directors began to transact business at their new house in Threadneedle Street. The business of the bank had previously been carried on at Grocers' Hall, in the Poultry. In the hall of the new building was erected a curious marble statue of King William III., with a Latin inscription, of which the following is a translation:—

> For restoring efficacy to the laws,
> Authority to the courts of justice,
> Dignity to the parliament,
> To all his subjects their religion and liberties,
> And
> For confirming these to posterity,
> By the succession of the illustrious House
> Of Hanover
> To the British Throne,
> To the best of Princes, WILLIAM III.,
> Founder of the Bank,
> This Corporation, from a sense of gratitude,
> Has erected this statue,
> And dedicated it to his Memory,
> In the year of Our Lord MDCCXXXIV.,
> And the first year of this building.

1737. Considerable public discussion about the propriety of again renewing the bank charter. The following extracts from the "London Magazine" of this year will show the sentiments which different writers entertained upon this subject:—

"The bank have power to lend money on land, and no doubt might have put out prodigious sums that way, and have had a better interest for their money than most private people. Had the bank, then, lent out their money on land, they would have strengthened their CREDIT and their INTEREST, and also extended their usefulness by relieving the landed property, of which there is a great deal at this time in mortgage, most unaccountably, at five per cent., while inferior securities bear a premium at three per cent.

"Another branch of business which the bank have power to transact, but yet never meddle with, is the remittance of money backwards and forwards to London from all the chief trading cities in England, for which they should have proper offices or inferior banks erected in all such cities and towns as they intend to manage a remittance with;—this, besides what profit might be expected upon the remittances, would naturally bring great part of the cash which is circulated in the country to be lodged in their hands.

"I must next observe that in that branch of business in which they do employ themselves, which is that of a *London banker*, they very much contract and narrow their dealings, by refusing to take in payment *the foreign coins*, for which reason it is impracticable with many traders to keep their cash with them.

"This very privilege which the bank has for so long enjoyed, I could demonstrate to be a most heavy burthen upon the people, and a great prejudice to the landed interest as well as the trading interest of this kingdom; for if it had not been for this privilege, we should have had a bank, perhaps, in every county in England, and probably half a dozen different banks in London, by which means no merchant of tolerable credit could ever have been straitened for want of ready money at a low interest when he had occasion for it, nor would any landed gentleman who had a good title to his estate have been obliged to pay such premiums to brokers, or such an interest to mortgagees as they have now generally to pay;—whereas our present bank has never, so far as I have heard, assisted any landed gentleman, nor any merchant, except in and about London only.

"I am of opinion that with respect to the banking trade and the trade to the East Indies, neither the one nor the other can be carried on with such success, or in such an extensive manner, by private adventurers, as by a public company with such an exclusive privilege as our present companies have. The circulating of bank bills or cash notes must certainly increase the current cash of any country, and must, therefore, be of great use in trade; consequently, the more extensive and the more general such a circulation is, the better will it be for the inland trade of that country. It is true, a private man or set of men may, by a long series of good management, gain a very extensive credit, but that credit can never come to be so extensive or near so general as the credit of a rich public company, that has supported itself with honour, perhaps, for some ages; because the credit of a private man always depends upon himself, so that when he dies, his credit, as to any further circulation, generally dies with him, for it must require some time before those who succeed can revive or regain it; whereas a public company never dies, nor can their credit meet with any such interruption; and as their managers are always chosen annually by the company, there is a greater security for its being under good management than a private bank, whose chief managers are appointed by the chance of natural or legal succession: therefore, I shall always think it better for a trading country to have a public bank than to trust entirely to private bankers.

"There certainly never was a body of men that contributed more to the public safety than the Bank of England. This flourishing and opulent company have, upon every emergency, always cheerfully and readily supplied the necessities of the nation, so that there never have been any difficulties—any embarrassments—any delays in raising the money which has been granted by parliament for the service of the public; and it may very truly be said that they have, in very many important conjunctures, relieved the nation out of the greatest difficulties, if not absolutely saved it from ruin."

1738. Dec. 14. The bank commenced issuing post bills, payable seven days after sight, that in case the mail was robbed the parties might have time to stop payment of the bills. Highway robberies appear to have been very frequent at this period.

1742. The bank charter was extended or renewed until the expiration of twelve months' notice, to be given after the first day of August, 1764, and until payment by the public to the bank of the demands in this Act specified, being an extension or renewal of the said charter for twenty-two years (15 Geo. II. c. 13). In consideration of obtaining this charter, the bank lent to government £1,600,000 without interest. To raise this sum the bank made a call upon the proprietors of £840,004 5s. 4d., which increased its capital to £9,800,000.

1745. A RUN upon the bank, occasioned by the rebellion in Scotland, and supposed to be for the purpose of supplying the rebels with gold. A public meeting was held, and one thousand one hundred and forty merchants signed a declaration expressing their readiness to take bank notes.

1746. By the Act 19 Geo. II. c. 6, the bank delivered up to be cancelled £986,000 exchequer bills, in consideration of an annuity of £39,472, being three per cent. per annum. To raise the above sum the bank made a call of ten per cent. upon its proprietors; this increased the bank capital from £9,800,000 to £10,780,000.

1750. A reduction took place in the interest of part of the national debt. The bank held a court at Merchant-Taylors' Hall, and consented to receive a reduced rate of interest upon £8,486,800 of the debt due to them by the government. The bank also agreed to advance to the government a sum of money to pay off the dissentients.

1751. In order to raise the sum promised to be lent to the government, the bank established what was called "Bank Circulation." Books were opened to the public, and any person might enter his name and the sum he was willing to lend to the bank, *in case it should be called for*. The books being closed, the bank had the power of calling for the whole or any part of the sum subscribed at any time it pleased. The subscribers were to receive 2s. per cent. on the total amount of their subscription, and £4 per cent. on the sum actually advanced.

1752. By 25 Geo. II. the balance of annuities granted by 8 Geo. I. was carried to a three per cent. stock, formed in 1731, and they were consolidated into one stock—the new stock is still called " Three per cent. *consols*." The word *consols* is a contraction for consolidated.

1757. The government stock, called " Three per cent. reduced," derives its name from the operation of this year. This stock had borne four per cent. until the year 1750; from that time it paid three and a half per cent., and this year it was *reduced* to three per cent.

1758. It was legally determined that those persons who had given value for bank notes stolen from the mail, had a right to receive payment of them from the bank.

In this year occurred the first instance of the forgery of a bank note. It was committed by a person named R. W. Vaughan, who had been a linendraper at Stafford. The note was for £20, the smallest amount then in circulation. He was convicted and executed.

1759. The bank commenced issuing notes and post bills of £15 and £10.

1764. The bank charter was extended or renewed until the expiration of twelve months' notice, to be given after the first day of August, 1786, and until payment by the public to the bank of the demands therein specified; being an extension or renewal of the said charter for twenty-two years (4 Geo. III. c. 25).

In consideration of obtaining this charter the bank advanced £1,000,000 on exchequer bills until the year 1766, and paid into the exchequer £110,000.

1775. Bankers were prohibited to issue notes of a less amount than 20s. (15 Geo. III. c. 51).

1777. Bankers were prohibited to issue notes of a less value than £5 (17 Geo. III. c. 30).

1781. The bank charter was extended or renewed until the expiration of twelve months' notice, to be given after the first day of August, 1812, and until payment by the public to the bank of the demands therein specified; being an extension or renewal of the said charter for twenty-six years (21 Geo. III. c. 60). In consideration of obtaining this renewal of their charter, the bank advanced to the government £2,000,000, for three years at three per cent.

It is legally decided that the bank is not liable to pay forged notes.

1782. A call of £862,400, making the total capital of the bank £11,642,400. There was no further increase of capital until the year 1816.

1786. Previous to this year the bank received an allowance from the government on account of the management of the public debt; that is, for trouble in paying the dividends, superintending the transfer of stock, &c., of £562 10s. a million. It was now reduced to £450 a million; the bank being at the same time entitled to a considerable allowance for trouble in receiving contributions on loans, lotteries, &c. This scale of allowance was continued until the year 1808.

1791. A bill was brought into parliament to render £500,000 of the unclaimed dividends on the public funds available for the service of the public; but the bank agreed to lend that sum to the government without interest, and the bill was withdrawn.

1793. An Act of Parliament was passed (33 Geo. III.

c. 32), declaring that the bank should not be subject to any penalties for advancing money to the government for the payment of bills of exchange, accepted by the commissioners of his Majesty's treasury, and made payable at the bank. The amount of sums so advanced was required to be annually laid before parliament. According to their original charter, the bank was prohibited lending money to the government without the consent of parliament, under a penalty of three times the sum lent: one-fifth part of which was to go to the informer.

This was a year of great commercial distress: twenty-two commissions of bankruptcy were issued against country bankers.

1794. The bank commenced issuing notes for £5.

1795. The bank having resolved to reduce their discounts, placed the following notice in the discount office:—

"Bank of England, 31st December, 1795.

"Pursuant to an order of the Court of Directors:

"Notice is hereby given,

"That no bills will be taken in for discount at this office after 12 o'clock at noon, or notes after 12 o'clock on Wednesday.

"That in future, whenever the bills sent in for discount shall in any day amount to a larger sum than it shall be resolved to discount on that day, a *pro ratâ* proportion of such bills in each parcel as are not otherwise objectionable, will be returned to the person sending in the same, without regard to the respectability of the party sending in the bills, or the solidity of the bills themselves.

"The same regulation will be observed as to the notes."

1797. THE SUSPENSION OF CASH PAYMENTS.

From the first establishment of the Bank of England down to this year, it had always paid its notes regularly when presented. But in the course of 1796 and the early part of 1797 there was, owing to the prevalence of reports of invasion, a pretty severe run upon the Bank of England, and it was at length apprehended that the bank might be obliged to make a temporary stoppage. To avert this contingency an Order in Council was issued on the 26th of February, authorizing the bank not to pay its notes in gold, in the following terms :—

"Upon the representation of the Chancellor of the Exchequer, stating that from the results of the information which he had received, and of the inquiries which it has been his duty to make, respecting the effects of the unusual demand for specie that has been made upon the metropolis, in consequence of ill-founded or exaggerated alarms in different parts of the country; it appears, that unless some measure is immediately taken, there may be reason to apprehend a want of a sufficient supply of cash to answer the exigencies of the public service. It is the unanimous opinion of the Board, that it is indispensably necessary for the public service, that the directors of the Bank of England should forbear issuing any cash in payment, until the sense of parliament can be taken on that subject, and the proper measures adopted thereupon, for maintaining the means of circulation and supporting the public and commercial credit of the kingdom at this important conjuncture; and it is ordered that a copy of this minute be transmitted to the directors of the Bank of England, and they are hereby required, on the grounds of the exigency of the case, to conform thereto until the sense of parliament can be taken as aforesaid."

Among the crowd assembled at the bank, with a view of demanding gold, handbills were distributed, of which the following is a copy:—

"Bank of England, Feb. 27th, 1797.

"In consequence of an order of his Majesty's Privy Council, notified to the bank last night, a copy of which is hereunto annexed, the governor, deputy-governor, and directors of the Bank of England think it their duty to inform the proprietors of the bank stock, as well as the public at large, that the general concerns of the bank are in the most affluent and prosperous situation, and such as to preclude every doubt as to the security of its notes. The directors mean to continue their usual discounts for the accommodation of the commercial interest, paying the amount in bank notes, and the dividend warrants will be paid in the same manner."

On the same day was held a meeting of merchants, bankers, and others, the Lord Mayor in the chair, when the following resolution was unanimously passed:—

"That we, the undersigned, being highly sensible how necessary the preservation of public credit is at this time, do most readily declare, that we will not refuse to receive bank notes in payment of any sum of money to be paid to us, and we will use our utmost endeavours to make all our payments in the same manner."

This resolution was left for signature at several of the most respectable taverns, and a similar resolution was subsequently adopted by other public assemblies.

Immediately afterwards, the House of Commons appointed a committee to inquire into the affairs of the bank. The committee reported, that "The total amount of outstanding demands on the bank, on the 25th of July, was £13,770,390; and that the total amount of the funds for discharging those demands (not including the permanent debt due from government of £11,686,800, which bears an interest of three per cent.) was £17,597,280; and the result is, that there was, on the 25th day of February last, a surplus of effects belonging to the bank, beyond the amount of their debts, amounting to the sum of £3,825,890, exclusive of the above-mentioned permanent debt of £11,684,800, due from government." From accounts since published, it appears that the amount of gold and silver in possession of the bank was reduced by the previous run to £1,086,170.

1797. March 3. The bank was authorized to issue notes under £5 (37 Geo. III. c. 28). It is entitled, "An Act to remove doubts respecting promissory notes of the Governor and Company of the Bank of England, for payment of sums of money under £5." Accordingly, on the 10th of March the bank issued, for the first time, notes for £1 and £2.

May 3. THE BANK RESTRICTION ACT PASSED. It is the 37 Geo. III. c. 45, and is entitled, "An Act for continuing, for a limited time, the restriction contained in the minute of council of the 26th of February, 1797, on payment of cash by the bank." By this Act the bank directors were indemnified against any legal proceedings on account of having complied with the order of council. They were not permitted to issue cash, except for any sum under twenty shillings. But if any person lodged *cash* in the bank, he might be repaid in cash to the extent of three-fourths of the sum lodged; but the sum lodged must not be less than £500. The bank was also allowed to advance to the bankers of London, Westminster, and Southwark, any sum of cash not exceeding in the whole £100,000; and also £25,000 each to the Bank of Scotland and the Royal

Bank of Scotland, during the continuance of this Act. The bank could not be sued for payment of any of its notes for which it was willing to give other notes; and no person could be held to special bail upon any process issuing out of any court, unless the affidavit made for the purpose, stated, also, that the party had made no offer to pay in bank notes. This Act was to be in force till the 24th day of the following June, a duration of fifty-two days.

1797. June 22. Another Act was passed, continuing the bank restriction until one month after the commencement of the then next session of parliament.

Nov. 30. A third Act passed, continuing the restriction until six months after the conclusion of the war.

An Act was also passed (37 Geo. III. c. 32) suspending the Acts passed in 1777, which prohibited bankers issuing notes below the amount of £5, and the country bankers commenced issuing notes of £1.

1799. Jan. 3. The bank gave notice, that on and after the 14th inst. it would pay in cash all fractional sums under £5; and that on and after the 1st day of February next, it would pay cash for all notes of £1 and £2 value that are dated prior to the 1st day of July, 1798, or exchange them for new notes of the same value, at the option of the holders.

1800. The bank charter was extended or renewed until the expiration of twelve months' notice, to be given after the 1st day of August, 1833, and until payment by the public to the bank of the demands therein mentioned; being an extension or renewal of the said charter for twenty-one years (40 Geo. III. c. 28). In consideration of obtaining this renewal of their charter, the bank agreed to lend the government the sum of £3,000,000 without interest for six years.

The 40 Geo. III. c. 36, was enacted to enable courts of

equity to compel a transfer of stock in suits, without making the Bank of England, or the East India Company, or the South Sea Company, partners in the sales.

1801. 41 Geo. III. c. 57, was enacted "for the better prevention of the forgery of the notes and bills of exchange of persons carrying on the business of bankers."

"After July 10th, 1801, no person shall use or make any frame or mould for making paper, with the name or firm of any persons or body corporate appearing in the substance of the paper, without a written authority for that purpose: or shall make or vend such paper, or cause such name or firm to appear in the substance of the paper, whereon the same shall be written or printed,—on penalty of being imprisoned for the first offence, not exceeding two years, nor less than six months; and for the second offence, transported for seven years.

"No person shall engrave, &c., any bill or note of any person or banking company, or use any plate so engraved, or any device for making or printing such bill or note, nor shall knowingly have in his custody such plate or device, or shall utter such bill or note, without a written authority for that purpose, under a like penalty.

"No person shall engrave, &c., on any plate, any subscriptions subjoined to any bill or note of any person or banking company, payable to bearer on demand, or have in his possession any such plate, on penalty, for the first offence, of being imprisoned not exceeding three years, nor less than twelve months; and for the second, transported for seven years."

1802. The war having been concluded by the peace of Amiens, the Bank Restriction Act would have expired six months afterwards, but it was by a new Act continued in force till the 1st day of March, 1803.

1803. Feb. 28. The Bank Restriction Act was continued until six weeks after the commencement of the next session of parliament.

Dec. 15. War having recommenced, the Bank Restriction Act was continued until six months after the conclusion of a definite treaty of peace.

The bank is said to have lost this year no less a sum than £300,000, through a fraud committed by one of its principal cashiers, Mr. Aslett.

In consequence of the scarcity of silver, the bank issued five-shilling dollars. These dollars had on the obverse side an impression of his Majesty's head, and the following superscription: "Georgius III. Dei Gratia Rex;" and on the reverse side, the impression of Britannia and the following: "Five shillings dollar. Bank of England, 1804." The bank subsequently issued silver tokens for three shillings, and for one shilling and sixpence. By an Act passed in 1812, the counterfeiting these dollars and tokens was liable to a punishment of fourteen years' transportation.

1808. The allowance from the government to the bank for managing the public debt, reduced from £450 a million to £340 a million, on six hundred millions of the debt, and to £300 a million on all that it exceeded that sum. This was exclusive of some separate allowances on annuities, &c.

By 48 Geo. III. c. 149, the following duties were imposed upon country bank notes:—

					£	s.	d.
Not exceeding £1 1s.		...	...	...	0	0	4
Exceeding	. .	1	1 not exceeding £2	2s.	0	0	8
,,	. .	2	2 ,,	5 5	0	1	0
,,	. .	5	5 ,,	20 0	0	1	6
,,	. .	20	0 ,,	30 0	0	3	0
,,	. .	30	0 ,,	50 0	0	4	6
,,	. .	50	0 ,,	100 0	0	7	6

These duties remained the same until the year 1815.

1810. THE BULLION COMMITTEE appointed by the House of Commons for the purpose of inquiring into the causes of the high price of gold bullion, and its effect on the circulating medium.

The committee delivered a very long report, in which they discussed a variety of matters connected with the currency, and concluded by recommending that the bank should resume cash payments at the end of two years. The following are extracts:—

"Your committee have found that the price of gold bullion which, by the regulation of his Majesty's mint, is £3 17s. 10½d. per ounce of standard fineness, was, during the years 1806, 1807, and 1808, as high as £4 in the market. Towards the year 1808 it began to advance very rapidly, and continued very high during the whole year 1809, the market price of standard gold fluctuating from £4 9s. to £4 12s. per oz. The market price at £4 10s. is about 15½ per cent. above the mint price.

"Your committee have likewise found, that towards the end of the year 1808 the exchanges with the continent became very unfavourable to this country, and continued still more unfavourable through the whole of 1809, and the three first months of the present year.

"Mr. Whitmore, the late governor of the bank, stated to the committee, that in regulating the general amounts of the loans and discounts, he did 'not advert to the circumstance of the exchanges, it appearing upon a reference to the amount of our notes in circulation, and the course of the exchange, that they frequently have no connection.'

"Mr. Pearse, now governor of the bank, agreed with Mr. Whitmore in this account of the practice of the bank, and expressed his full concurrence in the same opinion. Mr. Pearse said: 'In considering this subject with reference to the manner in which bank notes are issued, resulting from the applications made for discounts to supply the necessary want of bank notes, by which their issue in amount is so controlled that it can never amount to an excess, I cannot see how the amount of bank notes issued can operate upon the price of bullion, or the state of exchanges; and therefore I am individually of opinion that the price of bullion or the state of the exchanges can never be a reason for lessening the amount of bank notes to be issued, always understanding the control which I have already described.'

" The bank directors, as well as some of the merchants who have been examined, showed a great anxiety to state to your committee a doctrine, of the truth of which they professed themselves to be most thoroughly convinced: that there can be no possible excess in the issue of Bank of England paper, so long as the advances in which it is issued are made upon the principles which at present guide the conduct of the directors—that is, so long as the discount of mercantile bills is confined to paper of undoubted solidity, arising out of real commercial transactions, and payable at short and fixed periods. That the discounts should be made only upon bills growing out of real commercial transactions, and falling due in a fixed and short period, are sound and well-established principles. But that while the bank is restrained from paying in specie, there need be no other limits to the issue of their paper than what is fixed by such rules of discount; and that during the suspension of cash payments, the discount of good bills falling due at short periods cannot lead to any excess in the amount of bank paper in circulation, appears to your committee to be a doctrine wholly erroneous in principle, and pregnant with dangerous consequences in practice.

"Upon a review of all the facts and reasonings which have been submitted to the consideration of your committee in the course of this inquiry, they have formed an opinion, which they submit to the House—That there is at present an excess in the paper circulation of this country, of which the most unequivocal symptom is the very high price of bullion; and, next to that, the low state of the continental exchanges: that this excess is to be ascribed to the want of a sufficient check and control in the issues of paper from the Bank of England, and originally to the suspension of cash payments, which removed the natural and true control.

"Your committee would suggest, that the restriction on cash payments cannot safely be removed at an earlier period than two years from the present time; but your committee are of opinion that early provision ought to be made by parliament for terminating, at the end of that period, the operation of the several statutes which have imposed and continue that restriction."

This report was delivered late in the session, and was not taken into consideration by the House until the following year.

1811. The commercial distress of the country had become so great, that parliament authorized the sum of six millions to be advanced to merchants on their giving sufficient security; but such had been the fall in the price of mercantile property, that not many could give the required security, and bankruptcies were numerous. Whether this distress arose from any preparations of the bank to return to cash payments, from the American embargo, or from Buonaparte's Berlin and Milan decrees, was a matter of much controversy. From the accounts since published, it does not appear that the bank had taken any measures to increase its stock of gold; but during the years 1810,

1811, and 1812, it considerably reduced its private securities and increased the amount of its public securities. Thus on the last day of February, 1810, the public securities were £14,322,634, and the private securities £21,055,946. On the same day, in 1813, the public securities were £25,036,626, and the private securities £12,894,324. This progressive reduction of the discounts no doubt occasioned great distress, though it was in some degree counteracted by an increase in the same period of above two millions in the circulation.

The report of the Bullion Committee was taken into consideration by the House of Commons, and after much discussion rejected. Instead of the measures recommended by the committee, the House adopted certain resolutions proposed by Mr. Vansittart (afterwards Lord Bexley), declaring that the value of bank notes was not depreciated, but that the value of gold was enhanced; and that the political and commercial relations of Great Britain with foreign States were sufficient to account for the unfavourable state of the foreign exchanges and the high price of bullion.

July 24. Lord Stanhope's Act passed. This Act (51 Geo. III. c. 127) is entitled, "An Act for making more effectual provision for preventing the current gold coin of the realm from being paid or accepted for a greater value than the current value of such coin; for preventing any note or bill of the Governor and Company of the Bank of England from being received for any smaller sum than the sum therein specified; and for staying proceedings upon any distress by tender of such notes." It enacts that the taking of gold coin at more than its value, or Bank of England notes for less than their value, shall be deemed a misdemeanour. This Act was to be in force until the 25th of March, 1812. It was introduced by the Earl of Stanhope, in consequence of the following notice having been addressed by Lord King to his tenantry:—

"By lease, dated 1802, you have contracted to pay the annual rent of £47 5s. in good and lawful money of Great Britain. In consequence of the late great depreciation of paper money, I can no longer accept any bank notes at their nominal value in payment or satisfaction of an old contract. I must, therefore, desire you to provide for the payment of your rent in the legal gold coin of the realm; at the same time, having no other object than to secure payment of the real intrinsic value of the same, stipulated by agreement, and being desirous to avoid giving you any unnecessary trouble, I shall be willing to receive payment in either of the manners following, according to your option:—1st. By payment in guineas: 2nd. If guineas cannot be procured, by a payment in Portugal gold coin, equal in weight to the number of guineas requisite to discharge the rent: 3rd. By a payment in bank paper, of a sum sufficient to purchase (at the present market price) the weight of standard gold requisite to discharge the rent. The alteration in the value of paper money is estimated in this manner: the price of gold, in 1802, the year of your agreement, was £4 an ounce; the present market price is £4 14s., arising from the diminished value of paper. In that proportion an addition of £17 10s. per cent. in paper money will be required as the equivalent for the payment of rent in paper."

1812. An Act passed "for the further prevention of the counterfeiting of silver tokens issued by the Governor and Company of the Bank of England, called *dollars*, and of silver pieces issued and circulated by the said Governor and Company, called *tokens*, and for the further prevention of frauds practised by the imitation of the notes or bills of the said Governor and Company" (52 Geo. III. c. 138).

Lord Stanhope's Act continued, by 52 Geo. III. c. 5, until three months after the commencement of the next session of parliament.

1814. Lord Stanhope's Act revived and continued, by 54 Geo. III. c. 52, during the continuance of the Bank Restriction Act.

1815. The following stamp duties were imposed upon the notes of country bankers (55 Geo. III. c. 184):

	£	s.			£	s.	s.	d.
Not exceeding	1	1	.	.	.	.	0	5
Exceeding	1	1	and not exceeding		2	2	0	10
,,	2	2	,,	,,	5	5	1	3
,,	5	5	,,	,,	10	0	1	9
,,	10	0	,,	,,	20	0	2	0
,,	20	0	,,	,,	30	0	3	0
,,	30	0	,,	,,	50	0	5	0
,,	50	0	,,	,,	100	0	8	6

1815. Peace being restored, the Bank Restriction Act would have expired six months afterwards, but it was continued by a new Act until the 5th July, 1816.

1816. The Bank Restriction Act continued from July, 1816, to July, 1818.

The bank was authorized to increase its capital from £11,642,400 to £14,553,000, being an addition of twenty-five per cent. to the stock of the several proprietors. This addition was made out of the surplus profits without any further call (56 Geo. III. c. 96). In consideration of obtaining this privilege, the bank agreed to lend the government the sum of £3,000,000 at three per cent.

1817. April 17. The bank gave notice that on and after the second day of May then next ensuing, it would pay cash for all notes of £1 and £2 value dated prior to the first day of January, 1816, or exchange them for new notes of the same value, at the option of the holders.

Sept. 18. The bank gave notice that on and after the first day of October then next ensuing, it would be ready to pay cash for their notes, of every description, dated prior to the first day of January, 1817.

1818. The Bank Restriction Act continued from the 5th July, 1818, to 5th July, 1819.

The bank had always followed the practice of detaining the forged notes offered for payment. But two persons who had forged notes returned to them by the bank, paid the amount and kept the notes. They were charged with having forged notes in their possession, and tried on this charge, but the juries acquitted them. In consequence of this decision the bank has since returned all forged notes to the parties presenting them, after having stamped them in several places with the word "forged."

1819. A bill passed through parliament in the course of two nights to restrain the bank from paying away any more gold under its notice of September, 1817, or any previous notice. A committee of the House of Commons had reported that the bank had paid away above five millions in gold; the greater part of which had been taken to the continent, and there re-coined into foreign money.

From an account submitted to parliament of the total amount of outstanding demands on the Bank of England, and the funds for discharging the same, it appears that there was a surplus in favour of the bank of £5,202,320, independently of its capital of £14,553,000.

Mr. Peel's Bill passed. This Bill (59 Geo. III. c. 49) contains the following provisions:—

1. The Bank Restriction Act was continued, absolutely, from the 5th of July, 1819, to February 1, 1820.

2. Between February 1 and October 1, 1820, the bank

was required to pay its notes in gold bullion of standard fineness at the rate of £4 1s. per ounce, but not to be liable to a demand for a less quantity than sixty ounces at one time.

3. Between October 1, 1820, and May 1, 1821, the bank was required to pay its notes in gold bullion upon the same plan, at the rate of £3 19s. 6d. per ounce.

4. Between May 1, 1821, and May 1, 1823, the bank was to pay in gold bullion upon the same plan, at the rate of £3 17s. 10½d. per ounce, which was the mint price of gold.

5. From May 1, 1823, the bank was to pay its notes in the gold coin of the realm.

6. But between February 1 and October 1, 1820, the bank might make payments at a less rate than £4 1s., and not less than £3 19s. 6d. per ounce; and between October 1, 1820, and May 1, 1821, the bank might pay at any rate less than £3 19s. 6d., and not less than £3 17s. 10½d., on giving three days' notice in the Gazette. Such payments to be made in ingots or bars of gold, of the weight of sixty ounces. The bank was also permitted to pay in gold coin on or after May 1, 1822.

7. All the laws which restrained the exportation of gold and silver coin were repealed, and the coin was allowed to be exported or melted without incurring any penalty.

The bill did not give satisfaction to the bank directors. They wished to be allowed to pay their notes in gold bullion at the market price of the day.

The 59 Geo. III. c. 76, was passed to prohibit the bank making advances to government without the authority of parliament. But the bank was allowed to purchase exchequer bills, or to advance money on them, but the amount of such bills was to be laid annually before parliament.

1820. An Act passed for the further prevention of forging and counterfeiting of bank notes (1 Geo. IV. c. 92). It also enacted, that the names of persons authorized by the bank directors to sign the notes, might be impressed by machine instead of being subscribed in the handwriting of such persons.

1821. The bank commenced paying off its notes under £5 in gold. The directors had procured an Act of Parliament, 1 & 2 Geo. IV. c. 26, permitting them to do so from the first day of May, 1821. The gold coins issued by the bank were not guineas, but sovereigns of the value of twenty shillings, which were now first coined. The gold coined at the mint this year amounted to £9,520,758, and the silver to £433,686.

1822. In this year an Act was passed permitting the country bankers to continue the issuing of notes under £5 until the expiration of the bank charter in 1833. As the law previously stood, their notes were prohibited on the resumption of cash payments by the bank. The directors made the following reference to this subject, in a memorandum they delivered to the parliamentary committee of 1832:—

"By the resolution of the House of Commons of 1819, the bank were required, within four years, to pay off in gold the amount of their one-pound notes then in circulation (about £7,500,000); further, to provide the coin for paying off the country small notes in 1825 (about seven or eight millions more); in addition to which the necessity was imposed of providing the requisite surplus bullion for insuring the convertibility of all their liabilities, which addition of bullion to their then stock could not be estimated at less than £5,000,000; making in the aggregate £20,000,000 of gold as necessary to be provided from foreign countries, within the space of four years from 1819.

"That the supply of gold could only be purchased by reduced prices of commodities; the bank withdrawing a given amount of securities in the first instance, the notes for which might be reissued in payment of the gold as imported. The low prices and general state of trade, from 1819 to 1821, and the withdrawal of the bank's securities, enabled the bank to cancel their small notes in the latter year; and in the following (1822), three years prior to the time fixed by parliament, they were in a situation to furnish the gold for paying off the country small notes, when, without any communication with the bank, the government thought proper to authorize a continuance of the circulation of the country small notes until 1833. The consequence of that measure was to leave in the possession of the bank an inordinate quantity of bullion (£14,200,000 in January, 1824); and further, to afford the power of extension to the country bankers' issues, which it is believed were greatly extended, fróm 1823 to 1825."

By a return from the Stamp Office, it appears that the number of country banks this year was five hundred and fifty-two, and the number of persons in those firms was one thousand six hundred and seventy-three.

In this year the government reduced the interest of the navy five per cents. to four per cent. Each holder of £100 stock received £105 new stock, bearing four per cent., with a guarantee that the interest should not be further reduced until the year 1829. The new stock was distinguished by the name of "new fours." The bank agreed to advance the money to pay off the dissentients.

1822. In consequence of the abolition of the notes under £5, the directors of the bank found they had many more clerks than was necessary. A good number were, therefore, discontinued; the bank giving them either a pension, or the value of a pension in ready money, at the option of the clerks. The conduct of the bank on this occasion was highly liberal, and met with universal approbation.

The bank engaged to advance to government, between April, 1823, and April, 1828, the sum of £13,089,419, for the purpose of defraying the charge of military and naval pensions, and to receive in lieu of this sum, £585,740 per annum; to commence from the 5th of April, 1823, and to continue for a term of forty-four years, and then to cease. This charge is commonly called " the dead weight."

In the latter end of this year the bank commenced advancing money upon the security of government stock. It also lent £1,500,000 to the East India Company.

1824. The bank extended its advances upon stock, and commenced lending money on mortgage.

The old four per cents. were reduced to three and a half per cent. The new stock is called "Three and a half per cent. reduced."

This and the subsequent year were remarkable for the commencement of a great number of joint-stock companies. The total number of projects was six hundred and twenty-four, and to carry them all into effect would have required a capital of £372,173,100. They have been thus classified: [1]—

		Capital.
		£
74	Mining Companies	38,370,000
29	Gas ditto	12,077,000
20	Insurance ditto	35,820,000
29	Investment ditto	52,600,000
54	Canal Railroad ditto	44,051,000
67	Steam ditto	8,555,500
11	Trading ditto	10,450,000

[1] See A Complete View of the Joint-Stock Companies formed during the years 1824 and 1825, by Henry English.

		Capital.
		£
26 Building Companies	. . .	13,781,000
24 Provision ditto	. . .	8,360,000
290 Miscellaneous ditto	. . .	148,108,600
624		£372,173,100

The above companies are divided by Mr. English into four classes. First, companies which continued to exist in the year 1827; secondly, companies whose shares had been sold in the market, but were afterwards abandoned; thirdly, companies which published prospectuses, or which were announced in the papers, but which are not known to have issued shares; fourthly, companies, the formation of which was noticed in the public papers, but the particulars not specified.

The following is the general summary:—

Companies.	Capital required.	Amount actually advanced.
	£	£
127 Companies existing in 1827	102,781,600	15,185,950
118 do. abandoned . . .	56,606,500	2,419,675
236 do. projected . . .	143,610,000	
143 do. do. not particularized .	69,175,000	
624	£372,173,100	£17,605,625

Besides the capital required for the above companies, large sums of money were granted as loans to foreign Powers, as appears from the following table:—

A list of the foreign loans contracted in England, with the amounts of the same, the names of the contractors, the years in which the contracts were made, and the prices at which they were issued.

	£	Per Cent.			Per Cent.
Austrian . . .	2,500,000	5	N. M. Rothschild . .	1823	82
Brazilian . . .	3,200,000	„	T. Wilson & Co. . .	1824	75
Ditto	2,000,000	„	N. M. Rothschild . .	1825	85
Buenos Ayres .	1,000,000	6	Baring Brothers . . .	1824	85
Chili	1,000,000	„	Hullett Brothers . .	1822	70
Columbian . .	2,000,000	„	Herring, Graham, & Co.	1822	84
Ditto	4,750,000	„	B. A. Goldschmidt & Co.	1824	88½
Danish . . .	5,500,000	3	T. Wilson & Co. . .	1825	75
Greek	800,000	5	Loughnan & Co. . .	1824	59
Ditto	1,000,000	„	Ricardos	1825	56½
Guatemala . .	1,428,571	6	I. & A. Powles . . .	1825	73
Guadaljara . .	600,000	5	W. Ellward, jun. . .	1825	60
Mexican . . .	3,200,000	„	B. A. Goldschmidt & Co.	1824	58
Ditto	3,200,000	6	Barclay, Herring, & Co.	1825	89¾
Neapolitan . .	2,500,000	5	N. M. Rothschild . .	1824	92½
Prussian . . .	5,000,000	„	Ditto	1818	72
Ditto	3,500,000	„	Ditto	1822	84
Portuguese . .	1,500,000	„	B. A. Goldschmidt & Co.	1823	87
Peruvian . . .	450,000	6	Frys and Chapman . .	1822	88
Ditto	750,000	„	Ditto	1824	82
Ditto	616,000	„	Ditto	1825	78
Russian . . .	3,500,000	5	N. M. Rothschild . .	1822	82
Spanish . . .	1,500,000	„	A. F. Haldimand . .	1821	56
Ditto	1,500,000	„	J. Campbell & Co. . .	1823	30¼

£52,994,571

1825. At the commencement of this year there was every appearance of general prosperity, but in December occurred "THE PANIC."

The course of exchange being unfavourable, had occasioned a demand for gold for exportation. The bank became under the necessity of restraining its issues.

The house of Sir Peter Pole and Co., who were agents to several country banks, stopped payment. This occasioned a general alarm, and the notes of private bankers became discredited throughout the country. As the bank had ceased to issue notes under £5, it was obliged to find gold for the country bankers to pay off their notes; but the gold failing, the bank reissued its £1 notes, some of which, happily, had not been destroyed. Notwithstanding the great liberality of the bank, several London bankers, and a much greater number of country bankers, were obliged to suspend their payments. Most of the joint-stock companies that had been formed in the season of speculation fell to the ground.[1]

The following is the opinion of J. H. Palmer, Esq., the governor of the bank, as to the causes of the wild spirit of speculation which had preceded the panic:—

"Will you state to the committee what, in your opinion, was the nature and the march of the crisis in 1825?—I have always considered that the first step towards the excitement was the reduction of the interest upon the government securities; the first movement in that respect was, I think, upon £135,000,000 of five per cents., which took place in 1823. In the subsequent year, 1824, followed the reduction of £80,000,000 of four per cents. I have always considered that reduction of interests, one-fifth in one case, and one-eighth in the other, to have created the feverish feeling in the minds of the public at large, which prompted almost everybody to entertain any proposition

---

[1] The crisis was at its height from Monday, the 12th, to Saturday, the 17th December. Up to the night of Wednesday the bank restricted its issues, to the ruin of houses of first-rate importance. Becoming sensible of its error, it discounted liberally the three last days of the week, issuing upwards of £5,000,000 of notes; otherwise, the ruin would have been universal.

for investment, however absurd, which was tendered. The excitement of that period was further promoted by the acknowledgment of the South American republics by this country, and the inducements held out for engaging in mining operations, and loans to those governments, in which all classes of the community in England seem to have partaken almost simultaneously. With those speculations arose general speculation in commercial produce, which had an effect of disturbing the relative values between this and other countries, and creating an unfavourable foreign exchange, which continued from October, 1824, to November, 1825, causing a very considerable export of bullion from the bank, about seven millions and a half. Commercial speculations had induced some bankers, one particularly, to invest money in securities not strictly convertible, to a larger extent than was prudent; they were also largely connected with country bankers. I allude to the house of Messrs. Pole and Co., a house originally possessed of very great property, in the persons of the partners, but which fell with the circumstances of the times. The failure of that banking-house was the first decisive check to commercial and banking credit, and brought at once a vast number of country bankers, which were in correspondence with it, into difficulties. That discredit was followed by a general discredit throughout London and the interior."

Some of the other witnesses considered the panic to have arisen from an over-issue of notes on the part of the Bank of England and the country bankers. But whatever may have been the cause, the bank certainly acted with great liberality at the period of the alarm, even at the risk of its own stoppage of payment.

"Will you describe the manner in which the bank lent its assistance at that time?—We lent it by every possible means, and in modes that we never had adopted before. We took in stock as security, we purchased exchequer bills, we made advances on exchequer bills, we not only discounted outright, but we made advances on deposit of bills of exchange to an immense amount; in short, by every possible means consistent with the safety of the bank; and we were not, upon some occasions, over nice; seeing the dreadful state in which the public were, we rendered every assistance in our power.

"Did any communication take place between the bank and the government respecting an order in council to restrain payments in gold at that period?—Yes; it was suggested by the bank.

"What answer did his Majesty's government give to that?—They resisted it from first to last.

"The Bank of England issued one-pound notes at that period. Was that done to protect its remaining treasure?—Decidedly; and it worked wonders, and it was by great good luck that we had the means of doing it: because one box containing a quantity of one-pound notes had been overlooked, and they were forthcoming at the lucky moment.

"Had there been no foresight in the preparation of these one-pound notes?—None whatever, I solemnly declare.

"Do you think that issuing of the one-pound notes did avert a complete drain?—As far as my judgment goes, it saved the credit of the country."

Evidence of Jeremiah Harman, Esq. (p. 154.)

On the last day of December, 1825, the coin and bullion in the bank amounted to only £1,260,890.

1826. Jan. 13. The government made a communication to the bank directors, stating its intention, in order to prevent a recurrence of panic, to propose to parliament the gradual abolition of country bank notes under £5, and also proposing to the bank,—

"First, That the Bank of England should establish branches of its own body in different parts of the country.

"Secondly, That the Bank of England should give up its exclusive privilege as to the number of partners engaged in banking, except within a certain distance from the metropolis."

The directors were at first unwilling to establish branches, but ultimately they acceded to both the above propositions.

The government also induced the bank to make advances upon the security of goods, and accordingly the bank established boards for this purpose at the following places, and advanced to the undermentioned amounts :—

	£		£
Manchester	115,490	Huddersfield	30,300
Glasgow	81,700	Birmingham	19,600
Sheffield	59,500	Dundee	16,500
Liverpool	41,450	Norwich	2,400

To carry these measures into effect several Acts of Parliament were passed, viz. :—

"An Act to facilitate the advancing of money by the Governors and Company of the Bank of England, upon deposits and pledges" (7 Geo. IV. c. 7). It was enacted that persons in possession of bills of lading, warrants, &c., should be deemed owners of the goods therein mentioned, so far as to make valid any contracts for the advance of money thereupon by the Bank of England.

"An Act to limit, and after a certain period to prohibit, the issuing of promissory notes, under a limited sum, in England" (7 Geo. IV. c. 6). By this Act, no further notes under £5 were allowed to be stamped, and those already stamped could not be issued or re-issued after the 5th of April, 1829, under a penalty of £20. The Bank of England was required to make monthly returns to the Treasury of the weekly amounts of their notes in circulation under £5, to be published in the Gazette, and laid before parliament. And after the 5th of April, 1829, all bankers' notes under £20 were to be made payable at the place of issue, though they might also be made payable at other places.

"An Act for the better regulating co-partnerships of certain bankers in England," &c. (7 Geo. IV. c. 46). According to this Act—

1. Banks having more than six partners might carry on business in England at a greater distance than sixty-five miles from London, provided they have no establishment as bankers in London, and that all the partners are liable for the whole debts of the bank.

2. The banks shall not issue their notes at a place within sixty-five miles from London, nor draw any bills on London for a less amount than £50.

3. The banks may sue, and be sued, in the name of their public officers; and when judgment is obtained against such public officers, execution may be issued against any member of the co-partnership.

4. Previous to issuing notes, the bank shall deliver to the Stamp Office, schedules containing the name or title of the bank—the names and places of abode of all the partners—the names of the places where the banks are established—and the names and descriptions of the public officers in whose name the bank wishes to sue and be sued.

5. These banks are allowed to compound for the stamp duties on their notes, at the rate of seven shillings per annum for every £100 in circulation.

By the fifteenth clause of this Act, the Bank of England was expressly authorized to establish branches. This was enacted to "prevent any doubts that might arise" upon the subject. The bank accordingly opened branches this year at Gloucester, Manchester, and Swansea.

The extension of the branches of the Bank of England this year occasioned great dissatisfaction among the country bankers. The establishment of rival banks in their own neighbourhood, was a circumstance that the country bankers could not view with indifference. They declared that the Bank of England, and not themselves, had been the cause of the previous spirit of speculation; that the Bank of England, by their advances to government and loans on mortgage, had made excessive issues, and that now to extend their influence, at the expense of the country bankers, was to reward the guilty and to punish the innocent. The country bankers had been accustomed to charge five per cent. on the bills they discounted, and at some places five or six shillings commission besides the discount, but the branches of the Bank of England charged only four per cent., without any commission. The country bankers were of course compelled to do business on the same terms, or to permit their customers to go to the branch. The chief advantage the country bankers possessed over the branch banks was, that they continued to allow interest on deposits, which the branch banks did not. But the additional confidence which was then possessed by the branch banks may, notwithstanding, have induced some depositors to give them a preference to the country bankers.

On December 7, the country bankers held a meeting at the London Tavern, Bishopsgate Street, where they passed several resolutions, and appointed a deputation to wait upon Lord Goderich, the first Lord of the Treasury, and Mr. Herries, the Chancellor the Exchequer. Among other resolutions were the following:—

"That the late measures of the Bank of England in the

establishment of branch banks have the evident tendency to subvert the general banking system that has long existed throughout the country, and which has grown up with, and been adapted to, the wants and conveniences of the public.

" That it can be distinctly proved that the prosperity of trade, the support of agriculture, the increase of general improvement, and the productiveness of the national revenue, are intimately connected with the existing system of banking.

" That the country bankers would not complain of rival establishments, founded upon equal terms; but they do complain of being required to compete with a great company, possessing a monopoly and exclusive privileges.

" That should this great corporation, conducted by directors who are not personally responsible, succeed, by means of these exclusive advantages, in their apparent object of supplanting the existing banking establishments, they will thereby be rendered masters of the circulation of the country, which they will be enabled to contract or expand according to their own will, and thus be armed with a tremendous power and influence, dangerous to the stability of property and the independence of the country."

At a meeting held at the same place, on the 16th of December, Sir John Wrottesley, Bart., M.P., the chairman, reported to the meeting the result of the interview of the deputation with Lord Goderich and the Chancellor of the Exchequer on that day, and read their answer as follows: " Lord Goderich and the Chancellor of the Exchequer stated to the deputation, that they were fully sensible of the great importance of the subjects which were brought before them by the deputation; and that, although it was obviously impossible that they could undertake, on the part of the government, to express upon that occasion any opinion upon the matters under consideration, they could assure the deputation that all that had been communicated should receive the most deliberate and serious attention."

The country bankers complained, too, that the branch banks, instead of meeting them on the footing of equality, had refused to take their notes, unless the bankers had previously opened accounts with the branch banks, and provided funds for the purpose.

1828. Another subject of complaint on the part of the country bankers.—The Bank of England had always issued its notes and post-bills unstamped, in consideration of paying, as a composition for the stamp duties, £3,500 per annum on every £1,000,000 in circulation. When the branches were established it issued bills, drawn upon the parent establishment in London, at twenty-one days after date, without being stamped, alleging that these were included in their composition. At the same time the country bankers could not draw bills upon London without paying the stamp duty. In a memorial presented to the government by the bankers in the town and neighbourhood of Birmingham, it was shown that the stamp duty on a bill drawn at twenty-one days on London, is three shillings and sixpence, while under the composition the Bank of England would pay but fivepence; and that a circulation throughout the year of £10,000, in bills of exchange of £20 each, would subject the Bank of England to a payment, in lieu of stamp duty, of only £35, while other banks would have to pay £650. An Act of Parliament (9 Geo. IV. c. 23) was accordingly passed, to enable country bankers to compound for their stamp duties on the same terms as the Bank of England, and to include bills drawn upon London at twenty-one days' date in the composition. By this law the country bankers have the advantage of paying duty only on the amount of notes in circulation.

1828. May 9. "The humble memorial of the country bankers in England and Wales" was presented to "the Lords Commissioners of his Majesty's Treasury" against the branch banks. It concludes thus:—

"Your memorialists therefore deeply regret that your lordships do not feel justified in adopting measures for the withdrawal of the branch banks, and they hope that your lordships will be pleased, as far as lies in your lordships' power, to prevent any interference with the business of your memorialists; and that your lordships will be pleased to institute an inquiry into the system of country banking, and take into your lordships' consideration the claims of the country bankers to be regarded as parties in the intended application for the renewal of the bank charter, and that no special privilege or monopoly be granted or continued to the governor and company of the Bank of England; but that they may be placed on a perfect equality with country bankers in the competition which, by means of their branches, they are now carrying on with your memorialists."

The government replied, that "the interests of the country bankers should not be neglected in any negotiation between the government and the Bank of England for the renewal of the bank charter."

1830. The government reduced the interest on the new four per cent. stock to three and a half per cent. This stock was formed in the year 1822, by the reduction of the navy five per cents. to four per cent. The holders had the option of receiving for every £100 new four per cents. either £100 stock at three and a half per cent., not redeemable until the year 1840, or £70 at five per cent., not redeemable until the year 1873. Most of the holders chose the former. This stock is called "*new* three and a half per cent.," and amounts to above £139,000,000. The other stock, formed by those who chose the £70, is called the new five per cents., and amounts to little more than £466,000.

1832. May 22. A committee of secrecy was appointed by the House of Commons, to inquire into the expediency of renewing the charter of the Bank of England, and into the system on which banks of issue in England and Wales are conducted.

On the 11th day of August the committee delivered the following report:—

"The secret committee appointed to inquire into the expediency of renewing the charter of the Bank of England, and into the system on which banks of issue in England and Wales are conducted, and to whom the petition of certain directors of joint-stock banking companies in England was referred, and who were empowered to report the minutes of evidence taken before them, have agreed upon the following report:—

"Your committee have applied themselves to the inquiry which the House has committed to them, by calling for all the accounts which appeared to them necessary for the purpose of elucidating the affairs of the Bank of England, and have examined evidence for the purpose of ascertaining the principles on which it regulates the issues of its notes, and conducts its general transactions. They feel bound to state that the directors of the Bank of England have afforded to them every facility in their power, and have most readily and candidly answered every question which has been put to them, and produced every account which has been called for. The committee have also examined such witnesses as appeared to them, from their practical knowledge and experience, most likely to afford information on the important subjects under their consideration, who have all been ready to give the committee the most ample information.

"The principal points to which they have directed their attention are—

"*First*.—Whether the paper circulation of the metropolis should be confined, as at present, to the issues of one bank, and that a commercial company; or whether a competition of different banks of issue, each consisting of an unlimited number of partners, should be permitted.

"*Secondly*.—If it should be deemed expedient that the paper circulation of the metropolis should be confined, as at present, to the issues of one bank, how far the whole of the exclusive privileges possessed by the Bank of England are necessary to effect this object.

"*Thirdly*.—What checks can be provided to secure for the public a proper management of banks of issue, and especially whether it would be expedient and safe to compel them periodically to publish their accounts.

"With respect to the circulation of paper in this country, the committee have examined,—*First*, into the effect produced by the establishment of the branch banks of the Bank of England; and *secondly*, into the expediency of encouraging the establishment of joint-stock banks of issue in the country.

"On all these, and on some collateral points, more or less information will be found in the minutes of evidence; but on no one of them is it so complete as to justify the committee in giving a decided opinion.

"The period of the session at which the committee commenced their labours, the importance and extent of the subjects, and the approaching close of the session, will sufficiently account to the House for the limited progress of the inquiry, and for the incompleteness of the materials which have been collected for the purpose of forming an opinion;—they have thought it better, therefore, to submit the whole of the evidence which they have taken, with a very few exceptions, to the consideration of the House.

"In their opinion, no public inconvenience will arise from this publication. The only parts of the evidence which they have thought it necessary to suppress, are those which relate merely to the private interests of individuals.

"The House will perceive that the committee have presented, as part of the evidence which they have taken, the actual amount of bullion at different times in the hands of the Bank of England. This information has never before been given to the public; it is, however, very essential to a complete knowledge of the subject, and if it had been suppressed by the committee, many parts of the evidence would have been unintelligible, and a false impression would have been produced in the minds of the public, that the bank were not so well provided with bullion as is desirable, which might have a very injurious effect. The House will, however, observe that the bank is amply provided with bullion at the present time; and it does not therefore appear to the committee that this information being now given to the public can be productive of any injurious consequences.

"The committee, however, by no means wish it to be understood, from their having felt themselves called upon to include this evidence in their report, that they have formed any opinion as to the propriety of periodically publishing the affairs of this or of any other bank of issue. There appears to be a difference between a publication of the affairs of the bank when an inquiry is instituted for the purpose of deciding whether the bank charter shall be renewed or not, and a periodical publication during the course of its ordinary transactions.

"Of the ample means of the Bank of England to meet all its engagements, and of the high credit which it has always possessed and which it continues to deserve, no man who reads the evidence taken before this committee can for a moment doubt; for it appears that, in addition to the surplus rest in the hands of the bank itself, amounting to £2,880,000, the capital on which interest is paid to the proprietors, and for which the State is debtor to the bank, amounts to £14,553,000, making no less a sum than £17,433,000 over and above all its liabilities."

1833. May 31. A meeting of the proprietors of bank stock was held at the Bank of England, to receive a communication from the court of directors, of the result of the negotiation with his Majesty's government, respecting the renewal of the bank charter. The following letter from Lord Althorp, the Chancellor of the Exchequer, was read by the secretary:—

"Downing Street, May 2, 1833.

"GENTLEMEN,

"After duly considering the conversation I have had with you, the substance of which I have reported to my colleagues, his Majesty's government have directed me to make the following proposals to you for the purpose of renewing the bank charter.

"1. We propose to renew the charter for twenty-one years, subject, however, to this condition:—that if at the end of ten years the then existing government should so think fit, they may give a twelvemonth's notice to the bank that the charter shall expire at the end of eleven years.

"2. That no banking company consisting of more than six partners shall issue notes payable on demand within the metropolis, or within sixty-five miles from the metropolis. Banking companies, however, consisting of any number of partners established at a greater distance from the metropolis than sixty-five miles, shall have the right to draw bills on London without restriction as to their amounts, and to issue notes payable in London.

" 3. Bank of England notes shall be a legal tender, except at the Bank of England, or at any of its branches.

" 4. Bills not having more than three months to run before they become due, shall not be subject to the usury laws.

" 5. An account, similar to that laid before the bank committee, of the amount of bullion and securities in the hands of the bank, and of the amount of notes in circulation, and of the deposits in the hands of the bank, shall be transmitted, as a confidential paper, weekly, to the Chancellor of the Exchequer: these accounts shall be consolidated at the end of each quarter, and the average state of the bank accounts for the preceding quarter published quarterly in the Gazette.

"A bill will also be introduced into Parliament, with the view of regulating country banks. The provisions of this measure will be such as to hold out an inducement to the establishment of joint-stock banks who will not issue their own notes.

" His Majesty's government desire me to call your attention to the advantages which these different propositions are likely to confer upon the bank. Their tendency must be to extend the circulation of its notes, and by relieving bills at short dates from the usury laws to facilitate its operations. While, on the other hand, the only relaxation in its exclusive privileges, as they at present exist, which is required is, the permission given to joint-stock banks, established at a greater distance than sixty-five miles from the metropolis, to draw bills and to issue notes payable in London. His Majesty's government, therefore, think that they have a right to expect some considerable pecuniary advantages from the bank in the management of the government business. They consequently propose that government should repay to the bank twenty-five per cent. of the debts of £14,500,000 now due, and that the bank should deduct from the payments made to them from the government for the transaction of the government business the annual sum of £120,000.

"I hope that this proposal will be satisfactory to the bank directors, and that by making this arrangement an end may be speedily put to the suspense now existing.

"I have the honour to be,
"Gentlemen,
"Your most obedient humble servant,
"ALTHORP.
"To the Governor and Deputy-Governor
of the Bank of England."

After some discussion, the further consideration of this letter was adjourned to a future meeting.

On the same evening Lord Althorp brought forward the subject in the House of Commons. Besides the measures that were connected with the Bank of England, he announced the measures for regulating country banks. These were—

1. That government should have the power of granting charters to joint-stock banks issuing notes beyond sixty-five miles from London, and to joint-stock banks within the sixty-five miles, provided they issued only the notes of the Bank of England.

2. That the joint-stock banks which issued notes should be required to pay up one-half of their capital, and all the shareholders be answerable individually to the full extent of their property.

3. That the joint-stock banks which did not issue their own notes should be required to pay up only one-fourth of

their capital, and the shareholders be responsible only to the amounts of their shares.

4. That the government when granting the charter should have the power to decide whether the amount of capital subscribed was a sufficient amount for the place in which the bank was situated.

5. That each private bank should be required to send a statement of its accounts to the government in London, as a strictly confidential paper, which was not to be published in a separate form, but, the accounts being added together, the total results should be given to the public periodically.

6. That to enable the government to know the total amount of notes in circulation, each private bank, as well as each joint-stock bank, should be compelled to compound for the stamp duties.

The Bank of England proprietors agreed, at a subsequent meeting, to the measures which had a reference to them. But the country bankers expressed great dissatisfaction; and on the 12th of June they presented a memorial to Earl Grey, the first Lord of the Treasury, and to Lord Althorp, the Chancellor of the Exchequer, upon the subject. In consequence of the opposition of the country bankers, Lord Althorp postponed his measures for the regulation of the private and joint-stock banks, and carried forward his plan for the renewal of the charter of the Bank of England. The following bill was ultimately passed into a law:—

An Act (3 and 4 Will. IV. c. 98) for giving to the corporation of the Governor and Company of the Bank of England certain privileges, for a limited period, under certain conditions, was passed August 29, 1833.

" Whereas an Act was passed in the 39th and 40th years of the reign of his Majesty King George III., intituled, An Act for establishing an agreement with the Governor and Company of the Bank of England, for advancing the sum of £3,000,000 towards the supply for the service of the year 1800: and whereas it was by the said recited Act declared and enacted, that the said governor and company should be and continue a corporation, with such powers, authorities, emoluments, profits, and advantages, and such privileges of exclusive banking, as are in the said recited Act specified, subject nevertheless to the powers and conditions of redemption, and on the terms in the said Act mentioned : and whereas an Act passed in the 7th year of the reign of his late Majesty King George IV., intituled, An Act for the better regulating co-partnerships of certain bankers in England, and for amending so much of an Act of the 39th and 40th years of the reign of his late Majesty King George III., intituled, An Act for establishing an agreement with the Governor and Company of the Bank of England for advancing the sum of £3,000,000 towards the supply for the service of the year 1800, as relates to the same: and whereas it is expedient that certain privileges of exclusive banking should be continued to the said governor and company for a further limited period, upon certain conditions: and whereas the said Governor and Company of the Bank of England are willing to deduct and allow to the public, from the sums now payable to the said governor and company for the charges of management of the public unredeemed debt, the annual sum hereinafter mentioned, and for the period in this Act specified, provided the privilege of exclusive banking specified in this Act is continued to the said governor and company for the period specified in this Act."

Bank of England to enjoy an exclusive privilege of banking upon certain conditions :—

"May it therefore please your Majesty that it may be enacted, and be it enacted by the King's most excellent Majesty, by and with the advice and consent of the lords spiritual and temporal, and commons, in this present Parliament assembled, and by the authority of the same, that the said Governor and Company of the Bank of England shall have and enjoy such exclusive privilege of banking as is given by this Act, as a body corporate, for the period and upon the terms and conditions hereinafter mentioned, and subject to termination of such exclusive privilege at the time and in the manner in this Act specified."

During such privilege, no banking company of more than six persons to issue notes payable on demand, within London or sixty-five miles thereof :—

"And be it further enacted, that during the continuance of the said privilege, no body politic or corporate, and no society, or company, or persons united or to be united in covenants or partnerships, exceeding six persons, shall make or issue in London, or within sixty-five miles thereof, any bill of exchange or promissory note, or engagement for the payment of money on demand, or upon which any person holding the same may obtain payment on demand, provided always, that nothing herein or in the said recited Act of the 7th year of the reign of his late Majesty King George IV. contained shall be construed to prevent any body politic or corporate, or any society or company, or incorporated company or corporation, or co-partnership, carrying on and transacting banking business at any greater distance than sixty-five miles from London, and not having any house of business or establishment as bankers in London, or within sixty-five miles thereof (except as hereinafter mentioned), to make and issue their bills and notes, payable on demand or otherwise, at the place at which the same shall be issued, being more than sixty-five miles from London, and also in London, and to have an agent or agents in London, or at any other place at which such bills or notes shall be made payable for the purpose of payment only, but no such bill or note shall be for any sum less than £5, or be re-issued in London, or within sixty-five miles thereof."

Any company or partnership may carry on the business of banking in London, or within sixty-five miles thereof, upon the terms herein mentioned:—

"3. And whereas the intention of this Act is, that the Governor and Company of the Bank of England should, during the period stated in this Act (subject, nevertheless, to such redemption as is described in this Act), continue to hold and enjoy all the exclusive privileges of banking given by the said recited Act of the 39th and 40th years of the reign of his Majesty King George III. aforesaid, as regulated by the said recited Act of the 7th year of his late Majesty King George IV., or any prior or subsequent Act or Acts of Parliament, but no other or further exclusive privilege of banking: and whereas doubts have arisen as to the construction of the said Acts, and as to the extent of such exclusive privilege; and it is expedient that all such doubts should be removed, *be it therefore declared and enacted, that any body politic or corporate, or society, or company, or partnership, although consisting of more than six persons, may carry on the trade or business of banking in London, or within sixty-five miles thereof, provided that such body politic or corporate, or society, or company, or partnership, do not borrow, owe, or take up in England, any sum or sums of money on their bills or notes payable on demand, or at any less time than six months from the borrowing thereof, during the continuance of the privileges granted by this Act to the said Governor and Company of the Bank of England.*"

4. All notes of the Bank of England, payable on demand, which shall be issued out of London, shall be payable at the place where issued, &c.:—

"Provided always, and be it further enacted, that from and after the 1st day of August, 1834, all promissory notes payable on demand of the governor and company of the Bank of England, which shall be issued at any place in that part of the United Kingdom called England, out of London, where the trade and business of banking shall be carried on for and on behalf of the said Governor and Company of the Bank of England, shall be made payable at the place where such promissory notes shall be issued; and it shall not be lawful for the said governor and company, or any committee, agent, cashier, officer, or servant of the said governor and company, to issue, at any such place out of London, any promissory note payable on demand which shall not be made payable at the place where the same shall be issued, anything in the said recited Act of the seventh year aforesaid, to the contrary notwithstanding."

Exclusive privileges hereby given, to end upon one year's notice, given at the end of ten years after August, 1834; and what shall be deemed sufficient notice :—

"5. And be it further enacted, that upon one year's notice given within six months after the expiration of ten years from the 1st day of August, 1834, and upon repayment by Parliament to the said governor and company, or their successors, of all principal money, interest, or annuities, which may be due from the public to the said governor and company at the time of the expiration of such notice, in like manner as is hereinafter stipulated and provided, in the event of such notice being deferred until after the 1st day of August, 1855, the said exclusive privileges of banking granted by this Act shall cease and determine at the expiration of such year's notice; and any vote or resolution of the House of Commons, signified by the Speaker of the said House in writing, and delivered at the public office of the said governor and company, or their successors, shall be deemed and adjudged to be a sufficient notice."

Bank notes to be a legal tender, except at the bank and branch banks:—

"6. And be it further enacted, that from and after the 1st day of August, 1834, unless and until Parliament shall otherwise direct, a tender of a note or notes of the Governor and Company of the Bank of England, expressed to be payable to bearer on demand, shall be a legal tender, to the amount expressed in such note or notes, and shall be taken to be valid as a tender to such amount for all sums above £5 on all occasions on which any tender of money may be legally made, so long as the Bank of England shall continue to pay on demand their said notes in legal coin: provided always, that no such note or notes shall be deemed a legal tender of payment by the Governor and Company of the Bank of England, or any branch bank of the said governor and company; but the said governor and company are not to become liable or be required to pay and satisfy, at any branch bank of the said governor and company, any note or notes of the said governor and company not made specially payable at such branch bank; but the said governor and company shall be liable to pay and satisfy at the Bank of England in London all notes of the said governor and company, or of any branch thereof."

Bills not having more than three months to run, not to be subject to usury laws:—

"7. And be it further enacted, that no bill of exchange or promissory note made payable at or within three months after the date thereof, or not having more than three months to run, shall, by reason of any interest taken thereon or secured thereby, or any agreement to pay, or receive, or allow interest in discounting, negotiating, or transferring the same, be void, nor shall the liability of any party to any bill of exchange or promissory note be affected by reason of any statute or law in force for the prevention of usury, nor shall any person or persons drawing, accepting, indorsing, or signing any such bill or note, or lending or advancing any money, or taking more than the present rate of legal interest in Great Britain and Ireland respectively for the loan of money on any such bill or note, be subject to any penalties under any statute or law relating to usury, or any other penalty or forfeiture; anything in any law or statute relating to usury in any part of the United Kingdom to the contrary notwithstanding."

Accounts of bullion, &c., and of notes in circulation to be sent weekly to the Chancellor of the Exchequer, &c. :—

"8. And be it further enacted, that an account of the amount of bullion and securities in the Bank of England belonging to the said governor and company, and of notes in circulation, and of deposits in the said bank, shall be transmitted weekly to the Chancellor of the Exchequer for the time being, and such accounts shall be consolidated at the end of every month, and an average state of the bank accounts of the preceding three months, made from such consolidated accounts as aforesaid, shall be published every month in the next succeeding 'London Gazette.'"

Public to pay the bank one-fourth part of the debt of £14,686,800 :—

"9. And be it further enacted, that one-fourth part of the debt of £14,686,800 now due from the public to the Governor and Company of the Bank of England, shall and may be repaid to the said governor and company."

Capital stock of the bank may be reduced :—

"10. And be it further enacted, that a general court of

proprietors of the said Governor and Company of the Bank
of England shall be held at some time between the passing
of this Act and the 5th day of October, 1834, to determine
upon the propriety of dividing and appropriating the sum
of £3,638,250, out of or by means of the sum to be repaid
to the said governor and company as hereinbefore mentioned, or out of or by means of the fund to be provided
for that purpose, amongst the several persons, bodies
politic or corporate, who may be proprietors of the capital
stock of the said governor and company on the said 5th
day of October, 1834, and upon the manner and the time
for making such division and appropriation, not inconsistent with the provisions for that purpose herein contained;
and in case such general court or any adjourned general
court, shall determine that it will be proper to make such
division, then, but not otherwise, the capital stock of the
said governor and company shall be, and the same is hereby
declared to be reduced from the sum of £14,553,000, of
which the same now consists, to the sum of £10,914,750,
making a reduction or difference of £3,638,250 capital
stock, and such reduction shall take place from and after
the said 5th day of October, 1834; and thereupon out of
or by means of the sum to be repaid to the said governor
and company as hereinbefore mentioned, or out of or by
means of the fund to be provided for that purpose, the sum
of £3,638,250 sterling, or such proportion of the said fund
as shall represent the same, shall be appropriated and
divided amongst the several persons, bodies politic or
corporate, who may be proprietors of the said sum of
£14,553,000 bank stock on the said 5th day of October,
1834, at the rate of £25 sterling for every £100 of bank
stock which such persons, bodies politic and corporate, may
then be proprietors of, or shall have standing in their respective names in the books kept by the said governor and

company for the entry and transfer of such stock, and so in proportion for a greater or lesser sum."

Governor, deputy-governor, or directors, not to be disqualified by reduction of their share of the capital stock :—

"11. Provided always, and be it enacted, that the reduction of the share of each proprietor of and in the capital stock of the said Governor and Company of the Bank of England, by the repayment of such one-fourth part thereof, shall not disqualify the present governor, deputy-governor, or directors, or any or either of them, or any governor, deputy-governor, or director who may be chosen in the room of the present governor, deputy-governor, or directors at any time before the general court of the said governor and company, to be held between the 25th day of March and the 25th day of April, 1835: provided that at the said general court, and from and after the same, no governor, deputy-governor, or director of the said corporation shall be capable of being chosen such governor, deputy-governor, or director, or shall continue in his or their respective offices, unless he or they respectively shall at the time of such choice have, and during such his respective office continue to have, in his and their respective names, in his and their own right, and for his and their own use, the respective sums or shares of and in the capital stock of the said corporation in and by the charter of the said governor and company prescribed as the qualification of governor, deputy-governor, and directors respectively."

Proprietors not to be disqualified :—

"12. Provided also, and be it enacted, that no proprietor shall be disqualified from attending and voting at any general court of the said governor and company, to be held between the said 5th day of October, 1834, and the 25th day of April, 1835, in consequence of the share of such proprietor of and in the capital stock of the said governor and company having been reduced by such repayment as aforesaid below the sum of £500 of and in the said capital stock: provided such proprietor had in his own name the full sum of £500 of and in the said capital stock on the said 5th day of October, 1834; nor shall any proprietor be required, between the said 5th day of October, 1834, and the 25th day of April, 1835, to take the oath of qualification in the said charter."

Bank to deduct the annual sum of £120,000 from sum allowed for management of national debt:—

"13. And be it further enacted, that from and after the said 1st day of August, 1834, the said governor and company, in consideration of the privileges of exclusive banking given by this Act, shall, during the continuance of such privileges, but no longer, deduct from the sums now payable to the said governor and company, for the charges of management of the public unredeemed debt, the annual sum of £120,000, anything in any Act or Acts of Parliament or agreement to the contrary notwithstanding: provided always that such deduction shall in no respect prejudice or affect the right of the said governor and company to be paid for the management of the public debt, at the rate and according to the terms provided in an Act passed in the 48th year of his late Majesty King George III., intituled 'An Act to authorize the advancing for the public service, upon certain conditions, a proportion of the balance remaining in the Bank of England, for payment of unclaimed dividends, annuities, and lottery prizes, and for regulating the allowances to be made for the management of the national debt.'"

Provisions of Act 39 and 40 Geo. III. to remain in force, except as altered by this Act:—

"14. And be it further enacted, that all the powers, authorities, franchises, privileges, and advantages given or recognized by the said recited Act of the 39th and 40th years aforesaid, as belonging to or enjoyed by the Governor and Company of the Bank of England, or by any subsequent Act or Acts of Parliament, shall be and the same are hereby declared to be in full force and continued by this Act, except as far as the same are altered by this Act, subject, nevertheless, to such redemption upon the terms and conditions following; (that is to say), that at any time, upon twelve months' notice, to be given after the 1st day of August, 1855, and upon repayment by Parliament to the said governor and company, or their successors, of the sum of £11,015,100, being the debt which will remain due from the public to the said governor and company after the payment of the one-fourth of the debt of £14,686,800 as hereinbefore provided, without any deduction, discount, or abatement whatsoever, and upon payment to the said governor and company and their successors of all arrears of the sum of £100,000 per annum, in the said Act of the 39th and 40th years aforesaid mentioned, together with the interest or annuities payable upon the said debt or in respect thereof, and also upon repayment of all the principal and interest which shall be owing unto the said governor and company and their successors, upon all such tallies, exchequer orders, exchequer bills, or parliamentary funds which the said governor and company or their successors shall have remaining in their hands, or be entitled to at the time of such notice to be given as last aforesaid, then and in such case, and not till then (unless under the proviso hereinbefore contained), the said exclusive privileges of banking granted by this Act shall cease and determine at the expiration of such notice of twelve months."

Act may be amended this session:—

"15. And be it further enacted, that this Act may be altered, amended, or repealed by any Act to be passed in this session of Parliament."

It will be seen by a reference to the 5th Section of this Act that the bank charter was renewed for certain for a further period of ten years (until the 1st day of August, 1844), but with the further proviso that if the then existing government did not see fit to give notice that the charter should expire within a twelvemonth from that date, the charter should in that case continue until the expiration of twelve months' notice to be given after the 1st day of August, 1855.

It will also be seen by the 13th Section that, "in consideration of the privileges of exclusive banking given by this Act," the bank was to deduct the annual sum of £120,000 from the allowance made to it by the government for the management of the public debt as fixed by Act 48 Geo. III. c. 4, passed in 1808.

1844. "Bank Act" passed. This Act is discussed at length elsewhere, and we need only refer to it here to say that by the 8th Section the above-mentioned deduction of £120,000 was repealed, and in its place, and "in consideration of the privileges of exclusive banking and the exemption from stamp duties given to them by this Act," a deduction of £180,000 from the allowance to the bank was substituted. But as this sum included £60,000 as composition for stamp duty on notes, the bank's allowance remained the same as it was left by Act 3 and 4 Will. IV. c. 98, viz.—£340 per million on six hundred millions of debt, and £300 per million on the excess of that sum.

The 27th Section of this Act continued the bank charter with all its powers and authorities, franchises, privileges, and advantages, until the expiration of twelve months' notice to be given after the first day of August, 1855, and upon repayment by Parliament of the public debt of £11,015,100 to the bank. It is under this enactment that the Bank of England possesses all its privileges at the present time, the public debt being still outstanding, and the requisite twelve months' notice not having been given.

1861. An inquiry having been instituted by the government in 1854 into their relations with the Bank of England, and a committee having been appointed in 1860 to report upon the results of that inquiry, the following rate of remuneration was proposed by the government and agreed to by the bank for the services of the latter in connection with the management of the public debt, viz.— £300 per million for the first six hundred millions of debt, and £150 per million for the excess of that sum. This scale of remuneration is now in force, and according to Act 24 Vict. c. 3, will exist till 5th April, 1886.

1870. With a view to the revision of the Statute Law, and particularly to the preparation of the revised edition of the Statutes then in progress, it was considered expedient to consolidate, with amendments, certain enactments relating to the National Debt. Accordingly, in this year was passed Act 33 and 34 Vict. c. 71, with the view of regulating the various denominations of the Funded Debt, the payments of the dividends, and the unclaimed dividends, thereon, the transfers thereof, &c. &c. Clause 72 of this Act enacts that the Bank of England for the purpose of the Act shall continue a corporation until all the public funds are duly redeemed by Parliament,—thus practically continuing the charter of the bank in perpetuity.

The government of the bank rests entirely with the court of directors, who may, if they please, change the whole system of management. The only check upon their proceedings consists in the publicity of their measures, the half-yearly meetings of their proprietors, and the communications between the court and the government. The directors are elected by the proprietors of bank stock at a general meeting. Eight directors go out and eight come in every year. The eight that come in are commended by the whole court—that is, a "house list" is sanctioned by the court; and though the proprietors are not required to vote for the names included in the list, yet these persons have always been elected. The qualification for governor is £4,000 bank stock; deputy-governor, £3,000; director, £2,000. The directors are not usually large holders of bank stock: none of them hold more than the qualification. The governor and deputy-governor are appointed by the directors, and usually continue in office for a year. The senior directors of the bank, who have passed the chair, form a select committee: to these are added the director immediately succeeding by rotation to the deputy chair. The governor and the select committee have the management of the bank in the intervals between the sittings of the court, but nothing of consequence is done without the knowledge and concurrence of the court of directors.

At the weekly meeting of the court of directors there is a statement read of the actual position of the bank in every department, of its securities, of its bullion, and of its liabilities. There is a committee of treasury, who may suggest any measure they think fit for the consideration of the court. The daily transactions of the bank are conducted by a committee of three, assisted by the governor or deputy-governor: no responsible action is taken by the committee without reference to the governor. All bills presented for discount are presented before that daily committee, and they determine upon the bills to be discounted. The bullion is purchased by the governor, who considers that he has no power to refuse the issue of notes for gold bullion brought to him at the bank. The purchasing price of gold has been fixed at £3 17s. 9d. per ounce. The price of silver is regulated by the course of the foreign exchanges.

On the opposite page is a Table of the dividends, including cash bonuses, paid by the Bank of England to the proprietors from the year 1695 to the present time.

In addition to the indicated dividends and cash bonuses there were distributed to the proprietors of the bank stock as further bonuses:—

In 1799, £1,164,240 in five per cent. Annuities of 1797, being ten per cent. on the bank's capital.

In 1801, £582,120 in Navy five per cent. Annuities, being five per cent. on the bank's capital.

In 1802, £291,060 in Navy five per cent. Annuities, being two and a half per cent. on the bank's capital.

In 1816, £2,910,600 taken from the bank's reserve fund and added to the capital stock of the bank, making it £14,553,000, the amount at which it stands at the present time. This bonus was equal to twenty-five per cent. on the previous capital of £11,642,400.

In the Table on page 96 will be found a more detailed account of all distributions made by the Bank of England amongst the proprietors of bank stock, whether by money payments, transfer of five per cent. Annuities, or otherwise, under the heads of bonus, increase of dividend, and increase of capital, betwixt the 25th February, 1797, and 31st March, 1832, in addition to the ordinary dividend of seven per cent. on the capital stock of that corporation existing in 1797; including therein the whole dividend paid since June, 1816, on their increased capital, stating the period when such distributions were made, and the aggregate amount of the whole.

Year.	Rate per cent.	Year.	Rate per cent.	Year.	Rate per cent.
1695	10	1733		1847	9
1696		to	5½	1848	8
1697	27½	1746		1849	9
1698	7	1747		1850	
1699	9½	to	5	to	7½
1700	10¾	1752		1852	
1701	9	1753		1853	8
1702	17	to	4½	1854	9
1703	19	1763		1855	8
1704	15¾	1764	4¾	1856	9½
1705	15½	1765		1857	
1706	18¼	to	5	to	10
1707	7¾	1766		1858	
1708	12½	1767	5¼	1859	8½
1709	16	1768		1860	9½
1710	7½	to	5½	1861	10
1711	7	1780		1862	8½
1712		1781	5¾	1863	8¾
to	8	1782		1864	11
1714		to	6	1865	10½
1715	7¾	1787		1866	11¾
1716		1788		1867	10
to	8	to	7	1868	8
1718		1803		1869	
1719	17½	1804		to	8¾
1720	7½	to	12	1871	
1721		1806		1872	9½
to	6	1807		1873	
1727		to	10	to	10
1728		1822		1874	
to	5½	1823		1875	9
1729		to	8	1876	9
1730		1838		1877	9½
to	5¾	1839		1878	9½
1732		to	7	1879	10½
		1846			

	£
In June, 1799, £10 per cent. bonus in five per cents., 1797, on £11,642,400 is	1,164,240
May, 1801, £5 ditto Navy five per cents. ditto .	582,120
Nov., 1802, £2½ ditto ditto ditto .	291,060
Oct., 1804, £5 ditto Cash ditto .	582,120
Oct., 1805, £5 ditto ditto ditto .	582,120
Oct., 1806, £5 ditto ditto ditto .	582,120
From April, 1807, to Oct., 1822, both inclusive . . . . { Increase of dividend at the rate of £3 per cent. per annum, on £11,642,400, is, 16 years . . }	5,588,352
From April, 1823, to Oct., 1831, both inclusive . . . . { Increase of dividend at the rate of £1 per cent. per annum, on £11,642,400, is, 9 years . . }	1,047,816
In June, 1816, increase of capital at £25 per cent. is .	2,910,600
From Oct., 1816, to Oct., 1822, both inclusive . . . . { Dividend at the rate of £10 per cent. per annum, on £2,910,600 increased capital, is, 6½ years }	1,891,890
From April, 1823, to Oct., 1831, both inclusive . . . . { Dividend at the rate of £8 per cent. per annum, on £2,910,600 increased capital, is, 9 years . }	2,095,632
Aggregate amount of the whole	17,318,070
Annual dividend payable on bank stock in 1797, on a capital of £11,642,400, at the rate of £7 per cent. per annum	814,968
Annual dividend payable since June, 1816, on a capital of £14,553,000 to October, 1822, inclusive, at the rate of £10 per cent. per annum	1,455,300
Annual dividend payable from April, 1823, to 31st March, 1832, both inclusive, on a capital of £14,553,000 at the rate of £8 per cent. per annum	1,164,240

We now proceed to give a statement of the capital stock of the bank, together with the date on which each addition was made, and the way in which it was raised:—

	£	s.	d.
1694. Original Subscription, 5 & 6 Wm. III. c. 20	1,200,000	0	0
1697. Public Subscription, 8 & 9 Wm. III. c. 20	1,001,171	10	0
(In 1707 the additional capital raised in 1697 was paid back, leaving the capital as it originally stood; but in 1709 a fresh subscription of £1,001,171 10s. was made, thereby again raising the capital to what it stood at in 1697.) 1709. Public Subscription, 7 Anne, c. 7	2,201,171	10	0
	4,402,343	0	0
1709. Call of about 15 per cent.	656,204	1	9
	5,058,547	1	9
1710. Further call of about 10 per cent.	501,448	12	11
1722. Public Subscriptions, 7 Geo. I. c. 5.	3,400,000	0	0
	8,959,995	14	8
1742. Call of about 9½ per cent., 15 Geo. II. c. 13.	840,004	5	4
	9,800,000	0	0
1746. Call 10 per cent., 19 Geo. II. c. 6	980,000	0	0
	10,780,000	0	0
1782. Call 8 per cent., 21 Geo. III. c. 60	862,400	0	0
Carried forward.	11,642,400	0	0

Brought forward	. . . .	£11,642,400	0	0
1816. Added to the stock of each proprietor 25 per cent. from the Rest	. . . . .	2,910,600	0	0
Capital at present time	. . .	£14,553,000	0	0

The following is a Table of the changes in the Bank of England minimum rate of discount from the year 1694 to the present time:—

Date.		Rate.	Remarks.	Date.		Rate.	Remarks.
1694	Aug. 8	6	On Foreign Bills.	1839	Aug. 1	6	Currency 95 days.
,,	Aug. 30	4½	,,	1840	Jan. 23	5	,, ,,
,,	Oct. 24	6	Inland Bills.	,,	Oct. 15	5	,, 65 days.
1695	Jan. 16	6	Foreign Bills three months to run.	1841	June 3	5	,, 95 days.
				1842	April 7	4	,, ,,
,,	,,	4½	Inland Bills to those who keep cash at Bank.	1844	Sept. 5	2½	Currency 95 days (Bills).
				,,	,,	3	Currency 95 days (Notes).
,,	,,	3	Foreign Bills do.				
,,	May 19	3	Running Notes and Bills do.	1845	Mar. 13	2½	,, 95 days.
				,,	Oct. 16	3	,, ,,
1704	Feb. 28	4	Foreign Bills made payable at Bank.	,,	Nov. 6	3½	,, ,,
				1846	Aug. 27	3	,, ,,
,,	,,	5	Do. not do.	1847	Jan. 14	3½	,, ,,
1710	June 22	5	Foreign Bills.	,,	Jan. 21	4	,, ,,
1716	July 26	4	Foreign and Inland Bills.	,,	April 8	5	,, ,,
				,,	Aug. 5	5½	,, ,,
1719	April 30	5	Bills and Notes.	,,	Sept. 2		(Advances 5%.)
1720	Oct. 27	5	Bills.	,,	Sept. 30	5½	Currency 1 month.
1722	Aug. 23	4	Do.			6	,, 95 days.
1742	Oct. 18	5	Do. drawn within the Kingdom.	,,	Oct. 25	8	,, ,,
							(Government Letter suspending Act of 1844.)
,,	,,	4	Do. without.				
1745	Dec. 12	4	Foreign Bills.				
1746	May 1	4	Foreign Bills.	,,	Nov. 27	7	Currency 95 days.
,,	,,	5	Inland Bills and Notes.	,,	Dec. 2	6	,, ,,
				,,	Dec. 23	5	,, ,,
1773	May 13	5	Foreign Bills.	1848	Jan. 27	4	,, ,,
1822	June 20	4	All Bills and Notes. Currency 95 days.	,,	June 15	3½	,, ,,
				,,	Nov. 2	3	,, ,,
1825	Dec. 13	5	,, ,,	1849	Nov. 22	2½	,, ,,
1827	July 5	4	,, ,,	1850	Dec. 26	3	,, ,,
1836	July 21	4½	,, ,,	1852	Jan. 1	2½	,, ,,
,,	Sept. 1	5	,, ,,	,,	April 22	2	,, ,,
1838	Feb. 15	4	,, ,,	1853	Jan. 6	2½	,, ,,
1839	May 16	5	,, ,,	,,	Jan. 20	3	,, ,,
,,	June 20	5½	,, ,,	,,	June 2	3½	,, ,,

PRACTICE OF BANKING.

Date.	Rate	Remarks.	Date.	Rate	Remarks.
1853 Sept. 1	4	Currency 95 days.	1860 May 10	4½	Currency 95 days.
,, Sept. 15	4½	,, ,,	,, May 24	4	,, ,,
,, Sept. 29	5	,, ,,	,, Nov. 8	4½	,, ,,
1854 May 11	5½	,, ,,	,, Nov. 13	5	,, ,,
,, Aug. 3	5	,, ,,	,, Nov. 15	6	,, ,,
1855 April 5	4½	,, ,,			(Withdrawal of gold by Bank of France.)
,, May 3	4	,, ,,			
,, June 14	3½	,, ,,			
,, Sept. 6	4	,, ,,	,, Nov. 29	5	Currency 95 days.
,, Sept. 13	4½	,, ,,	,, Dec. 31	6	,, ,,
,, Sept. 27	5	,, ,,	1861 Jan. 7	7	,, ,,
,, Oct. 4	5½	,, ,,	,, Feb. 14	8	,, ,,
,, Oct. 18	6	,, 60 days.	,, Mar. 21	7	,, ,,
	7	,, 95 days.	,, April 4	6	,, ,,
1856 May 22	6	,, ,,	,, April 11	5	,, ,,
,, May 29	5	,, ,,	,, April 27		(Civil War in America.)
,, June 26	4½	,, ,,			
,, Oct. 1	5	,, ,,	,, May 16	6	Currency 95 days.
,, Oct. 6	6	,, 60 days.	,, Aug. 1	5	,, ,,
	7	,, 95 days.	,, Aug. 15	4½	,, ,,
,, Nov. 13	7	,, ,,	,, Aug. 29	4	,, ,,
,, Dec. 4	6½	,, ,,	,, Sept. 19	3½	,, ,,
,, Dec. 18	6	,, ,,	,, Nov. 7	3	,, ,,
1857 April 2	6½	,, ,,	1862 Jan. 9	2½	,, ,,
		(Advances 7%. Indian Mutiny.)	,, May 22	3	,, ,,
			,, July 10	2½	,, ,,
,, June 2	6	Currency 95 days. (Advances 8%.)	,, July 24	2	,, ,,
			,, Oct. 30	3	,, ,,
,, July 16	5½	Currency 95 days.	1863 Jan. 15	4	,, ,,
,, Oct. 8	6	,, ,,	,, Jan. 29	5	,, ,,
,, Oct. 12	7	,, ,,	,, Feb. 19	4	,, ,,
,, Oct. 19	8	,, ,,	,, April 23	3½	,, ,,
,, Nov. 5	9	,, ,,	,, April 30	3	,, ,,
,, Nov. 9	10	,, ,,	,, May 16	3½	,, ,,
,, Nov. 9		Failure of Western Bank of Scotland.	,, May 21	4	,, ,,
			,, Nov. 2	5	,, ,,
			,, Nov. 5	6	,, ,,
,, Nov. 12		(Government Letter suspending Act of 1844.)	,, Dec. 2	7	,, ,,
			,, Dec. 3	8	,, ,,
			,, Dec. 24	7	,, ,,
,, Dec. 24	8	Currency 95 days.	1864 Jan. 20	8	,, ,,
1858 Jan. 7	6	,, ,,	,, Feb. 11	7	,, ,,
,, Jan. 14	5	,, ,,	,, Feb. 25	6	,, ,,
,, Jan. 28	4	,, ,,	,, April 15	6	
,, Feb. 4	3½	,, ,,			(Advances 7%.)
,, Feb. 11	3	,, ,,	,, April 16	7	Currency 95 days.
,, Dec. 9	2½	,, ,,	,, May 2	8	,, ,,
1859 April 28	3½	,, ,,	,, May 5	9	,, ,,
		(War between France and Austria.)	,, May 19	8	,, ,,
			,, May 26	7	,, ,,
			,, June 16	6	,, ,,
,, May 5	4½	Currency 95 days.	,, July 25	7	,, ,,
,, June 2	3½	,, ,,			(Advances 8%.)
,, June 9	3	,, ,,	,, Aug. 4	8	Currency 95 days.
,, July 14	2½	,, ,,	,, Sept. 8	9	,, ,,
1860 Jan. 19	3	,, ,,	,, Nov. 10	8	,, ,,
,, Jun. 31	4	,, ,,	,, Nov. 24	7	,, ,,
,, Mar. 29	4½	,, ,,	,, Dec. 15	6	,, ,,
,, April 12	5	,, ,,	1865 Jan. 12	5½	,, ,,

Date.	Rate.	Remarks.	Date.	Rate.	Remarks.
1865 Jan. 25	5	Currency 95 days.	1870 Aug. 25	4	Currency 95 days.
,, Mar. 2	4½	,, ,,	,, Sept. 1	3½	,, ,,
,, Mar. 30	4	,, ,,	,, Sept. 15	3	,, ,,
,, May 4	4½	,, ,,	,, Sept. 29	2½	,, ,,
,, May 25	4	,, ,,	1871 Mar. 2	3	,, ,,
,, June 1	3½	,, ,,	,, April 13	2½	,, ,,
,, June 15	3	,, ,,	,, June 15	2¼	,, ,,
,, July 27	3½	,, ,,	,, July 13	2	,, ,,
,, Aug. 3	4	,, ,,	,, Sept. 21	3	,, ,,
,, Sept. 28	4½	,, ,,	,, Sept. 28	4	,, ,,
,, Oct. 2	5	,, ,,	,, Oct. 7	5	,, ,,
,, Oct. 5	6	,, ,,	,, Nov. 16	4	,, ,,
,, Oct. 7	7	,, ,,	,, Nov. 30	3½	,, ,,
,, Nov. 23	6	,, ,,	,, Dec. 14	3	,, ,,
,, Dec. 28	7	,, ,,	1872 April 4	3½	,, ,,
1866 Jan. 4	8	,, ,,	,, April 11	4	,, ,,
,, Feb. 22	7	,, ,,	,, May 9	5	,, ,,
,, Mar. 15	6	,, ,,	,, May 30	4	,, ,,
,, May 3	7	,, ,,	,, June 13	3½	,, ,,
,, May 8	8	,, ,,	,, June 20	3	,, ,,
,, May 10		(Overend, Gurney & Co. failed.)	,, July 18	3½	,, ,,
			,, Sept. 18	4	,, ,,
,, May 11	9	Currency 95 days.	,, Sept. 26	4½	,, ,,
,, May 12	10	,, ,,	,, Oct. 3	5	,, ,,
		(Government Letter of 11th suspending Bank Act 1844.)	,, Oct. 10	6	
			,, Oct. 21		(Advances 7%.)
			,, Nov. 8		(Advances 8%.)
			,, Nov. 9	7	Currency 95 days.
,, June 13		(War between Prussia and Austria.)	,, Nov. 12		(Advances 9%.)
			,, Nov. 28	6	Currency 95 days.
			,, Dec. 12	5	,, ,,
,, Aug. 16	8	Currency 95 days.	1873 Jan. 9	4½	,, ,,
,, Aug. 23	7	,, ,,	,, Jan. 23	4	,, ,,
,, Aug. 30	6	,, ,,	,, Jan. 30	3½	,, ,,
,, Sept. 6	5	,, ,,	,, Mar. 26	4	,, ,,
,, Sept. 27	4½	,, ,,	,, May 7	4½	,, ,,
,, Nov. 8	4	,, ,,	,, May 10	5	,, ,,
,, Dec. 20	3½	,, ,,	,, May 17	6	,, ,,
1867 Feb. 7	3	,, ,,	,, June 4	7	,, ,,
,, May 30	2½	,, ,,	,, June 12	6	,, ,,
,, July 25	2	,, ,,	,, July 10	5	,, ,,
1868 Nov. 19	2½	,, ,,	,, July 17	4½	,, ,,
,, Dec. 3	3	,, ,,	,, July 21	4	,, ,,
1869 April 1	4	,, ,,	,, July 31	3½	,, ,,
,, May 6	4½	,, ,,	,, Aug. 21	3	,, ,,
,, June 10	4	,, ,,	,, Sept. 25	4	,, ,,
,, June 24	3½	,, ,,	,, Sept. 29	5	,, ,,
,, July 15	3	,, ,,	,, Oct. 14	6	,, ,,
,, Aug. 19	2½	,, ,,	,, Oct. 18	7	,, ,,
,, Nov. 4	3	,, ,,			(Advances 8%.)
1870 July 21	3½	,, ,,	,, Nov. 1	8	Currency 95 days.
					(Advances 10%.)
		(War between France and Prussia.)	,, Nov. 7	9	Currency 95 days.
					(Advances 12%.)
,, July 23	4	Currency 95 days.	,, Nov. 20	8	Currency 95 days.
,, July 28	5	,, ,,	,, Nov. 27	6	,, ,,
,, Aug. 4	6	,, ,,	,, Dec. 4	5	,, ,,
,, Aug. 11	5½	,, ,,	,, Dec. 11	4½	,, ,,
,, Aug. 18	4½	,, ,,	1874 Jan. 8	4	,, ,,

PRACTICE OF BANKING.

Date.		Rate.	Remarks.	Date.		Rate.	Remarks.
1874	Jan. 15	3½	Currency 95 days.	1878	Mar. 26	3	Currency 95 days.
,,	April 30	4	,, ,,	,,	May 30	2½	,, ,,
,,	May 28	3½	,, ,,	,,	June 27	3	,, ,,
,,	June 4	3	,, ,,	,,	July 4	3½	,, ,,
,,	June 18	2½	,, ,,	,,	Aug. 1	4	,, ,,
,,	July 30	3	,, ,,	,,	Aug. 12	5	,, ,,
,,	Aug. 6	4	,, ,,	,,	Oct. 2		(Failure of City of Glasgow Bank.)
,,	Aug. 20	3½	,, ,,				
,,	Aug. 27	3	,, ,,	,,	Oct. 14	6	Currency 95 days.
,,	Oct. 15	4	,, ,,	,,	Nov. 21	5	
,,	Nov. 16	5	,, ,,				(Failures of J. and J. Fenton and Sons, Rochdale, Nov. 30; West of England Bank, Bristol, Dec. 14; Tweedy, Williams and Co., Truro, Jan. 4, 1879.)
,,	Nov. 30	6	(Advances 7%.)				
1875	Jan. 7	5	Currency 95 days.				
,,	Jan. 14	4	,, ,,				
,,	Jan. 28	3	,, ,,				
,,	Feb. 18	3½	,, ,,				
,,	July 8	3	,, ,,				
			(Heavy failures; Collie and others.)	1879	Jan. 16	4	Currency 95 days.
,,	July 29	2½	Currency 95 days.	,,	Jan. 30	3	
,,	Aug. 12	2	,, ,,				(Failure of Vivian, Grylls, Kendal and Co., Helston, Feb. 4.)
,,	Oct. 7	2½	,, ,,				
,,	Oct. 14	3½	,, ,,				
,,	Oct. 21	4	,, ,,				
,,	Nov. 18	3	,, ,,	,,	Mar. 13	2½	Currency 95 days.
,,	Dec. 30	4	,, ,,	,,	April 10	2	
1876	Jan. 6	5	,, ,,				(Failure of Swann, Clough and Co., York, May 8.)
,,	Jan. 27	4	,, ,,				
,,	Mar. 23	3½	,, ,,				
,,	April 6	3	,, ,,	,,	Nov. 6	3	Currency 95 days.
,,	April 20	2	,, ,,	1880	June 17	2½	,, ,,
1877	May 3	3	,, ,,				
,,	July 5	2½	,, ,,				
,,	July 12	2	,, ,,				
,,	Aug. 23	3	,, ,,				
,,	Oct. 4	4	,, ,,				
,,	Oct. 11	5	,, ,,				
,,	Nov. 29	4	,, ,,				
1878	Jan. 10	3	,, ,,				
,,	Jan. 31	2	,, ,,				

The establishment of joint stock banks at a distance beyond sixty-five miles from London having been permitted by Act, 7 Geo. IV. c. 46, 26th May, 1826, it is desirable to present in the following Table the average Bank rate for each year from that period until now.

Year.	Average Bank Rate.			Year.	Average Bank Rate.		
	£	s.	d.		£	s.	d.
1826	5	0	0	1853	3	13	10
1827	4	10	2	1854	5	2	3
1828	4	0	0	1855	4	17	9
1829	4	0	0	1856	6	1	3
1830	4	0	0	1857	6	12	11
1831	4	0	0	1858	3	4	7
1832	4	0	0	1859	2	14	8
1833	4	0	0	1860	4	3	7
1834	4	0	0	1861	5	4	11
1835	4	0	0	1862	2	10	6
1836	4	7	9	1863	4	8	2
1837	5	0	0	1864	7	7	0
1838	4	2	6	1865	4	15	4
1839	5	2	0	1866	6	18	11
1840	5	1	3	1867	2	10	9
1841	5	0	0	1868	2	1	11
1842	4	5	3	1869	3	4	2
1843	4	0	0	1870	3	1	11
1844	3	10	4	1871	2	17	8
1845	2	13	7	1872	4	1	11
1846	3	6	6	1873	4	15	10
1847	5	3	8	1874	3	13	10
1848	3	14	5	1875	3	4	8
1849	2	19	0	1876	2	12	2
1850	2	10	1	1877	2	18	0
1851	3	0	0	1878	3	15	7
1852	2	3	0	1879	2	10	3

SECTION IV.

THE LONDON BANKERS.

AFTER the establishment of the Bank of England, the goldsmiths or "new-fashioned bankers" continued their business in the same manner as before. In the year 1705 they obtained greater facilities, from an alteration in the laws respecting promissory notes. It had been held that promissory notes, whether issued by bankers or others, could not be legally transferred to a third party, and that no action at law could be sustained against the issuer, unless brought by the person to whom the note was originally granted. But, by 3 and 4 Anne, c. 8, all doubts were removed; and it was enacted, that after the 1st of May, 1705, all notes in writing made and signed by any person or persons, bodies politic or corporate, or by the servant or agent of any corporation, banker, goldsmith, merchant, or trader, who is usually entrusted to sign such promissory notes, shall be assignable or endorsable over, in the same manner as inland bills of exchange.

In the year 1714 the legal interest of money was reduced from six to five per cent. The reduction of the rate of interest was probably the effect of the abundance of money produced by the issue of Bank of England notes, and the increase of deposits with the private bankers. The various small sums of money which had remained idle in the hands of individuals were collected into large deposits in the hands of the bankers. Hence the supply of capital was increased, and the rate of interest consequently fell.

About the year 1775 the London bankers who lived in the city established what is called "the Clearing House," for the purpose of facilitating their exchanges with each other. By this means each banker is enabled to pay the cheques drawn upon himself by the cheques he holds upon other bankers. And hence he is not under the necessity of keeping so large an amount of money unemployed in his till.

The London banks have long ceased to be banks of circulation: they are now banks of deposit, banks of discount, and banks of agency to country bankers.

The oldest banking houses in London are Messrs. Child and Co., of Temple Bar, and Messrs. Hoares, of Fleet Street; these were established previous to the Bank of England. The others are comparatively of recent date. In the year 1810 the number of banking houses who settled their accounts with each other at the Clearing-House was forty-six.

SECTION V.

COUNTRY BANKS.

WE have no authentic details of the rise and progress of country banking. It is generally understood that very few country banks existed previous to the American war; that they rapidly increased after the termination of that war; that they received a severe check in the year 1793, when twenty-two became bankrupt; and that they increased with wonderful rapidity after the passing of the Bank Restriction Act.

The country banks are banks of deposit, banks of discount, and banks of remittance; many of them are also banks of circulation.

As banks of deposit, they allow interest upon deposits; as banks of discount, they discount for parties who keep with them a current account; as banks of remittance, they conduct their business through the agency of the London bankers; they also receive through the London agents the dividends on the public funds, on account of the stockholders in the neighbourhood. The holders of stock grant in the first instance to the London banker a power of attorney to receive the dividends, which, when received, are placed to the credit of the country banker, by whom they are paid to the holders. This facility of receiving dividends in all parts of the country, has, no doubt, induced many persons to become holders of government securities, and thus the country banks have assisted in supporting public credit.

The country banker pays his London agent either by a *balance*, by a *commission*, or by an *annual fixed amount*. In the case of a balance, the country banker agrees to keep in the hands of the London banker a certain sum, for which he is to receive no interest. The amount of this deposit varies, according to the extent of the business. If the country banker keeps less than the stipulated amount, he is liable to be charged interest for the deficiency, as upon an overdrawn account; but as he frequently keeps more than this amount, the overplus is usually regarded as a set-off against the deficiency, and no interest is charged, provided it is seen that the *spirit* of the arrangement is fairly adhered to. In the case of a commission, the country banker pays at the end of each year a certain rate of commission on the transactions of the year; the charge is made upon the amount of the debit side of his account. Some country bankers, instead of a commission, prefer paying a fixed sum per annum. In this case the charge does not vary with the amount of transactions as in the case of commission, but whether the transactions be great or small the payment remains the same.

By 3 and 4 William IV. c. 83, passed in 1833, banks issuing promissory notes were required to make returns to the Stamp Office of the average amount of notes in circulation in the quarters ending the first day of January, April, July, and October in each year. The quarterly average is to be formed from the amount in circulation at the end of each week. But the Bank Act of 1844 enacted that every issuing banker in England should, once a week, make a return to the Stamp Office of the amount of his notes in circulation on every day during the preceding week, ending with Saturday, together with a return of the average amount in circulation during the same period. He was moreover required, on the completion of every successive period of four weeks, to annex to such return an account of the average amount of notes in circulation during the said four weeks, and also a statement of the amount of notes which he was authorized to issue under the provisions of the Act. The monthly average was to be ascertained by taking the amount of notes in circulation on every business day during the period of four weeks, and dividing the aggregate thereof by the number of working days during the same period.

The legislation with regard to the averages of the Irish and Scotch issues was somewhat different. By Acts 8 and 9 Victoria, c. 37 and 38, passed in 1845, it was enacted that every bank in Ireland and Scotland should once a week return to the Stamp Office an account of the notes in circulation at the close of business on the next preceding Saturday, together with an account of the gold and silver coin held at the head office of the bank on each day of the week ending with the same Saturday; and also an account of the total amount of gold and silver coin held by the bank each Saturday. And on completion of each successive period of four weeks each bank was required to annex to its return the average amount of notes in circulation, and the average amount of the gold and silver coin held at the head office during the said four weeks: each bank was also required to annex a statement of the amount of the authorized issue. The monthly average was to be ascertained by taking the amount of notes in circulation every Saturday during the four weeks, and then dividing the aggregate by the four weeks. The monthly average of gold and silver coin was to be ascertained in the same way.

In the memorial presented by the committee of country bankers to Earl Grey and Lord Althorp, June 12, 1833, they make the following observations upon the circulation of the country banks:—

"Your memorialists are prepared to prove that the issues of country bankers have less tendency to promote fluctuations in the country than those of the Bank of England; and that their effect in throwing the exchanges against the country is comparatively insignificant. The slightest attention to facts would indicate the truth of these positions. It has been established by parliamentary evidence that the issues of country bankers fluctuated much less between the years 1817 and 1826 than those of the Bank of England; and it is indisputable that adverse exchanges, which endanger the bank, always succeed great importations of foreign produce, and that they never can be occasioned by large exportations of domestic productions. Now it is notorious that the circulation of country bankers acts almost exclusively in promoting these productions: and that, when it is in an extended state, the direct and proper influence even of an alleged excess of that circulation, would be to provide the means of paying for the importations of foreign produce without causing so great an export of gold as to derange and endanger the monetary system of the country. This is looking at the separate and distinctive character of the issues of country bankers; if regarded as a part of a whole, any excess in which must bear its relative proportion of effect in producing derangement, that proportion can never exceed one-tenth; because, assuming that all paper currency has an equal bearing upon depreciation and appreciation, the issues of country bankers never amounted to one-tenth part of that which is used for effecting the interchanges of commodities and property in the country. All experience shows that great fluctuations have originated in the speculations of influential merchants, and never originated in the channels to which the issues of country bankers are confined; their source is in great mercantile cities, and they are promoted by the issues of the Bank of England. That this is the invariable course which fluctuations resulting in excess and derangement take, is proved by the evidence of Mr. Ward and others, before the bank charter committee, and is fully explained by the speeches of the king's ministers in the year 1826. The debts of a few speculative merchants who failed in a single year in the town of Liverpool, where country bankers' notes never circulated, amounted to between seven and eight millions sterling, and their bills were either lodged in the Bank of England for loans, or were current in all parts of the country, stimulating circulation and promoting excess.

"Then, with regard to the alleged tendency of many sources of issue to promote fluctuation—the rivalry of numerous banks of issue was set up by the government of 1826 as a principle which insures solidity and equability to the circulation, 'from the constant exchange of notes between the different banks, by which they become checks upon each other, and by which any over-issue is subject to immediate observation and correction.' That was the report of the Lords' committee, after full and complete investigation. The government of 1833 is proceeding with a measure founded on the principle that rival banks of issue promote fluctuation; this, however, is before investigation. Deposits and cash credits were declared by the witnesses from Scotland to be absolutely dependent on local bank issues, and the government of 1826 admitted the validity of the plea; the government of 1833 concludes that the system of deposits and cash credits may be maintained in England without local issues, but this conclusion is adopted without any inquiry into the case. It would be fruitless to dwell on this contradictory conduct in two administrations professing to be guided, in dealing with the currency, by the same policy. Admitting that by one source of issue, the actual amount of notes payable on demand might be kept more equal than by many, it does not follow that their distribution would not be infinitely more unequal—every man possessed of practical information who understands the subject knows that by giving the exclusive circulation of notes to the Bank of England abundance will be created in the money market, and in the great commercial emporiums—raising the price of public securities, and stimulating the produce markets—while unexampled scarcity will be the consequence in the country, producing embarrassment and discontent among the cultivators of the soil and all who are dependent upon them. Therefore the real practical point to be determined concerning the tendency of different issues is, whether £2,000,000, or any given sum, laid out in purchasing French rentes in Paris, and indigo in Calcutta, or in replenishing with stock the exhausted corn and pasture fields of England, have the most effect in drawing gold out of the country. It is hardly possible to imagine any measure of greater danger than the projected plan of government. The present bank directors may be men of unimpeachable integrity; but others less scrupulous may succeed them; and it is within the range of possibility for a man of influence who had obtained a seat at their board, to make a speculation by purchasing indigo in Calcutta, and then proceed to stimulate the market for that commodity in London, just before the sale at the East India House, by discounting the bills of favoured connections; then, at nearly the same period, he might cause instructions to be given to the manager of the branch bank in Manchester to contract the customary and stipulated discounts; which would have the effect of depressing the market for cotton twist and piece goods, which are the principal commodities transmitted to India in exchange for the produce of that country. By this double operation the produce of a director's capital employed in Hindostan might be temporarily raised in price in the London market, and the produce of English capital and labour sunk to favour the interests of one bank director or of several. The same result might be produced by the importer of Baltic produce: indeed, the importation of corn in 1831 probably created that state of things, which suggested to the government the plan of suppressing all local issues as the remedy for an alleged evil in the country bank system. It is hardly necessary to disclaim all personal imputation in this illustration. The Chancellor of the Exchequer has taken the self-interest of country bankers to be an element of so much danger, from its tendency to induce them to extend their issues, as to adopt it as a principle in framing a legislative measure of the most hazardous character. Is the danger of the operation of the same principle to be disregarded when it might be exercised, not in a manner where it would be open to 'immediate observation and correction,' but in secret, where it could not be detected and challenged? The history of national banks proves that their funds may be applied by their directors to far more daring private speculations than is described by this supposititious case.

"If all bankers should be compelled to supply their customers with the notes of the Bank of England, a charge of seven per cent. for the interest of loans to graziers, farmers, and dealers in agricultural produce would not remunerate the country bankers so well as four or five per cent. does now upon the present system. The contemplated change in the usury laws, if intended to afford to your memorialists some advantage for that of which it is intended to deprive them, would give them some satisfactory compensation, but its tendency is to disorder or change that system upon which loans are made by country bankers with promptitude, facility, and comparative uniformity and cheapness; the distinctive characteristics of their business are regularity and the absence of extortionary charges. In the event of the subversion of that system it would be impossible for a great corporation, forming rules of conduct in London, and thence directing their application, to appoint agents competent to conduct the pecuniary affairs of the productive portion of the community. Those affairs, as far as banks are concerned with them, always demand peculiar local knowledge, and are in a great measure based on the confidential intercourse of fellowship and neighbourhood; they frequently require personal knowledge of the circumstances and character of individuals, and the closest sympathy with the feelings arising from family difficulties, or family expectations and prospects. The governing principles, therefore, for conducting those important pecuniary affairs are totally incompatible with any that can govern the conduct of an hired agent in attempting to conduct the same. From these premises it results that the free application of labour to land would be prevented, the cost of cultivation enhanced, markets and the sale of produce impeded, and the pursuits of agriculture deeply injured.

"Then with respect to miners and manufacturers, any system which would bring them into immediate contact with the operation of the bank for regulating the foreign exchanges, without the protection and defence from those convulsive changes which the local circulations afford, would be a system pregnant with indescribable hazard. Many of the bank directors are connected by friendship or commercial dealings with the great speculators in London and the populous towns, whose transactions mainly cause excess of circulation and an adverse state of the exchanges. In this class any contraction of the paper currency for the rectification of derangement, upon the present system, acts: but upon the projected plan, parliamentary evidence, as well as the nature of things, shows that the contracting force will be put into operation by the branch bank managers at a distance from London, and produce confusion in the affairs of mining and manufacturing industry, and discontent among a dense and excitable population. It may, under such a state of things, be rationally apprehended that occasions will arise when workmen will be suddenly dismissed for the want of the power to pay them their wages, shopkeepers deprived of their weekly receipts, and the regular custom at markets for the supply of agricultural produce impaired."

In reply to a question, "What effect do you suppose that an increase or decrease of London bank notes has upon the issues of country bankers?" J. H. Palmer, Esq., replied:—

"A material increase of the bank in London tends, in the first instance, to reduce the value of money, and, consequently, the rate of interest, upon all negotiable securities. That abundance of money renders it difficult for the country bankers to find beneficial investment for that part of the country money sent up to the capital for employment, consequently they are forced to resort to their immediate neighbourhoods for new channels for investing their surplus money; and which tends to create additional issues in the country at an early period after the London increase has taken place. But it does not follow that a diminution of issues has an equally rapid effect in reducing the issues of the interior."

SECTION VI.

JOINT-STOCK BANKS.

IN the year 1708, a clause was inserted in the charter of the Bank of England, prohibiting the establishment of any other bank having more than six partners. This clause prevented the formation of any other joint-stock bank; and, as the increasing wealth and commerce of the nation occasioned a demand for banks, a great number, each having no more than six partners, rose into existence, as they were successively required by the wants of the country. The charter of the Bank of England had no reference to Scotland, which, at the period of the grant of the charter, was a separate kingdom. Hence, with the increasing wealth of Scotland, joint-stock banking companies were formed; and at present they conduct nearly the whole of the banking business of that country. But with every renewal of the charter of the Bank of England, this clause was retained, and hence has arisen the difference which subsists between the Scotch and the English systems of banking. In the year 1826, an Act of Parliament was passed to permit the formation of banks having more than six partners, at a greater distance than sixty-five miles from London; with a provision, however, that such banks should not make their notes payable in London, nor draw bills upon London for a less amount than £50. By an Act passed in 1833, these banks have the privilege of drawing bills on their London agents, either on demand or otherwise, and for sums less than £50.

The advocates of joint-stock banks allege that they possess the following advantages over private banks:—

1. Joint-stock banks possess greater security than private banks.

Security is of the first importance to a bank. One branch of the business of a banker is to take charge of money committed to his care. But who will entrust money to a banker who is not known to be, or, at least, supposed to be rich? And if a banker be rich, but afterwards, by mismanagement or misfortune, become poor, and fail, what dreadful misery is inflicted upon those who have money in his hands! How many respectable individuals may be suddenly bereft of their whole dependence! How many industrious tradesmen may become bankrupts! What distrust, what inconvenience, what interruption of business is occasioned, even to those who can bear the loss! But by a joint-stock bank all these evils are avoided. Another branch of the business of a bank is to remit money from one part of the country to another; but who will trust them with money to remit when they may fail before they have executed their trust? Banks, too, issue their own notes, and thus supply the circulating medium of the country. Here wealth and security are more necessary than ever. In the former cases, the creditors of the banker may have had some opportunity of judging of his safety, and would probably make previous inquiries upon the subject. But when the notes of a banker have become the circulating medium of a neighbourhood, they are readily taken without any inquiries about his solvency. And, indeed, in some cases, if the notes were suspected, they could not be refused. If a tradesman will not deliver goods to his customers for such notes as they offer him, they will take the notes to some other tradesman. Men who receive wages must receive them in such notes as the master chooses to pay. Since, then, each banker supplies the circulating medium of a large district, and the notes are thus circulated among all classes, some of whom have not the option of refusing them, nor the ability to judge of their value, it is of the utmost importance that banks should be established on those principles which will prevent their failure.

That a bank having a great number of partners should be more secure than a bank consisting of only a few partners, seems a very obvious proposition; and it has received abundant confirmation from the numerous failures that have occurred among the bankers in England, and the few failures that have occurred in Scotland. This is a fact that demonstrates the superior security of joint-stock banks. If a bank of this kind has a charter, it must previously possess a large fund, which forms a guarantee for the punctual payment of its notes or deposits. If the bank has no charter, then every individual shareholder is answerable for all the debts of the bank to the whole extent of his property, as fully as though he had incurred those debts himself. In either case the security is greater than can be offered by any one individual, or by any four or five individuals, however respectable they may be.

2. A joint-stock bank is less liable to runs.

A run is a sudden and general demand for the payment of notes or deposits. It is not sufficient that a banker be safe: it is also necessary that he should be believed to be safe. He derives the larger portion of his gains from the confidence which is placed in him by others. Confidence is money. However wealthy or respectable a banker may be, he may not always be believed to be so. The misfortunes of others may cause him to be suspected. But no banker has always in his coffers all the sums necessary to pay all the claims that may be made upon him. If he were to do this, from what quarter would he obtain his profits? What, then, is he to do in case of a run? He must at all events obtain money to meet the demands made upon him; for if he once suspend his payments, all his credit is destroyed, and his business is broken up. Hence he may be compelled to borrow money at a high rate of interest, or to sell stocks or estates below their value, and to incur great expense, in order that the money may arrive in time to meet the demand. But the effects of a run are not confined to the banker himself. One run is over, but another may come. He will be anxious to be better provided next time. He will be more cautious. He will call in the money he has lent. He will lend no more. He will discount fewer bills. Those tradesmen and others who have been accustomed to obtain from the banker facilities for carrying on their business, can obtain them no longer. Some have depended on these facilities, and will now fail; others will circumscribe their business; labourers will be thrown out of work, and trade will be obstructed and depressed.

Such are the effects of a run when the banker is solvent, and the run is met with promptitude. But the banker may be good, and yet the run may cause him to stop payment. In this case, though the banker may ultimately pay the whole of his debts, yet this stoppage will produce for a while the same effects as though he were insolvent. But it is possible that he might have been solvent before the run, and have been rendered insolvent by the run. The sacrifices he may have been compelled to make for the purpose of raising the money in time to meet the demand, may have absorbed the whole of his property.

Now, what is it that causes a run? It is merely an apprehension that the banker cannot discharge the whole of his obligations, and hence each creditor tries to be first, that he may secure the full amount of his own claim. But no apprehension of this kind can exist in reference to a joint-stock bank. Everybody knows that all the partners are liable for the debts of the bank to the full extent of their property; and each creditor, feeling assured that even should the bank fail his property is secure, abstains from engaging in a run whereby he can gain no advantage.[1]

3. Another advantage which joint-stock banks are alleged to possess, consists in the prudence of their management.

A joint-stock bank is managed by a board of directors, men of character and ability, who are chosen to fill the office from their superior knowledge of mercantile and banking business. The united knowledge and wisdom of a number of individuals must be greater than that of two or three individuals. They are not so liable to be imposed upon by false representations, to be deluded by false reasonings, or to be biassed by personal attachments. As among many persons there is sure to be a difference of opinion on almost every question brought before them, it is certain that no measure will be adopted without having first received a full discussion.

On the other hand the management of a private bank is too frequently intrusted to one or two of the partners; men who cannot be expected to act with the caution and prudence of an elected body, answerable for their conduct to the great body of proprietors; men, too, who have their

[1] The text was written prior to the passing of the various Limited Liability Acts, and was at the time to a great extent true. But since the passing of these Acts, under which many banks have registered, the same cannot now be said. Indeed a recent instance, in the beginning of 1879, of a foolish run, which lasted for several hours, upon one of the largest London joint-stock banks with a large liability on its shares, shows that the most perfect system cannot protect a bank from the wicked designs of unprincipled persons when they have a feverish public and anxious times to work upon.

prejudices to indulge, their friends to please, and their partialities to gratify. Not so with the directors of a joint-stock bank, where the follies of an individual would be checked, and his deficiencies would be supplied by his colleagues. It often happens, too, that the partners of a private bank are engaged in some branch of manufactures or commerce; and in this case the bank will be made subordinate to the trading concern. The banking merchant or manufacturer will extend his business, or engage in speculation, under the consciousness of being able to make good his purchases. The trading concern will have an account at the bank, and will always be overdrawn. The money which ought to be employed by the bank in discounting bills for their customers, will be absorbed by the trade of the partners. If the trading concern fails, the bank too must fail: the one involves the ruin of the other. Perhaps, indeed, the bank, by supplying money in the first instance for the parties to speculate with, may have been the cause of the ruin. Even when the partners of a private bank are not themselves engaged in any other employment, the bank often becomes connected with some large manufacturing or commercial establishments. Such establishments are useful to the bank, by enabling them to circulate a considerable amount of their notes. Hence the bank is induced to make large advances to them. Afterwards a further advance is necessary. A run upon the bank compels them to call in the money they have advanced. The money cannot suddenly be replaced. Hence all the parties become bankrupts. From all these evils joint-stock banks are alleged to be free.

Whatever the opinion, whether for or against, that may be entertained respecting joint-stock banks, the fact is undeniable that competition is, in most cases, good for the public. And hence, perhaps, the best system of banking is, when private banks and joint-stock banks are intermingled with each other. The rivalry of the private banks may induce the public banks to act with promptness and liberality: while the rivalry of the public banks may induce the private banks to guard against any measure that might shake their credit, and tend to weaken the public confidence in their stability.

SECTION VII.

BRANCH BANKS.

THE establishment of branch banks may be considered as the effect of the formation of joint-stock banks. A bank consisting of only six partners is seldom sufficiently well known over a great extent of country to be able to open many branches. The credit of such a bank would be liable to be shaken at one or other of its branches, and this might throw a suspicion on the whole establishment. But a joint-stock bank, possessing undoubted credit, may extend its branches with confidence wherever adequate business can be obtained. The comparative merits of an independent private bank, and a branch of a joint-stock bank, and the effects they are adapted to produce in any town in which they may be introduced, form a useful subject of inquiry.

In the first place, the branch bank may be supposed to possess greater security. The branch, however small, would possess all the security that belonged to the whole establishment. The notes issued at the branch would be as valid as notes issued at the head office; and deposits made at the branch would be recoverable from all the partners in the whole bank. In case a run were upon even the smallest branch, the directors would be as anxious to meet the demand as though the run were directed against the largest. A small private bank, on the other hand, would have its only resource within itself. Its own capital would form its only guarantee; and, in case of a sudden demand, it must expect but little assistance from its neighbours.

Secondly, a branch bank would command the use of greater capital.

Every joint-stock bank would call upon its shareholders for a supply of capital equal to the carrying on of the business. This capital would be kept in a disposable form, and, not like the capital of some private banks, locked up in loans upon inconvertible security. The confidence the bank possessed would create more banking capital, by attracting deposits and facilitating the issue of notes. Some banks create more capital than they can employ; such is the case when the amount of notes and deposits is greater than that of the loans and discounts. Others employ more than their banking capital. And some banks employ more at one season of the year, and less at another. In such cases a branch bank would be fed with capital from the parent bank, as its wants might demand. If it yielded more capital than it required, the parent bank would employ it elsewhere. If it wanted capital the parent bank would grant an ample supply. But in these cases a private bank would be troubled with an excess of capital which it might not be able to employ advantageously for a short period, or it might be distressed to raise capital to meet the wants of its customers.

Thirdly, a branch bank would probably do business with the public on lower terms.

A bank having many branches usually charges the same rate of interest at all the branches. The Bank of England discounts at all its branches on the same terms as in London. This cheapness of discount occasioned a great reduction of profits to the private bankers. A branch bank, too, conducted on the principle of allowing interest on deposits, will probably allow a higher rate, because the money can always be employed at some one or other of the branches, and it will return the deposits at a shorter notice, because the funds of the whole bank are ready to meet the call. In the transmission of money, a system of branch banks has a decided advantage, because the branches draw direct upon each other, and discount bills payable at all the branches respectively. In a system of independent banks the transmission of money from one to another is usually effected by a bill on London; and bills drawn by one town on another are obliged to be made payable in London.

Branch banks are enabled to charge less than private bankers, from their expenses and their expected profits being less. If a country bank, having many branches, employs a London agent, the charge for agency will be much less than if the branches were all independent banks. A branch bank is not under the necessity of keeping in its coffers so large a stock of gold as though it were an independent bank, because, in case of emergency, it is sure of obtaining supplies. The rate of profit, too, expected from a branch bank is much less than would be expected by a private banker. A banking company would be induced to establish a branch, could they be assured of obtaining one or two per cent. clear profit on their capital above the market rate of interest. But a private banker, who may be supposed already a wealthy man, would not consider that amount a sufficient remuneration for his own trouble and superintendence. Hence, his charges must be higher, to meet this increased rate of profit. Were the profits of a private banker, in proportion to the amount of capital employed, to be reduced to the average rate of profit of joint-stock banks, he would very soon think of retiring from business.

A branch bank may thus be established in a place where

a private bank could not exist. It may also be opened in places not sufficiently wealthy to furnish capital for a joint-stock bank, and where the people have no banking facilities; branches being opened in such places, prevent the formation of banks with insufficient capital. For, to be without a bank is felt to be so great an inconvenience that, if a good bank cannot be obtained, a bad one will, for a while, be supported. Hence, shopkeepers and others have become bankers; and, having but a small capital, and being unacquainted with their business, they have, ultimately, involved themselves and others in irretrievable ruin.

I have hitherto only compared a branch bank with an independent private bank. I will now compare it with an independent joint-stock bank. Several of the advantages already specified will apply as justly in this case as in the other. The branch may in this case also be supplied with a greater amount of capital if it could be profitably employed, or it may have better means of disposing of its surplus capital. The charges of the branch, especially for the transmission of money by letters of credit, or by discounting bills, may also be less at the branch. In point of security, the two banks may be considered as on an equality; though, perhaps, in some cases, the advantage may be in favour of the branch.

The expense of managing a branch must be less than that of managing an independent bank, as a less number of directors would be necessary. The directors or managers of a branch, too, acting under the direction of a superior board, are less liable to be involved by indiscreet advances of loans from personal friendship or imperfect information. The transactions are more thoroughly sifted, and no important measure adopted without full discussion. The very circumstance of being accountable to a superior board would render the agents at the branch more scrupulous and cautious than they might otherwise be. And the periodical returns made to the head office would constantly bring all the business of the branch under the notice of experienced and unbiassed inspectors.

There are, however, some disadvantages attending a branch bank. As a branch bank is a mere colony, the agents must be directed by the commands they receive from the seat of government. And the branch may be directed, in some cases, to adopt measures more adapted to promote the welfare of the whole establishment than to advance the interest of that particular branch. The Bank of England, for instance, may engage to lend, on advantageous terms, a certain sum of money to the government; and, for the purpose of raising this money, they may direct their agents at the branches to limit their discounts. As it is the duty of the directors to consult the interest of the whole establishment, they might consider themselves justified, as commercial men, in adopting this line of conduct. At the same time, it would be a great inconvenience to the persons resident at the places where the branches are established to be deprived of their usual discounts.

Another possible inconvenience to a branch arises from the circumstance, that most cases of importance are necessarily referred for the consideration of the head office; not that these cases are more difficult than ordinary cases, but because they are deviations from the usual course of business, or they belong to a class of transactions which is reserved for the decision of the highest authority. Hence, persons who have dealings with the branch may be obliged to wait the return of post, or a still longer term, before they can obtain answers to important inquiries. This inconvenience may, however, be largely diminished by giving to the managers or agents a high degree of discretionary power, reserving as few cases as possible for the decision of the board of directors.

The respective claims of these three different kinds of banks as far as regards any particular place, must depend on local circumstances. It is easy to imagine cases wherein a private bank of undoubted wealth and judicious management is superior to either a branch bank or an independent joint-stock bank. But private banks depend entirely upon the persons by whom they are managed. And these persons, whatever other endowments they may possess, are not endowed with immortality, nor with the power of bequeathing their good qualities to their successors. Leaving private banks out of the question, a branch bank seems best adapted for a small town: and an independent joint-stock bank for a large one. When banking is left perfectly free, the natural force of competition will soon enable each town to provide itself with that kind of bank which is best adapted to its own wants and circumstances.

The Bank of England has several branches. The business of the branches consists in discounting bills; in receiving deposits; in issuing bills on the London bank, at seven, fourteen, and any greater number of days after date; and in the transmission of money to and from London. Each branch issues its own notes, which are payable at the place of issue, and in London. The rate of discount is the same as in London; no interest is allowed on deposits; no charge is made for a fourteen-day bill on the parent establishment: but if money be lodged at the branch, to be received the following day in London; or lodged in London, to be received at the branch, a charge is made for commission. The charge to parties who have accounts at a branch, or in London, is at a reduced rate.

SECTION VIII.

BANKS OF DEPOSIT.

BANKING is a kind of trade carried on for the purpose of getting money. The trade of a banker differs from other trades, inasmuch as it is carried on chiefly with the money of other people.

The trading capital of a bank may be divided into two parts: the invested capital, and the banking capital. The invested capital is the money paid down by the partners for the purpose of carrying on the business. This may be called the real capital. The banking capital is that portion of capital which is created by the bank itself in the course of its business, and may be called the borrowed capital.

There are three ways of raising a banking or borrowed capital. First, by receiving deposits; secondly, by the issuing of notes; thirdly, by the drawing of bills. If a person will lend me £100 for nothing, and I lend that £100 to another person at four per cent. interest, then, in the course of a year, I shall gain £4 by the transaction. Again, if a person will take my "promise to pay," and bring it back to me at the end of the year, and pay me four per cent. for it, just the same as though I had lent him 100 sovereigns, then I shall gain £4 by that transaction; and again, if a person in a country town brings me £100 on condition that, twenty-one days afterwards, I shall pay the same amount to a person in London, then whatever interest I can make of the money during the twenty-one days, will be my profit. This is a fair representation of the operations of banking, and of the way in which a banking capital is created by means of deposits, notes, and bills.

The profits of a banker are generally in proportion to the amount of his banking or borrowed capital. If a banker employ only his real or invested capital, it is impossible he should ever, in the ordinary course of business, make any profits. Bankers can seldom attain more upon their advances than the market-rate of interest; and that may be obtained upon real capital, without the expense of maintaining a banking establishment. If, after deducting the expenses, the profits amount to nothing more than the market-rate of interest upon the invested capital, the bank may be considered to have made no profits at all. The partners have received no higher dividend upon the capital invested in the bank than they would have received if the same money had been laid out in government securities. To ascertain the real profit of a bank, the interest upon the invested capital should be deducted from the gross profit, and what remains is the banking profit.

A bank that receives lodgments of money, is called a bank of deposit. A bank that issues notes, is called a bank of circulation. Each bank attempts to procure a banking capital, but by different means. When a bank of deposit is opened, all the people in the district, who have money lying idle in their hands, will place the money in the bank. This will be done by the merchants and tradesmen, who are in the habit of keeping by them a sufficient sum of money to answer daily demands; by the gentry, and others out of business, who receive their rents, dividends, or other moneys, periodically, and disburse them as they have occasion. The various small sums of money which were lying unproductive in the hands of numerous individuals, will thus be collected into one sum in the hands of the banker. The banker will retain a part of this sum in his till, to answer the cheques the depositors may draw upon him; and with the other part he will discount bills, or otherwise employ it in his business. But if, instead of a bank of deposit, a bank of circulation *only* be established, then the several small sums of money will remain unproductive as before in the hands of various individuals; and the banker, in discounting bills, will issue his own promissory notes.

Now, it is obvious that these two kinds of banking are adapted to produce precisely the same effects. In each case a banking capital is created, and each capital is employed in precisely the same way; namely, in the discounting of bills. To the parties who have their bills discounted, it matters not from what source the capital is raised,—the advantage is the same to them,—the mode in which they employ the money is the same,—and the effects upon trade and commerce will be the same. Let us suppose that in each case the banking capital created is £50,000. Now, the bank of circulation will have increased the amount of money in the country by £50,000. The bank of deposit will not have increased at all the amount of money in the country, but it will have put into motion £50,000 that would otherwise have been idle. Here, then, is a proof that to give increased rapidity to the circulation of money, has precisely the same effects as to increase the amount. Here, too, is a proof of the ignorance of banking on the part of those writers who consider that the banks which issue notes are the sole cause of high prices, overtrading, and speculation; whereas it is obvious, that if those effects are to be attributed to banking at all, they may as fairly be ascribed to banks of deposit as to banks of circulation.

Even those bankers who do not issue notes, create a banking capital by the discounting of bills. They render their discounts subservient to the increase of their deposits. The London bankers will not discount except for those persons who have deposit accounts with them. A party who has had bills discounted, and has paid interest on the whole amount, must leave some portion of that amount in the hands of the banker without interest. By this means the banker obtains more than the current rate of interest on the money actually advanced, and raises a banking capital to the amount of the balance left in his hands. "A good account," in the language of the London bankers, is an account on which there is a large deposit—a bad account is that on which the sum deposited is small. A person who keeps a good account may have his bills discounted readily, but a person who keeps a bad account will have his bills more severely scrutinized. The depositors are aware of this; and therefore they endeavour to keep a fair account with the banker, that they may at all times be able to obtain such accommodation in the way of discounts as they may require. This mode of raising a banking capital by means of discounts, without allowing interest on the deposits, appears to be less advantageous to the borrower than by means of notes. In the one case, the borrower has to lodge some portion of his money in the hands of the banker, but in the other case he has only to take the banker's notes, which are probably as serviceable to him as gold. Hence, such banks appear adapted for the service of the rich rather than the poor—a young tradesman who is commencing business with a slender capital, will hardly find it worth his while to open an account at a banker's unless he has always by him a certain portion of his capital, which he is obliged to keep unemployed.

The London private bankers usually grant no interest for money placed in their hands, nor charge any commission upon the amount of the transactions. Their customers pay them for the trouble of conducting their accounts by keeping a certain balance to their credit. The amount of the balance is never definitely fixed, but is regulated very much by the good sense and proper feeling of the parties. The number of cheques a party draws—the degree of accommodation he receives by discount or otherwise, these and other circumstances are taken into consideration; and though the amount of the balance is not expressly stipulated, yet few people of business habits are at a loss to judge whether the average balance of their account throughout the year is sufficient to remunerate the banker.

By the Scotch banks, deposit accounts are divided into two classes—" accounts current," and " deposit receipts;" the "accounts current" are similar to the "current accounts" kept by merchants, traders, and others in the English banks. The party pays his money into the bank, and makes all his payments by cheques upon the bank. The deposit receipts are similar to what the English bankers call " dead accounts." The depositor pays his money into the bank, and there it lies " dead" until he has occasion for it, and then he produces his receipt and withdraws the whole amount, or takes a new receipt for any part he wishes to leave. The deposit receipts are chiefly for the use of those who lodge their money in the bank merely for the purpose of security and interest. The accounts current are for those who, in addition to security and interest, wish to make use of the bank as a means of facilitating their pecuniary transactions. As far as regards the circulation of the bankers' notes, each kind of account has the same effect; but as the operations on the current accounts are more frequent, they put into circulation a larger amount.

When a banker's own notes are lodged on a deposit

account, they do not diminish the amount of his banking capital. The banking capital raised by his notes is diminished, but that raised by his deposits is in the same proportion increased. If, however, the interest he allows upon the deposits is greater than the expense of the wear and tear of his notes, then will his banking capital be diminished in the more profitable, and increased in a less profitable direction. But when a deposit consists of notes of other banks, his banking capital is increased by that amount. Hence, if a banker could know that the money deposited in his hands would consist chiefly of his own notes, it might not be for his advantage to allow any interest on deposits. It would be better for him that his notes should remain in circulation.

It will be observed that the amount of notes issued on deposit accounts, depends not on the banker but upon the depositors. They lodge money in his bank, and draw it out when they please. The deposit system, therefore, cannot place in circulation any additional amount of money. The depositors cannot draw out of the bank more money than they had deposited. After the deposits are made, the amount of money in existence is precisely the same as before. The only difference is, that what was previously in the hands of many individuals, is now in the hands of the banker—and until he has made use of this money in the way of discounts or loans, or in some other mode, no effect whatever can be produced upon the trade and commerce of the district. All the advantage the people of the neighbourhood obtain by the deposit system, considered by itself, consists in having a place of security in which they may lodge their money—in receiving interest for the sums thus deposited—and in the saving of time and trouble in effecting their pecuniary transactions. But although the deposit system does not affect the amount of the currency, it changes its character. As the lodgments will be made in the previously existing currency—whether gold, or silver, or notes of other banks—and all the issues will be in the banker's own notes—the effect will be, that in course of time all the previous currency will have passed into the bank, and all the existing currency will consist exclusively of the banker's own notes—and the more frequent and heavy are the operations on the deposit accounts, the more rapidly will this effect be produced.

Banks of deposit serve to economize the use of the circulating medium. This is done upon the principle of transfer. The principle of transfer was one of the first which was brought into operation in modern banking. The bank of Amsterdam was founded upon this principle. Any person who chose, might lodge money in the bank, and might then transfer it from his own name to that of another person. All foreign bills of exchange were required, by law, to be paid by such transfers. Although the money might at any time be drawn out, either by the original depositor or by the party into whose name it had been transferred, yet, in fact, this was seldom done, because the bank money was more valuable than the money in common use, and consequently bore a premium in the market. The transfer of lodgments is extensively practised in our own times. If two persons, who have an account in the same bank, have business transactions with each other, the debtor will pay the creditor by a cheque upon the bank. The creditor will have this cheque placed to his credit. The amount of money in the bank remains the same, but a certain portion is transferred into a different name in the banker's books. The cheque given by the debtor is an authority from the debtor to the banker to make this transfer.

Here the payment between the creditor and debtor is made without any employment of money. No money passes from one to the other: no money is paid out or received by the banker. Thus it is that banks of deposit economize the use of the circulating medium, and enable a large amount of transactions to be settled with a small amount of money. The money thus liberated is employed by the banker in making advances, by discount or otherwise, to his customers. Hence the principle of transfer gives additional efficiency to the deposit system, and increases the productive capital of the country. It matters not whether the two parties who have dealings with each other keep their accounts with the same banker or with different bankers; for, as the bankers exchange their cheques with each other at the clearing-house, the effect, as regards the public, is the same. The deposit system might thus, by means of transfers, be carried to such an extent as wholly to supersede the use of a metallic currency. Were every man to keep a deposit account at a bank, and make all his payments by cheques, money might be superseded, and cheques become the sole circulating medium. In this case, however, it must be supposed that the banker has the money in his hands, or the cheques would have no value.

Since 1825, the following facilities have been granted by the Bank of England to those who have deposit accounts; or, as they are called, "drawing accounts," at the bank:—

1. The bank receives dividends, by power of attorney, for all persons having drawing accounts at the bank.

2. Dividend warrants are received at the drawing office for ditto.

3. Exchequer bills and other securities are received for ditto—the bills exchanged, the interest received, and the amount carried to their respective accounts.

4. Cheques may be drawn for £5 and upwards, instead of £10 as heretofore.

5. Cash boxes taken in, contents unknown, for such parties as keep accounts at the bank.

6. Bank notes are paid at the counter, instead of drawing tickets for them on the pay clerks as heretofore.

7. Cheques on city bankers, paid in by three o'clock, are received and passed to account the same evening.

8. Dividend warrants taken in at the drawing office until four in the afternoon, instead of till three as heretofore.

9. Credits paid into account are received without the bank book, and are afterwards entered therein without the party claiming them.

10. Bills of exchange, payable at the bank, are paid with or without advice; heretofore with advice only.

11. Notes of country bankers, payable in London, are sent out the same day for payment.

12. Cheques are given out in books, and not in sheets as heretofore.

SECTION IX.

BANKS OF REMITTANCE.

IN the infancy of commerce, all trade was carried on with ready money. Before good roads are formed, and posts are established, trade between distant places is carried on by merchants, who associate together in considerable numbers, and meet at fixed times at particular places, whence they commence their journey to the country with which they intend to traffic. When arrived at the place where the market is held, they dispose of their goods for ready money; they then lay out their money in the purchase of other goods, with which they return. Such was the practice with the merchants of the East, who formed the immense caravans that formerly traded between Europe and India; and such is the practice of similar caravans that now trade between Egypt and Mecca. In such cases all the transactions are carried on with ready money. The bankers, if such they may be called, are mere money-changers, who exchange the money of the country in which they live for the money of other countries.

The labour of carrying money from one country to another was considerably diminished by the invention of bills of exchange; but the same mode of remittance was continued, even in England, until a very recent period, with regard to the transmission of money through the provinces. When a country is considerably improved, good roads are established, and places hitherto obscure become seats of manufacturing and agricultural industry; an interchange of commodities will take place between the provinces; the produce of one district will be transported to another: hence will arise the necessity of having some means of transmitting money in payment of these respective commodities, and banks will consequently be established. It is not the banks that give rise to the trade, it is the trade that gives rise to the banks: though, after the trade is established, the introduction of a bank extends the trade.

The most effectual means of transmitting money throughout a country is by an extensive establishment of banks; banks transmit money by means of their agencies, by means of their branches, and by means of the circulation of notes.

First.—Banks transmit money by means of their agencies. This is the way in which it is carried on by the country bankers. Each country banker employs a London agent to pay his notes or bills, and to make payments in London; and, on the other hand, to receive sums that may be lodged by parties residing in London for the use of parties residing in the country. As each country bank is thus connected with London, it is virtually connected with all the other banks in the country; as far, at least, as concerns the transmission of money.

Money is remitted from London to a country town by being paid into a London bank, to the credit of the country bank, for the use of the party who resides in the country. Money is remitted from a country town to London by being paid into a country bank, to the credit of their London agents, for the use of the party who resides in London, or by remitting to the party a bill drawn by the country upon the London bank. Money is remitted from one country town to another by paying the money into the country bank, to be paid by their London agents to the

London agent of the country bank established in the town to which the money is to be remitted, or by sending direct to the party a bill drawn by the country upon the London bank, which bill will be discounted by the bank established in the place to which the bill is sent.

Secondly.—Banks remit money from one place to another by means of their branches. Money is received at the head office for the credit of any branch; and money is received at each of the branches for the credit of the head office; and letters of credit are also granted at every branch upon all the other branches. The Bank of England transmits money from London to a branch; and *vice versâ,* for only the charge of postage. The branches also draw bills upon the parent establishment at fourteen days' date without any charge.

Thirdly.—Banks remit money from one place to another by means of their circulation. Every bank of circulation will necessarily become a bank of remittance, whether it carry on the remitting of money as a branch of business or not. Some of the notes which are issued will be sent as payments from one place to another. This will be more frequently the case if the notes are payable at any place besides the place of issue, or the bank that issues them has credit over a great extent of country: thus, Bank of England notes serve the purpose of remittance all over the kingdom. They are usually cut in halves and sent by post, one half being retained till the receipt of the first is acknowledged. The issue of bank post bills, payable seven days after sight, and granted in favour of the party to whom the payment is to be made, has still farther increased the efficiency of the Bank of England as a bank of remittance.

The extent of the remittance of any place must depend in a great degree upon its trade—that is, upon its exports and its imports. Money must be sent *from* a place to pay for its imports, and money must be *received* in exchange for exports. Both these branches of remittance, as far as regards provincial towns, are effected through the banks. Exporters and importers, residing in a city or town, do not meet together, like the merchants engaged in a foreign trade, and traffic from their bills, but both parties go to the bank. The exporter draws bills which he discounts with the bank; the importer obtains from the bank bills or letters of credit, which he remits in payment of his imports. The amount of this kind of business must, of course, depend upon the amount of the trade. When the imports are great, there will be demand for bills, or other modes of remittance upon the banker. When the exports are great, bills will be brought to him for discount, or lodgments will be made to his credit at his agents. By comparing the sums which are thus transmitted in different directions, a banker can, merely by a reference to his own books, ascertain the balance of trade between the place in which he resides and any other place with which it may have commercial intercourse. If he finds his exchanges with the neighbouring bankers are unfavourable, he may infer that the balance of trade is against the place in which his bank is established. And if, on the other hand, the exchanges are in his favour, he may infer the balance of trade is favourable. It will generally be found, that the trade between seaport and inland towns is always in favour of the former. Manufacturing towns and large cities have usually the balance in their favour. It may be observed, however, that the balance of remittances will not *always* show the balance of trade. With regard to places of fashionable resort, for instance, there must be a great consumption of commodities imported from other places, and at the same time there is no commodity exported,—

here the balance of trade is unfavourable: at the same time there must be great remittances, in money, to the parties residing there, to enable them to pay for the commodities they consume. Thus, too, when large sums are remitted from England to absentee landlords, or as loans to foreign powers, the balance of remittance may be against England, while the balance of trade may be in her favour.

The remitting of money to London by a country bank diminishes the currency to that amount in the place where the bank is established. If a person at Birmingham takes one hundred sovereigns to the branch of the Bank of England, and obtains a bill at fourteen days on the parent establishment in London, then there is a banking capital created for fourteen days. If, when the bill becomes due, the Bank of England pay the bill in gold, the banking capital is destroyed. The currency of Birmingham is now one hundred sovereigns less, and that of London is one hundred sovereigns more. During the existence of the bill there were one hundred sovereigns less in circulation, and these one hundred sovereigns were represented by the bill. Some country bankers, instead of drawing bills upon their London agents, reissue the bills they have discounted. By this means the banker saves the expense of remitting the discounted bill to London, and the person taking it saves the expense of the stamp for a new bill.

Banks of remittance encourage the trade of a district in two ways: First, by diminishing the prices of commodities. The facility of conveying money has the same effect upon trade as a facility of conveying commodities. The opening of good roads diminishes the expense of the conveyance of goods. This cheapness in the conveyance causes the commodities to be sold at a lower price. As the imports into the town are sold at a cheaper rate, and the exports are also sold at a lower price at the place of consumption, the increased cheapness in both cases increases the demand, and hence trade is advanced. The cheapness of conveying money operates in the same way as cheapness in the conveyance of goods. After the goods are sold, the money must be transmitted. The expense of remitting the money, like the expense of conveying the goods, must be regarded as an item in the cost of production, and be taken into account in fixing the price at which the goods must be sold. Banks remit money at a less expense than it can be remitted in any other way. Hence the merchants are enabled to sell their merchandise at a lower price, and thereby consumption is increased and trade is extended.

The second way in which banks of remittance promote trade is by enabling capital to revolve more rapidly. They cause money to be remitted in a shorter space of time. For instance,—an Irish butter-merchant may purchase of a farmer a quantity of butter, and ship it for London. He may, on the same day, draw a bill for the value of the butter, and have it discounted at the bank. With this money he may purchase a further quantity of butter against which he may draw another bill and have it discounted. This operation, if he be in good credit, may be repeated as often as he pleases. Now, if there be no bank in the district, he could not get the money for the first shipment of butter until the return of post from London, and then he would receive large Bank of England notes, which he might not easily be able to get changed. During this interval he can make no purchases for want of money, and the farmer has no sale for his butter. Thus the banks enable the merchants' capital to revolve several times more rapidly than it could otherwise do. To increase the rapidity of the returns of capital has the same effect as to increase its amount. If any given amount of capital, that now revolves once in a year, be made to revolve twice in a year, it will have the same effect upon trade as if the amount of capital were doubled and its progress remained the same.

Banks of *deposit* encourage the trade and wealth of a district by collecting together the various small amounts of money that previously lay idle in the hands of the depositors, and employing this sum in advances, by way of loan or discount, to the productive classes of the community. The commodities thus produced are remitted to a distant place for sale. But in the interval, between the transmission of the goods and the return of the money for which they may be sold, the manufacturer is deprived of the use of this amount of capital. Banks of *remittance* guard against this inconvenience, and advance immediately to the manufacturer the value of the goods, by discounting his bill upon the party to whom they are consigned. By this means he has all the advantage to be gained from the higher prices at a distant sale, in connexion with that prompt payment he would obtain from a home market. Thus it is, that while banks of deposit enable the capital of any district to revolve more rapidly *within the district*, banks of remittance enable it to revolve more rapidly with reference to other places. Both produce the same effect as that positive increase of capital which is introduced by banks of circulation.

SECTION X.

BANKS OF CIRCULATION.

A BANK that issues notes is called a bank of circulation. The amount of notes that any bank has in circulation is usually called by bankers "*the circulation.*" Banks of circulation, both in England and Scotland, have all of them had to sustain heavy accusations. I shall notice some of these charges, not with a view of rebutting them in regard to any individual bank, but in order to discuss the general principles by which we should be guided, in judging of the effects produced by banks of circulation.

The most common charge against banks of circulation is, that they have issued an excessive amount of their notes; and thus have encouraged speculation, raised the price of commodities, and led to commercial convulsions similar to that of December, 1825.

Before entering upon the consideration of these charges, I shall point out the checks that operate against an overissue of notes.

I have already stated that similar accusations may be as justly advanced against banks of deposit as against banks of circulation; for to give increased motion to the currency has the same effect as to increase its amount. If a million of money be taken from the counting-houses of the merchants, and the tills of the shopkeepers, and lodged in the hands of a London banker, for him to employ in advancing loans or discounting bills, this has the same effect as though he issued for the same purposes a million of his own promissory notes. There is, however, one difference. The advances of a London banker are limited by the amount of his lodgments. If the money be not placed in his hands, he cannot issue it; and hence he may be regarded as merely an agent regulating the distribution of the previously existing currency. But the country banker having the power of making money, the amount of his advances is not subject to this restraint.

But the amount of notes issued by a bank must be limited by the demand of its customers. No banker is so anxious to put his notes into circulation that he gives them away. He advances them either by way of loan or discount; and he always believes that the security on which he makes his advances is sufficiently ample. He expects that the money will be repaid with interest. It is true, that like other commercial men, he is sometimes deceived in his customers; and by placing too much confidence in them, he sustains losses. But this is a misfortune against which he is always anxious to guard. The issues of bankers are limited, therefore; on the one hand by the wants of the public, and on the other by the bankers' desire to protect their own interests.

A further check upon the issues of banks is, that all their notes are payable on demand. Although a banker has the power of issuing his notes to excess, either by advancing them as dead loans or on slender security, yet he has not the power of keeping them out; their remaining in circulation depends not on him, but on the public; and the uncertainty as to the time of their return for payment compels him to keep at all times a sufficient stock of money to meet the most extensive demand that is likely in the ordinary course of business to occur.

Another check upon an excessive issue of notes, is the system of exchanges that is carried on between the banks.

Every banker that issues notes has an interest in withdrawing from circulation the notes of every other banker, in order to make more room for his own. When a banker receives the notes of another banker, he never reissues them. If the two bankers live in the same place, they meet once or twice a week, as they may find convenient, and exchange their notes. The balance between them, if any, is paid by a draft on London payable on demand; or, which amounts to the same thing, the London agent of the one party is directed to pay the amount to the London agent of the other party. If the country banker lives at a distance from the banker whose notes he has received, he sends them to his London agent to present for payment. Hence it is that country notes seldom travel far from the place of issue: they are sure to be intercepted by some of the rival banks; and in a country where banks are so numerous as in England, it is obvious that the notes of any individual bank must move in a very limited circle. If a banker attempts to force out a higher amount of notes than the wants of this circle require, he will soon find that the notes will be returned to him in the exchanges with neighbouring bankers, or else they will speedily find their way for payment to his London agent.

Another check upon an over-issue on the part of the banks is their practice of allowing interest upon money lodged in their hands. No man will keep money lying idle in his hands if he can obtain interest for it, and have it returned to him upon demand. If a banker attempts to force out a large amount of notes, they will get into the hands of somebody. And those who do not employ them in their trade will take them back to the bank and lodge them to their credit, for the purpose of receiving the interest. Thus, if the notes of a banker are put in motion by the operations of commerce, they are soon intercepted by rival bankers; and if they attain a state of rest, they are brought back and lodged upon interest; so that in either case they are withdrawn from circulation.

Banks of circulation have also been accused of encouraging a spirit of speculation.

To obtain clear ideas as to the justice of this charge, it will be necessary to define accurately the nature of speculation, and to view the circumstances by which it is governed.

Between the producer and the consumer of any commodity, there are generally two or more parties, who are merchants or dealers. The demand for any commodity is either a speculative or a consumptive demand. The demand by the consumers who purchase for immediate use, is always a consumptive demand. But if the commodity purchased be not intended for immediate use, but is purchased at any given time, merely because the purchaser apprehends that its price will advance, then is that demand a speculative demand. So, if a merchant purchase of a manufacturer, or a farmer, such a quantity of commodities as in the ordinary course of his trade he is likely to require, that demand may be considered a consumptive demand; but if, in expectation of a rise in price, he fills his warehouses with goods for which he has no immediate sale, then is that demand a speculative demand. A speculation, then, is that kind of traffic in which the dealer expects to realize a profit, not by the ordinary course of trade, but by the intervention of some fortuitous circumstance that shall change the price of the commodity in which he deals.

A speculation in any commodity, therefore, is occasioned by some opinion that may be formed of its future price. It is well known that the price of commodities is governed by the proportion that may exist between the supply and the demand. Whatever increases the supply, or diminishes the demand, will lower the price; and, on the contrary, whatever diminishes the supply, or increases the demand, will advance the price. The greater part of our food, and the materials of most of our clothing, are produced by the seasons; and the quantity produced in each year depends, in a great degree, upon the most uncertain of all things,—the weather. Here, then, is a wide field for speculation. If our food, like the manna in the wilderness, were supplied to us day by day, in exactly the quantity that each individual required, it would furnish no subject for speculation. But as long as the seasons are variable in the quantity of their productions, so long will speculation exist. Many commodities, too, besides being influenced by the seasons, are influenced by several other circumstances,—as a state of peace or war,—the opening of new markets,—the discovery of cheaper modes of production,—or the substitution of a rival commodity; all these circumstances have an effect upon price, and the dealer who buys or sells any commodity in expectation that an alteration in price will be produced by such causes, is a speculator.

Now, it is obvious that no system of banking can prevent speculation, and that speculations would be formed, even were there no bank in existence. We learn from Holy Writ, that the owners of corn sometimes refused to sell, in expectation of an advance of price. These were speculations, though Judæa had neither banks nor paper money. If it be said that the country banks are the cause of speculation, I will ask how it is that speculations exist in countries where there are no country banks? If it be said that the issuing of country notes is the cause of speculation, I will ask how it is that Liverpool is the most speculative place in England, although the Liverpool bankers do not issue notes? If it be said that the speculations of 1825 were produced by the country banks, I will ask, what produced similar speculations in 1720, when there was not a single country bank in the kingdom?

It must not, however, be denied that all banking gives to speculation facilities that would not otherwise be so easily supplied. It is the object of banking to give facilities to trade, and whatever gives facilities to trade gives facilities to speculation. Trade and speculation are in some cases so nearly allied, that it is impossible to say at what precise point trade ends and speculation begins. When a banker discounts a bill, he does not usually ask the party how he intends to employ the money; and, for aught he knows, it may be employed in speculation. Wherever there are banks, capital is more readily obtained, and at a cheaper rate. The cheapness of capital gives facilities to speculation just in the same way as the cheapness of beef and of beer gives facilities to gluttony and drunkenness.

The legitimate operations of banking, however, are such as to place speculation under some degree of restraint. As to men of large capital and immense wealth, they may speculate as much as they please; over *them* the bankers have no control. But if men of moderate means engage in speculation beyond their capital, it is not the interest of the banker to support them. For such persons to carry speculation to any great extent, it is necessary either that they raise money on slender security, or that the money be advanced for a considerable length of time. It is not the interest of a banker to meet their wishes in either of these respects. It is not his interest to advance his money on insufficient security. It is not his interest to advance money as a dead loan. The security a banker requires ought to be both ample and convertible. It is contrary to all sound principles of banking for a banker to advance money on dead security. In the first place, such loans do not create any banking capital; and, in the second place, they cannot be suddenly called up, in case any contraction of the banking capital should render it necessary.

In admitting that banking, by granting facilities to trade, necessarily grants facilities, to a certain extent, to speculation, it is not admitted that bankers generally have granted facilities to speculation beyond the fair operations of their trade. All speculation, by increasing the number and amount of commercial transactions, puts into motion a greater quantity of money. This money is supplied by the bankers either in the way of repayment of deposits, or of discounting of bills, or by loans. Now as increased issues on the part of the banks are almost simultaneous with a spirit of speculation, it has been inferred that the issues of the notes have excited the spirit of speculation, whereas it has been the spirit of speculation that has called out the notes. In the years 1824 and 1825, as the speculations increased, the issues of notes increased; and when the speculations were over, the notes returned. This was the case not merely in England, but also in Scotland, though none of the Scotch banks sustained the least diminution of public confidence.

Another charge that has often been preferred against banks of circulation is, that by an increased issue of their notes they have caused a general rise in prices.

In investigating this charge, it will be proper to inquire what are the cases in which an increased issue of notes may produce a rise in prices.

It cannot be denied that if any bank have the privilege of issuing notes, not convertible into gold—that is, not payable in gold on demand—the notes may be issued to such an amount as to cause a considerable advance in prices. It is now generally believed that the issues of the Bank of England during the operation of the Restriction

Act did produce this effect. It may also be admitted that in a country where there is one chief bank, possessing an immense capital and unbounded confidence, the notes of such a bank, even if payable in gold, may be issued to such an extent as to cause an advance of prices, until an unfavourable course of the exchange shall cause payment of the notes to be demanded in gold. For gold will not be demanded until the course of the exchange is so unfavourable as to cause the exportation of gold to be attended with profit. Hence the issues of the Bank of England being at present under no other restraint than liability to pay in gold on demand, may for a time cause an advance in prices.

In cases where the increased issue of notes is caused by the increased quantity of commodities brought to market, the additional amount of notes put into circulation does not cause any advance of prices. In all agricultural districts there is a great demand for notes about the season of harvest, to pay for the produce then brought to market. In the south of Ireland the amount of notes in circulation is much greater in the winter, when corn and bacon are being exported, than in the summer months. Almost every trade and every kind of manufacture is carried on with more activity at some periods of the year than at others; and during the active seasons when money is in demand, more notes are in circulation. These notes are at such periods drawn out of the banks, either as repayments of money lodged, or by discount of the bills drawn against the exported commodities.

An increased issue of notes often causes the production of an additional quantity of commodities, and in this case does not produce an advance of prices. The issue of notes will be either in the form of discounts, or loans, or the repayment of deposits. In either case the parties receiving the money will spend it, and a demand will thus be occasioned for a certain class of commodities. If this demand should not exceed the quantity that can be readily supplied, there will be no advance of price. The parties who receive the money from the banker may give it to the dealer in exchange for the articles they purchase. The dealer wishes to replace the goods he has sold, and passes the money for more goods to the manufacturer. The manufacturer consequently buys more raw material and employs more labourers. An increased quantity of goods is thus produced, and exchanged against the increased quantity of money. But while the supply can keep pace with the demand, the price will remain the same; it is only when the demand exceeds the supply, and the commodities are consequently comparatively scarce, that the price will advance.

In many cases, an increased issue of notes is not the *cause*, but the *effect* of an advance of prices. If a Yorkshire clothier sells a thousand pounds' worth of goods to a London merchant, he will draw a bill for a thousand pounds, and take it for discount to a country banker, whose notes for a thousand pounds may thus be put into circulation; but if, in consequence of a scarcity of wool, or from any other cause, the goods that were sold for a thousand pounds are now worth two thousand pounds, then will the banker discount a bill for two thousand pounds, and put into circulation two thousand pounds of his notes. In this case it is obvious that the issue of notes is not the cause of the high price of wool; but that the high price of wool is the cause of the increased issue of notes. Such is often the case with many other commodities; a real or apprehended scarcity causes an advance in price. The same commodity exchanges for a greater quantity of money. The bills are drawn for higher sums, and the bankers who discount these bills issue, of course, a greater amount of notes. The rise in price, too, renders more capital necessary to carry on the same extent of business. Many persons who had money in the bank on interest will now draw it out, to employ it in their trade, and these operations will occasion a still farther issue of notes. A rise in the price of one commodity will sometimes advance the price of other commodities, and hence similar banking operations are effected by persons engaged in other branches of trade. The process by which high prices cause an increase in the amount of notes in circulation, can thus be easily and obviously traced.

In cases where an increased issue of notes does cause an advance of price, the advance can be but temporary, and this advance may generally be ascribed to a spirit of speculation on the part of the dealers, and not to an excessive issue on the part of the banks. As the prices of all commodities are regulated by the proportion that may exist between the demand and the supply, whenever an increased issue of notes raises prices, it must be either by increasing the demand for commodities, or diminishing the supply. The cases in which an increased issue of notes may cause an advance of prices, are chiefly those in which the money is employed in purchasing such commodities as cannot be readily produced by human labour. Thus, if a banker lend money to a corn merchant to purchase a stock of corn, he increases the demand for corn. If he lend money to a farmer to enable him to pay his rent without selling his corn, he diminishes the supply. In both cases he may cause an advance in price. But even in this case, the most unpopular that can well be imagined, the effect on price will be but temporary; for these speculations do not diminish the quantity of corn in the country. The supplies now withheld must ultimately be sold, and in proportion as they advance the price when withheld, will they lower the price when brought to market. A degree of speculation in some commodity or other is always on foot, and occasions fluctuations in the price. The banks have no control over these speculations, and ought not to be deemed answerable for the changes they occasion. To suppose that the banks can so regulate their issues as to maintain permanent prices, is to ascribe to them a power which they do not possess, and which, if they did possess, they ought never to use.

There are various cases wherein an increased issue of notes causes a reduction of prices. The speculations which advance prices are chiefly those carried on by *dealers*. The speculations of *producers* who invest their capital in new undertakings, with the view of producing any given commodities at a less cost, will, if successful, reduce the price to the consumer, and so far as such speculations are assisted by the banks, the issue of notes thus occasioned tends to the reduction of prices. An advance of money which enables a farmer to bestow a higher degree of cultivation on his land—which enables a manufacturer or a tradesman to extend his business—has the effect of increasing the quantity of commodities offered for sale, and consequently to reduce the price. The banks, too, by advancing capital on lower terms than it could be otherwise obtained, diminish the cost of production, and consequently the price. The banks still farther reduce prices by destroying monopoly. In towns where there are no banks, a few moneyed men have all the trade in their own hands: but when a bank is established, other persons of character are enabled to borrow capital of the bankers. Thus monopoly is destroyed, competition is produced, and prices fall. Hence it is obvious, that *in the ordinary course of business* the issues of the banks tend not to advance but to lower prices.

The effect which the amount of notes in circulation has upon the foreign exchanges has been the subject of much discussion. One party contended, that as the amount of notes increases, the exchange must become unfavourable. Another party maintained, that the exchanges were not at all affected by the issue of notes, but by the state of foreign trade. The authors of the Report of the Bullion Committee expressed the former opinion, some of the Bank directors maintained the latter.

It is obvious that the exchanges are regulated by the amount of gold that is required to be sent abroad, either to pay the balance of trade, or to pay our armies, or to subsidize foreign Powers, or as rents to absentees, or for some other purpose. Now it is clear that an increased or diminished issue of notes will in no way diminish the amount of gold that is to be sent abroad, and, therefore, can have no *direct* effect upon the exchanges. If we owe the gold, we must pay it. We may diminish our issues of notes, but that will not pay our debts. If, then, the issues of notes have any effect upon the exchanges it must be in an *indirect* way.

I have already stated that an increased issue of notes can have no effect upon the prices of commodities at home, but by influencing either the supply or the demand. If the increased quantity of money raises the demand for commodities beyond a certain point, it will advance the price. And if it increases the supply it will lower the price; but in no way can the quantity of money in circulation affect the price of commodities but through the channels of supply and demand. Just so with the foreign exchanges. An unfavourable course of exchange arises generally from our owing a sum of money which we have to pay in consequence of our imports having exceeded our exports. An increased quantity of money, therefore, to affect the exchanges must diminish the amount of our foreign debt, and it can do this only by either increasing our exports or diminishing our imports. When money is abundant our merchants can import more than formerly. This increases our debt. The importers are disposed to lay in stocks of goods, and the competition between the importers raises the price they give to the foreigner. Hence there are heavy sums to be sent abroad. It is true that when money is abundant our manufacturers and exporters can also export more goods, but the competition among exporters diminishes the price to the foreigner, and hence we have a less proportionate sum to receive. The exporter, too, having abundance of money, gives the foreigner long credit, and hence the money is not received in England for a considerable time after the goods have been shipped. In the mean time the exchanges become unfavourable, and gold must be sent abroad. Now suppose in this state of things the bank contracts its issues; money becomes scarce—bills cannot be discounted, and trade is dull. Now, then, the importer having already a heavy stock of goods, will buy no more; he is anxious to sell, for he has not now sufficient capital to keep so large a stock. A general desire of selling will cause a fall of price. Fewer commodities will now be imported, and these obtained at a less price, hence there is less money due to the foreigner. The exporters, on the other hand, deprived also of their usual accommodation, cannot carry on business to the same extent—the supply will be reduced—the competition is less, and prices rise to the foreigner. The exporters, too, cannot give such long credit as formerly; they will call in the sums due to them, and hence more money must come in from abroad. As, then, we have to pay other nations a less amount of money for our imports, and they have to pay us a greater amount for our exports, the exchanges will become favourable. It is obvious that this operation will cause great embarrassment in trade; in fact, it is only by producing embarrassment that a contraction of the currency can affect the exchanges.

The amount of notes in circulation affects the foreign exchanges in another way. When an increased issue takes place, money becomes more abundant; the lenders are more numerous, and the supply of capital is increased. Hence the price given for the loan of money, that is, the rate of interest, falls. Persons who have money to employ will find they cannot obtain the same interest as formerly, hence they will be disposed to invest it in the foreign funds, where it can be employed to greater advantage. In order to remit this money they will purchase foreign bills; this demand for foreign bills will advance their price, and the exchanges will, consequently, be unfavourable. On the other hand, when the circulation is considerably reduced, money becomes scarce, a higher price will be given for the use of it, the rate of interest rises; persons who have property abroad will be disposed to bring it home, where it can be more profitably invested; they will draw bills against it and sell them in the market. This new supply of bills will lower the price, and make the exchanges favourable.

It should always be recollected that the transmission of money as subsidies, loans, or for investment in the foreign funds, will have the same effect upon the exchanges as though it were transmitted in payment of commodities imported. Whenever, therefore, the issue of notes shall, directly or indirectly, cause a transmission of money from one country to another, the exchanges will be affected. But when this shall not be the case, the expansion or contraction of the currency will have no effect upon the foreign exchanges.

SECTION XI.

BANKS OF DISCOUNT.

A CONSIDERABLE branch of the business of modern banking consists in discounting bills of exchange. As they have only a short time to run before they fall due, the capital advanced soon returns; and being transferable, they can, if necessary, be re-discounted.[1] Hence they are admirably adapted for the purposes of the bankers: for as the advances of bankers to their customers are made with other people's money, and that money may at any time be withdrawn, it becomes necessary that the securities on which those advances are made should rapidly revolve and be at all times convertible. By means of bills of exchange bankers can easily extend or diminish their advances in proportion to the capital they may have to employ. If they find that the amount of their deposits or the amount of their circulation is diminishing, they will diminish their discounts. If these increase, they may increase their discounts.

I. *Nature and Origin of Bills of Exchange.*—Bills of exchange are said to have been invented in the fourteenth century by the Jews or the Lombards, for the purpose of withdrawing their property from the countries from which they were expelled. The drawer and the acceptor of a bill

---

[1] None of the London or the Scotch banks re-discount their bills, but it is a common practice with some of the English provincial and some of the Irish banks.

were two persons, residing at two distant places, and the bill was probably nothing more than a written order delivered to a third person, who was going to visit the place where the debtor resided, and who would return with the money to the drawer. But it might happen that this person might not be going to return; in this case he might advance to the creditor the amount of the order, and receive the money again from the debtor when he arrived at his journey's end. But this third person might not be going to the place where the debtor resided, he might be going only a part of the way, and he might then fall in with some other person who was going the other part; he would then request this other person to advance him the money in exchange for the order he had received from the creditor, and the order would then be transferred. It would thus be discovered that as a creditor might give an order upon his debter to a third person, this third person might transfer the order to a fourth, the fourth to a fifth, and so on. To effect these transactions it would be necessary that each person receiving the order, or bill, had confidence in the drawer or some of the endorsers, and also that each person receiving it should have some compensation for the trouble it occasioned him. If the order were not payable on demand, but at some months after date, the compensation would be increased by the amount of interest for the time the order had to run before it would be payable.

Such is at present the case. The drawer of a bill on a person residing out of the country *sells* it on the exchange. Foreign bills are never said to be *discounted*, but to be *sold;* for the person who gives the drawer the amount, is supposed to deduct not only the interest on the bill, but also the expense of its transmission. The buyer of a bill is a person who owes a sum of money to a person in another country (say in France), and who wants a bill to remit thither to pay his debt. The seller of a bill is a person who has exported a quantity of goods to France, and who draws a bill for the amount: it will be for the convenience of these two people to deal together: the buyer will give his money in exchange for the bill, which he will send to his creditor in France, and the seller will give his bill in exchange for the buyer's money, by which he is paid for the goods he has exported. If this money is equal to the amount of the bill, minus only what may be deemed equal to the discount and the expense of transmission, the exchange is said to be at par; but there are various circumstances which may cause the exchange to be either above or below par, and the price given for bills of exchange will vary accordingly.

When two nations exchange their commodities with each other to exactly the same amount, the buyers will be just as numerous as the sellers. The demand for bills and the supply of bills will be equal; the exchange will now be at par; but it rarely or never happens that the exports and imports between any two countries are precisely the same; and as gold is the medium of traffic between nations as well as between individuals, the balance or difference between the purchases and the sale must be remitted in that metal. Now the expense in freight and insurance of sending a quantity of gold from one country to another will not be inconsiderable. If, then, I owe a sum of money to a merchant in France, I would be willing to give something more than that sum for a bill, rather than submit to the expense and trouble of remitting gold. But if the bill would cost more than the expense at which I could send the gold, why, then, the gold should go. It is evident, then, that in that nation which is in debt to another nation, and which, consequently, has to send gold to pay its debts, the demand for bills of exchange will be greater than the supply. These bills will be sold for more than the amount of the money for which they are drawn; they are then at a premium, but this premium never can rise higher than the expense of remitting an equal amount in gold: for if it were cheaper to remit gold, the gold would be remitted.

The price of bills in the market is usually called the rate of exchange, and when the balance of trade is against a country, and gold must be remitted to pay that balance, and, consequently, the price of foreign bills rises beyond their real value or par, then the course of exchange is said to be against that country: thus, for instance, if in London I can sell a bill on Paris for more than the amount for which it is drawn, then the course of exchange is said to be against England and in favour of France; but if I am obliged to sell my bill for less than the amount, then the exchange is against France and in favour of England. The price of bills is regulated entirely by the proportion that may exist between the demand and the supply, and the demand and the supply are regulated chiefly by the state of trade between the respective countries.

The trafficking in bills of exchange is now a distinct branch of business. When bills, say on France, are at a high premium in our market, a house in London will draw bills upon a house in Paris, and the bills will be sold at a good price. On the other hand, when bills on England are at a high premium in the Paris markets, a house in Paris will draw upon a house in London, and sell the bill in the Paris market. This seems to be a very honourable kind of business, but it is said that some inferior persons engaged in this traffic sometimes have recourse to unjustifiable means of raising or lowering the price of bills, in the same way as stockjobbers are said to do to affect the value of the public funds.

Not only are bills employed as the means of transmitting money from one country to another, but also as the means of making remittances from one town to another. If a person in a country town wishes to send money to London, he can go to the bank and procure a bill upon a banker in London. If he wants to receive money from London, he will draw a bill upon his debtor, and get the money for it at the bank. If he wishes to send money from one provincial town to another, he will get from the bank a bill upon a London banker and send it to his correspondent by post. When the country banker discounts, or, as it is called in the foreign market, *buys* a bill, he usually charges, in addition to the discount, a commission to pay the expense of its transmission and collection. And when he issues or sells a bill, he usually gives in exchange for cash a bill at a certain number of days after date. Hence the number of days at which a provincial banker is in the habit of drawing upon his London agent is usually called the *par of exchange* between that place and London.

II. *Advantages of Bills.*—Besides their utility as a means of transferring money from one place to another, bills have the following advantages:—

1. Bills are a means of transferring debts from one person to another. If I owe a man £100 and another man owes me £100, I will draw a bill for that amount on my debtor and give it to my creditor. I have thus transferred the debt from my debtor to my creditor, and my own debt is liquidated. My debtor, instead of paying me the money he owed me, will pay it to the holder of the bill. My creditor will now look for payment to my debtor, and consider me simply as a guarantee for the payment of the bill. If he wishes to make use of the bill he will again transfer the debt to another party, placing his own name on the bill as an additional guarantee. The bill may thus pass through a variety of hands, and liquidate a great

number of debts, before it becomes due. When due, it will be paid by the acceptor, who was the original debtor, and all these intermediate transactions will be closed. Hence, in Lancashire, bills of exchange have served the purpose of a circulating medium, in the same way as bank notes. The only difference is, that in transferring a bank note you are not responsible for its ultimate payment; but in passing a bill of exchange you place your name on it as a guarantee. A bill of exchange, too, cannot always be passed for its full amount, but you will have to pay a discount according to the time it has to run before it will fall due.

2. Bills fix the period for the payment of debts, and in case of litigation they afford an easy proof of the debt. A person will have little scruple in putting off a tradesman to whom he owes money, and the creditor dares not be urgent lest the debtor should no longer deal with him, hence the time of payment can never be calculated upon with certainty. But if the customer has given a bill for the amount he owes, that bill will circulate into the hands of other persons who will be more peremptory in demanding payment, and whose applications cannot be disregarded with impunity. Besides, if a man dishonour his acceptance, his character is stamped at once in the commercial world as being either very poor, very negligent, or very unprincipled, and at no future time will he be able to raise money upon the credit of his name. Hence many persons who are very tardy in paying a book debt, are very punctual in paying their bills. In case, too, a tradesman is under the necessity of bringing an action at law against his customer, he will have to prove the actual delivery of every article mentioned in his account. This, at a distance of time, is often difficult to do; but if a bill has been accepted for the amount, it is only necessary to prove that the acceptance is in the defendant's handwriting.

3. Bills enable a tradesman to carry on a more extensive business with the same amount of capital. If, by the custom of trade, a dealer gives his customers three months' credit, he can, during that period, make no use of that portion of his capital which is invested in the commodities they have purchased; but if they accept his bills, drawn at three months after date, he can, if in good credit, get those bills discounted at the bank in his town, and then employ this money in the further extension of his business. He will thus, while selling on credit, obtain nearly the same advantages as though he sold for ready money. Should he, instead of having these bills discounted, pay them to the manufacturer or wholesale house of whom he makes his purchases, it will amount to nearly the same thing. The whole of his capital is thus kept in motion, and is not diminished by any amount of outstanding debts. To give credit without drawing bills requires that a tradesman should have a large capital. To give no credit will restrict his business. By means of bills he is enabled to give credit and to extend his business, without requiring any addition to his capital.

4. Bills afford an easy way of giving a guarantee. A person may wish to borrow money of me, and I may be unwilling to lend it to him unless he procure a more wealthy person to guarantee the repayment at a given time. If he has a friend that will do this, the most easy way of effecting the guarantee is by means of a bill drawn by the borrower upon his friend. This, in point of security, is the same thing as a letter of guarantee; but it has also this additional advantage, that if I should want the money before the time fixed for its repayment, I can get this bill discounted and reimburse myself the money I have advanced. Bills of this description are called accommodation-bills, or wind-bills, or kites. When employed only as a

means of affording occasional assistance to a needy friend, or for raising a sum of money for a short time, to meet an unexpected call, they do not appear to be very objectionable; but when systematically pursued for the purpose of raising a fictitious capital whereon to trade, they uniformly indicate the folly, and effect the ruin, of all the parties concerned.

5. Bills are the means of facilitating the removal of capital from one branch of trade to another as circumstances may require. When the demand for any commodity increases, the price advances, and more capital is put into requisition to increase the supply. When the demand for any commodity declines, the price falls, the trade is bad, and capital will be withdrawn to be invested in a more profitable employment. Every branch of trade is liable to fluctuations from an alteration in the proportion between the demand and the supply, and hence capital is continually undergoing a transfer from the production of those articles for which there is a less demand to the production of those articles for which there is a greater demand. But in what way is this transfer effected? Is it by a manufacturer leaving one employment for another? No. The manufacturer in the declining trade will reduce his capital, while the manufacturer in the prosperous trade will augment his capital; and the transfer of capital from one trade to the other is effected chiefly by bills of exchange. The manufacturer who has sold a less quantity of commodities will have fewer bills for his banker to discount; the other, having sold a greater quantity of commodities, has more bills for discount. The banker's capital, which he employs chiefly in the discount of bills, is thus easily transferred from one branch of manufacture to another, in exact proportion to the circumstances of the respective parties. On this subject we quote Mr. Ricardo:

"In all rich countries there is a number of men forming

what is called a moneyed class. These men are engaged in no trade, but live on the interest of their money, which is employed in discounting bills, or in loans to the more industrious part of the community. The bankers, too, employ a large capital on the same objects. The capital so employed forms a circulating capital of a large amount, and is employed in larger or smaller proportions by all the different trades of a country. There is, perhaps, no manufacturer, however rich, who limits his business to the extent that his own funds alone will allow; he has always some portion of this floating capital increasing or diminishing according to the activity of the demand for his commodities. When the demand for silks increases, and that for cloth diminishes, the clothier does not remove with his capital to the silk trade, but he dismisses some of his workmen, and he discontinues his demand for loans from bankers and moneyed men: while the case of the silk manufacturer is the reverse; he wishes to employ more workmen, and thus his motive for borrowing is increased; he borrows more, and thus capital is transferred from one employment to another without the necessity of a manufacturer discontinuing his usual occupation."[1]

III. *Classes of Bills.*—The bills presented to a bank for discount may generally be divided into the following classes:

1. Bills drawn by producers or manufacturers upon wholesale dealers.
2. Bills drawn by wholesale dealers upon retail dealers.
3. Bills drawn by retail dealers upon consumers.
4. Bills not arising out of trade, but yet drawn against value, as rents, &c.
5. Kites, or accommodation bills.

[1] Ricardo's "Principles of Political Economy," page 84.

The first two classes of bills are the best, and are fair legitimate bills for bankers to discount.

The third class ought not to be too much encouraged. They are for comparatively small amounts, and are drawn by shopkeepers and tradesmen upon their customers. To discount these bills freely would encourage extravagance in the acceptors; and ultimately prove injurious to the drawers. When a man accepts bills to his butcher, baker, tailor, upholsterer, &c., he may fairly be suspected of living beyond his income. Solvent and regular people pay their tradesmen's accounts with ready money.

The fourth class of bills, though sometimes proper, ought not to be too much encouraged. Persons out of trade have no business with bills.

The last class of bills should almost always be rejected. To an experienced banker, who knows the parties, the discovery of accommodation bills is by no means difficult. They are usually drawn for even amounts, for the largest sum that the stamp will bear, and for the longest term that the bank will discount, and are presented for discount soon after they are drawn. The parties are often relations, friends, or parties who, from their avocations, can have no dealings with each other.

Not only the parties and the amounts of bills are matters of consideration to a banker, but also the time they have to run before they fall due. A bill drawn for a long term after date, is usually styled, not perhaps very properly, *a long dated bill*. A bill drawn at a short term, is styled a short dated bill.

Query.—Is it most for the interest of a bank to discount long dated bills or short dated bills?

Short Bills versus *Long Bills.*—First, There is more safety in discounting short bills, because the parties may fail before the long ones become due. Secondly, If any given amount of capital be employed in discounting bills, it will accumulate more rapidly by discounting short bills than long bills, operating in the same way as money placed at compound interest, which increases the faster, as the times of paying the interest are more frequent. Thirdly, If a bank charges commission on the amount of the bills discounted, the commission will be more in the course of a year upon any given amount of capital employed in discounting short bills than employed in discounting long bills. Fourthly, If a bank issues notes, a greater amount of notes will be issued in discounting a succession of short bills, than by discounting long bills. Thus if I discount a bill for £1,000 drawn at twelve months after date, I issue only £1,000 of notes; but if I discount in succession four bills each, having only three months to run, I issue, in the course of the year, £4,000 of notes. Fifthly, Long dated bills lock up the funds of a bank so that they cannot be discounted with safety but from the bank's own capital: for if a bank employs its deposits or its circulation in discounting long dated bills, and payment of the notes or deposits should be demanded, the long dated bills could not be re-discounted, and the bank must stop. Sixthly, Long bills may encourage speculation. Persons may purchase large quantities of commodities in the expectation that the price will advance before the long bills which they accept in payment shall fall due. But if the bills are of short date, the speculation will be prevented.

Long Bills versus *Short Bills.*—First, The amount of discount is greater on a long bill than on a short bill. If, therefore, a gentleman out of business wants a temporary advance, and proposes to draw a bill on his friend, it is better to advise him to draw a long bill than a short one. Secondly, Long bills will employ a larger amount of capital. If a banker discounts any given amount per week, he will always have twice the amount of bills current, if they are drawn at four months' date, than he will have if they are drawn at two months. And, as bankers wish to employ their capital, it will be more for their advantage to discount such bills as will employ the largest amount. Thirdly, The discounting of long dated bills, being a more permanent advance of capital, is more beneficial to the commercial and agricultural classes in the district. If a retail dealer can get long bills discounted, he can afford to give longer credit, and this will induce his customers to buy more goods of him, and he will do more business. If a manufacturer or wholesale dealer can get his long bills discounted, he also can give longer credit, and will sell more goods. If a landlord can get a long bill on his tenant discounted, he need not urge him for rent, and the money may, in the interim, be employed in improving the land. The discounting of long bills is similar to a permanent advance of capital. The money may be profitably employed, and be reproduced before the long bill may become due, but if the bill be short this cannot be done.[1]

IV. *Notaries Public.*—"A notary was anciently a scribe that only took *notes* or minutes, and made short drafts of writings and other instruments, both public and private. But, at this day, we call him a notary public who confirms and attests the truth of any deeds or writings, in order to render the same authentic."[2] This part of the business of a public notary must have been very necessary before the

---

[1] Bills are drawn usually at three, four, or six months. Bills for longer than six months may be quite legitimate if drawn under special circumstances—as collateral security for fixed advances, or for the payment of capital out of a firm to a retiring partner, for instance. The Bank of England discount no bills having over ninety-five days to run.

[2] Burns' "Ecclesiastical Law," vol. iii. page 1.

discovery of the art of printing, and when many of the first men in the State were unable to read or write. We find that some public documents have been attested by notaries in the following form :—" As my Lord Bishop is unable to write, I do hereby certify, that the above is his mark." These notaries were appointed by the Archbishop of Canterbury, and took an oath of fidelity on receiving their appointment. All instruments made by them were considered public instruments, and were received as evidence in the courts of law.

The business of a notary includes the making of wills, drawing up powers of attorney, bonds of arbitration, bills of sale, charter-parties, and attestations. The drawing of instruments of this description constitutes almost the sole employment of some few notaries; while the chief, indeed, the sole business of the majority, consists in noting and protesting bills of exchange. Some notaries are translators of languages, but more frequently they employ a foreigner for this purpose.

The difference between the noting and the protesting of a bill of exchange for non-payment, is this : In noting, the notary, after having presented the bill at the proper place, and demanded payment, attaches to it a small piece of paper, on which he writes the amount of his charge and the reason why the bill is not paid—such as "no effects," "no advice," "out; no orders," "will be paid to-morrow," &c. This piece of paper is called "the notary's ticket," and the writing on it is called "the notary's answer." Some notaries have their name and address printed on their tickets. The notary also places on the bottom part of the bill, in front, the initials of his name, the amount of his fee, and the date of the noting. The same form is used in noting a bill for non-acceptance.

The practice of noting bills of exchange is said to have

taken its rise from the following circumstance: After the modern system of banking was established, and bills of exchange became numerous, it was customary for one of the clerks of the banking-house to act as a notary. If the bill had been presented in the morning and was not paid, he called in the evening to ask the reason of its non-payment, and he charged a small fee for this additional trouble. By degrees this practice became established, and, ultimately, a notary public was employed for the purpose.

A protest is a legal instrument, drawn on stamped paper, generally according to the following form:—

On this day,   , the   day of   , one thousand eight hundred and   , I, A. B., Public Notary, by legal authority, admitted and sworn, dwelling in the city of   , did present for *payment* the original bill (a true copy whereof is within written), to a *woman* at   , who replied, *that said bill could not then be paid*.

Wherefore, I, the said notary, do solemnly protest against the drawer and endorsers of the said bill, and all others therein concerned, for all exchange, re-exchange, losses, costs, interest and damages, suffered and to be suffered, for want of *payment* of said bill. This done in my office, the day and year aforesaid,

Which I attest,
A. B., Not. Pub.

If a bill has been protested for non-acceptance, it must, when due, be presented for payment, and if payment be refused it must be again protested for non-payment. The holder of a protested bill should immediately send the protest to the party of whom the bill had been received. If the bill was only noted, the party should receive due notice.

If an action be brought upon a bill which has been only noted, it will be necessary to produce a witness in court, to prove that the bill was duly and properly presented for payment: but if the bill has been protested, the production of the protest will be sufficient evidence.[1] But if the bill has been duly noted, a protest may be drawn up at any time previous to the commencement of a suit, without a second presentation of the bill at the place where it was payable.

An inland bill may be protested for non-acceptance if it be above £5, if drawn after date, and if the value is stated therein to be received. Inland bills, in such cases, may also be protested for non-payment, if they have been accepted. No other inland bills can legally be protested. This excludes bills drawn after sight, or for a less sum than £5.

Although every foreign bill must be protested, yet it is not considered absolutely necessary that an *inland* bill should be either noted or protested, in order to sustain an action for the amount.

A bill is usually noted or protested for non-payment after bank hours, on the evening of the day on which it falls due. But if not done then, it may, provided the notary himself made a due demand of payment, be noted or protested at any subsequent time. The omission of the noting or protesting by the holder does not nullify his claims upon any of the antecedent parties, provided they received due notice of the dishonour.[2] Foreign bills should

[1] The law seems to be different with respect to bills drawn in a foreign country upon parties in this country. In such cases, in an action brought to recover from an endorser in this country, it would be necessary to prove the proper presentment of the bill by the person so presenting it.

[2] It is absolutely necessary to have foreign bills protested for non-acceptance and non-payment in order to retain the liability of the endorsers.

be noted on the day that acceptance or payment was refused. Inland bills may also be noted on that day, but a protest for non-payment of an inland bill is not usually made out until the day after it is due.

If a bill be refused acceptance by the drawee, and another party accept it for honour of the drawer or of an endorser, it must again be protested for non-payment by the drawee before an action can be sustained against the acceptor.

In London it is not the custom to protest inland bills at all. And in case of non-acceptance, they are not even noted, unless drawn after sight. It is then necessary that they should be noted in order to fix the time on which they fall due. Inland bills are always noted for non-payment. Foreign bills are protested both for non-acceptance and for non-payment. Bills drawn from Ireland or from Scotland are regarded as foreign bills. The notary's charge for noting a bill within the site of the ancient walls of the city of London, is 1*s.* 6*d.* Beyond those limits the charges are 2*s.* 6*d.*, 3*s.* 6*d.*, 5*s.*, and 6*s.* 6*d.*, &c., according to the distance. The charge for protesting a bill under £20 is 5*s.* 6*d.*,—from £20 to £100 it is 6*s.* 6*d.*,—£100 to £500 it is 7*s.* 6*d.*—£500 to £2,000 it is 10*s.*, and for every additional thousand, 1*s.* extra. The charges of notaries in London are not fixed by law, but are regulated by a society which they have established themselves, and which issues printed rules, a copy of which is given to each notary. Mr. Justice Bayley has stated positively, that if a bill be paid when presented by the notary, the acceptor is not bound to pay the expense of noting. But this is contrary to the usual practice. In such cases, the notaries always refuse to take the money for the bill, unless they are paid the noting fees at the same time.

It is customary for the country bankers to re-issue the London bills they have discounted. In this case they always endorse the bills, and place on them a "case of need." A case of need is a reference for payment to a merchant or banker in London if the bill should not be paid by the party on whom it is drawn. This reference is made by writing on the back of the bill at bottom [1]—"In case of need apply to Messrs. A. B. & Co." If, then, the bill should not be paid, Messrs. A. B. & Co. will pay it for honour of the endorser. The advantage of placing a case of need upon a bill is, that the party endorsing it receives it back sooner in case of non-payment. It also makes the bill more respectable, and secures its circulation. The notaries always observe these "cases or need," and after having noted the bill apply to the referee.

In the year 1801, an Act of Parliament was passed for the better regulation of public notaries in England. It enacts, that from and after the first day of August, 1801, no person shall be admitted as a notary, unless he shall have served as an apprentice for seven years to a public notary, or to a scrivener, being also a public notary. Within three months after the date of the indenture of apprenticeship, one of the subscribing witnesses must make an affidavit of the fact before the Master of the Faculties of his Grace the Lord Archbishop of Canterbury, in London, his surrogate, or commissioner. This affidavit is to be entered in a book, for which the clerk may charge the sum of 5s., and this book may be searched by any person on paying the sum of 1s. for each search. Every person, previous to being enrolled as a notary, must also make an affidavit that he has served an apprenticeship of seven years, and that during the whole of that time he has been actually employed in the business. No public notary can have an apprentice but while he actually practises. Persons

[1] A foreign case of need is generally written on the front of the bill, and the notary presents it the day after due.

applying for a faculty to become notaries within the jurisdiction of the Company of Scriveners, must previously take their freedom of that company. Any person doing anything belonging to the office of the notary, without being enrolled, shall forfeit the sum of £50.

In the year 1833, an Act was passed to alter and amend the Act of 1801. It limits the operation of the former Act to the city of London and liberties of Westminster, the borough of Southwark, and the circuit of ten miles from the Royal Exchange, in the said city of London. Beyond those limits the Archbishop of Canterbury may authorize attorneys, solicitors, and proctors, to practise as notaries within any district in which it shall be made to appear to the master of the Court of Faculties, that there is not (or shall not hereafter be) a sufficient number of such notaries public (3 & 4 Will. IV. c. 70).

In default of a notary public, a bill may be protested for non-acceptance or non-payment by any other substantial person of the city, town, or place where such bill or note shall be so dishonoured, in the presence of two or more credible witnesses, which protest shall be made and written under a fair written copy of such bill or note.

V. *The Rate of Discount.*—During the Middle Ages it was believed that all interest taken for the loan of money was unjust and unscriptural, and the lender was stigmatized as a usurer.

Though this notion has been altogether discarded in modern times, it may not have been either pernicious or absurd at the time it was introduced. It originated when the population was purely agricultural. That a man who borrows money with a view of making a profit by it, should give some portion of his profit to the lender, is a self-evident principle of natural justice. A man makes a profit usually by means of traffic. But in a country purely agricultural, and under such a government as was the feudal system, there can be but little traffic, and hence but little profit. Besides, in an agricultural country a person seldom wants to borrow money except he be reduced to poverty or distress by misfortune. Now for a rich man who has money which he cannot profitably employ, to charge interest for a loan to a man in distress, appears to be consistent with neither justice nor benevolence.

Erroneous views are often entertained of the Mosaic laws, from neglecting to consider the state of the people to whom those laws were given. It was the object of the Jewish legislator to make the Jews a purely agricultural people. The promotion of agriculture was, as Montesquieu would say, the SPIRIT of his laws. Hence he prohibited the taking of interest for the loan of money. By this means he interdicted commerce. His design was to prevent the Israelites associating with the surrounding nations and learning their idolatrous practices. But even Moses permitted the Jews to take interest for money lent to strangers; a circumstance which proves that the prohibition was only a political and not a moral precept. If the taking of interest for money were morally wrong, it would have been forbidden in all cases. But in the Middle Ages the political and the moral laws of Moses were confounded together, and all of them were supposed to be of perpetual obligation upon all nations. These opinions, which might have been useful in a purely agricultural State, were still indulged when a change of manners required that this country should become commercial. If we admitted the unlawfulness of taking interest for money we might on the same principle condemn all kinds of commerce, and even all profitable investment of capital. Where is the difference between taking money for the use of money, and taking money for the use of commodities that are purchased with money? If I lay out £100 in the purchase of a house, I am allowed to take rent for the use of that house. Why, then, if I lend to a friend the £100 with which he purchases a house, am I to receive no remuneration? If we are not allowed to receive any money for the loan of money, why are we allowed to receive money for the loan of a house or a coach, or any other article? An exorbitant charge for interest is certainly unjust, but so is an exorbitant charge for anything else.

After it had been admitted that it was lawful to take interest for the loan of money, the government thought proper to limit the amount. In the reign of Henry VIII. interest was limited to 10 per cent. James I. reduced it to 8 per cent.; at which rate it remained till the reign of Charles II., when it was reduced to 6 per cent.; and finally, in the reign of Queen Anne, it was reduced to 5 per cent., in Ireland the legal rate of interest being higher. However inapplicable these laws may be to our own times, they were probably beneficial at the time they were enacted. In our time capital has accumulated, money is abundant, the lenders are numerous, hence competition is sure to take place, and the value of money will be regulated in the same way as that of any other commodity in the market. But, in those times, the lenders were few, and might easily combine to fix the rate of interest as they pleased. They had, in fact, though not a legal, yet an actual monopoly, and hence it was necessary that they, like other monopolists, should be placed under restraint. In our times, it is the rate of profit which regulates the rate of interest. In those times, it was the rate of interest which regulated the rate of profit. If the money-lender charged a high rate of interest to the merchant, the merchant must have charged a high rate of profit on his goods. Hence, a large sum of money would be taken from the pockets of the purchasers to be put into the pockets of the money-lenders. This additional price, too, put upon the goods, would render the public less able and less inclined to purchase them. The laws, therefore, which restricted the rate of interest were, probably, in those times, friendly to trade.

Sir Josiah Child, in his excellent Essay on Trade, accuses the "new-fashioned bankers" of being "the main cause of keeping the interest of money at least two per cent. higher than otherwise it would be; for, by allowing their creditors six per cent., they make monied men sit down lazily with so high an interest, and not push into commerce with their money, as they certainly would do, were it at four or three per cent., as in Holland. This high interest also keeps the price of land at so low as fifteen years' purchase. It also makes money scarce in the country, seeing that the trade of bankers being only in London, it very much drains the ready money from all other parts of the kingdom."

That we may be able to judge of the truth of these accusations, it will be necessary to make some observations upon those circumstances which influence the rate of interest.

It has been the opinion of most of our political economists, that the rate of interest is regulated by the rate of profit. This sentiment has, however, been attacked. It has been contended, that the rate of interest is not influenced by the average rate of profit, but by the quantity of moneyed capital in the market, compared with the wants of the borrowers. In other words, that the price of money is influenced by the proportion between the demand and the supply.

This sentiment is undoubtedly right; but it does not overthrow the proposition against which it is advanced. The price of money, or of the loan of money, is no doubt, like the price of every other commodity, regulated *at any particular time* by the proportion between the supply and the demand. But does not the rate of profit regulate the supply and the demand? Will any commercial man borrow money when he must give a higher interest for it than he can make profit by its use? Or will any man lend money at a very low interest when, by engaging in business, he can make a very high profit? It is true that, on particular occasions, and under particular circumstances, some individuals may do this, but not permanently and universally. It is obvious, then, that a high rate of interest, in proportion to profits, increases the supply of money, and diminishes the demand; and a low rate of interest, in proportion to profits, increases the demand for the loan of money, and diminishes the supply. The rate of interest, therefore, is ultimately regulated by the rate of profits.

When we say the price of cotton is regulated by the cost of production, we do not mean to deny that the market price of cotton is fixed by the proportion between the demand and the supply. On the contrary, this is admitted; but then it is contended, that the supply itself is regulated by the cost of production. If the market price of cotton were so low as not to furnish to the grower a fair average of profit on the capital employed, then would capital be removed, after a while, from the cultivation of cotton to some other employment. And if the price of cotton were so high as to furnish more than a fair average of profit, then, after a while, more capital will find its way into that employment, the supply would be increased, and the prices would fall; but it is only by influencing the supply that the cost of production has any effect upon the price. Thus, although the cost of production may be the same for a number of years, the price may be perpetually varying. The price may, from a variety of causes, be in a state of constant vibration: but it cannot *permanently* deviate on one side or the other much beyond the line marked out by the cost of production.

It is the same with the interest of money. It is subject to perpetual fluctuation from the proportion between the demand and the supply, but it will not deviate far from the line marked out by the rate of profit. For the rate of profit not only influences the supply (as with cotton) but also influences the demand.

The above reasoning is founded on the supposition that those who borrow money, borrow it for the purpose of investing it in trade, or of making a profit by its use. But this is not always the case; and is never the case with the government of a country, who always borrow for the purpose of spending. Now we can form a judgment as to what portion of his profits a merchant is willing to give for the loan of a sum of money, but we can form no judgment as to the conduct of a profligate rake who wants money to spend on his follies. A king or a government is in the same state. They will borrow money as cheaply as they can; but, at all events, money they will have. We cannot, therefore, infer that, because Charles II. gave, at times, to the new-fashioned bankers, thirty per cent. for money, the average rate of profit exceeded thirty per cent. May not, then, these advances to the king have had the effect of raising the interest of money, and thus justify the accusations of Sir Josiah Child?

When a number of commercial men borrow money of one another, the *permanent* regulator of the rate of interest is the rate of profit; and the *immediate* regulator is the proportion between the demand and the supply. But when a new party comes into the market, who has no common interest with them, who does not borrow money to trade with, but to spend, the permanent regulator (the rate of profit) loses its influence, and the sole regulator is then the proportion between the demand and the supply. The loans to the king created a much greater demand for money, and the rate of interest consequently rose. These demands were to so great an amount, and were so frequently repeated, that the rate of interest became permanently high. Many individuals would, no doubt (as Sir Josiah Child states they did) withdraw their capital from trade, and live upon the interest of their money. And others, who were in business, would employ their superfluous capital in lending it at interest, rather than in extending their business. Those commercial men who now wanted to borrow money must give a higher interest for it than they did before. To enable themselves to do this, they must charge a higher profit on their goods. Thus then, in this artificial state of the money market, it appears reasonable to suppose that the rate of interest may have regulated the rate of profits, instead of the rate of profits regulating the rate of interest, which is the natural state.

As the rate of interest is regulated by the proportion between the demand and the supply of money, it will vary, not only in different countries, but in different provinces of the same country, according to the proportions found to exist. In the London money market the rate of interest is usually much less than in the country. The price of any commodity when purchased in large quantities at a wholesale warehouse, is always less than that at which it is retailed to the consumer. So the price of the loan of money at the Stock Exchange, where it is advanced in large masses upon government security, will always be less than when advanced in small sums upon individual security. A low rate of interest in London, however, will, after a while, have the effect of lowering the rate of interest in the country *upon those securities which are negotiable in*

London. For if the country banker insists on a high rate of discount for bills drawn upon good London houses, the drawer will send them to a bill broker in London, who will get them discounted and remit the money to the drawer. But with regard to those bills which are not payable in London, a higher rate of discount may be obtained.

The cheapness of money in London has the effect of diminishing the number of bills drawn upon London. A London merchant who sends an order for goods to a country manufacturer, instead of saying, "Draw upon me at two months," will say, "Allow me the discount, and I will send you the cash." If he can get an allowance of four per cent. discount, and borrow the money in London at two per cent., he will make an additional profit on this transaction. As the surplus quantity of money in London thus becomes diffused throughout the country, the rate of discount will gradually advance in London and fall in the country.

Although a low rate of interest indicates the abundance of capital, and hence may be considered as a favourable circumstance in the condition of any nation, yet it produces some injurious effects: it occasions the removal of capital to foreign countries; it weakens the inducements to frugality and accumulation; and it encourages speculative and hazardous undertakings. Persons who can obtain but a low rate of interest for their money, are often induced to engage in speculations which promise to yield a more profitable return. All seasons of speculations have been preceded by a low rate of interest.

In the year 1818, a select committee of the House of Commons was appointed to consider the effects of the laws which regulate or restrain the interest of money, and to report their opinion thereupon to the House. After examining twenty-one witnesses upon the subject, the committee delivered the following report:—

"1. *Resolved*,—That it is the opinion of this committee, that the laws regulating or restraining the rate of interest have been extensively evaded, and have failed of the effect of imposing a maximum on such rate; and that of late years, from the constant excess of the market rate of interest above the rate limited by law, they have added to the expense incurred by borrowers on real security; and that such borrowers have been compelled to resort to the mode of granting annuities on lives,—a mode which has been made a cover for obtaining higher interest than the rate limited by law, and has further subjected the borrowers to enormous charges, or forced them to make very disadvantageous sales of their estates.

"2. *Resolved*,—That it is the opinion of this committee, that the construction of such laws, as applicable to the transactions of commerce as at present carried on, has been attended with much uncertainty as to the legality of many transactions of frequent occurrence; and, consequently, been productive of much embarrassment and litigation.

"3. *Resolved*,—That it is the opinion of this committee, that the present period, when the market rate of interest is below the legal rate, affords an opportunity peculiarly proper for the repeal of the said laws."

In the Bill passed in 1833 for the renewal of the charter of the Bank of England, a clause was introduced, which exempted bills not having more than three months to run, from the operations of the laws against usury.[1]

VI. *Effect of Discounts on the Circulation.*—The discounting of bills, by banks of circulation, will have the same effect in changing the currency as the deposit accounts,

---

[1] The laws against usury have been repealed.

but will not operate so rapidly. When a bill is discounted, the banker issues his own notes to that amount; and when the bill is paid, he receives a part of the amount in gold, or silver, or in notes of other banks. If, however, the bill be not a local bill, that is, if it be not payable in the place in which the bank is established, it will be paid in the currency of the place where it is payable, and its payment will not have the effect of diminishing the local currency.

While the issue of notes upon the deposit accounts depends altogether upon the depositors, the issues in the way of discount depend altogether upon the banker—he may discount, or not discount, as he pleases. If he discounts with real capital, he does not thereby increase the amount of the currency—for that capital must, in some way or other, have been previously employed. If he discounts with that portion of his banking capital which is raised by deposits, he does not increase the amount of the currency, but gives it increased rapidity. If he discounts with that portion of his banking capital which is raised by notes, he increases the amount of the currency. As banks of circulation always issue their own notes, it would seem that their discounting business is carried on exclusively with this last description of capital, but it is not so. It is very possible for a banker to issue his own notes for all the bills he discounts, and yet nine-tenths of the bills in his possession shall represent real capital. For, although in the first instance, the banker's notes are given for the bill, yet these notes may not stay in circulation until the bill becomes due: the bill may have three months to run, the notes may return in three days. If the notes given in exchange for the bills remain in circulation until the bills become due, then do the discounts create a banking capital equal to their own amount. But if the bills have three months to run, and the notes remain out only one month, then they create a capital to only one-third of their amount, and the other two-thirds must consist of capital derived from other sources. If the notes remain out beyond the time the bill falls due, then do the discounts create a banking capital beyond their own amount.

It may be observed, that in order to trace the effects of banking, it is necessary to mark particularly the way in which the bankers employ their money. It is not by the creation of a banking capital, but by the way in which that capital is applied, that the greatest effects are produced upon the currency, and upon the trade and commerce of a country. Money employed in discounting bills drawn for value will encourage trade—if employed in discounting accommodation bills, it will promote speculation—if advanced as dead loans to persons out of trade it may lead to extravagance—if invested in the funds, it will raise their price and reduce the market rate of interest—if kept in the till, it will yield no profit to the banker, and be of no advantage to the community.

SECTION XII.

CASH CREDIT BANKS.

A CASH credit is an understanding on the part of the bank to advance to an individual such sums of money as he may from time to time require, not exceeding in the whole a certain definite amount; the individual to whom the credit is given entering into a bond, with securities, generally two in number, for the repayment, on demand, of the sums actually advanced, with interest upon each issue from the day upon which it is made.

A cash credit is, in fact, the same thing as an overdrawn current account, except that in a current account the party overdraws on his own individual security, and in the cash credit he finds two securities who are responsible for him. Another difference is, that a person cannot overdraw his current account without asking permission each time from the bank, whereas the overdrawing of a cash credit account is a regular matter of business; it is, in fact, the purpose for which the cash credit has been granted.

The following considerations will show that a person who has occasion for temporary advances of money will find it more advantageous to raise these sums by a cash credit than by having bills discounted:—

First. In a cash credit the party pays interest only for the money he actually employs.

If a person wants to make use of £100, and has a bill for £150, he will get the bill discounted, and thus pays interest for £50 for which he has no use. But if he has a cash credit he draws only £100, and pays interest for that amount.

Secondly. In a cash credit he can repay any part of the sum drawn whenever he pleases.

If a trader has a bill for £150 discounted to-day, and should unexpectedly receive £150 to-morrow, he cannot re-discount the bill, but has actually paid interest for money he does not want. But if he draws £150 upon his cash credit account to-day, and to-morrow receives £150, he takes this money to the bank, and will have to pay the interest upon £150 for only one day.

Thirdly. In a cash credit he has the power of drawing whenever he pleases, to the full amount of his credit; but in the case of discounting bills, he must make a fresh application to the bank to discount each bill, and if the bank have at any time more profitable ways of employing their money, or if they suspect the credit of the applicant, they may refuse to discount, but this would not be the case if he had a cash credit.

Fourthly. In a cash credit the party does not pay the interest until the end of the year; whereas, in the other case, he pays the interest at the time the bill is discounted.

Cash credits are granted not only upon personal security, but also upon the security of the Public Funds.

This furnishes great facilities for raising money to those who possess property which they are not disposed to sell. A person who is a holder of government stock may sell out a portion to supply his temporary necessities; and when he wishes to replace it he finds the price of stock has risen, and it will cost him more money to repurchase than he received when he sold. But if he transfers the stock to a bank as a security for a cash credit, he may repay the money whenever he pleases; and if, in the meantime, the value of the security should have risen, all the advantage will be his own.

The effects of cash credits are thus described by Adam Smith:—

"The commerce of Scotland, which at present is not very great, was still more inconsiderable when the two first banking companies were established, and those companies would have had but little trade had they confined their business to the discounting of bills of exchange. They invented, therefore, another method of issuing their promissory notes, by granting what they call cash accounts, that is, by giving credit to the extent of a certain sum (two or three thousand pounds, for example,) to any individual who could procure two persons of undoubted credit and good landed estate to become surety for him, that whatever money should be advanced to him within the sum for which the credit had been given should be repaid upon demand, together with the legal interest. Credits of this kind are, I believe, commonly granted by banks and bankers in all different parts of the world. But the easy terms upon which the Scotch banking companies accept of repayment are, so far as I know, peculiar to them, and have perhaps been the principal cause both of the great trade of those companies, and of the benefits which the country has received from it.

"Whoever has a credit of this kind with one of those companies, and borrows a thousand pounds upon it, for example, may repay this sum piecemeal, by twenty and thirty pounds at a time, the company discounting a proportional part of the interest of the great sum, from the day on which each of those small sums is paid in, till the whole be in this manner repaid. All merchants, therefore, and almost all men of business, find it convenient to keep such cash accounts with them, and are hereby interested to promote the trade of those companies by readily receiving their notes in all payments, and by encouraging all those with whom they have any influence to do the same. The banks, when their customers apply to them for money, generally advance it to them on their own promissory notes. These the merchants pay away to the manufacturers for goods; the manufacturers to the farmers, for materials and provisions; the farmers to their landlords for rent; the landlords repay them to the merchants for the conveniences and luxuries with which they supply them; and the merchants again return them to the banks, in order to balance their cash accounts, or to replace what they may have borrowed of them: and thus almost the whole money business of the country is transacted by means of them. Hence the great trade of those companies.

"By means of those cash accounts every merchant can, without imprudence, carry on a greater trade than he otherwise could do. If there are two merchants—one in London and the other in Edinburgh—who employ equal stocks in the same branch of trade, the Edinburgh merchant can, without imprudence, carry on a greater trade and give employment to a greater number of people than the London merchant. The London merchant must always keep by him a considerable sum of money, either in his own coffers, or in those of his banker, who gives him no interest for it, in order to answer the demands continually coming upon him for payment of the goods he purchases upon credit. Let the ordinary amount of this sum be supposed five hundred pounds. The value of the goods in his warehouse must always be less by five hundred pounds than it would have been had he not been obliged to keep such a sum unemployed. Let us suppose that he generally disposes of his whole stock upon hand, or of goods to the value of his whole stock upon hand, once in the year. By being obliged to keep so great a sum unemployed, he must sell in a year five hundred pounds' worth less goods than he might otherwise have done. His annual profits must be less by all that he could have made by the sale of five hundred pounds' worth more goods, and the number of people employed in preparing his goods for market must be less by all those that five hundred pounds more stock could have employed. The merchant in Edinburgh, on the other hand, keeps no money unemployed for answering such occasional demands. When they actually come upon him he satisfies them from his cash account with the bank, and gradually replaces the sum borrowed with the money or paper which comes in from the occasional sales of his goods. With the same stock, therefore, he can, without imprudence, have at all times in his warehouse a larger quantity of goods than the London merchant, and can thereby both make a greater profit himself and give constant employment to a greater number of industrious people who prepare those goods for the market. Hence, the greater benefit which the country has derived from this trade.

"The facility of discounting bills of exchange, it may be thought, indeed, gives the English merchants a convenience equivalent to the cash accounts of the Scotch merchants. But the Scotch merchants, it must be remembered, can discount their bills of exchange as easily as the English merchants, and have, besides, the additional conveniency of their cash account."[1]—*Wealth of Nations*, Book ii. chap. 2.

Query.—Is it better for a bank to make advances of

[1] A fuller account of the system of cash credits will be found, further on, in The Practice of Banking.

money on cash credits, or by discounting bills of exchange?

Bills of Exchange versus *Cash Credits.*—1. Cash credits, when once granted, are not usually suddenly called up, but bills of exchange soon fall due, and you can refuse to discount again.

2. If you discount bills of exchange, they can be re-discounted to supply the bank with funds, if necessary, but advances on cash credits cannot be replaced.

3. In case of a panic or a run upon the bank, the persons having cash credits might have occasion to draw upon the bank, and the notes would immediately be returned upon the bank for payment in gold; but you could refuse to discount bills of exchange until the run was over.

Cash Credits versus *Bills of Exchange.*—1. A higher interest is charged upon cash credits than upon bills of exchange.

2. Cash credits, being of the nature of a permanent advance, are more beneficial to the parties; hence trade is more promoted, and the benefit to the bank must ultimately be greater.

3. Parties having cash credits are more closely connected with the bank, and hence would use their influence to prevent any run upon the bank, and to promote the prosperity of the bank.

4. The mode of recovering an advance upon a cash credit is more summary and certain, as the bond can be put into execution immediately, but an action for the recovery of an unpaid bill is very tedious, and may be frustrated by informality, &c.

A cash credit operates much in the same way as a discount account and a current account combined. It resembles a discount account inasmuch as a banker is usually in advance to his customer. It resembles a current account, as it is required that there be frequent operations upon it; that is, that there be perpetual payings in and drawings out of money. The bankers expect that a cash credit shall maintain a banking capital equal to its own amount. As the banker is usually in advance, a cash credit can create no banking capital by means of deposits; it can be done only by means of the notes. If then, the operations on a cash credit are sufficient to keep in circulation an amount of notes equal to the amount of the credit, then it gives satisfaction to the banker; but not otherwise. Previous to granting a cash credit, the banks always make inquiries to ascertain if this is likely to be the case; and even after it is granted it is liable to be called up if it has not accomplished this object. Hence, cash credits are denied to persons who have no means of circulating the banker's notes, or who wish to employ the money as a dead loan. And in all cases they are limited to such an amount as the party is supposed to be capable of employing with advantage to the bank.

SECTION XIII.

LOAN BANKS.

LOAN banks are banks formed for the purpose of advancing loans upon articles of merchandise. Some are carried on for the purposes of gain, others from motives of charity.

The Bank of England was empowered by its charter to carry on the business of a loan bank. The following is the twenty-sixth section of the Act:—" Provided that nothing herein contained shall in anywise be construed to hinder the said corporation from dealing in bills of exchange, or in buying or selling of bullion, gold or silver, or in selling any goods, wares, or merchandise whatever, which shall really and *bonâ fide be left or deposited with the said corporation for money lent or advanced thereon*, and which shall not be redeemed at the time agreed on, or within three months after, or from selling such goods as shall or may be the produce of lands purchased by said corporation." In pursuance of the privilege granted by this clause, the directors gave public notice that they would lend money at four per cent., on " plate, lead, tin, copper, steel, and iron."

The Bank of Scotland was also authorized to act as a loan bank. The following is one clause of the Act by which it was established in 1695:—" And it is further hereby statute and ordained, that it shall be lawful for the said governor and company to lend, upon real or personal security, any sum or sums, and to receive annual rent for the same, at six per cent., as shall be ordinary for the time : as also that if the person borrowing, as said is, shall not make payment at the term agreed upon with the company, that it shall be lawful for the governor and company to sell and dispose of the security or pledge by a public roup, for the most that can be got, for payment to them of the principal annual rents and reasonable charges, and returning the overplus to the person who gave the said security or pledge."

The Royal Bank of Scotland was also empowered by its charter, " to lend to any person or persons, bodies politic or corporate, such sum and sums of money as they should think fit, at any interest not exceeding lawful interest, on real or personal security, *and particularly on pledges of any kind whatsoever, of any goods, wares, merchandises, or other effects whatsoever,* in such way and manner as to the said company should seem proper and convenient."

"The Hibernian Joint-Stock Loan Company," usually called the Hibernian Bank, was formed in 1825, " for the purpose of purchasing and selling annuities, and all public and other securities, real and personal, in Ireland, and to advance money and make loans thereof, on the security of such real and personal security, at legal interest, and on the security of merchandise and manufactured goods." This company, however, has never carried on the business of a loan bank, but has confined its transactions to the business of a commercial bank. It has not the power of issuing notes, but it is a bank of discount and of deposit.

Capital advanced, by way of loan, on the securities of merchandise, would produce the same effects as if advanced in the discounting of bills. If a party borrows £100 on the security of his merchandise, it is the same as though he had sold his merchandise for a £100 bill, and got it discounted with the banker. By obtaining this advance he is enabled to hold over this merchandise for a better market, and avoids a sacrifice which, otherwise, he might be induced to make, in order to raise the money for urgent purposes.

Every advance of money by a banker, let it be made in what way soever, is in fact a loan. To discount a £100 bill that has three months to run, is much the same as to lend that amount for three months. The difference is, that the banker has two or more securities instead of one—the time of repayment is fixed; and the interest on the whole sum is paid at the time it is advanced. But let one trader draw bills upon his customers, and take them to the bank for discount—let another trader give his customers three months' credit without drawing bills, and borrow of the banker the amount of the goods sold; it is obvious that in each case the traders receive the same accommodation, and the effect on commerce will be the same. The bill is merely a transfer of the debt from the drawer to the banker, with the drawer's guarantee. Cash credits are loans—the amount of the loan varies every day, but the maximum is fixed. If a trader who has a cash credit for £500 has always £300 drawn out, it is nearly the same thing as though he had a loan for £300. The advantage to him is, that he can draw exactly such a sum as he may need—that he can replace it whenever he pleases, and in such portions as he may find convenient; and he pays interest only for the sum drawn out. It is unnecessary to say that overdrawn accounts, mortgages, and all advances of money on pledges or securities of any kind are loans.

It is contrary to all sound principles of banking for a banker to advance money in the form of permanent loans, or as they are called, dead loans. In the first place, those dead loans do not create any banking capital—and, secondly, they cannot be suddenly called up. For a banker to lend out his banking capital in the way of permanent loan is obviously imprudent, as he knows not how soon that capital may be taken out of his hands; and it is almost equally imprudent to advance his real capital in that way, as the real capital ought to be kept in a disposable form, so that it may be rendered available in case of any sudden contraction of the banking capital. The investing of money in the public funds is not strictly an operation of banking. It does not increase the banking capital. Yet it is necessary that a banker should lay out some portion of his capital in this way, because he can so easily realize the money in case a run should be made upon his bank. The portion thus invested is probably less productive than any other part of his capital, except the sums kept in his till to meet occasional demands. Sometimes, however, a rise in the funds will be the means of affording him a considerable profit.

The second class of loan banks arose from motives of charity.

These institutions were first established in the fifteenth century, for the purpose of checking the extortions of usurers, by lending money to the poor upon pledges, and without charging interest.[1] They were originally supported by voluntary contributions; but as these were found insufficient to support the necessary expenses, it became necessary that the borrowers should be charged interest for the loans. These banks were at first distinguished by being called *montes pietatis*. It appears that the word, mont, or mount, was at an early period applied to any pecuniary fund, and it is probable that the promoters of this system added "pietatis" to give it an air of religion, and thus to procure larger subscriptions. A bank of this

[1] See Beckmann's "History of Ancient Institutions."

kind was formed at Perugia in the year 1464; another at Rome in 1539; one at Naples, which was considered the greatest in Europe, in the following year, and it took the name of *banco dei poveri*—the bank of the poor. These institutions were opposed in France. An attempt was made to introduce them under Louis XIII. in 1626, but the managers were threatened with punishment, and the undertaking was relinquished. The Mont de Piété, at Paris, was established in the year 1777; and so largely has the public taken advantage of the accommodation this afforded, that it has been known to have in its possession forty casks filled with gold watches.

These banks were not only called Mounts of Piety, but they were also called Lombards, from the name of the original bankers, or money-lenders. A loan-bank, or a Lombard, was established in Russia in 1772,[1] to prevent the usury and the oppression to which the poor were exposed, and the profit was given to the foundling hospital of St. Petersburg. The "Lombard" lent on gold and silver three-fourths of the value, on other metals it lent one-half the value, and on jewels as much as the circumstances of the times would allow, the estimate being made by sworn appraisers. The rate of interest was established throughout the empire, in 1786, at five per cent. At the Lombard, one year's interest is taken in advance. Pledges that are forfeited are publicly sold; and if they produce more than the loan, the interest, and the charges, the overplus is given to the owners.

In 1695, Sir Francis Brewster published his Essay on Trade and Navigation, "printed for T. Cockerell, at the Three Legs, in the Poultry, over against the Stocks-market." He has a section upon "Banks and Lumbers."[2] He recommends that in every shire a bank should be

[1] Oddy, on European Commerce.   [2] Lumbers, *i. e.* Lombards.

erected by Act of Parliament; and he states that it would be "the most effectual way for suppressing highwaymen; for that no man need travel with more than pocket-money for his expenses, when he may have bank tickets to any part of the kingdom where he goes." He afterwards observes, "that lumbers for poor artizans and others is an appendix to banks, and may by funds out of them in each county be supplied so as that the poor men have money to carry on their trade and employment on the pawns that may be so easy, and with the advantage of selling in public sales what they leave in pledge. And that what they borrow should be of more advantage and easy to them than if the money were lent them gratis, and may be of great use in the employment, and encouraging the manufactures of the nation, which are much discouraged by the necessities and hardships that are put upon the poor."

Loan banks for charitable purposes, have, for a considerable time past, existed in Ireland. A voluntary association of this kind was established in the year 1756. This society was incorporated in 1780, under the title of "The Charitable Musical Society." They had their meetings at St. Ann's vestry-room, Dublin, on the first and second Tuesday in every month, for the purpose of lending money, interest free, to indigent tradesmen, in sums of not less than two pounds to any one person at one time, which sums are to be repaid at sixpence in the pound, weekly.

The Meath Charitable Loan Society was established in 1807. The committee of managers lent sums, not under five, and not exceeding twenty pounds, free of interest, to be repaid by weekly instalments of 1s. 6d. for £5; 3s. for £10; 6s. for £20. Donations of £10 and upwards being vested in government securities, the interest only to be applicable to the fund, or thrown into the floating capital, at the option of the donor.

It seems highly desirable that in England also charitable loan banks should be taken under the protection of the legislature. These institutions might be organized in the same manner as savings' banks. In most parts of England there are probably some persons of affluence who would become personally bound for the repayment of such sums as the government might be disposed to advance; or, in other parts, the necessary funds might be raised by private donations. The funds might be employed in such a way as the committee might deem best adapted to promote the object of the institution. The loans might be made either in money, in raw produce, or in implements of labour. These might be recovered, if necessary, by summary process. The state would thus become the Bank of the Poor. It would sustain the same relation to the humbler classes which ordinary banks sustain to the commercial classes. It would be an intermediate party between the borrowers and the lenders. It could borrow, by means of savings' banks, from those who had money to lend; and lend, by means of loan banks, to those who wished to borrow.

SECTION XIV.

SAVINGS' BANKS.

SAVINGS' banks are banks formed to promote saving. They are purely banks of deposit; they differ, however, from other banks of deposit in the following particulars:—First. Very small sums are received as deposits. Secondly. All the money deposited is lent, upon interest, to the government. Thirdly. The depositors are restricted as to the amount of their lodgments; these restrictions are designed to exclude from the banks all except the humbler classes of the community.

Loan banks, or institutions for lending money to the poor, are of ancient date; but savings' banks, or institutions for borrowing money of the poor, are entirely of modern invention. They were first urged upon the attention of the public and the legislature of this country in the years 1815 and 1816, by the late Right Hon. George Rose. In his pamphlet upon the subject, he thus traces the origin of these establishments:—

" The idea was first suggested by the Society for Bettering the Condition of the Poor, of which I have long been a member, and it has been acted upon in Edinburgh and Bath with such a degree of talent, zeal, and perseverance, as to manifest the great advantage of it.

" In other parts of Great Britain, however, the principle has been acted upon on a small scale, especially in Scotland, where the *parochial* institutions for savings are called Maneges; so full an account of these is given by Mr.

Duncan, the early promoter of them, as to render it quite unnecessary to enter on any particulars respecting them here. But however well intended they are, there are strong objections to them. In any event, extended establishments are infinitely more to be desired, on account of the preferable management of them, as well as for the safe custody of the money. By a large district being included, gentlemen of property are found to become trustees and managers; and a fund is easily furnished by small voluntary subscriptions at first, and by the surplus of the interest allowed to the depositors afterwards, to meet all the expenses of the institution.

"Since the first publication of these observations, a controversy has arisen by Mr. Duncan, the promoter of the parochial banks, insisting upon his having (by the establishment of the one at Ruthwell) been the first to bring the banks for savings into notice, in an address to Mr. Forbes, a gentleman of the highest respectability in Edinburgh, who was a zealous promoter of the banks there. The truth is, that the two establishments are perfectly dissimilar, as above stated, which will appear more manifestly to whomsoever will take the trouble of reading the pamphlet of Mr. Duncan and the answer of Mr. Forbes to it. As far as respects Scotland, it would seem that the Edinburgh plan has the merit of priority, *for general advantage;* but it may be hoped that in future there may be no contention, except how the public can be most benefited—it is of very little importance from whence the suggestion originated."

Mr. Rose proceeds to explain in detail the nature of these institutions, and points out the advantages they may be expected to confer upon different classes of the community:—

"Apprentices, on first coming out of their time, who

now too frequently spend all their earnings, may be induced to lay by five shillings to ten shillings a week, and sometimes more, as in many trades they earn from twenty-four to fifty and sixty shillings a week.

"The same observation applies, though somewhat less forcibly, to journeymen in most trades (whose earnings are very considerable), from not beginning so early, and to workmen in several branches. With respect to these, it has been made evident to me, and to many members who attended the mendicity committee in a former session of parliament, that in numerous instances when the gains have been as large as above stated, the parties have been so improvident as to have nothing in hand for the support of themselves and families when visited with sickness, and have consequently with their families fallen immediately upon the parish. In some instances the tools and implements of their trade have been carried to the pawnbroker during illness, whereby difficulties were thrown in the way of their labour being resumed on the restoration of health.

"Domestic servants, whose wages are frequently more than sufficient for their necessary expenses.

"Carmen, porters, servants in lower conditions, and others may, very generally, be able to make small deposits, without finding the slightest inconvenience from the diminution of their income occasioned thereby.

"With respect to day labourers, the full advantage cannot be expected to be derived at first, as far as relates to married men with families: it too frequently happens that when there are two or three children, it is all that the father can do to support himself and those dependent upon him with his utmost earnings; but the single man, whose wages are the same as those of his married fellow-labourers, may certainly spare a small weekly sum, by doing which he would, in a reasonable time, have saved enough to enable him to marry with a hope of never allowing any one belonging to him to become a burthen to the parish.

"Nothing is so likely as a plan of this sort to prevent early and improvident marriages, which are the cause, more than any others, of the heavy burthen of the poor-rates. When a young single man shall acquire the habit of saving, he will be likely to go on till he shall get together as much as will enable him to make some provision towards the support of a family before he thinks of marrying.

"The welfare of the lower classes of society cannot be a matter of indifference to any, nor can it be doubted that their situation will be ameliorated by the adoption and promotion of these banks. The industry, sobriety, and economy among the lower orders of the people will thus be promoted by their being encouraged to make little savings for a provision against want and distress; and their moral improvement will be advanced, while their social comfort is augmented. By the plan which I here recommend, this beneficent and most important object will be obtained at no expense to the higher orders, or at so trifling a one as to be utterly unworthy of notice.

"This plan has in it the germ of valuable moral principles, and if it can be fairly brought into action, will tend more than anything to lessen the enormous and increasing burthen on the middle and higher classes, and at the same time to infuse into the minds of the lower order a legitimate spirit of independence. Its merits are so well expressed where its advantages were early experienced, that I cannot do so well as to quote a few words from one of the Edinburgh reports:—'It secures independence without inducing pride—it removes those painful misgivings which render the approaches of poverty so appalling, and often paralyze the exertions that might ward off the blow. It leads to temperance and the restraint of all disorderly passions, which a wasteful expenditure of money nourishes. It produces that sobriety of mind and steadiness of conduct which afford the best foundation for the domestic virtues in humble life. The effects of such an institution as this upon the character of the people, *were it to become universal, would be almost inappreciable.*' "

In the year 1817, Mr. Rose obtained an Act of Parliament, entitled, "An Act to encourage the Establishment of Banks for Savings in England." About the same time an Act was passed, entitled, "An Act to encourage the Establishment of Banks for Saving *in Ireland;*" the provisions of which were similar to the preceding.

The establishment of Post-office Savings' Banks in 1861 (24 Vic. c. 14) has, by the greater facilities, and by the undoubted security which they afford, largely reduced the number of the (old) savings' banks, and still more largely the funds lodged in them.[1] Government and the public

---

[1] Returns of savings' banks, which brought up their accounts to the end of 1869, show that at that date the number of banks closed were, in England, 119; in Wales, 9; in Scotland, 6; in Ireland, 11; giving a total of 145 banks closed. The number of depositors' balances, on 20th of November, previous to date of notice to close, was, in England, 134,183; in Wales, 3,280; in Scotland, 2,034; in Ireland, 2,082. The amounts of the balances were, in England, £3,083,648 14s. 6d.; in Wales, £72,147 18s. 2d.; in Scotland, £19,944 4s. 4d.; in Ireland, £52,527 17s. 8d. Thus the total number of depositors' balances throughout the United Kingdom, in the banks about to close, was 141,579, the total amount, £3,228,268 14s. 8d. The number of accounts thence transferred to post-office savings' banks was, in England, 73,911; in Wales, 782; in Scotland, 238; in Ireland, 360: total number, 75,291. The amounts transferred were, in England, £1,785,552 13s. 6d.; in Wales, £20,110 8s.; in Scotland, £634 9s. 3d.; in Ireland, £10,037 9s. 8d.: total amount, £1,816,335 0s. 5d. These amounts were transferred by *transfer* certificates only; but in addition to them it was estimated by the post-office authorities that £194,000 were paid in cash by about 9,800 of the depositors in these closed savings' banks to the post-office savings' banks.

are indebted to Mr. Sikes, manager of the Huddersfield Banking Company, for the suggestion, and for an outline of the plan, as well, of making the Money Order offices contributory to the development of savings' banks.

Scotland has always had the advantage of savings' banks by means of the deposit system, which is a regular branch of the business of the commercial banks. The deposit system of banking is universally considered to be one cause of the prudence and frugality by which the lower classes of the people of Scotland are distinguished.

In every point of view the savings' banks appear calculated to produce unmingled good. They extend to persons of small means all the benefits of banking. The industrious have thus a place where their small savings may be lodged with perfect security from loss, and with the certainty of increase. They tend to foster that disposition to accumulate which is usually associated with temperance and prudence in all the transactions of life. Upon the mercantile interests of society they have the same effect as commercial banking. The various small sums which were previously lying unproductive in the hands of many individuals, are collected into one sum and lodged in the public funds. The tendency of this, in the first place, is to raise the price of the funds. This advanced price may cause some of the holders to sell out and to employ their money in trade and commerce. Thus the savings' banks augment the productive capital of the nation.

It is much to be regretted that the advocates for savings' banks should ever have proposed these institutions as substitutes for benefit societies. Cannot the interest of one excellent institution be promoted but at the expense of another? Savings' banks are a useful addition to benefit societies, but cannot supply their place. A labourer pays to a benefit club about thirty shillings per annum, and for that payment he receives about eight shillings per week during the time of illness. If this sum be lodged in a savings' bank, how soon will a few weeks' illness exhaust the whole. It is no doubt the revelling and excess that have too often attended the meeting of benefit societies at public-houses that have given rise to objections against them. It may be expected, however, that as our labourers and mechanics become better instructed these excesses will be avoided.

But while savings' banks do not supersede benefit societies, neither do benefit societies supersede the necessity for savings' banks. The benefit society is of use only in case of illness—in no other case has a member any claim upon its funds. He cannot draw out money to support his wife, to furnish his house, or to educate his children. The benefit societies are only to guard against calamity, not to increase enjoyment. By these, labourers may be saved from the parish workhouse, but they must also become depositors in a savings' bank if they wish to acquire independence.

As it is always interesting and useful to note the progress of the savings of a nation such as ours, we append tables showing the amount of the deposits in the Post-office Savings' Banks, and in the old Savings' Banks under trustees. These tables are taken from the statistical abstract of the United Kingdom, and range from 1864 (the year when first the abstract was presented to Parliament) till the end of 1878.

I.

SAVINGS' BANKS UNDER THE POST-OFFICE.

TOTAL AMOUNT RECEIVED from, and PAID to, DEPOSITORS in the POST-OFFICE SAVINGS' BANKS, and of the COMPUTED CAPITAL of those SAVINGS' BANKS at the end of each Year.[1]

		ENGLAND AND WALES.	SCOTLAND.	IRELAND.	UNITED KINGDOM.
		£	£	£	£
1864	RECEIVED	3,242,088	89,219	121,044	3,452,351
	PAID	1,685,730	64,831	85,494	1,836,056
	CAPITAL	4,687,803	123,747	181,484	4,993,124
1865	RECEIVED	3,630,432	94,645	126,810	3,851,887
	PAID	2,156,781	70,670	91,160	2,318,611
	CAPITAL	6,161,488	147,775	217,137	6,526,400
1866	RECEIVED	4,335,449	99,798	134,583	4,569,830
	PAID	2,776,956	83,013	115,086	2,975,055
	CAPITAL	7,719,981	164,560	236,634	8,121,175
1867	RECEIVED	4,578,309	106,263	192,692	4,877,264
	PAID	3,068,061	78,269	102,180	3,248,510
	CAPITAL	9,230,229	192,554	327,146	9,749,929
1868	RECEIVED	5,247,761	120,818	237,288	5,605,867
	PAID	3,475,843	83,696	129,602	3,689,141
	CAPITAL	11,002,147	229,676	434,832	11,666,655
1869	RECEIVED	5,676,849	132,805	274,956	6,084,610
	PAID	3,965,773	95,734	165,549	4,227,056
	CAPITAL	12,713,223	266,747	544,239	13,524,209
1870	RECEIVED	5,891,508	146,429	295,145	6,333,082
	PAID	4,442,862	108,941	206,384	4,758,187
	CAPITAL	14,161,869	304,235	633,000	15,099,104

[1] In this table the amounts received include interest.

		England and Wales.	Scotland.	Ireland.	United Kingdom.
		£	£	£	£
1871	Received.	6,546,826	155,881	338,660	7,041,367
	Paid..	4,769,687	119,359	226,421	5,115,467
	Capital .	15,939,008	340,757	745,239	17,025,004
1872	Received.	7,567,034	189,074	373,887	8,129,995
	Paid..	5,402,644	140,630	293,386	5,836,660
	Capital .	18,103,398	389,201	825,740	19,318,339
1873	Received.	7,898,200	193,020	342,371	8,433,591
	Paid..	6,084,166	177,453	322,562	6,584,181
	Capital .	19,917,432	404,768	845,549	21,167,749
1874	Received.	8,319,179	184,432	362,204	8,865,815
	Paid..	6,410,824	171,264	294,007	6,876,095
	Capital .	21,825,787	417,936	913,746	23,157,469
1875	Received.	8,779,880	185,448	390,108	9,355,436
	Paid..	6,864,838	160,171	300,551	7,325,560
	Capital .	23,740,829	443,213	1,003,303	25,187,345
1876	Received.	8,963,813	187,883	449,985	9,601,681
	Paid..	7,311,152	151,753	329,571	7,792,476
	Capital .	25,393,490	479,343	1,123,717	26,996,550
1877	Received.	9,140,998	196,516	490,684	9,828,198
	Paid..	7,560,170	166,144	357,677	8,083,991
	Capital .	26,974,318	509,715	1,256,724	28,740,757
1878	Received.	9,483,248	214,389	487,363	10,185,000
	Paid..	7,919,462	176,451	418,281	8,514,194
	Capital .	28,538,104	547,653	1,325,806	30,411,563

II.

SAVINGS' BANKS UNDER TRUSTEES.

Total Amount Received and Paid by Trustees of Savings' Banks from and to Depositors in each Year, and of the Computed Capital of Savings' Banks at the end of each Year.

		England.	Wales.	Scotland.	Ireland.	United Kingdom.
		£	£	£	£	£
1864	Received	6,580,322	177,369	953,138	463,850	8,174,679
	Paid	8,837,626	233,228	1,093,803	617,172	10,781,829
	Capital	33,743,143	984,910	2,819,033	1,973,250	39,520,336
1865	Received	6,104,130	174,572	967,663	438,272	7,684,637
	Paid	7,731,845	191,523	1,007,652	626,052	9,557,072
	Capital	33,052,171	997,091	2,859,377	1,836,659	38,745,298
1866	Received	5,767,410	159,880	945,945	352,574	7,225,809
	Paid	8,631,762	209,044	1,134,046	678,141	10,652,993
	Capital	31,100,486	976,198	2,751,166	1,554,266	36,382,116
1867	Received	5,582,409	159,069	1,055,784	463,569	7,260,831
	Paid	6,607,107	186,472	938,243	428,238	8,160,060
	Capital	30,974,031	976,621	2,949,732	1,632,819	36,533,203
1868	Received	5,587,104	155,627	1,164,659	503,813	7,411,203
	Paid	6,545,968	176,000	984,007	370,943	8,076,918
	Capital	30,850,166	984,656	3,218,843	1,813,792	36,867,457
1869	Received	5,699,654	169,099	1,278,858	520,124	7,667,735
	Paid	6,212,191	168,341	1,066,074	410,485	7,857,091
	Capital	31,038,966	1,013,927	3,526,285	1,974,568	37,553,746
1870	Received	5,537,136	162,404	1,372,110	500,017	7,571,667
	Paid	6,353,980	175,584	1,175,130	463,089	8,167,783
	Capital	31,038,029	1,029,468	3,828,294	2,062,758	37,958,549
1871	Received	5,804,984	178,303	1,487,970	566,765	8,038,022
	Paid	6,204,795	170,889	1,309,144	465,685	8,150,513
	Capital	31,413,002	1,066,543	4,119,735	2,220,283	38,819,663
1872	Received	6,134,089	205,537	1,702,497	520,848	8,562,971
	Paid	6,193,165	168,883	1,491,596	532,540	8,386,184
	Capital	31,872,535	1,133,346	4,452,330	2,221,669	39,679,880
1873	Received	6,344,132	242,479	1,765,176	436,598	8,788,385
	Paid	6,600,535	195,292	1,705,241	570,176	9,071,244
	Capital	32,501,383	1,213,587	4,638,608	2,146,557	40,500,135

		ENGLAND.	WALES.	SCOTLAND.	IRELAND.	UNITED KINGDOM.
		£	£	£	£	£
1874	RECEIVED	6,521,344	256,825	1,879,858	408,647	9,066,674
	PAID	6,742,373	218,939	1,683,493	571,520	9,216,325
	CAPITAL	33,225,029	1,288,070	4,935,909	2,017,391	41,466,399
1875	RECEIVED	6,656,900	229,086	1,959,444	450,085	9,295,515
	PAID	7,049,457	251,491	1,752,994	455,277	9,509,219
	CAPITAL	33,745,130	1,259,312	5,322,065	2,061,022	42,387,529
1876	RECEIVED	6,588,701	198,956	1,995,125	511,097	9,293,879
	PAID	7,034,866	257,208	1,784,523	461,098	9,537,695
	CAPITAL	34,206,556	1,201,286	5,697,649	2,177,967	43,283,458
1877[1]	RECEIVED	6,590,428	173,260	2,090,480	504,463	9,363,631
	INTEREST CREDITED	984,996	34,142	165,956	61,638	1,246,732
	PAID	7,031,233	224,434	1,927,283	472,185	9,655,135
	CAPITAL	34,750,747	1,189,254	6,026,802	2,271,883	44,238,686
1878[1]	RECEIVED	6,496,927	164,494	2,061,099	436,098	9,158,618
	INTEREST CREDITED	990,957	33,308	175,400	62,013	1,261,678
	PAID	7,493,766	236,667	2,054,766	550,398	10,385,597
	CAPITAL	34,744,865	1,150,389	6,178,535	2,219,596	44,293,385

[1] Prior to the year 1877 the amount of Interest Credited was not separately distinguished, although it was included in the Capital.

SECTION XV.

THE NATURE OF BANKING.

"WHAT is it that we call a Banker? There is in this city a company or corporation, called goldsmiths, and most of those called bankers are of that corporation; but so far as I know, there is not a company or corporation in England called bankers, nor has the business any definition or description either by common law or by statute. By custom we call a man a banker who has an open shop, with proper counters, servants, and books, for receiving other people's money, in order to keep it safe, and return it upon demand; and when any man has opened such a shop we call him a banker, without inquiring whether any man has given him any money to keep or no: for this is a trade where no apprenticeship is required, it having never yet been supposed that a man who sets up the trade of banking could be sued upon the statute of Queen Elizabeth, which enacts, that none shall use any art or mystery then used, but such as have served an apprenticeship in the same."[1]

A banker is a dealer in capital, or more properly a dealer in money. He is an intermediate party between the borrower and the lender. He borrows of one party, and lends to another; and the difference between the terms at which he borrows and those at which he lends, forms the source

---

[1] Speech, delivered in the House of Commons, in 1746.—See the "London Magazine" for that year, page 1_0.

of his profit. By this means he draws into active operation those small sums of money which were previously unproductive in the hands of private individuals; and at the same time furnishes accommodation to those who have need of additional capital to carry on their commercial transactions.

Banks have been divided into private and public. A private bank is that in which there are but few partners, and these attend personally to its management. A public bank is that in which there are numerous partners, and they elect from their own body a certain number, who are entrusted with its management. The latter are usually called Joint-stock banks.

The business of banking consists chiefly in receiving deposits of money, upon which interest may or may not be allowed;—in making advances of money, principally in the way of discounting bills;—and in effecting the transmission of money from one place to another. Banks in metropolitan cities are usually the agents of the banks in the provinces, and charge a commission on their transactions. In making payments many country banks still issue their own notes.

The disposable means of a bank consist of—First, the capital paid down by the partners, or shareholders. Secondly, the amount of money lodged by their customers. Thirdly, the amount of notes they are able to keep out in circulation. Fourthly, the amount of money in the course of transmission—that is, money they have received, and are to repay, in some distant place, at a future time.

These disposable means are employed—First, in discounting bills. Secondly, in advances of money in the form of cash credits, loans, or overdrawn accounts. Thirdly, in the purchase of government or other securities. Fourthly, a part is kept in the banker's till, to meet the current demands. Of these four ways of employing the capital of a bank, three are productive, and one is unproductive. The discounting of bills yields interest—the loans, and the cash credits, and the overdrawn accounts, yield interest—the government securities yield interest—the money in the till yields no interest.

The expenses of a bank may be classified thus: rent, taxes, and repairs of the house in which the business is carried on; salaries of the officers; stationer's bill for books, paper, notes, stamps, &c.; incidental expenses, as postages, coal, &c.

The profits of a bank are that portion of its total receipts—including discount, interest, dividends, and commission—which exceeds the amount of the expenses.

SECTION XVI.

THE UTILITY OF BANKING.

IN the first place, banks are useful as places of security for the deposit of money. The circumstance which gave rise to the business of banking in this country, was a desire on the part of the merchants of London to obtain a place where they might lodge their money in security. Every one who has had the care of large sums of money knows the anxiety which attends their custody. A person in this case must either take care of his money himself, or trust it to his servants. If he take care of it himself, he will often be put to inconvenience, and will have to deny himself holidays and comforts, of which a man who is possessed of much money would not like to be deprived. If he entrust it to others, he must depend upon their honesty and their ability. And, although in many important cases a master is compelled to do this, yet he does not feel the same satisfaction as if the money was actually under his own care. Some instances of neglect or of dishonesty will necessarily occur, and these will occasion suspicion in reference to other parties against whom no suspicion ought to be entertained. Besides, in both these cases, the money is lodged under the owner's own roof, and is subject to thieves, to fire, and to other contingencies, against which it is not always easy to guard.

All these evils are obviated by means of banking. The

owner of money need neither take the charge of it himself, nor trust to his dependents. He can place it in the hands of his bankers. They are wealthy men, and are responsible to him for the amount. If they are robbed, it is no loss to him: they are pledged to restore to him the amount of his deposit when he shall require it. Whenever he wants money he has only to write an order, or draft, upon his banker, and the person to whom he is indebted takes the draft to the bank, and without any hesitation or delay receives the money.

2. The bankers allow interest for money placed in their hands on deposit.

By means of banking, the various small sums of money which would have remained unproductive in the hands of individuals, are collected into large amounts in the hands of the bankers, who employ it in granting facilities to trade and commerce. Thus banking increases the productive capital of the nation. At the origin of banking, "the new-fashioned bankers," as they were called, allowed a certain rate of interest for money placed in their hands. The banks of Scotland carry this practice to the greatest extent, as they receive upon interest so low an amount as ten pounds, and also allow interest on the balance of a running account. Many of the country bankers in England allow interest on the balance of a running account, and charge commission on the amount of the money withdrawn. The London bankers generally do not allow interest on deposit, but neither do they charge commission. All their profits are derived from the use of their customers' money. The banks of Scotland do not charge commission, although they allow interest on deposits; but then those banks have a profit by the issue of their notes. The London bankers do not issue notes.

3. Another advantage conferred upon society by bankers

is, that they make advances to persons who want to borrow money. These advances are made—by discounting bills —upon personal security—upon the joint security of the borrower and two or three of his friends—and sometimes upon mortgage. Persons engaged in trade and commerce are thus enabled to augment their capital, and consequently their wealth. The increase of money in circulation stimulates production. When bankers are compelled to withhold their usual accommodation, both the commercial and the agricultural interests are plunged into extreme distress. The great advantage arising to a neighbourhood from the establishment of a bank, is derived mainly from the additional supplies of money advanced in the form of loans, or discounts, to the inhabitants of the place. This principle is so well understood in Scotland, that branch banks are sometimes established in poor districts, with a view of obtaining a future profit from the prosperity which the bank will introduce.[1]

4. Another benefit derived from bankers is, that they transmit money from one part of the country to another.

There is scarcely a person in business who has not occasion sometimes to send money to a distant town. But how is this to be done? He cannot send a messenger with it on purpose—that would be too expensive. He cannot send it by post—that would be too hazardous. Besides, the sum may be some fraction of a pound, and then it cannot go by post. The post, too, takes a considerable time, as three letters at least must pass on the transaction. If he live in London he may obtain a bank post bill, but he cannot obtain that in the country; and he may not be able to obtain it in London for the exact sum he wants. How, then, is the money to be sent? Every country

[1] Evidence before the Select Committee of the House of Commons, upon the Abolition of Small Notes, p. 43. Report.

banker opens an account with a London banker. If, then, a person lives at Penzance, and wants to send a sum of money to Aberdeen, he will pay the money into the Penzance bank, and his friend will receive it of the Aberdeen bank. The whole transaction is this: the Penzance bank will direct their agent in London to pay the money to the London agent of the Aberdeen bank, who will be duly advised of the payment. A small commission charged by the Penzance bank, and the postages, constitute all the expenses incurred, and there is not the least risk of loss.

Commercial travellers, who go collecting money, derive great advantage from the banks. Instead of carrying with them, throughout the whole of their journey, all the money they have received, when perhaps it may be wanted at home, they pay it into a bank, by whom it is remitted with the greatest security, and at little expense; and they are thus delivered from an incumbrance which would have occasioned great care and anxiety.

5. Wherever a bank is established, the public are able to obtain that denomination of currency which is best adapted for carrying on the commercial operations of the place. In a town which has no bank, a person may have occasion to use small notes, and have none but large ones; and at other times he may have need of large notes, and not be able to obtain them. But where a bank is established there can be no difficulty of this kind. The banks issue that description of notes which the receivers may require, and are always ready to exchange them for others of a different denomination. Banks, too, usually supply their customers and the neighbourhood with silver; and if, on the other hand, silver should be too abundant, the banks will receive it, either as a deposit, or in exchange for their notes. Hence, where banks are established, it is easy to obtain change. This is very convenient to those who have

to pay large sums in wages, or who purchase in small amounts the commodities in which they trade.

6. By means of banking there is a great saving of time in making money transactions. How much longer time does it take to count out a sum of money in pounds, shillings, and pence, than it does to write a draft. And how much less trouble is it to receive a draft in payment of a debt, and then to pay it into the banker's, than it is to receive a sum of money in currency. What inconveniences would arise from the necessity of weighing sovereigns. What a loss of time from disputes as to the goodness or badness of particular pieces of money.

Besides the loss of time that must necessarily occur on every transaction, we must also reckon the loss which every merchant or tradesman, in an extensive line of business, would certainly sustain in the course of a year from receiving counterfeit or deficient coin, or forged notes. From all this risk he is exempt by keeping a banker. If he receives payment of a debt, it is in the form of a draft upon his customer's banker. He pays it into his own banker's, and no coin or bank notes pass through his hands. If he draws bills, those bills are presented by his banker: and if his banker take bad money it is his own loss.

7. A merchant or tradesman who keeps a banker saves the trouble and expense of presenting those bills or drafts which he may draw upon his customers, or which he may receive in exchange for his goods. He pays these into the hands of his banker, and has no further trouble. He has now no care about the custody of his bills—no anxiety about their being stolen—no danger of forgetting them until they are over-due, and thus exonerating the endorsers—no trouble of sending to a distance in order to demand payment. He has nothing more to do than to

see the amount entered to his credit in his banker's books. If a bill be not paid it is brought back to him on the day after it falls due, properly noted. The banker's clerk and the notary's clerk are witnesses ready to come forward to prove that the bill has been duly presented, and the notary's ticket attached to the bill assigns the reason why it is not paid. But if any endorser of the bill has given a reference in case of need—that is, if any endorser has written on the back of the bill that some other party will pay it in case the accepter does not, then the notary takes the bill to the referee, and procures the money from him.

This circumstance alone must cause an immense saving of expense to a mercantile house in the course of a year. Let us suppose that a merchant has only two bills due each day. These bills may be payable in distant parts of the town, so that it may take a clerk half a day to present them. And in large mercantile establishments it would take up the whole time of one or two clerks to present the due bills and the drafts. The salaries of these clerks are therefore saved by keeping an account at a banker's. Besides the saving of expense, it is also reasonable to suppose that losses upon bills would sometimes occur from mistakes, or oversights—from miscalculation as to the time a bill would become due—from errors in marking it up—from forgetfulness to present it—or from presenting it at the wrong house. In these cases the endorsers and the drawers are exonerated; and if the accepter do not pay the bill the amount is lost. In a banking-house such mistakes are not so likely to occur, though they do occur sometimes; but the loss falls upon the banker, and not upon his customer.

8. Another advantage from keeping a banker in London is, that by this means you have a continual referee as to

your respectability. If a mercantile house in the country write to their agent, to ascertain the respectability of a firm in London, the first inquiry is, Who is their banker? And when this is ascertained, the banker is applied to through the proper channel, and he gives his testimony as to the respectability of his customer. When a trader gives his bill, it circulates through the hands of many individuals to whom he is personally unknown; but if the bill is made payable at a banking-house, it bears on its face a reference to a party to whom the accepter is known, and who must have some knowledge of his character as a tradesman. This may be an immense advantage to a man in business, as a means of increasing his credit; and credit, Dr. Franklin says, is money.

9. The keeping an account at a banking-house enables a trader not only to give a constant reference as to his own respectability, but it also enables him to ascertain the respectability of other persons who keep bankers. There are numerous cases in which a trader may wish to know this. A stranger may bring him a bill, and want goods in exchange: or he may have drawn a bill upon a customer, and wishes to ascertain if this bill would be paid before he gave him any further credit. If this bill is not made payable at a banking-house he can obtain no information. But suppose the bill is made payable at a banking-house; even then he can obtain no information unless he himself has a banker. If he take the bill to the banker's, at whose house it is made payable, and say, "Gentlemen, I will thank you to inform me if the accepter of this bill be a respectable man—may I safely give goods or money in exchange for it?" they will reply, "Sir, we never answer such questions to strangers." But if the holder of this bill keeps an account at a banker's, he has only to ask his banker to make the inquiry for him, and he will easily

obtain the most ample information. Among nearly all the bankers in London the practice is established of giving information to each other as to the respectability of their customers. For as the bankers themselves are the greatest discounters of bills, it is their interest to follow this practice; and indeed the interest of their customers also, of those at least who are respectable.

10. By means of banking, people are able to preserve an authentic record of their annual expenditure.[1] If a person pays in to his banker all the money he receives in the course of a year, and makes all his payments by cheques—then by looking over his bank-book at the end of the year he will readily see the total amount of his receipts, and the various items of his expenditure. This is very useful to persons who have not habits of business, and who may therefore be in danger of living beyond their means. It is useless to advise such persons to keep an account of their expenses—they will do no such thing; but when short of money at Christmas to pay their tradesmen's bills, they may take the trouble of looking over their bank-book, and noticing how many cheques were drawn for the purchase of unnecessary articles. A bank account is useful also in case of disputed payments. People do not always take receipts for money they pay to their tradesmen, and when they do the receipts may be lost or mislaid. In case of death, or of omission to enter the amount in the creditor's books, the money may be demanded again. Should the payment have been made in bank notes or sovereigns, the payer can offer no legal proof of having settled the account; but if the account

---

[1] In the year 1849 a committee of investigation into the affairs of a railway company reported that the company had kept no books for eighteen months, and knew their transactions only from their bankers' pass-book.

was discharged by a cheque on a banker, the cheque can be produced, and the payment proved by the officers of the bank, who can be subpœnaed for that purpose.

11. Another advantage resulting from keeping a banker in London, is, that the party has a secure place of deposit for any deeds, papers, or other property that may require peculiar care. Any customer who pleases may have a tin box, which he may leave with his banker in the evening, and call for it in the morning. In this box he might place his will, the lease of his house, policies of insurance, or any other documents he wished to preserve against fire. Stockbrokers and others who have offices in the city, and live out of town, have such boxes, which they leave overnight with their banker for the sake of security, in preference to leaving them in their own office. If a party were going to the country he might send his plate or jewellery to his banker, who will lock it up in his strong room, and thus it will be preserved from fire and thieves until his return. Solicitors and others, who have deeds or other writings of importance left in their custody, can send them to the bank during the night, and thus avoid the danger of fire.

12. By keeping a banker, people have a ready channel of obtaining much information that will be useful to them in the way of their business. They will know the way in which bankers keep their accounts; they will learn many of the laws and customs relating to bills of exchange. By asking the banker, or any of the clerks, they may know which is the readiest way of remitting any money they have to send to the country or to the Continent. If they have to buy or sell stock in the public funds, the banker can give them the name of a respectable broker who can manage the business; or should they be about to travel, and wish to know the best way of receiving money abroad;

or be appointed executors to a will, and have to settle some money matters—the banker will in these, and many other cases, be able to give them the necessary information.

13. Banking also exercises a powerful influence upon the morals of society. It tends to produce honesty and punctuality in pecuniary engagements. Bankers, for their own interest, always have a regard to the moral character of the party with whom they deal; they inquire whether he be honest or tricky, industrious or idle, prudent or speculative, thrifty or prodigal, and they will more readily make advances to a man of moderate property and good morals, than to a man of large property but of inferior reputation. Thus the establishment of a bank in any place immediately advances the pecuniary value of a good moral character. There are numerous instances of persons having risen from obscurity to wealth only by means of their moral character, and the confidence which that character produced in the mind of their banker. It is not merely by way of loan or discount that a banker serves such a person. He also speaks well of him to those persons who may make inquiries respecting him, and the banker's good opinion will be the means of procuring him a higher degree of credit with the parties with whom he trades. These effects are easily perceivable in country towns; and even in London, if a house be known to have engaged in gambling or smuggling transactions, or in any other way to have acted discreditably, their bills will be taken by the bankers less readily than those of an honourable house of inferior property.

It is thus that bankers perform the functions of public conservators of the commercial virtues. From motives of private interest they encourage the industrious, the prudent, the punctual, and the honest—while they discountenance the spendthrift and the gambler, the liar and the knave.

They hold out inducements to uprightness, which are not disregarded by even the most abandoned. There is many a man who would be deterred from dishonesty by the frown of a banker, though he might care but little for the admonitions of a bishop.

SECTION XVII.

BANKING TERMS.

QUERY I.—Is the word Bank a singular or a plural noun?

The word BANK, being a noun of multitude, may have verbs and pronouns agreeing with it in either the singular or the plural number, yet not without regard to the import of the term as conveying unity or plurality of idea. In the use of this term the following rules are usually observed:—

1. When any operation or feeling of the mind is ascribed to a bank, the verbs and pronouns are placed in the plural—as, "The bank *were anxious* to meet the wishes of the public." "The bank *have concurred* in the measure proposed." "Are you one of the persons who tried the question with the Bank of Ireland, whether *they conceived themselves* bound to pay in gold at *their* branches?" "The Bank of England petitioned against this bill, and *were* heard by *their* Counsel; but *their* representations produced no effect, and the bill having passed through both Houses, received the Royal assent." The following examples, wherein mental operations are ascribed to a neuter pronoun, are violations of this rule: "The bank *allows* the party having the cash credit to liquidate any portion of his debt to the bank at any time that may suit his convenience, and reserves to *itself* the power of cancelling, whenever *it shall think fit*, the credit granted." "It is usual for the

bank when *it* gives a cash credit *to keep a watchful eye* over the person having that cash credit."

2. When a reference is made to a bank merely as an institution, the term is considered to belong to the singular—as, "The Bank of Scotland continued the only bank from the date of *its* establishment, in 1695, to the year 1727. In that year a charter of incorporation was granted to certain individuals named therein, for carrying on the business of banking, under the name of the Royal Bank; and subsequent charters were granted to this establishment, enlarging *its* capital, which now amounts to two millions." "The National Bank of Scotland *has* 1,238 partners." "If this measure be carried into effect, the Provincial Bank must instantly be deprived of any sufficient means of reimbursing *itself* for the heavy expense to which *it has* been subject." "*Has* your bank an establishment at Kirkcudbright?" "The Bank of England *has* the control of *its* issues entirely within *itself*."

3. When we notice the rules or habitual acts of a bank, the word belongs to the singular—as, "The Provincial Bank *allows* interest at the rate of two per cent." "The bank *draws* bills upon London at twenty-one days after date." "The bank *discounts* bills at the rate of four per cent." "The bank *issues* notes payable in gold at the place of issue." "The London and Westminster *grants* interest upon deposits—*it does* not allow *its* officers to receive Christmas presents from *its* customers." In reference to cases that fall under this rule, there is, however, some contrariety of practice: "*Do* the Provincial Bank *issue* post bills? *They do* not." "Have the Bank of Ireland at *their* branch at Cork been in the habit of receiving gold to any amount in payments?" "*Have* the Bank of Ireland any deposits at the Cork branch? Do you know how *their* notes get into circulation? Do *they* pay any interest on

their deposits? *They have* a great quantity of notes in circulation—*have they* not?"

4. When the word bank is connected with a past participle by means of the neuter verb *to be*, it usually belongs to the singular—as, " I am a director of the Bank of Scotland, which *is established* by Act of Parliament; *it does* not hold a charter from the Crown, but in common language *it is called* a chartered bank." " Suppose a bank *was enabled* to take 6 per cent. on a cash credit, instead of 4." " The Falkirk Union Banking Company *has been returned* to this house, as sequestrated in the month of October, 1816." " A new bank *was constituted* as a fund, upon which the sum of £2,564,000 should be raised, and *it was called* the Land Bank, because established on land securities."

5. When the word bank is preceded by the indefinite article, *a, an*—by the demonstrative pronoun, *this, that*—or by the words *each, any, every, one*—it belongs to the singular; as, " Do you not think that *a* bank that *is* possessed of a capital of one million, may and will do more business than *a* bank that *is* only possessed of half a million?" " In a moment of pressure, an emergency like the present, *that* bank would get into great disrepute who called up any one of *its* cash credits." " What is the amount of the small note circulation in *that* bank, as connected with *its* whole circulation?" " *Each* bank *has* an interest to issue as much of the small note circulation as *it* can?—Certainly *it has*, provided the small notes can be kept out; but, as *every* bank *makes* an exchange at Glasgow twice every week, and the exchanges of *each* bank come back upon *itself*, and the balance is paid by a draft on Edinburgh at sight," &c. " I believe almost *every* bank in Scotland *has* an agent in Glasgow." " Suppose *one* bank in Scotland made *its* notes payable in Scotland, at the

place where the notes were issued." " Is there *any* bank in Cork now that *issues* notes?"

6. When the word bank is introduced in either the singular or the plural number, the same number should be preserved throughout the sentence. Hence, the following sentence of Smollett's is inaccurate: "By the same Acts the bank *was* required to advance a sum not exceeding £2,500,000 towards discharging the national debt, if wanted, on condition that *they* should have £5 per cent. for as much as *they* might advance, redeemed by Parliament."

7. When the word bank is used in the singular number, it is considered as a substantive of the neuter gender, and hence is associated with the relative pronoun, *which;* but when used in the plural number, it implies the idea of persons, and has accordingly the personal relative, *who;* as, "The Bank with *which* he kept his account *has* stopped payment;" or, "The bank with *whom* he kept his account *have* stopped payment." "The bank, *whose* interests are affected by the proposed measure, *have* petitioned against it." The bank upon *whom* the cheque was drawn *have* refused to honour it." The following sentence is not in accordance with this rule: "In a moment of pressure, an emergency like the present, that bank would get into great disrepute *who* called up any of *its* cash credits."

I have not observed that any *English* writer, except Mr. McCulloch, considered a bank to be a lady; and this is only in the case of an Irish bank. Under the article "Banking," in his Commercial Dictionary, he says, "The Bank of Ireland draws on London, at twenty days' date. *She* neither grants cash credits, nor allows any interest on deposits; *she* discounts at the rate of £5 per cent." This mode of expression is, however, very common with American writers.

II. Should we write *accepter* or *acceptor* of a bill of exchange? The name of the agent to any verb is usually formed, in our language, by the addition of *r* or *er* to the verb; as, *indorser, talker, walker, speaker*. What reason, then, can be assigned why, in the present case, we should depart from the analogy of the language? We do not say, the drawor, the holdor, the payor of a bill; why then should we say the acceptor? When we speak of the accepter of a bill, why should we not spell the word in the same way as when we speak of the accepter of a present, or of a fee? Yet all our English legal authors write, acceptor: "A person who accepts for honour, is only liable if the original drawee do not pay; and to charge such *acceptor*, there must be a presentment for payment to such original drawee."—*Bayley.* "A foreign bill is binding in this country on the *acceptor*, though he accepted by parol, or by writing unconnected with the instrument."—*Chitty.* "Where the *acceptor* of a forged bill pays it, and is guilty of any negligence, or want of due caution in making such payment, he cannot recover the money so paid, from the innocent party to whom he paid it."—*Roscoe*. Scotch authors, however, write *accepter*. "An English inland bill has generally three parties to it—the drawer, *accepter*, and payee; whereas, in Scotland, most of the inland bills have, at first, but two parties, the drawer and the *accepter*; and they are made payable to the drawer or his order."[1]

III. Should we write *indorse* or *endorse?* Indorse is derived direct from the Latin, *in dorsum*, on the back. *Endorse* is derived from the Latin, through the French, *endosser*. In such cases, most writers adopt the Latin mode of spelling, in preference to the French, as *indorse, inquire, intire;* not *endorse, enquire, entire*. All legal authors write indorse. "A promise to *indorse*, though on

[1] See Glen on the Law of Bills of Exchange in Scotland.

sufficient consideration, cannot be treated as an actual *indorsement*."—*Bayley.* "The liability of the *indorser* is discharged by want of notice, as in the case of the drawer." —*Roscoe.* "A person who draws or *indorses* a bill, or *indorses* a note for the accommodation of the acceptor or maker, or payee, or prior *indorsers*, has on paying the instrument, a remedy over thereon against the acceptor or maker, or prior party."—*Chitty.* "A drawer or *indorser* cannot, in the character of *indorsee*, maintain an action against the accepter, where the indorsement is after the refusal of payment."—*Glen.*

IV. Should we say *indorsement* or *indorsation?* In England we always use the word indorsement. "No particular words are essential to an *indorsement*; the mere signature of the indorser is, in general, sufficient."—*Bayley.* "The *indorsement* may be upon the face, or at the back of the bill."—*Chitty.* "An attesting witness to an *indorsement* is necessary, when the bill is for a less sum than £5."—*Chitty.* In Scotland the term more generally used is indorsation. "If a bill or note be granted to a woman while single, and she afterwards marry, the right to transfer it by *indorsation* would vest in the husband." "After a bill has been paid no *indorsation* can take place, so as to affect the accepter, or any of the parties who would otherwise be discharged."—*Glen.* The word indorsement is also used in Scotland, though more rarely. Both words appear to have precisely the same meaning. "An *indorsation* is made, either by the indorser's writing, and subscribing an order to pay the contents of the bill to some particular person mentioned by name, which is styled a *full indorsement*, or by merely signing his name on the bill, and delivering it to the indorsee, or person to whom it is indorsed, which is termed *a blank indorsation*." —*Glen.* "A fictitious *indorsement* to a bill is a forgery;

such *indorsation* is clearly giving it a false credit."—*Glen.*

V. Should we say the *presentment* or the *presentation* of a bill of exchange? All writers agree in using presentment. "If upon the *presentment* of the bill for acceptance to the drawee, he refuse or neglect to accept it, the drawer is immediately responsible to the holder, although the bill has not become due according to its tenor."—*Chitty.* "If the bill be payable after sight, and the drawee detain it some days without declaring his intention to accept, and afterwards incline to do so, the acceptance must be from the date of the first *presentment.*"—*Glen.* "*Presentment* for payment must be made by the holder of the bill, or by an agent competent to give a legal receipt for the money."—*Glen.* "Upon a *presentment* for acceptance, the bill should be left with the drawee twenty-four hours, unless in the interim he either accept, or declare a resolution not to accept. But a bill or note must not be left (unless it be paid) on a *presentment* for payment; if it be, the *presentment* is not considered as made, until the money is called for."—*Bayley.*

VI. Should we write *draught* or *draft?* This word is derived from the verb *to draw*, and probably was originally written and pronounced *drawght*. But custom, which is the law of language, has changed both the pronunciation and the spelling to *draft*. In the former editions of this work, I mentioned that Mr. Justice Bayley had always spelled this word *draught;* but in a recent edition of his work, since published, I find that *draught* has been changed to *draft*.

VII. Should we write *check* or *cheque?* This word is derived from the French, *echecs, chess*. The chequers placed at the doors of public-houses, are intended to represent chess-boards, and originally denoted that the game of chess was played in those houses. Similar tables were employed in reckoning money, and hence came the expression—to check an account; and the Government Office, where the public accounts were kept, was called the Exchequer. It probably obtained this name from the French *exchiquier*, a chess-board, though Blackstone states that this court was called the exchequer, from the chequered cloth which covered the table. Of the two forms of writing this word, *check* and *cheque*, the latter seems preferable, as it is free from ambiguity, and is analogous to EX-CHEQUER, the public treasury. It is also used by the Bank of England, "CHEQUE-OFFICE." In *Bayley* both forms are employed. "A *cheque* upon a banker was lost, and paid to a stranger the day before *it bore date*: the banker was obliged to repay the money to the loser." "By the usage of trade, a banker in London will not render himself responsible by retaining a *check* drawn on him, provided he return it at any time before five o'clock on the evening of the day in which it was drawn."

SECTION XVIII.

THE GENERAL ADMINISTRATION OF A BANK.

To be a good banker requires some intellectual and some moral qualifications. A banker need not be a man of talent, but he should be a man of wisdom. Talent, in the sense in which the word is ordinarily used, implies a strong development of some one faculty of the mind. Wisdom implies the due proportion of all the faculties. A banker need not be a poet or a philosopher—a man of science or of literature—an orator or a statesman. He need not possess any one remarkable quality by which he may be distinguished from the rest of mankind. It is only necessary that he should possess a large portion of that practical quality which is called common sense. Banking talent (using the word *talent* here in the sense of adaptation of character to any particular pursuit) consists more in the union of a number of qualities, not in themselves individually of a striking character, but rare only in their combination in the same person. It is a mistake to suppose that banking is such a routine employment that it requires neither knowledge nor skill. The number of banks that have failed within the last fifty years are sufficient to show, that to be a good banker requires qualities as rare and as important as those which are necessary to attain eminence in any other pursuit. The dealer in money exercises intellectual faculties of a high order, and of great value to the community. His profession has a powerful bearing on the practical happiness of mankind.

"The philosophy which affects to teach us a contempt of money, does not run very deep; for, indeed, it ought to be still more clear to the philosopher than it is to the ordinary man, that there are few things in the world of greater importance. And so manifold are the bearings of money upon the lives and characters of mankind, that an insight which should search out the life of a man in his pecuniary relations, would penetrate into almost every cranny of his nature. He who knows, like St. Paul, both how to spare and how to abound, has a great knowledge: for if we take account of all the virtues with which money is mixed up—honesty, justice, generosity, charity, frugality, forethought, self-sacrifice,—and of their correlative vices—it is a knowledge which goes near to cover the length and breadth of humanity: and a right measure and manner in getting, saving, spending, giving, taking, lending, borrowing, and bequeathing, would almost argue a perfect man."[1]

But though wisdom—or, in other words, a high degree of common sense—does not imply the possession of any remarkable talent (the undue development of any one faculty), it always implies the absence of any remarkable defect. One great defect in a banker is a want of decision. A banker ought to know how to balance the evidence on each side of a question, and to arrive speedily at a just conclusion.

"Indecisiveness will be, *cæteris paribus*, most pernicious in affairs which require secrecy. 1st, Because the greatest aid to secrecy is celerity. 2nd, Because the undecided man, seeking after various counsel, necessarily multiplies confidences. The pretext for indecisiveness is commonly mature deliberation; but, in reality, indecisive men occupy

[1] Taylor's Notes on Life.

themselves less in deliberation than others; for to him who fears to decide, deliberation (which has a foretaste of that fear) soon becomes intolerably irksome, and the mind escapes from the anxiety of it into alien themes. Or, if that seems too open a dereliction of its task, it gives itself to inventing reasons of postponement. And the man who has confirmed habits of indecisiveness, will come in time to look upon postponement as the first object in all cases, and wherever it seems to be practicable, will bend all his faculties to accomplish it."[1]

Another defect is a want of firmness. A banker having, after a mature consideration, made up his mind, should be capable of a strict adherence to his previous determination: he should know when to say, *No;* and having once said No, he should adhere to it. Another defect is a hasty or impetuous temper. Another is that of being swayed by any personal or constitutional prepossession. Almost every man has a sin by which he is most easily beset; a constitutional defect, against which it is necessary he should be upon his guard.

It is a great advantage to a banker, and indeed to every one else, to know himself. He should know wherein he excels, and wherein he is deficient. He ought to know whether he is disposed from his temperament to be excessively cautious, or excessively liberal—whether his manners are courteous or abrupt—whether he is apt to view matters on their gloomy or on their bright side—whether social intercourse renders him more or less fit for his official engagements—whether the presents and civilities he receives from his customers do, or do not, affect his transactions with them in matters of business. When he has made a loss, he should examine whether the loss was occasioned by

---

[1] Taylor's Statesman.—I would advise all bankers, and all other persons at the head of large establishments, to read this little work.

the ordinary operation of events, or produced by any little weaknesses of his own character. He should record all those instances in which he has shown a want of firmness, of discretion, of discrimination, or of perseverance; and should guard in future against the exhibition of any similar defect:

"Man, know thyself; all wisdom centres there."

But while a banker should make himself acquainted with his own defects, he ought not to let his customers become acquainted with them. All wise men know their own defects; none but fools publish them. Crafty men, who often have occasion to borrow money, are quick in perceiving the weaknesses of their banker. And if they find that by coaxing, or flattering, or gossiping, or bribing, or threatening, they can influence his conduct, he will always be at their mercy. On this account it is, perhaps, advisable that a banker should not have too much social intercourse with those of his customers who have occasion to ask him for any large amount of accommodation.

Wisdom implies prudence and discretion, and these should regulate the whole conduct of a banker, not merely when engaged in banking transactions, but at all other times. We may apply to a banker the language we have elsewhere applied to a merchant:

"The amusements of a merchant should correspond with his character. He should never engage in those recreations which partake of the nature of gambling, and but seldom in those of a frivolous description. A judge is not always on the bench, a clergyman is not always in the pulpit, nor is a merchant always on 'Change; but each is expected at all times to abstain from any amusements which are not consistent with his professional character. The credit of a merchant depends not merely on his wealth, but also upon the opinion generally entertained of his personal qualities; and he should cultivate a reputation for prudence and propriety of conduct, as part of his stock in trade." [1]

A banker should have a talent for selecting suitable instruments. He ought not only to know himself, he ought also to have a capacity for judging of others. He should know how to choose proper clerks for the discharge of the duties of the office. He should know also what parties to employ to procure him confidential information as to the character and circumstances of commercial houses, or of individuals. He should know how to choose his partners or coadjutors, and should endeavour to select those who possess qualifications in which he is himself deficient. In all cases when he has any object to effect he should know how to make use of other men. We may here, as in some other cases, apply to a banker the observations Mr. Taylor applies to a statesman:

"The most important qualification of one who is high in the service of the State, is his fitness for acting through others, since the operations vicariously effected ought, if he knows how to make use of his power, to predominate greatly over the importance which can attach to any man's direct and individual activity." [2]

A neglect of this rule has occurred in the history of some joint-stock banks, where the manager has impaired his own health, and damaged his bank, by taking upon himself a vast variety of duties which should have been assigned to others; forgetful that in large establishments the chief officer should confine his personal attention to those duties which are intellectual, or which are of the chief importance;

[1] Lectures on the History and Principles of Ancient Commerce. By J. W. Gilbart.
[2] Taylor's Statesman.

while the duties which are of a mere manual, or less important character, should be performed through the instrumentality of assistants.

A banker should know how to economize his own time. One mode of doing this will be, as we have intimated, to assign inferior duties to others. His accountant should keep his books, and make his calculations. His secretary should write his letters (except those of a private or confidential nature), and he should only sign them. His chief clerk should attend to the discipline of the office. A banker at the head of a large establishment should not only be acquainted with the art of banking—he ought also to be acquainted with the art of government. He ought to put a clever man at the head of each department, and reserve to himself only the duty of general superintendence. He should give these parties a pretty wide discretion, and not encourage them to ask his instructions about matters of comparatively trifling importance. If he does this, they will never learn to think for themselves,—never feel that wholesome anxiety which results from a sense of responsibility,—and never acquire that decision of mind which arises from the necessity of forming an independent judgment. Consequently, they will be less useful to him in their present position, and never become qualified for higher offices.

Another mode of economizing time is to observe a principle of order. A banker should come to the bank every day at the same hour; attend to his affairs, one by one, in the same order, and leave the bank at his usual time. By observing this routine, he will not only save much time, but he will avoid tumultuous feelings, and maintain a calmness of mind and of manner, that will be useful in all his affairs. He will also acquire from habit a coolness of investigation, and a promptness of decision ; and he will get through a great deal of work without ever appearing to be in a hurry.

Another mode of economizing time is, to make his interviews with his customers, or with other parties, as short as he can. He should not encourage conversation upon any other topic than that which is the occasion of the interview. He had better receive his customers standing; as in that case they will stand too, and are not likely to remain so long as if they were to sit down. And the furniture of the room should be so arranged that the customer, if he sit down, should sit near the door, so that he may depart whenever disposed. He is not likely to remain so long as if seated comfortably by the fire-side. It is also desirable that his room should be so placed, with reference to the other parts of the building, that while it has one door open to the public, it should have another door opening into the office; so that he may easily pass into the office, to ascertain the state of a customer's account, or to consult with himself or another person, in doubtful cases, as to the course to be adopted. It is not advisable that the customer who applies, for instance, to have a heavy bill discounted, should witness the hesitation or the deliberation of the banker. Hence it is better, when it can be done, to establish the practice of the customer giving the bills to a clerk, who shall bring them into the banker's room, and take back his reply.

A banker will take means for obtaining and recording information. He should not, as we have said, keep any books himself. But he ought always to have in his room, ready for immediate reference, if necessary, "the General Balance Book," containing the weekly balances of the general ledger, which will show the weekly progress of his business for several years past,—"the Daily Balance Book," showing the daily balance to the credit of each of his customers in the current-account ledger,—" the Weekly Discount Balance Book," showing the amount of discounts, loans, or other advances which each customer has every Saturday night,—" the Inspection Book," showing the amount of bills bearing the names of houses who do not keep an account with him,—" the Information Book," containing the character of all the houses about whom he has had occasion to make inquiries,—and, finally, "a Private Memorandum Book," in which is entered any special agreements that he has made with his customers. It is also useful to a banker to have a list of his customers, classified according to their trades or professions—such as corn merchants, leather factors, grocers, solicitors, &c., &c. The banker would thus see at a glance among what classes of society his connections lie. When any public event was likely to affect any class—such, for instance, as the corn merchants—he would see how many of his customers are likely to be affected. By thus, too, bearing in mind the trade or profession of his customers, he would be able to judge more readily whether the bills they brought him for discount had arisen out of their business transactions.

Of these books, one of the most important is the "Information Book."[1] There is no doubt that a banker of great experience, and of a strong memory, may always bear in his mind a very correct estimate of the standing and character of all the houses that usually come under his notice. But this does not supersede the necessity for recording his information in a book. His memory may fail, and that too on important occasions; and certainly

[1] It is now the almost universal practice in London to record the information obtained, on cards, instead of in an "Information Book." The cards are arranged alphabetically in drawers, and the information on each can be added to from time to time much more readily, and is more accessible, than if recorded in a book.

if he leave the bank for a short time, as he must sometimes have occasion to do, he will carry his memory with him. But if the "Information Book" be closely kept up, he will record his knowledge for the use of those who will have to take his place. It is no valid objection to the keeping of such a book to say that the position of houses is perpetually changing. Those changes should be recorded, so that their actual standing should always be readily referred to. If a banker is requested by a customer to make inquiry about a house, he should record the information he gets for his own guidance, in case any bills on that house should afterwards be offered him for discount.

A banker will get information about parties from inquiry at their bankers, as we have mentioned at page 219. This information may be defective in two ways. In the first place, their banker may judge of them from the account they keep—that is, from the balance to their credit—and thus he may give too good an account of them. Or, secondly, their banker may have an interest in keeping up their credit, and under this bias he may not give them so bad a character as they actually deserve. Another source of information is from parties in the same trade. Houses in the same trade know pretty well the standing of one another. Wholesale houses are well acquainted with the retail shopkeepers who buy of them. Most bankers have among their own customers some houses in almost every trade, who can give them any information respecting other houses which they may require. The bills that pass through his hands will also often give him some useful hints respecting the parties whose names are upon them.

It is of great importance to a banker to have an ample knowledge of the means and transactions of his customers. The customer, when he opens his account, will give him some information on this subject. The banker will afterwards get information from his own books. The amount of transactions that his customer passes through his current account will show the extent of his business. The amount of his daily balance will show if he has much ready cash. The extent and character of the bills he offers for discount, will show if he trusts large amounts to individual houses, and if these are respectable. On the other hand, the bills his customer may accept to other parties, and his payments, will show the class of people with whom he deals, or who are in the habit of giving him credit. But one main source of information is to see the man. This, like other means of information, will sometimes fail; but, generally speaking, the appearance and manners of a man will show his character. Some people always send their clerk to the banker with bills for discount, &c. This is all very well if they want no extraordinary accommodation; but if they ask for anything out of the usual way, the banker had better say that he wishes to see the principal. And if he had a doubt whether his customer was tricky or honest—speculative or prudent—let him be guided by his first impression—we mean the impression produced by the first interview. In nine cases out of ten the first impression will be found to be correct. It is not necessary to study physiognomy or phrenology to be able to judge of the character of men with whom we converse upon matters of business.

A country banker has greater facilities than a London banker of ascertaining the character and circumstances of other parties. In a country town everything is known about everybody; a man's parentage and connections—his family and associates—the property he has already received, and what he may expect to receive from his relations—and, above all, his personal habits and disposition. Upon the last point, we will make a short extract from an excellent series of "Letters to a Branch Manager," published in the "Banker's Magazine," under the signature of "Thomas Bullion."

"Next in importance to a study of his accounts, the habits and character of a client are deserving of your attentive consideration. If a man's style of living, for example, becomes extravagant, and he gives himself over to excess, you cannot too promptly apply the curb, however regular the transactions upon his account may seem; because years may elapse before mere irregularity of living will make any impression on his banking account; whereas irregularity in business will exhibit itself immediately, and for this reason,—that whereas improvident habits of living involve a continuous waste in small sums, spreading over tolerably long periods, improvidence in business may involve in one fell swoop the loss perhaps of thousands. I hold, then, that you are not warranted in all cases in feeling satisfied of a man's perfect responsibility *until* his banking account exhibits indubitable evidence to the contrary."

A banker should always have general principles; that is, he should have fixed rules for the government of his bank. He should know beforehand whether he will or will not advance money on mortgage, or upon deeds, or upon bills of lading, or warrants; or whether he will discount bills based upon un-commercial transactions, or having more than three months to run. These are only a few of the cases in which a banker will find it useful to store his mind with general principles.

One advantage of this adoption of general principles is, that it saves time. If a banker can say, in reply to a customer, "It is contrary to the rules of our bank to advance money upon bills of lading," the reply is conclusive. But if he had not previously adopted any rule upon the subject, the reply would have taken up much more time. Another advantage is, that it gives decision of mind, and saves the banker from being "talked over" by any of his customers who may possess fluency of speech, or dexterity in debate. In this case, the banker whose mind is stored with general principles, though he may listen patiently to all his customer shall advance, will give the same reply which he would have given had the application been made in fewer words.

But although a banker ought to have a large stock of general principles—and this stock will increase as his experience increases—yet it may not be always wise to explain these principles to his customer. It is generally best, when a banker gives a refusal, to give no reasons for that refusal. Banking science is so little understood, that the public generally are unable to appreciate its principles. Besides, a man who wants to borrow money can never be convinced by reasoning that his banker is right in refusing to lend it to him; nor, in fact, did the banker himself acquire his knowledge of banking by reasoning. He acquired it not by reasoning, but by experience; and he must not expect that his customers, who have had no experience, will, by reasoning alone, readily acquiesce in the banking principles he may propound to them. In most cases, therefore, he had better keep his reasons to himself.

Nevertheless, while we contend that every banker should have general principles, we do not say that in no possible case should he depart from them. But he should not look for such cases; they are rare, and when they do occur they will force themselves upon his attention. If under shelter of the truism, "All rules have their exceptions," he departs from his general principles whenever he finds it convenient or profitable to do so, he may as well have no general principles at all.

It seems desirable that a banker in a large city should mark out for himself one or two main branches of business, rather than attempt to carry on banking in all its branches. We see this line of conduct adopted by some of the most eminent London bankers. A west-end banker will not discount a bill: a city banker will not lend money on mortgage.[1] Different kinds of banking exist in different parts of the country, according to the character and circumstances of the district. And in London the classes of people are numerous, and it may be both proper and advantageous for a banker to adapt his mode of business chiefly to the requirements of some one particular class. Different banks may thus pursue different courses, and all be equally successful.

A banker will exercise due caution in taking new accounts. He will expect the new customer to be introduced by some person to whom he is personally known. The more respectable the introducer, the higher opinion will the banker entertain of the party introduced. If a party apply to open an account without such an introduction, he is asked to give references to some well-known houses. He is expected to state to the banker the kind of business in which he is engaged, and the extent of accommodation, if any, that he is likely to require. He will state the kind and character of the bills he will have to offer to discount, and mention any peculiarity in his business or circumstances that may occasionally require especial consideration. It is a great folly in a party opening an account to make any representation that will not afterwards turn out to be correct. Every banker is anxious to avoid taking shabby accounts; and especially such as are opened for the purposes of fraud, or to obtain a fictitious credit, or to get

[1] Exceptions occasionally occur; but, as a general rule, these statements hold good.—EDITOR.

undue accommodation. It is considered to be not advisable to take the account of a party who has another banker, especially if he opens the account for the purpose of getting additional discount. The object of a party keeping two bankers is usually to get as much accommodation as he can from each. If an account is brought from another bank, the reason of the removal should be distinctly stated, and the banker will accept or reject it, according to circumstances. It is bad policy in a banker to attempt to draw away the connections of another bank, by offering them greater accommodation. It is also usually bad policy to take the accounts of parties residing at a distance, as their transactions do not come under the notice of the banker; and the fact of their passing by the banks in their neighbourhood to go elsewhere, is one that should excite suspicion. It is not advisable for London bankers to take the accounts of private individuals who reside in the country. They should be referred to the bankers in their own districts.

A small banker should not attempt to take large accounts. Banks, otherwise well administered, have been ruined by one large account. If this account requires accommodation, it will absorb the banker's funds, so that he will be compelled to stint his other customers, or to have recourse to re-discount, or other modes of raising money. Even if it be only a deposit account, it may produce inconveniences. A small banker cannot so readily employ this large deposit profitably, and yet have it at command whenever required; and the additional amount he must keep in his till will be proportionably greater than would be kept by a large banker. Thus, if £100,000 be placed in a bank that has already £2,000,000 of deposits, the additional sum kept in the till to meet daily demands may not be much increased; but should it be lodged with a banker whose deposits are only £300,000, the increase of notes to be kept in his till will be very considerable. This shows that large deposits are not so profitable to small banks as to large ones. There is also a danger that a small banker will employ his large deposits in such a way as shall render him less ready to repay them punctually. Instances have occurred of small banks being greatly inconvenienced by the repayment of large deposits, which had been placed in their hands by railway companies. It is prudent, therefore, in a banker to apportion the amount of his transactions to the extent of his business.

A very important part of the business of a banker consists in the discounting of bills.

In doubtful cases, the banker, before discounting a bill, will probably look through his books, and satisfy himself with regard to the following inquiries:—

What is the character of the customer? This inquiry will be answered from the Information Book. What is the usual balance of his cash accounts? This will be answered by the Daily Balance Book. What amount has he now under discount? This will be answered from the Discount Ledger, and will suggest other inquiries. Is that amount greater or less than usual? What proportion does that amount bear to the average amount of his cash balance? Is the amount chiefly upon few parties, or is it divided among a number? Have their bills been discounted chiefly upon the strength of the customer, or upon the strength of other parties? Are his bills generally paid? He will then proceed to inquire about the other parties to the bill. What is the character of the accepter in the Information Book? What is the nature of the transactions between the customer and the accepter, as far as can be ascertained? Has he had any bills upon him before, and have they been punctually paid? Are there any bills upon him now running, and how soon will they become due?

In the discount of bills it is necessary to guard against forgeries. It has happened that parties carrying on a great business in London, have presented to their banker, for discount, bills drawn upon all parts of the country; which bills, upon inquiry, have turned out to be purely fictitious. This is an additional reason for bankers making inquiry about the accepters of the bills they discount, even when they think they have reason to be satisfied with the drawers. Even this is no protection against forgery. Sometimes the name of a most respectable house in a provincial town has been forged. Where the amount is large, therefore, it seems advisable to send the bill down to some banker in the town, and ask his opinion as to the genuineness of the signature. Of course in these, and many other cases in which a banker is liable to be cheated, much must depend upon personal discretion; no rules can be given for all cases.

To facilitate the detection of forged CHEQUES, it is advisable that the banker should have a printed number placed on every cheque, in every cheque-book, and keep a record of the name of the customer to whom each book is given. When a cheque with a forged signature appears, the banker can then turn to this registry, and see to which of his customers he had given out this cheque. This plan has been found useful in tracing forgeries that have been perpetrated by the clerks or servants of the party keeping the account. Some bankers, moreover, place on their cheque-books a printed label, requesting the customer at all times to keep the book under his own lock and key.

To guard against forgery in the case of DEEDS or BONDS, all these documents should be witnessed by an officer of the bank. And when a letter of guarantee is given by a third party, it should not be taken by the banker from the party in whose favour it is given, but the letter should be signed at the bank, and the signature witnessed by one of the clerks. A banker is also liable to loss from the alteration of cheques. The words six, seven, eight, and nine, can easily be changed, by the addition of y, or ty, into sixty, seventy, eighty, or ninety. Sometimes, too, when cheques are drawn for less than £10, if a space be left open before the word, another word may be introduced. Thus, a short time ago a cheque was drawn on a banker for £3, and the party who obtained it wrote the word sixty before the word three, and thus cheated the banker out of £60. Letters of credit, as well as cheques, have heretofore been altered, by the original sum being taken out, and a larger sum being substituted. This is now prevented by staining the paper with a chemical preparation. Country banks also stamp upon their drafts the words "under ten pounds," "under twenty pounds," and so on, to prevent an alteration to any sum beyond those amounts.

The re-discounting of bills of exchange is an operation of much importance, and has a great influence on the monetary operations of the country. We quote from a former work of our own upon this subject:—

"Banks situated in agricultural districts have usually more money than they can employ. Independently of the paid-up capital of the bank, the sums raised by circulation and deposits are usually more than the amount of their loans and discounts. Banks, on the other hand, that are situated in manufacturing districts, can usually employ more money than they can raise. Hence, the bank that has a superabundance of money, sends it to London, to be employed by the bill-brokers, usually receiving, in return, bills of exchange. The bank that wants money sends its bills of exchange to London, to be re-discounted. These banks thus supply each other's wants, through the medium of the London bill-brokers."

But this principle of the re-discount of bills has been, in some cases, grossly abused, by being employed to give a sort of vitality to dead loans. A country banker lends upon mills and manufactories a larger amount of money than he can conveniently spare; then he asks the manufacturer to accept a bill for the amount, which the banker gets discounted in London or elsewhere. This bill, when due, is renewed, and the renewal is again replaced by another, and so the game goes on. As long as money is abundant all parties are pleased; the manufacturer gets his advance, the banker gets his commission, and the London bill-broker gets employment for his funds. But a pressure comes. The London bill-broker can discount no more, because the funds placed in his hands by his depositors have been withdrawn. The banker cannot get the new bills discounted elsewhere, and is unable to take up the old bills that are returned to him with his endorsement. The manufacturer, of course, cannot pay the money; the banker stops payment, and the manufacturer is ruined. The places at which this system has been chiefly carried on, are Manchester and Newcastle-upon-Tyne; and it is in these places that the greatest failures have taken place among the joint-stock banks. In fact, I believe it must be confessed, that the joint-stock banks have carried on this practice to a much greater extent than it was ever carried on by the private bankers. This has arisen from the greater credit which they possessed: it is one of the forms of the abuse of credit.

A London banker is always anxious to avoid dead loans. Loans are usually specific advances for specified times, either with or without security. In London, advances are generally made by loans; in the country, by overdrafts. The difference arises from the different modes of conducting an account. In London, the banker is paid by the balance standing to the credit of the account. A customer who wants an advance, takes a loan of such an amount as shall not require him to keep less than his usual balance. The loan is placed to the credit of his current account, until the time arrives for its repayment, and then he is debited for the principal and the interest. The country banker is paid by a commission, and hence the advance to a customer is made by his overdrawing the account, and he is charged interest only on the amount overdrawn.

Loans are divided into short loans and dead loans. Short loans are usually the practice of the London bankers: a time is fixed for their repayment. Dead loans are those for the payment of which there is no specified time; or where the party has failed to make the repayment at the time agreed upon. In this case, too, the loan has usually been made upon *dead*—that is, upon inconvertible security. Without great caution on the part of the banker, *short* loans are very apt to become *dead* loans. A loan is first made for two or three months; the time arrives, and the customer cannot pay; then the loan is renewed, and renewed, and renewed, and ultimately the customer fails, and the banker has to fall back upon his securities. The difference between *short* loans and *dead* loans may be illustrated by a reference to Liverpool and Manchester. The Liverpool bankers make large advances by way of loan, but usually on the security of cotton. The cotton is sold in a few months, and the banker is paid. At Manchester, the banker advances his loans on the security of mills and manufactories; he cannot get repaid; and after a while the customer fails, and the mill or manufactory, when sold, may not produce half the amount of the loan.

Dead loans are sometimes produced by lending money to rich men. A man of moderate means will be anxious not to borrow of his banker a loan which he will not be able punctually to repay, as the good opinion of his banker is necessary to his credit. But a man of property has no scruples of the kind: he has to build a house, to improve his estate, or to extend his manufactory; and he is unreasonable enough to expect that his banker will supply him with the necessary funds. He believes it will be only a temporary advance, as he will shortly be in possession of ample means. The banker lends the sum at first desired; more money is wanted; the expected supplies do not arrive; and the advance becomes a dead lock-up of capital. The loan may be very safe, and yield a good rate of interest, but the banker would rather have the money under his own control.

Dead loans are sometimes produced by lending money to parties to buy shares in public companies. There was too much business of this kind transacted by some bankers a few years ago. The party did not at first, perchance, apply to his banker to enable him to purchase the shares; but the calls were heavy, and his ready money was gone; he felt assured, however, that in a short time he should be able to sell his shares at a high profit; he persuaded his banker to pay the calls, taking the shares as security. Other calls were made, which the banker had to pay. The market fell; and the shares, if sold, would not pay the banker's advances. The sale, too, would have caused an enormous loss to the customer. The advances became a dead loan, and the banker had to wait till a favourable opportunity occurred for realizing his security.

In this, and in other ways, a banker has often much difficulty with customers of a speculative character. If he refuses what they ask, they remove their account, and give him a bad name; if he grants them their desires, they engage in speculations by which they are ruined, and probably the banker sustains loss. The point for the banker to decide is, whether he will lose them or ruin them. It is best in this case, for the banker to fix upon what advance he should make them, supposing they conduct their affairs prudently; and if they are dissatisfied with this, he had better let them go; after they have become bankrupts he will get credit for his sagacity.

The discounting of bills is an ordinary matter of business, and the banker has only to see that he has good names to his bill; but in regard to loans, a banker would do well to follow the advice which Mr. Taylor gives to individuals, and not to make a loan, unless he knows the purpose for which it is borrowed, and to form his own judgment as to the wisdom of the party who borrows, and as to the probability of his having the means of repayment at the time agreed upon.[1]

Sometimes, when an advance of money is wanted for two or three months, the party gives a note of hand. This is better than a mere loan, as it fixes the time of payment, and keeps the transaction fresh in the recollection of the borrower. But care must be taken that the note, by repeated renewals, does not in fact become a dead loan. Hence, when a renewal cannot be avoided, attempts should be made to reduce the amount. When public companies, of only a short standing, and not fully constituted, wish to borrow money of their banker, it is sometimes expedient to take the joint and several promissory note of the directors. By this means the banker avoids all knotty questions connected with the law of partnership; and the directors will, for their own sakes, see that the funds of

---

[1] *Vide* "Notes from Life," by Taylor.

the company shall, in due time, be rendered available for the repayment of the loan.

We have said that dead loans are usually advanced upon inconvertible security. Sometimes that security consists of a deposit of deeds relating to leasehold or freehold property. In London, however, this kind of security is not considered desirable, and the following rules are usually observed:—

No advances are made upon the security of deeds alone; they are taken only as collateral security; and then only to cover business transactions, and in cases where the parties are supposed to be safe independently of deeds.

The value of the property should be much higher than the sum it is intended to guarantee. When this is the case, and the parties fail, their creditors may take the deeds, and pay the debt due to the bank. The main use of taking deeds is to have something to fall back upon in this way. A customer should never receive more accommodation from having deposited his deeds than that to which he is legitimately entitled. No banker takes deeds if there is the slightest probability of his being compelled to realize the property, as the legal difficulties are very great.

In all cases in which deeds are taken, they are submitted to the inspection of the banker's solicitor, who makes a written report upon the value of the property, as far as it can be discovered by the deeds, and upon its legal validity as a security to the bank.

The rule of a banker is, never to make any advances, directly or indirectly, upon deeds, or any other *dead* security. But this rule, like all other general rules, must have exceptions, and when it is proper to make an exception is a matter that must be left to the discretion of the banker. He should, however, exercise this discretion with caution and prudence, and not deviate from the rule without a special reason to justify such deviation.

Among country bankers, in agricultural districts, advances upon deeds are not considered so objectionable as in London. A landed proprietor, who wants a temporary advance, places his deeds in the hands of his banker, and takes what he requires. The banker thinks he can have no better security; but the loan is usually for only a moderate amount, and is paid off within a reasonable time. In the country the character and circumstances of every man are known. A landlord who wants an advance to meet immediate demands, until his rents come in, seems fairly entitled to assistance from his banker. But should a landlord who is living beyond his income, ask for an advance almost equal to the value of his deeds, he would not be likely to obtain it.

Another kind of security is bills of lading, and dock warrants. Advances upon securities such as these must be considered as beyond the rules which prudent bankers lay down for their own government; they can only be justified by the special circumstances of each case. In advancing upon bills of lading, the banker must see that he has *all the bills of the set;* for if he has not *all*, the holder of the absent bill may get possession of the property. It is also necessary that he should have the policy of assurance, that, in case the ship be lost, he may claim the value from the insurers. In advances upon dock warrants, the banker should know that the value of the goods is equal to his advances, and will also give him a margin, as a security against any fall in the market price. But, in truth, no banker should readily make advances upon such securities. Now and then he may take them as collateral security, for an advance to a customer who is otherwise respectable. But if a customer requires such advances frequently, not to say constantly, it shows that he is conducting his business in a way that will not ultimately be either for his own advantage, or that of his banker.

A banker should never make any advances upon life policies. They may become void, should the party commit suicide, or die by the hand of justice, or in a duel; or if he go without permission to certain foreign countries. The payment may be disputed, upon the ground that some deception or concealment was practised, when the policy was obtained. And, in all cases, they are dependent upon the continued payment of the premiums. The value of a policy, too, is also often overrated. The insured fancies that his policy increases in value in exact proportion to the number of premiums he has paid; but if he offers it to the company, he will find that he gets much less than he expected. The policy is valued in a way that remunerates the office for the risk they have run during the years that are past; and the valuation has a reference only to the future.[1]

There are certain signs of approaching failure, which a banker must observe with reference to his customer. Thus—if he keeps a worse account than heretofore, and yet wants larger discounts—if the bills offered for discount are drawn upon an inferior class of people—if, when his bills are unpaid, he does not take them up promptly—if he pays his money late in the day, just in time to prevent his bills or cheques being returned through the clearing; but, above all, if he is found cross-firing: that is, drawing bills upon parties who at the same time draw bills upon him; as soon as a banker detects a customer in fair credit engaged in this practice, he should quietly give him reason for removing his account.

[1] The surrender value of a life policy in ordinary cases is roughly about one-third of the amount of premiums paid.

Sometimes two parties, who keep different bankers, will adopt a practice of exchanging cheques. Their cheques are paid into the banks too late to be cleared on the same day; and hence the parties' accounts appear better the next day than they otherwise would be. Some failing parties, too, have recourse to forged or fictitious bills, which they put into circulation to a large amount. The best way for a banker to guard against loss from this practice is, to inquire in all cases about the accepters of the bills that he discounts, not only when his customers are doubtful, but even when they are deemed respectable. Indeed, it is only people in good credit that can pass fictitious bills.

The banker's rule is, that they who have discounts must keep a proportionate balance: this is useful, as the amount of balance kept is an indication of the circumstances of the party. When a customer has heavy discounts, and keeps but a small balance, it may usually be inferred that he is either embarrassed in his affairs, or he is trading beyond his capital.

The operation which is called "nursing an account," sometimes requires considerable prudence, tact, and perseverance. A banker having made considerable advances to a customer, suddenly discovers that the party is not worthy of the confidence he has placed in him. If these advances should be called up, or discontinued, the customer will break, and the banker sustain loss. The banker must be governed by the circumstances of each case. It is sometimes best to continue to discount the good bills, and refuse those of a different character; and thus gradually weed the account of all the inferior securities. Sometimes he may get the customer to stipulate that he will diminish his advances by certain fixed amounts, at certain periods; and thus, by alternately refusing and complying, the banker may at length place himself in a state of security. At other times, the banker may offer to make still further advances, on condition of receiving good security also for what has been already advanced. This plan is advisable when the additional advance is not proportionably large, and the security is not inconvertible, otherwise the plan is sometimes a hazardous one. It requires some courage to look a loss in the face. And it has occurred that a banker, rather than sustain a small loss, will consent to make a further large advance upon inconvertible security; and the locking up of this large advance for an indefinite period has proved the greater evil of the two. In fact, some of the largest losses of fallen banks have been made in this way. They have, in the first instance, made an imprudent advance; rather than sustain this loss at once, they have made a further advance, with a view to prevent it. The advance has at last become so large, that if the customer falls, the bank must fall too; for the sake of self-existence, further advances are then made; these too are found ineffectual, and ultimately the customer and the bank fall together.[1]

---

[1] The evil effects of the weakness here alluded to have been very forcibly emphasized by the failures of the City of Glasgow Bank and the West of England Bank in 1878, both disasters having been brought about by the pernicious habit of "nursing" irredeemably bad debts.

SECTION XIX.

THE ADMINISTRATION OF A BANK WITH REGARD TO PROCEEDINGS ON BILLS OF EXCHANGE.

WHEN a banker has discounted a bill, it is handed to the accountant, who will see that it is drawn on a right stamp. The accountant will read it through, and see that it is properly drawn, and will observe that the sum in writing corresponds with the sum expressed in figures, and that no alteration has taken place in the amount, the date, the term, or the place at which it is made payable; for these are *material* alterations, and would affect the validity of the bill. He will then calculate the time at which it falls due, and place this date upon the bill, or, if it was there before, he will check it, and see that it is right. He will then turn it over, and see that it is indorsed by the party in whose favour it is drawn, and also that the subsequent indorsements are regular and properly spelled; for if there be a variation of a single letter in the spelling of a name, the payment of the bill could not be legally enforced. He will also observe that the bill is indorsed by the party for whom it is discounted. He will then pass the bill through the books, and at the close of the day deliver it with the others to the banker. The banker will, on the following morning, put these bills away in his bill-case according to the dates at which they fall due. This point should be recollected by persons who have to get bills from a banker before they are due; for, after they have given the amount and the names, the next question asked them will be,

"When is it due?" for among a multitude of bills, the only way of readily finding any individual bill is to turn to those that fall due on the same day. Every day the banker looks out the bills that fall due on the following day, and hands them to the chief clerk (or, in some cases, the chief clerk himself has the charge of the bills), who, after checking them against the books, distributes them among the clerks who are to collect them. If the bill be not paid, it is noted on the same evening, and on the following morning returned to the customer for whom it was discounted, and his account is debited for the amount. But if the party has not the sum to his credit, and the banker does not like to trust him, he merely receives notice of its dishonour; and notice is also given to every other party to the bill, with a demand for immediate payment. The bill has now become that hated object, a "past due bill;" and after a while, if the parties are supposed to be "worth powder and shot," it is handed to the bank's solicitor.

I shall give a short description of Bills of Exchange, and notice a few of those points of law and of business which are of most importance to practical bankers.

A bill of exchange is a written order from one person to another, directing him to pay a sum of money either to the drawer or to a third person at a future time. This is usually a certain number of days, weeks, or months, either after the date of the bill, or after sight; that is, after the person on whom it is drawn shall have *seen* it, and shall have written on the bill his willingness to pay it. The party expresses this willingness by writing on the bill the word "*accepted*," and his name.[1] If the bill be drawn after sight, he also writes the date of the acceptance.

[1] [A common practice having grown up, especially in Scotland, in the acceptance of bills, whereby an accepter simply signed his name across

If the party in whose favour the bill is drawn wishes to transfer it, he writes his name on the back. This is called an *indorsement;* and may be either special or general. A special indorsement is made to a particular party; as, "Pay to Messrs. John Doe & Co. or order." A general, or blank indorsement, is when the person merely writes his name. It is held by the lawyers[1] that a special indorsement cannot *follow* a general indorsement, and that in such a case the holder may sustain an action for the amount though the bill be not endorsed by the party to whom it is thus specially assigned. In practice, however, this is very common; and bankers always refuse to pay bills not properly endorsed, even though previous indorsements may be general. But, in regard to post bills, the Bank of England pays no regard to any special indorsement that may follow a general indorsement.

The following is the form of a Bill of Exchange:—

£1000.   London, 1st of May, 1827.

Two months after date, pay to the order of Messrs. Quick, Active, and Co. (or me or my order) the sum of One Thousand Pounds, for value received.

Hearty, Jolly, & Co.

To Messrs. John Careful & Co.
Southwark.

Accepted, payable at
Messrs. Steady & Co., Bankers.
John Careful & Co.

---

the face of the bill without prefixing the word "accepted," and a County Court Judge in the North of England having held that a bill so accepted did not bind the drawee, a declaratory Act was passed on 28th March, 1878 (41 and 42 Vict. c. 13), which declared that "an acceptance of a bill of exchange is not and shall not be deemed to be insufficient by reason only that such acceptance consists merely of the signature of the drawee written on such bill."]

[1] If a bill be once indorsed in blank, though afterwards indorsed in full, it will still as against the drawer, the payee, the accepter, the blank

A Promissory Note is as follows:—

£1000.   London, 1st of May, 1827.

Two months after date, we promise to pay Messrs. Hearty, Jolly, & Co., or their order, the sum of One Thousand Pounds, for value received.

John Careful & Co.

At Messrs. Steady & Co.,
    Bankers,
    Lombard Street.

The acceptance is usually written across a bill, but should always be on the front, not on the back of the bill. An indorsement, as the name implies, should be placed on the back.

The person who draws a bill is called the drawer; the person on whom it is drawn is called the drawee: after the bill is accepted the drawee is called the accepter. The person who indorses a bill is called the indorser; the person to whom it is indorsed is the indorsee. The person who pays a bill is the payer; the person to whom it is paid is the payee. These and similar terms may be illustrated by a circumstance said to have occurred on the cross-examination of a witness, on a trial respecting a mortgage.—*Counsellor.* "Now, sir, you are a witness in this case; pray do you know the difference between the mortgager and the mortgagee?"—*Witness.* "To be sure I do. For instance, now suppose I nod at you, I am the nod-er, and you are the nod-ee." The word discountee, denoting the person for whom a bill is discounted, is not used in England, but I observe in the parliamentary evidence that it was employed by some of the witnesses from Scotland.

All bills, except those payable on demand or at sight, indorser, and all indorsers before him, be payable to bearer, though as against the special indorser himself title must be made through his indorsee.—*Serjeant Byles on Bills of Exchange,* p. 115.

are allowed three days' grace. Thus, a bill drawn at two months from the 1st of May, will fall due on the 4th of July; but if that day be a Sunday, or a public holiday,[1] the bill will be due on the day before. Some bills, instead of being drawn after date or sight, state the time of payment, as "On the first of August pay, &c." These bills are allowed the usual three days of grace. Such a bill would fall due on the 4th of August.

[1] To remove all doubts upon this subject, an Act of Parliament was passed (7th and 8th Geo. IV. chap. 15), which enacts "that from and after the tenth day of April, one thousand eight hundred and twenty-seven, Good Friday and Christmas-day, and every day of fast or thanksgiving appointed by his Majesty, is and shall for all purposes whatever, as regards bills of exchange and promissory notes, be treated and considered as the Lord's-day, commonly called Sunday." This Act does not extend to Scotland, but it has since been extended to Ireland. This Act does not vitiate a bill *dated* on a Sunday.

[The law relating to the day on which bills falling due on any public holiday shall be payable was affected by Act 34 Vict. c. 17 (25th May, 1871), introduced by Sir John Lubbock. This Act enacts that in England and Ireland, Easter Monday, the Monday in Whitsun week, the first Monday in August, and the twenty-sixth day of December, if a week day, should be kept as close holidays, and that all bills falling due on these days should be payable on the next following day: and similarly in Scotland, New Year's Day, Christmas Day, Good Friday, the first Monday of May, and the first Monday of August should be kept as close holidays, and bills falling due thereon should be payable next day. But if either New Year's Day or Christmas Day happens to fall on a Sunday, the Act enacts that the following Monday shall be the statutory bank holiday.

As regards England and Ireland, Good Friday and Christmas Day being already bank holidays as explained above, no reference is made to these days in this Act. Bills falling due on these days, therefore, in England and Ireland are payable on the previous day, and in Scotland on the following day.

The effect of the passing of this Act was to give several additional legalized holidays to the banking community, for which that community—and indeed the public generally, for these holidays are now almost universally observed—are indebted to Sir John Lubbock.]

Some parties, when they indorse a bill, write at bottom, "In case of need, apply to Messrs. C. D. & Co." That is, if the bill be not paid when due, Messrs. C. D. & Co. will on the day after it is due pay it for the honour of the indorsers. The notaries always observe the "cases of need" upon the bills that come into their hands, and apply to the proper parties. The advantage of placing a case of need upon a bill is, that the party endorsing it receives it back sooner in case of non-payment. It also makes the bill more respectable, and secures its circulation.

Were it not for the space it occupies, it would be very desirable that the indorser of a bill of exchange should be compelled to state also his address. This would prevent forged and fictitious indorsements, and give a banker who discounts a bill, a better opportunity of ascertaining the respectability of the parties. In case, too, the bill was unpaid, he might immediately apply to all the indorsers, whereas now he has to find them out in the best way he can. The indorsers and drawer of a bill would have earlier notice of its non-payment, and have a better opportunity of obtaining their money from the antecedent parties.

Bills are divided into Inland and Foreign. Inland bills are those in which both the drawer and the accepter reside in the British Islands.[1] If a foreign bill be refused acceptance or payment, it should be immediately protested and returned. An inland bill is only noted, and then only when refused payment. A foreign bill may be accepted verbally, or by letter; but no acceptance of an inland bill is valid, unless written upon the bill itself.[2]

When a merchant in one country draws bills upon a merchant residing in another country, he usually draws them

---

[1] For stamp duty, bills drawn from the Isle of Man and the Channel Islands are regarded as foreign bills, and they must bear foreign bill stamps.   [2] See 1 and 2 Geo. IV. cap. 78.

in sets: that is, he draws two, three, or more bills of the same tenor and date. These bills are sent to his correspondent by different ships. Thus he secures the swiftest conveyance, and his remittances will not be delayed by any accident that may happen to an individual ship. In drawing these bills, it is always expressly stated whether each bill be the first, second, or third of a set; as, "Pay this my *first* of exchange (the second and third not being paid)." On the payment of any one bill, the others are of no value. If a merchant, say at Paris, has a set of bills drawn on a merchant at London, he will sometimes send over the first bill to his correspondent in London, to get it accepted, and to retain it until claimed by the holder of the second. The merchant at Paris will then write on the second bill, that the first lies accepted at such a house in London. He will then sell it or pay it away. By this means he is sure that the bill he negotiates will not be returned to him, and greater value is given to his bill, not only as it has the additional security of the accepter's name, but, if it be drawn after sight, it will become due so much the sooner. When the second bill arrives in London, the holder takes it to the house where the first is deposited, and it is immediately given up to him.

Foreign bills are often drawn at a "usance" after date. A usance from Amsterdam, Rotterdam, Hamburgh, or any place in Germany, is one month; from France, thirty days; from Spain and Portugal, two months; from Sweden, seventy-five days; from Italy, three months. Where it is necessary to divide a month upon a half usance, which is the case when the usance is either one month or three, the half month is always fifteen days. Bills drawn from Russia are dated according to the old style, and twelve days must be added to the date, in order to ascertain at what time they fall due.

A bill is sometimes accepted *for the honour* of the drawer, or of one of the indorsers. Thus, if a bill from Hamburgh be drawn upon a person in London, who refuses to accept it, another party, knowing the drawer or one of the indorsers to be a respectable man, may accept the bill himself, for the honour of the party with whom he is acquainted. By this means he prevents the bill being returned with expenses. This kind of acceptance renders him liable to pay the bill on the day after it is due, but he can afterwards recover the amount from the party for whose honour he had accepted it, and, of course, from all preceding parties. But, to secure himself, he must not accept the bill until after it has been protested for non-acceptance, and he must write, "Accepted for the honour of A. B. & Co.," upon the face of the bill. And when the bill is due, he must not pay it, until it has been presented for payment to the drawee.

Bills accepted, and made payable at a banking-house, in the usual manner, without the addition of the word ONLY, may be presented either at the banking-house, or at the residence of the accepter. In either case, it is a legal presentment,[1] as far as regards the accepter. In practice, however, bills are always presented at the place where they are made payable. If a bill be addressed to a banking-house or any other place ONLY, the payment cannot be enforced until it has been presented at that place. If any particular place of payment be mentioned in the body of a promissory note, it must be presented there.

When bankers receive any unaccepted bills, they send them out for acceptance, if they have four days to run. They are left at the house of the drawee, and are called for on the following day. On the day the bills are due, the tellers present them in the morning, at the place where

---

[1] 1 and 2 Geo. IV. cap. 78.

they are made payable. If not paid when presented, they leave a printed notice or direction, of which the following is a copy :—

Bill for £
Drawn by Mr.
On Mr.
Lies due at Messrs. Steady & Co.,
   No. Lombard Street.

Please call between Two and Four o'clock.

If not paid by five o'clock, the bill is sent to the notary's. It is brought to the banking-house the following morning, with the notary's ticket attached to it, stating the reason why it is not paid. The bill is then returned to the customer. If it be a foreign bill, that is, drawn from any foreign land, it must be protested. Foreign bills are also protested for non-acceptance; but inland bills are not, nor even noted, but the party who remitted the bill to the banking-house is advised of the circumstance.

The following is the form of a Draft or Cheque:—

No. 457.   *London, May 1, 1827.*
  Messrs. Hope, Rich, & Co., Lombard Street.
 Pay John Doe, Esq., or bearer, the sum of One Hundred Pounds.
£100.   *Peter Thrifty & Co.*

A bill given for an illegal consideration cannot be enforced by the drawer, but it may be enforced by an innocent holder who had no knowledge of the illegal consideration, and who received the bill before it was due. The principal illegal considerations are those arising from usury, gambling, and smuggling. But by the Act 17 and 18 Vic. c. 90, passed in the year 1854, the laws of usury are abolished.

The following are the Tables of Stamp Duties upon Bills of Exchange, corrected down to, and including 33 and 34 Vic. cap. 97, 1870.

	s.	d.
SECT. 47. *Bill of Exchange*, payable on demand	0	1

Bill of Exchange of any other kind whatsoever (*except a Bank Note*) and *Promissory Note* of any kind whatsoever (*except a Bank Note*)—drawn, or expressed to be payable, or actually paid or indorsed, or in any manner negotiated *in* the United Kingdom:

	s.	d.
Where the amount or value of the money for which the bill or note is drawn or made does not exceed £5.	0	1
Exceeds £5 and does not exceed £10.	0	2
„ £10 „ £25.	0	3
„ £25 „ £50.	0	6
„ £50 „ £75.	0	9
„ £75 „ £100.	1	0
„ £100 for every £100, and also for any fractional part of £100, of such amount or value	1	0

Exemptions.

Bill or note issued by the Governor and Company of the Bank of England or Bank of Ireland.

Draft or order drawn by any banker in the United Kingdom upon any other banker in the United Kingdom, not payable to bearer or to order, and used solely for the purpose of settling or clearing any account between such bankers.

Letter written by a banker in the United Kingdom to any other banker in the United Kingdom, directing the payment of any sum of money, the same not being payable to bearer or order, and such letter not being sent or delivered to the person to whom payment is to be made, or to any person on his behalf.

Letter of credit granted in the United Kingdom authorizing drafts to be drawn out of the United Kingdom payable in the United Kingdom.

Government Drafts, Orders, and Bills.

Coupon or warrant for interest attached to and issued with any security.

SECT. 48. The term "bill of exchange" for the purposes of this Act includes also draft, order, cheque, and letter of credit, and any document or writing (*except a bank note*) entitling or purporting to entitle any person, whether named therein or not, to payment by any other person of or to draw upon any other person for, any sum of money therein mentioned.

An order for the payment of any sum of money by a bill of exchange or promissory note, or for the delivery of any bill of exchange or promissory note in satisfaction of any sum of money, or for the payment of any sum of money out of any particular fund which may or may not be available, or upon any condition or contingency which may or may not be performed or happen, is to be deemed for the purposes of this Act a bill of exchange for the payment of money on demand.

An order for the payment of any sum of money weekly, monthly, or at any other stated periods, and also any order for the payment by any person at any time after the date thereof of any sum of money, and sent or delivered by the person making the same to the person by whom the payment is to be made, and not to the person to whom the payment is to be made, or to any person on his behalf, is to be deemed for the purposes of this Act a bill of exchange for the payment of money on demand.

SECT. 49. The term "promissory note" means and includes any document or writing (*except a bank note*) containing a promise to pay any sum of money.

A note promising the payment of any sum of money out of any particular fund which may or may not be available, or upon any condition or contingency which may or may not be performed or happen, is to be deemed for the purposes of this Act a promissory note for the said sum of money.

SECT. 50. The fixed duty of one penny on a bill of exchange for the payment of money on demand may be denoted by an adhesive stamp, which is to be cancelled by the person by whom the bill is signed before he delivers it out of his hands, custody, or power.

SECT. 51. The *ad valorem* duties upon bills of exchange and promissory notes drawn or made *out* of the United Kingdom are to be denoted by adhesive stamps.

Every person into whose hands any such bill or note comes in the United Kingdom before it is stamped shall, before he presents for payment, or indorses, transfers, or in any manner negotiates, or pays such bill or note, affix thereto a proper adhesive stamp or proper adhesive stamps of sufficient amount, and cancel every stamp so affixed thereto.

Provided as follows:

> If at the time when any such bill or note comes into the hands of any *bonâ fide* holder thereof there is affixed thereunto an adhesive stamp effectually obliterated, and purporting and appearing to be duly cancelled, such stamp shall, so far as relates to such holder, be deemed to be duly cancelled, although it may not appear to have been so affixed or cancelled by the proper person.

If at the time when any such bill or note comes into the hands of any *bonâ fide* holder thereof there is affixed thereto an adhesive stamp not duly cancelled, it shall be competent for such holder to cancel such stamp as if he were the person by whom it was affixed, and upon his so doing such bill or note shall be deemed duly stamped, and as valid and available as if the stamp had been duly cancelled by the person by whom it was affixed.

But neither of the foregoing provisoes is to relieve any person from any penalty incurred by him for not cancelling any adhesive stamp.

SECT. 52. A bill of exchange or promissory note purporting to be drawn or made *out* of the United Kingdom is, for the purposes of this Act, to be deemed to have been so drawn or made, although it may in fact have been drawn or made *within* the United Kingdom.

SECT. 53. Where a bill of exchange or promissory note has been written on material bearing an impressed stamp of sufficient amount but of improper denomination, it may be stamped with the proper stamp on payment of the duty, and a penalty of forty shillings if the bill or note be not then payable according to its tenor, and of ten pounds if the same be so payable.

Except as aforesaid, no bill of exchange or promissory note shall be stamped with an impressed stamp after the execution thereof.

SECT. 54. Every person who issues, indorses, transfers, negotiates, presents for payment, or pays any bill of exchange or promissory note liable to duty and not being duly stamped shall forfeit the sum of ten pounds, and the person who takes or receives from any other person any such bill or note not being duly stamped either in payment or as a security, or by purchase or otherwise, shall not be entitled to recover thereon, or to make the same available for any purpose whatever.

Provided that if any bill of exchange for the payment of money on demand, liable only to the duty of one penny, is presented for payment unstamped, the person to whom it is so presented may affix thereunto a proper adhesive stamp, and cancel the same, as if he had been the drawer of the bill, and may, upon so doing, pay the sum in the said bill mentioned, and charge the duty in account against the person by whom the bill was drawn, or deduct such duty from the said sum, and such bill is, so far as respects the duty, to be deemed good and valid.

But the foregoing proviso is not to relieve any person from any penalty he may have incurred in relation to such bill.

Sect. 55. When a bill of exchange is drawn in a set according to the custom of merchants, and one of the set is duly stamped, the other or others of the set shall, unless issued or in some manner negotiated apart from such duly stamped bill, be exempt from duty; and upon proof of the loss or destruction of a duly stamped bill forming one of a set, any other bill of the set which has not been issued or in any manner negotiated apart from such lost or destroyed bill may, although unstamped, be admitted in evidence to prove the contents of such lost or destroyed bill.

Prior to the passing of the 33 and 34 Vict. c. 93 (the Married Woman's Property Act, 1870), if a woman accepted a bill and married before it became due, her husband could be sued for the amount, but she could not; but by the above Act this is not so now, for that statute (sec. 12), enacts that "a husband shall not by reason of any marriage which shall take place after this Act has come into operation, be liable for the debts of his wife contracted before marriage, but the wife shall be liable to be sued, and any property belonging to her for her separate use, shall be liable to satisfy such debts as if she had continued unmarried." If a bill be indorsed to a woman, who afterwards marries, her husband must indorse the bill, unless she indorses it as the agent and by the authority of her husband. Should she have occasion to sue any of the antecedent parties to a bill, the action may be brought in the name of the husband, where the bill is drawn to "order," otherwise it must be brought in the joint names of the husband and the wife. If a woman who is actually married accepts a bill by and with the authority of her husband, the acceptance is binding on the husband; but if she accepts a bill without his authority, he cannot be legally compelled to pay it, unless it were given for articles necessary to her support.

A person under twenty-one years of age, whether acceptor, drawer, or indorser of a bill of exchange, cannot be sued at law, except the bill be drawn upon him for necessaries; but if he draw a bill, and transfer it to a third person, the third party may sue the accepter. The term "necessaries" is generally considered to include not only those things which are essential to existence, but those also which are suitable to the rank of the party. Many articles are considered necessary to the son of a nobleman which would not be necessary to a man of an inferior station in society.

If the drawee refuse to accept a bill, the holder may immediately bring an action for the amount against all the other parties, without waiting until the bill becomes due. And should the word "at" be written before the name of the drawee, it makes no difference, especially if it be written in such a manner as if designed to escape observation. But it is the practice of the London bankers to hold bills refused acceptance, and merely give notice of the circumstance to the party who sent it to the bank. If, however, it be an inland bill, drawn after sight, the bill is noted for non-acceptance. If it be a foreign bill, it is protested, and the protest sent to the last indorser. If the bill be not paid when due, it is then protested for nonpayment, and with the second protest returned to the last indorser. When a bill is drawn after sight, the day on which it is noted or protested for non-acceptance is regarded as the day on which the drawee has sent it, and the time on which it will become due is calculated accordingly.

If the accepter, drawer, and all the indorsers to a bill become bankrupts, the holder may prove for the full amount under each commission, and receive a dividend under each, provided he do not receive altogether more than 20s. in the pound. But if he receive a dividend under one commission before proving under the others, he can only prove for the balance.

If a bill be lost, immediate notice should be given to the accepter, and to the bankers or other parties at whose house it may be made payable. If, after such notice, they pay the bill to any person who has not given value for it, they are accountable to the loser. But a person who has given value for a lost or stolen bill, to a thief, or to a finder, can recover the amount from all the parties in the same way as though he had received it in the course of business from the last indorser, provided the bill was not specially indorsed. But if it was specially indorsed, and the thief or finder should have forged the indorsement, the holder cannot recover the amount, even though he may have given value for the bill, but he must sustain the loss.

If a lost bill should have been specially indorsed, or if the loser can prove that the bill has been destroyed, he can bring an action against the accepter for the amount. But if he cannot prove that the bill is actually destroyed, and it was indorsed in blank, he cannot recover from the accepter. For it is possible that a finder may pass it for a valuable consideration to another party, who would thus be a *bonâ fide* holder, and might compel the accepter to pay him the amount. In this case, therefore, the loser has no redress in *law*, but he may apply to a court of equity, and *might* obtain an order upon the accepter to pay the amount of the lost bill upon receiving a satisfactory indemnity. The loser of a bill should cause payment to be demanded from the accepter the day it falls due, and give notice of dishonour to the drawer and indorsers, in the same way as though he had the bill in his possession.

A country banker gave change for a Bank of England note for £100 which had been stolen. It was done at the time of the races, and immediately on opening the bank. The party who brought it stated he had some bets to pay at the racecourse, and gave a fictitious address, which was written on the note. The loser of the note brought an action against the banker, and recovered the amount. The judge who tried the cause stated that in his opinion there had been laches, *i.e.*, neglect on the part of the bankers in not making further inquiry, and under his direction the jury returned a verdict for the plaintiff.

Referring to the above decision, Serjeant Byles observes:—

"But it is now definitely settled that if a man takes *honestly* an instrument made or become payable to bearer, he has a good title to it, with whatever degree of negligence he may have acted, unless his gross negligence induce the jury to find fraud."[1]

The following case was tried in the Court of Queen's Bench:—

[1] Byles on Bills of Exchange, page 126.

The question involved was the right of money-changers to take Bank of England notes in disregard of notices that they had been stolen. The action was brought by Messrs. Adam Spielmann and Co., of London, as correspondents of Messrs. Meyer Spielmann and Co., of Paris, to recover the amount of two Bank of England notes for £500 each, which had formed portions of notes, for the value in all of £3,000, stolen from Messrs. Brown, Shipley, and Co., of Liverpool. The notes were stolen in November, 1852, and it was proved that notices of the robbery were delivered at the places of business of both firms. One of the notes was alleged to have been received by Meyer Spielmann and Co., in Paris, from a person giving the name of G. F. Howard, and the other from A. Monteaux, a money-changer in Paris, which note also had the name of G. F. Howard upon it. Both notes were remitted by Messrs. Meyer Spielmann and Co. to Messrs. Adam Spielmann and Co., and received by them in London. On behalf of the plaintiff it was contended that, the notes having been taken in the ordinary course of business, he was entitled to recover upon them. Lord Campbell left to the jury the question whether Meyer Spielmann took the notes *bonâ fide* and for value; whether Adam Spielmann received them *bonâ fide* as a remittance; and whether the notices were left at the places of business of both parties. The jury found that Meyer Spielmann and Co. did not take the notes *bonâ fide* for value; that Adam Spielmann and Co. did take them *bonâ fide* as a remittance; and that the notices were duly received. Upon this finding, Lord Campbell directed a verdict to be entered for the Bank of England."

The Editor of the "Bankers' Magazine" observes:—

"It is hoped that this decision will have the effect of preventing the practice, which has become too common, of taking stolen notes, which cannot be passed in England, to the chief cities of Europe, and there obtaining the amount through money-changers, who afterwards claim the value from the Bank, on the ground that the notes have been taken in due course of business, although, in fact, no sufficient inquiry has been made as to the *bona fides* of the transaction, or the respectability of the parties presenting them."[1]

But in a similar action brought by Messrs. Raphael and Co. on the part of Messrs. St. Paul and Co., of Paris, against the Bank of England, for the amount of another of these stolen notes, the verdict was for the plaintiff. The following were the points on which the jury were directed to decide :—

"1. Was the money paid? 2. Were the notices served on St. Paul and Co.? 3. Did they know of, and had they the means of knowledge of the robbery at the time they discounted the note? The jury, after retiring for three-quarters of an hour, found, in answer to these questions: —1. That Messrs. St. Paul gave full value for the note. 2. That the notices were served. 3. That the notices were not taken proper care of, and that St. Paul had the means of knowledge if he had taken proper care of the notices, but that he did not know of the loss at the time; and, lastly, that the plaintiff took the note *bonâ fide*.

"Verdict for the plaintiff—£534. Execution to be stayed, but no points reserved."

Any material alteration of a bill of exchange vitiates the bill, and it cannot be legally enforced against any of the parties, unless the alteration be made before the bill be accepted, and also before it has passed out of the hands of the drawer.

Thus, if a bill be left for acceptance by the drawer, and the drawee alter the date, time, or the amount of bill,

[1] "Bankers' Magazine," March, 1855.

and then accept it, the alteration does not affect the validity of the bill: but if the bill be left for acceptance by a third party, and the drawee then alters and accepts the bill, the bill is vitiated. Any alteration in the date, sum, time, name of drawer or payee, or appointing a new place of payment, is a material alteration, and requires a new stamp. But any alteration made only with a view of correcting a mistake does not vitiate a bill, provided it be made with the concurrence of all the parties. If a drawee accepts a bill, and before he gives the bill out of his possession cancels his acceptance, he cannot be compelled to pay it.

A bill must be presented in *reasonable time*. But what is a *reasonable time* is a question of consideration for the jury, and the decision has varied according to circumstances. If a bill be presented at a banker's after the hour of business, the presentment is not in reasonable time. Nevertheless such a presentment is a legal presentment, if the banker or any person on his behalf should be there to give an answer to the party presenting it.

Cheques, and notes payable on demand, should also be presented for payment within a *reasonable time* after they are received. It has been held that a person who receives a cheque is not bound to present it at the banker's till the next morning; and if the bank was at a distance, he was not bound to put the cheque into the post-office until the next day. But, perhaps, it would not be safe to rely upon these decisions. No general rule can be given; for the time which may be *reasonable* in one case may be unreasonable in another.

If a banker receives a bill or note by post, he is not required to present it until the next day.

"A man taking a bill or note payable on demand, or a cheque, is not bound, laying aside all other business, to present or transmit it for payment the very first opportunity. It has long since been decided, in numerous cases, that, though the party by whom the bill or note is to be paid live in the same place, it is not necessary to present the instrument for payment till the morning next after the day on which it was received. And later cases have established, that the holder of a cheque has the whole of the banking hours of the next day within which to present it for payment." [1]

In the following case it was decided that the presentment of a bill of exchange at the Clearing-house is a legal presentment.

"On the 11th September, between one and two o'clock, the defendants gave the plaintiffs a cheque upon Bloxam and Co., the bankers, in payment for goods. The plaintiffs lodged the cheque with Messrs. Harrison, the bankers, a few minutes after four; and they presented it between five and six to Bloxam and Co., who marked it as good. It was proved to be the usage among London bankers not to pay any cheque presented by or on behalf of another banker after four o'clock, but merely to mark it if good, and pay it next day at the clearing-house. On the 12th at noon Harrison's clerk took this cheque to the clearing-house, but no person attended for Bloxam and Co., who stopped payment at nine on that morning, and the cheque was therefore treated as dishonoured. The plaintiffs, in going with the cheque to Harrison's, passed Bloxam's house. On a case stating these facts, the court held that there had been no laches in the plaintiffs, in not presenting the cheque to Bloxam and Co. on the 11th for payment, or in his bankers in not presenting it at the banking house, but merely at the clearing-house, and therefore gave judgment for the plaintiff." [2]

[1] Byles's Law of Bills of Exchange, page 123.
[2] Bayley on Bills of Exchange.

Bills may be negotiated after they are due, but the party receiving an over-due bill cannot acquire a claim which the party holding the bill did not possess. For instance, one party may draw an accommodation bill upon another. As in this case no value had been given, the drawer could not sue the accepter for the amount. But if the drawer had passed this bill *for value* to a third party *before it became due*, that party could sue the accepter. But if the drawer passed it to a third party even for value *after it became due*, the third party could not sue the accepter, but would stand in the same situation as the drawer.

If a party lodge bills with a banker for the purpose of being collected, and the amount when received to be placed to his credit, and the banker gets them discounted, and applies the money to his own use, the customer has no redress except against the banker. The party who has given value for the bills to the banker can enforce payment of them.

As the giving notice of the dishonour of a bill or cheque is of considerable practical importance, I shall make a few extracts upon the subject from Mr. Justice Bayley's treatise on Bills of Exchange :—

"Though no prescribed form be necessary for notice of the dishonour of a bill or note, it ought to import that the person to whom it is given is considered liable, and that payment from him is expected.

"And the notice ought to import that the bill or note has been dishonoured : a mere demand of payment and threat of law proceedings in case of non-payment is not sufficient.

"Especially if such demand be made on the day the bill or note becomes due.

"Notice must be given of a failure in the attempt to procure an acceptance, though the application for such acceptance might have been unnecessary ; otherwise the person guilty of the neglect may lose his remedy upon the bill.

"The notice must come from the holder, or from some party entitled to call for payment or reimbursement.

"A notice from the holder or any other party will insure to the benefit of every other party who stands between the person giving the notice, and the person to whom it is given. Therefore, a notice from the last indorsee to the drawer will operate as a notice from each indorsee.

"It is, nevertheless, prudent in each party who receives a notice, to give immediate notice to those parties against whom he may have right to claim; for the holder may have omitted notice to some of them, and that will be no protection, or there may be difficulties in proving such notice.

"A notice the day the bill or note becomes due is not too soon; for though payment may still be made within the day, non-payment on presentment is a dishonour.

"To such of the parties as reside in the place where the presentment was made, the notice must be given at the farthest by the expiration of the day following the refusal: to those who reside elsewhere, by the post of that or the next post day. Each party has a day for giving notice, and he is entitled to the whole day; at least, eight or nine o'clock at night is not too late. He will be entitled to the whole day, though the post by which he is to send it goes out within the day; and though there be no post the succeeding day for the place to which he is to send. Therefore, where the notice is to be sent by the post, it will be sufficient if it be sent by the post of the following day. Or, if there be no post the following day, the day after.

"Where a party receives notice on a Sunday, he is in the same situation as if it did not reach him till the Monday: he is not bound to pay it any attention till the Monday, and has the whole of Monday for the purpose. So, if the day on which notice ought thus to be given be a day of public rest, as Christmas-day or Good Friday, or any day appointed by proclamation for a solemn fast or thanksgiving, the notice need not be given until the following day.

"And it has been held that where a man is of a religion which gives to any other day of the week the sanctity of Sunday, as in the case of the Jews, he is entitled to the same indulgence as on that day.

" Where Christmas-day, or such day of fast or thanksgiving, shall be on a Monday, notice of the dishonour of bills or notes due or payable the Saturday preceding need not be given until the Tuesday.

"And Good Friday, Christmas-day, and any day of fast or thanksgiving, shall, from 10th April, 1827, as far as regards bills or notes, be treated and considered as Sunday.

" But these provisions do not apply to Scotland.

" If the holder of a bill or note place it in the hands of his banker, the banker is only bound to give notice of its dishonour to his customer, in like manner as if the banker were himself the holder, and his customer were the party next entitled to notice.

" And the customer has the like time to communicate such notice, as if he had received it from a holder.

"And therefore, by thus placing a bill or note in a banker's hands, the number of persons from whom notice must pass is increased by one.

" Thus notice sent by a London banker to a London customer, the day after the dishonour, is in time; and if the customer communicate that notice the day following, that will be in time also.

" It is no excuse for not giving notice the next day after a party receives one, that he received his notice earlier than the preceding parties were bound to give it; and that he gave notice within what would have been proper time if each preceding party had taken all the time the law allowed him. The time is to be calculated according to the period when the party in fact received his notice. Nor is it any excuse that there are several intervening parties between him who gives the notice, and defendant to whom it is given; and that if the notice had been communicated through these intervening parties, and each had taken the time the law allows, the defendant would not have had the notice sooner.

"Sending a verbal notice to a merchant's counting-house in the ordinary hours of business, at a time when he or some of his people might reasonably be expected to be there, is sufficient; it is not necessary to leave or to send a written notice, or to send to the house where he lives. Sending notice by the post is sufficient, though it be not received; and where there is no post, it is sufficient to send by the ordinary mode of conveyance.

"And it is not essential the notice should be sent by the post where there is one; sending to an agent by a private conveyance, that he may give the notice, is sufficient, if the agent give the notice, or take due steps for the purpose, without delay.

"Notice to one of several partners is notice to all: and when a bill has been drawn by a firm upon one of the partners, and by him accepted and dishonoured, it is unnecessary to give notice of such dishonour to the firm; for this must necessarily be known to one of them, and the knowledge of one is the knowledge of all.

"Upon an acceptance payable at a banker's, notice of non-payment need not be given to the accepter, for he makes the bankers his agents; presentment to them is presentment to him.

"A person who has been once discharged by laches from his liability on a bill or note, is always discharged. And, therefore, where two or more parties to a bill or note have been so discharged, but one of them, not knowing of the laches, pays it, he pays it in his own wrong, and cannot recover the money from another of such parties."

Formerly bills of exchange constituted a large proportion of the circulating medium of Lancashire, and supplied the place of country notes. The following account is given by J. Gladstone, Esq., M.P., before a Parliamentary Committee:—

"We sell our goods, not for payments in cash, such as are usual in other places, but generally at credits from ten days to three months, to be then paid for in bills on London at two or three months' dates; those bills we pay to our bankers, and receive from them bills or cash when we have occasion for either, to make our payments. The bank notes or gold we require for our ordinary purposes and charges of merchandise of every description. The account is kept floating. The interest on both sides is calculated at the same rate, at present five per cent. Last year the rate was reduced to four; and the banker charges a commission of a quarter per cent. on the amount of one side of the account; that charge is his remuneration, and that of his bankers in London, for paying our acceptances there, both inland and foreign. The account fluctuates, depending on the confidence the banker may have in his customers; if that confidence is entire, the customer is occasionally in his banker's debt, but more frequently the balance is in his favour.

"Does that extend to the whole of Lancashire?—I believe the system at Manchester, Preston, and the other principal towns, is similar; I am not aware of any other. There are some small country bankers in the neighbourhood of Manchester, who issue promissory notes, but I do not know anything of their practice: none of the more respectable banks in Lancashire do issue them."[1]

"If I sell a thousand pounds' worth of goods to a wholesale grocer, or any other person who again distributes them to his customers in the country, when he comes to pay me the £1,000, he will do so in bills, running from £10 to any other sum; the £1,000 may be paid in twenty or thirty bills of exchange, drawn on London, and generally at two and sometimes three months' date."[2]

Mr. Lewis Loyd, of the firm of Messrs. Jones, Loyd, and Co., estimated in 1826 that the circulation of Manchester consists of nine parts bills of exchange, and the tenth part gold and Bank of England notes. Others think the proportion is as high as twenty to one, or even fifty to one.[3] Mr. Loyd stated he had seen bills of £10 with 120 indorsements upon them; and when the stamp duties were lower, bills were drawn of a less amount. He gives the following *criteria* of accommodation bills: "Bills that are issued for speculation generally travel to London very rapidly, with very few indorsements upon them; they are wanted to be converted into bank notes immediately, and come quite clean, and without any marks of negotiation upon them; and besides that, we know the parties upon them pretty well." In Scotland an accommodation bill is called a wind bill.

It may be mentioned, that after the establishment of branches of the Bank of England at Manchester and Liverpool, the bill circulation of Lancashire was considerably diminished. Most of the banks made agreements with the branch Bank, stipulating that, in consideration of having a

---

[1] Lords, 216, Gladstone.   [2] Lords, 227, Gladstone.
[3] See Evidence of Lewis Loyd, Esq., and of Mr. Henry Burgess, before the Committee of the House of Lords, pp. 294, 298.

certain amount of discount at a reduced rate of interest, they would not issue for local circulation any bills they had discounted for their customers. These agreements have been modified since the Act of 1844, but still the main circulation of Lancashire consists of Bank of England notes. It would not now be possible to find a bill with 120 indorsements.

As many bills drawn in foreign languages pass through the hands of a London banker, it may be useful to give a list of some of those words which express the amount and the time, the two main points in a bill of exchange:—

English	One	Two	Three	Sixty	Ninety.
German	Ein	Zwei	Drei	Sechzig	Neunzig.
Dutch	Een	Twee	Drie	Zestig	Negentig.
French	Un	Deux	Trois	Soixante	Quatre-vingt-dix, *or* Nonante.
Italian	Uno	Due	Tre	Sessanta	Nonanta, *or* Novanta.
Spanish	Uno	Dos	Tres	Sesenta	Noventa.
Portuguese	Hum	Dous	Tres	Secenta	Noventa.
Swedish	En	Twa	Tre	Sexti	Nitti.
Danish	Een	To	Tre	Tredsindstyve	Halvfemtesindstyve.

English	Two Months after date.
German	Zwei Monate nach dato.
Dutch	Twee Maanden na dato.
French	A deux mois de date.
Italian	A due mesi dopo data.
Spanish	{ A dos meses de la fecha. A dos meses data.
Portuguese	A dous mezes de data.
Swedish	Twa Manander ifran dato.
Danish	To maaneder efter dato.
English	Three days after sight.
German	Drei tage nach sicht.
Dutch	Drie dagen na zigt.

French	A trois jours de vue.
Italian	{ A tre giorni vista. { A tre giorni dopo vista.
Spanish	A tres dias vista.
Portuguese	A tres dias vista.
Swedish	Tre dagar efter sigt.
Danish	Tre dage efter sigt.[1]

In all the above languages, "at sight" is usually expressed by *a vista*, except the French, which expresses it by *à vue*. "At usance" is expressed by *a uso* or *ad uso*. The names of the months so nearly resemble the English, that a mistake can but rarely occur.

The following are forms of bills in each of the above-mentioned languages:—

FRENCH.

Lille, le 28 Septembre, 18 .   *Bon pour £158 9 Sterlings.*

Au vingt-cinq Décembre prochain, payez par ce mandat à l'ordre de nous-mêmes la somme de cent cinquante-huit livres sterlings 9 schellings valeur en nous-mêmes et que passerez suivant l'avis de

A Messrs._____ .
   à Londres.

GERMAN.

Nürnberg, den 28 October, 18 .   *Pro £100 Sterling.*

Zwei Monate nach dato zahlen Sie gegen diesen Prima Wechsel an die Ordre des Herrn_____ Ein Hundert Pfund Sterling den Werth erhalten. Sie bringen solche auf Rechnung laut Bericht von der

Herren_____
   London.

---

[1] These phrases are taken from a small pamphlet, called "The Interpreter," compiled and translated by a Member of the Society of Public Notaries in London.

Dutch.

Grouw, den 1st *November,* 18 . *Voor* £59 17 6

Twee maanden na dato gelieve UEd te betalen voor dezen onzen prima Wisselbrief de secunda niet betaald zynde aan de ordre van de Heeren ─────────── negen & vyftig Ponden zeventien schelling en zespences sterling, de waarde in rekening UEd stelle het op rekening met of zonder advys van.

de Heer───────────
    te London.

Italian.

Livorno, le 25 *Settembre,* 18 . *Per* £500 *Sterlins.*

A Tre mesi data pagate per questa prima de Cambio (una sol volta) all' ordine ─────────── , la somma di Lire cinque cento sterline valuta cambiata, e ponete in conto M. S. secondo l'avviso Addio

Al ───────────
    Londra.

Spanish.

Malaga, á 20 *de Setb^{re} de* 18 . *Son* £300.

A noventa dias fecha se serviran V^a mandar pagar por esta primera de cambio á la orden de loss S^{res} ─────────── Tres cientas libras Esterlinas en oro o plata valor recibido de dhos S^{res} que anotaran valor en cuenta segun aviso de

A los S^{res} ───────────
    Londres.

Portuguese.

£600 *Esterlinas.* *Lisbon, aos* 8 *de Dezembro de* 18 .

A Sessenta dias de vista precizos pagará V ─────────── por esta nossa unica via de Letra Segura, à nos ou à nossa Ordem a quantia acima de Seis Centas Livras Esterlinas valor de nos recebido em Fazendas, que passera em Comta segundo o aviso de

Ao Senr ───────────
    Londres.

SWEDISH.

Bjorneberg, den 23 September, 18 .   *For £ Sterl.* 100.
   Nittio Dagar efter dato behagade H. H. emot denna prima Wexel (secundo obetald) betala till Herr_____elle ordres Etthundra Pund Sterling som stalles i rakning enligt avis.

Herrar_____
   London.

DANISH.

Kjobenhavn, 9 December, 18 .   *Rbae* 4,000.
   Tre maaneder efter dato behager de at betale denne Prima Vexel, secunda ikke, til Herr_____eller ordre med Fire Tusinde Rigsbank Daler, Valutta modtaget og stilles i Regning ifölge advis.

Herrer_____
   London.

The following quotations from Waterston's "Commercial Dictionary"[1] will serve to explain the operations connected with foreign bills of exchange:—

"A foreign bill of exchange is an order addressed to a person residing abroad, directing him to pay a determinate sum of foreign money to the person in whose favour it is drawn, or to his order. The amount of foreign money, therefore, to be paid is fixed by the bill; but the amount of British money (or money of the country in which the drawer resides), to be given for the purchase of the bill, is by no means fixed, but is continually varying."

"Of the two terms of comparison between the money of one place and that of another, one is fixed, the other

---

[1] "A Cyclopædia of Commerce, Mercantile Laws, Finance, Commercial Geography, and Navigation," by William Waterston, Esq.

is variable. The place whose money is reckoned at the fixed price is, in commercial language, said to *receive* the variable price: the other is said to *give* the variable price. Hence the higher the exchange between any two places, the more it is in favour of that which receives the variable price; the lower, the more in favour of that which gives the variable price;—the exchange being said to be favourable or unfavourable to any place, according as a smaller or larger amount of the currency of that place is required for discharging a given amount of foreign payments. Thus London receives from Paris a variable number of francs and centimes for £1 sterling; and taking the par at 25 francs 34 centimes for £1, exchange will be 5 per cent. in favour of London when it rises to 26 francs 62 centimes, and about 5 per cent. against London when it falls to 24 francs 7 centimes."

" Bill merchants study the exchanges, not only between the place at which they reside and all other places, but also between all those other places themselves, by which means they are generally enabled to realize a profit by buying bills in one place and selling them in another;— in this way preventing any great fall in the price of bills in those countries in which the supply exceeds the demand, and any great rise in those countries in which the supply happens to be deficient. Sometimes exchange operations are conducted with little outlay of capital. Thus, if a bill merchant in London can sell a bill on Amsterdam at half per cent. premium, and buy one at Paris at half per cent. discount, and with the latter buy one at Paris on Amsterdam at par, he will have gained 1 per cent. by the transaction, without the employment of any capital;—the bill remitted from Paris to Amsterdam arriving in time to meet the bill drawn there upon his correspondent. Again; a bill merchant, in order to take advantage of a premium on the exchange, may obtain a credit abroad upon which he may draw bills, under the calculation that at some future and not very distant period he will be able to replace the funds at a lower rate of exchange, and thereby realize a profit by the operation. The central points for such transactions are Hamburgh, Amsterdam, Vienna, Paris, New York, and above all, London, the great money change of the world."

"In this country the buying and selling of bills on foreign countries is conducted by brokers, all such transactions centring in the metropolis. In London the days for the negotiation of foreign bills are Tuesdays and Fridays, the *foreign post days*, as they are still called. The brokers go round to the principal merchants, and discover whether they are buyers or sellers; and a few of the more influential, after ascertaining the state of the market, suggest a price at which the greater part of the transactions are settled, with such deviations as particular bills may be subject to from their high or low credit. For the bills they buy on one post-day, houses of established credit pay on the following post-day, when they receive the second and third bills of the set; foreign bills being usually drawn in sets of three. The brokerage charged on bills is 1 per mille, or one-tenth per cent.

"On the evenings of Tuesdays and Fridays, the market rates for bills on all the principal foreign cities, with the current prices of bullion, are published in Wetenhall's 'Course of the Exchange.'"

The real par of exchange between two countries is that by which an ounce of gold in one country can be replaced by an ounce of gold of equal fineness in the other country. In England gold is the legal tender, and its price is fixed at £3 17s. $10\frac{1}{2}d.$ per ounce.

SECTION XX.

THE ADMINISTRATION OF A BANK WITH REGARD TO THE EMPLOYMENT OF ITS SURPLUS FUNDS.

THE means of a London banker consist mainly of his capital and his deposits. A certain portion of this sum is kept in the till, to meet daily demands; another portion is advanced in the way of discounts or loans to his customers. The remainder forms his surplus fund, of which a part will probably be invested in Government securities; loans to bill brokers, payable on demand; in short loans on the Stock Exchange, or in first-rate bills obtained through the bill brokers, and hence styled brokers' bills. The Government securities are the more permanent of these investments. The amount will seldom vary. It is not deemed creditable for a bank to speculate in the funds, or to buy and sell stock frequently, with a view of making a profit by the difference of price; hence a banker sells his Government securities only in a season of pressure, as a means of precaution, or in order to meet urgent demands. On other occasions, he will, when necessary, reduce his short loans or brokers' bills. These form his fluctuating investments. In seasons when money is abundant his deposits will increase, and perchance, at the same time, the demand of his customers for loans or discounts will diminish. His surplus funds will thus increase. But these temporary surplus funds he will on no account invest in Government securities, as his deposits will be certainly, and perhaps suddenly, reduced, and he might have to realize his Government securities at a loss. He will in this case increase his loans to brokers, and his brokers' bills. And though he will get as much interest as he can, he will take a very low interest rather than keep the money unproductive in his till, or invest it in a more permanent form. We will now take a short review of the different kinds of investment we have mentioned. The three grand points for consideration are, convertibility—exemption from loss—and a good rate of interest. But first we will notice those circumstances which regulate the amount of cash to be kept in the till.

The amount of money which a banker will keep in his till depends upon circumstances. First, the amount of his deposits. It is natural to suppose that when his deposits are large, he will keep more money to meet them than when his deposits are small.—Secondly, the amount of his daily payments. These will not at all times correspond with the amount of the deposits; for some accounts are more *operative* than others. On commercial accounts, for instance, the payments will be much heavier in proportion to the average balance than on accounts which are not commercial. The City bankers pay much larger sums every day, in proportion to the amount of their deposits, than the bankers at the West-end.—Thirdly, if a banker issues notes, he will keep a less amount of other money in his till. The popular opinion is, that he keeps more, as he has to provide payment for his notes as well as his deposits. This is true in seasons of pressure. But in ordinary times he keeps less, as he pays the cheques drawn on account of his deposits with his notes, and these notes often get into the hands of another banker, with whom he settles by a draft on London. His reserve to meet his notes is kept, not in his own till, but in London, where it probably yields him interest. Indeed, when his deposits are withdrawn in large amounts, they are more usually withdrawn by a draft on London than in any other way.—Fourthly, the number of the branches. If a bank has many branches, the total amount of cash kept in the tills of the head office and all the branches put together will be considerably more than would be required if the whole of the business were collected into one place. In the case of a run the difference is considerable, as every point open to attack must be well fortified. The stoppage of one branch, even for a short time, would bring discredit upon the whole establishment.—Fifthly, in London the amount of notes to be kept in the till will be affected by the privilege of clearing. Those bankers that "clear," can pay bills and cheques upon them by the bills and cheques they have upon other bankers. Those banks that do not clear must pay all the bills and cheques upon them in bank notes before they receive payment of the bills and cheques they have upon other bankers.[1] Hence they must lock up every night with a larger amount of cash in their vaults.

We need hardly say, that with every banker the amount in the till will fluctuate from day to day. Though a banker has a certain average amount in his own mind, below or above which he does not swerve very widely, yet the cash-book will seldom be exactly this amount. Sometimes he will strengthen his till, in the prospect of large payments that may come upon him suddenly. At other times he will run his till low for a day or two, in expecta-

---

[1] The practice in this respect is changed now. Nearly all the London bankers keep an account at the Bank of England, and the non-clearing banks pay all bills and cheques upon them by what is called a Transfer Cheque upon the Bank of England. This transfer cheque is a simple request to the Bank of England to transfer a certain sum of money from the account of the banker who grants it to the account of the banker who presents the bills and cheques for payment. This practice now renders it unnecessary for non-clearing banks to keep any unusual amount of cash in their tills.

tion of large sums that will shortly be due to him. During the day, too, either the receipts or the payments may be heavier than he expected; and hence, now and then, the cashier reports to the chief clerk or to the banker the state of the till, in order, that, if necessary, it may be replenished. The temperament of a banker, too, has some effect in this case. Some bankers are so cautious that they will "lock up" with a large amount of cash; others are so anxious to make profit, that they will keep their cash very low. The state of the money market will also influence the tills of the bankers. When money is abundant, a banker will lock up with more money than he wants, because he cannot employ his funds. When money is so scarce as to betoken a pressure, he will also lock up strong, so as to be prepared for any emergency. In fact, there can be no general rule for regulating the amount of the till. Every banker must be guided by the experience of his own bank. The directors of the Bank of England consider that their reserve in bank notes and gold should be equal to about one-third of their deposits. From the accounts published by some of the London joint-stock banks, it would appear that the "cash in hand" is equal to about one-eighth or one-tenth of their liabilities. Even this, we conjecture, is a higher proportion than that which is generally kept by London bankers, especially by those who settle their accounts with each other at the Clearing-house.

To resume:—After a banker has furnished his till, and supplied his customers with such loans and discounts as they may require, he has a surplus of cash. This surplus may be considered as being divided into two parts—though it is never actually so divided—the permanent surplus, which the banker is not likely to require, except in seasons of extreme pressure, and the temporary surplus, arising from fluctuations in the deposits. We shall now notice those modes of investment to which we have referred.

With regard to Government securities, we have high authority from the testimony of practical bankers. The following are quotations given before the Joint-Stock Bank Committee, in the year 1836, by the late Vincent Stuckey, Esq., the founder of Stuckey's Joint-Stock Banking Company, in Somersetshire, and the late James Marshall, Esq., the Secretary of the Provincial Bank of Ireland.

Mr. V. Stuckey :—

"What is your reason for keeping so large a sum in Government stock?—I have always found from my experience, except two days in my life, that I could get money more easily upon those securities than any other.

"Is it easier, in times of emergency, to obtain money on Government stock than on good mercantile bills?—I have always found it so.

"You do not concur with any witnesses who state that they have found good negotiable bills more easy to obtain money upon than Government stock?—No: I have never found that with a good bill, even of the house of Baring, I could get money more easily than on Government stock.

"Do you consider that, generally speaking, in London the rate of interest at which you borrow money on exchequer bills and stock is notoriously lower than that at which you borrow on bills of exchange?—Yes, it is lower, and for that reason we generally adopt it."

Mr. James Marshall :—

"Will you inform the Committee whether it is the usage of the Provincial Bank to invest any portion of its funds in the public securities?—It has been its uniform practice so to do.

"By public securities, what do you understand?—The

Consols, for instance: there are various kinds of Government stock; exchequer bills, and Bank of England stock, are generally considered as a public sort of security.

"Do you hold stock in London only, or in Dublin as well as in London?—In Dublin but to a limited amount, because it is not easily convertible there.

"On what ground is it that it is not easily convertible in Dublin?—From the limited nature of the market as compared with London; we could not sell even an immaterial sum without lowering considerably the price.

"Have there not been at various times, from various causes, runs on the Provincial Bank, which rendered it necessary to supply large amounts of specie to that country?—There have, repeatedly.

"Do you consider, from your experience, that it would have been competent to the bank to have maintained its full security, with satisfaction to the directors, if they had not been possessed of very considerable funded property in this country?—Certainly not: speaking of the last run that happened, especially, I must say that that differed from any former run in this respect.

"You were conversant with the management of the Scotch banks prior to your connection with the Provincial Bank?—Yes.

"Is it not the usage of all the Scotch banks in like manner to maintain a very considerable portion of their funds invested in the Government securities?—I believe the practice with all is generally so, but I can speak particularly to that of the three oldest banks—as they are commonly called, the three chartered banks,—the Bank of Scotland was erected by Act of Parliament, the Royal Bank of Scotland and the British Linen Company were erected by charter, but have been recognized in the same way, so that there are three public banks in distinction to any of the subsequently-formed banks.[1] I can state, from personal knowledge, that these banks have had always a very large sum indeed invested in the funded property of the kingdom.

"Do you consider it would be a safe system of banking, if the capital of the bank was altogether invested in commercial bills?—Certainly not."

Of the various kinds of Government stock, consols are the best, as there is a more ready market for this kind of stock, and money can usually be borrowed on them until the next account day: so that, if a banker has only a temporary demand for money, he may thus obtain it at a moderate interest, when, by selling his stock at that time, he might sustain loss. The Bank of England has recourse, sometimes, to this mode of strengthening its reserve. Sometimes, too, a banker may make a profit by lending his consols. At the monthly settlings, among the brokers, stock is sometimes in demand and money may be obtained upon consols, until the next settling, without paying any interest; and the banker may employ the money in the mean time. As, however, the rate of interest is usually low in such seasons, his profit will rarely be great.

There are no time bargains in the reduced 3 per cents., or in the new 3 per cents.; but in ordinary times money can be borrowed upon them at the market rate of interest. In seasons of pressure these are not so saleable as consols. Bank stock, India stock, and long annuities, not being readily convertible, are not generally good investments for bankers.

Some bankers avoid all Government stock, and give a preference to exchequer bills. They have some advantages. As the Government must pay the amount demanded in March or June, when they become due, there

[1] The Commercial Bank of Scotland and the National Bank of Scotland are also Incorporated by Royal Charter.

can be no loss beyond the amount of the premium at which they were purchased. A banker, too, can borrow money upon them quietly and secretly. A transfer of stock is always known, and, if for a large amount, will, when money is scarce, excite notice, and give the impression that the banker is compelled to realize some of his securities, to meet demands made upon him by his depositors.[1] But a banker can hand his exchequer bills to a stock-broker, who will bring him the money, and the party who has granted the loan will know nothing about the party for whom it was required. On the other hand, there are some disadvantages. Almost every change in the market value of money affects the price of exchequer bills; and whenever money becomes abundant, the Government are very apt to reduce the rate of interest much below that which can be obtained from consols. But a greater objection is, that even in ordinary times, they are hardly saleable in large amounts. There are not now so many exchequer-bill jobbers as formerly, and hence these bills are not so readily saleable. On this account, the Bank of England, who were formerly large holders of exchequer bills, have changed their system, and are now holders of stock. The City bankers, too, prefer placing their money with the bill-brokers, to investing it in exchequer bills. But they are still a favourite mode of investment with bankers at the West-end.

East India bonds yield a higher interest than exchequer bills, and the interest cannot be reduced until after twelve months' notice from the Governor of India in Council.

---

[1] Since 1863 Government have given facilities for converting consols into what are called "Consol Certificates," which pass from hand to hand by simple delivery, and bankers can borrow on these certificates as quietly and secretly as on exchequer bills. The conversion is made by the Bank of England at a charge of two shillings per cent.

But they are by no means so saleable. Money, however, may generally be borrowed upon them; and the loans of the Bank of England are always announced to be granted on "exchequer bills, India bonds, and other approved securities."

Bonds of corporations, or of public companies, are by no means proper investments for a banker, except to a very moderate amount, and when they have a short time to run. They may, however, be taken as security for temporary advances to respectable customers.

Good commercial bills, of short dates, have this advantage over Government stock or exchequer bills, that a banker is sure to receive back the same amount of money which he advanced. He can calculate, too, upon the time the money will be received, and make his arrangements accordingly. And if unexpectedly he should want the money sooner, the bills can, in ordinary times, be rediscounted in the money market.[1] Another advantage is, that he is able to avail himself of any advance in the current rate of interest. He will get no higher dividend from his investment in Government stock, should money afterwards become ever so valuable. But with regard to bills as they fall due he will receive a higher rate of discount with the new bills he may take, and thus, as the market rate of interest advances, his profits will increase.

The bankers of Lancashire usually keep the whole of their reserves in bills of exchange. If they have a "good bill case," that is, a large amount of good bills in their case, they think themselves prepared to meet any emergency. Their objection to Government securities is founded, first, upon the low rate of interest which they yield; and, secondly, the possibility of loss, from fluctua-

---

[1] See note on page 157. It would very materially injure the credit of such banks as are not in the habit of re-discounting were they to do so in times of pressure.

tions in price. They contend, too, that good bills of exchange are more convertible than even exchequer bills; and, even if not convertible, the money comes back as the bills fall due, and thus the reserve is constantly replenished.

The authority of Mr. Samuel Gurney, from his high standing in the City, is so constantly referred to upon this subject, that we copy his evidence. It was given before the Committee on Joint-Stock Banks, in the year 1836; previous, of course, to the passing of the Act of 1844.

"Would not the result from that opinion be, that a properly-conducted establishment, whether a private or a joint-stock bank, should have some Government securities or exchequer bills on which always to rely as a resource in a moment of such emergency?—Experience has shown that it is not needful; bills of exchange are quite as good a security to hold in time of difficulty as exchequer bills or stock; in most respects very much better.

"Cannot you conceive a state of things in the money market—a state of mercantile discredit, for instance—when it might be possible to procure money on Government securities when it could not be procured on private security in the shape of bills?—Such difficulty may possibly exist under very peculiar circumstances; but I repeat my opinion, that bills of exchange have proved themselves to be a better investment for bankers than stock or exchequer bills.

"It is quite intelligible why, in ordinary times, bills of exchange should be a preferable investment for money, inasmuch as there is no risk of loss by variation of premium in the purchase and resale; but would you wish the committee to suppose that in the case supposed by the question, of a great degree of mercantile discredit and doubt, an amount of exchequer bills would not be a more certain security on which to raise money than the bills of private merchants?—That is a difficult question to answer; I doubt it.

"Supposing a period of difficulty to arise, and two country bankers came up to London, one who could exhibit Government stock to the extent of £25,000 and £25,000 in bills of exchange, and the other banker exhibiting £50,000 in bills of exchange only, which do you think would have the best means of procuring accommodation in the London market to pay his engagements?—My apprehension is, that they would both get their supplies upon any particular emergency: it is my judgment, that to a banker a good supply of bills of exchange of first-rate character is a better investment for his funds, for which he is liable to be called upon on demand, than exchequer bills or any Government security."

A London banker never considers as a part of his reserve the bills he has discounted for his customers. Nothing could damage his credit more than any attempt to rediscount these bills. During the war, the London bankers had discount accounts with the Bank of England; and in the panic of 1825, it is well known they discounted largely with that establishment. But since that period they have not done so, and their indorsements are never seen in the money market. The practice is now more general of lodging money at call with the large money dealers. And it is in this way that the London bankers make provision for any sudden demand. It is rarely, however, that any large demand comes so suddenly as to occasion any inconvenience. And it may be observed that such bankers as are members of the Clearing-house have the whole day to make preparation—one of the circumstances which enables them to lock up at night with a smaller amount of cash.

In the morning the banker looks at his "Cash-book,"

and observes the amount with which he "locked up" the preceding night. He then looks at the "Diary," which contains his receipts and payments for that day, as far as he is then advised. He then opens the letters, and notices the remittances they contain, and the payments he is instructed to make. He will learn from these items whether he "wants money," or has "money to spare." If he wants money, he will "take in" any loans that may be falling due that day, or he may "call in" any loans he may have out on demand, or he may go farther, and borrow money for a few days on stock or exchequer bills. Should he have money to spare, he will, peradventure, discount brokers' bills, or lodge money on demand with the bill-brokers, or lend it for fixed periods upon stock or exchequer bills. The bill-brokers usually make their rounds every morning, first calling on the parties who supply them with bills, and then calling on the bankers who supply them with money. The stock-brokers, too, will call after "the market is open," to inform the banker how "things are going" on the Stock Exchange, what operations are taking place, and whether money is abundant or scarce "in the house;" also what rumours are afloat that are likely to affect the price of the funds. It is thus that a banker regulates his investments, and finds employment for his surplus funds.

In our opinion, it is best for a banker not to adopt exclusively any one of the investments we have noticed, but to distribute his funds among them all. We have seen that practical bankers of high standing have been in favour of Government securities, as being at all times convertible. The objection on the part of others has been, that the value of these securities very much fluctuates, and as their realization will be required only in seasons of pressure when the funds are low, it is sure to be attended with loss.

On the other hand, it may be stated, with regard to "loans on demand," that the recent failures of bill-brokers have shown that the "demand" may not always be readily met. And with regard to "brokers' bills," the numerous failures among houses of the first standing have proved that great losses and most inconvenient "locks-up" may occasionally take place from such securities. Without condemning other modes of investment, we are strongly inclined to favour Government securities, though fully conscious of the losses they may occasionally produce.[1] There is one consideration that must be taken into account: a bank that has large surplus funds, if it makes no investments in Government securities, will be strongly tempted to invest its funds elsewhere in other securities that may not be so convertible. It is true that more interest may for a time be obtained,[2] but ultimately the bank may,

---

[1] In the books of all well-regulated banks consols are written down to much below the market price, so that in seasons of pressure when sales are necessary the loss sustained does not come out of profit and loss, and does not affect the dividend, nor, consequently, the credit of the bank.

[2] At the meeting of the London and Westminster Bank, July, 1855, the Chairman, J. L. Ricardo, Esq., M.P., made a comparison between the interest obtained on money invested in the funds and that employed with bill-brokers. Upon an average of twelve years the following is the result: On the 2nd January, 1843, the price of consols was 94¼, which yields an interest per annum of £3 3s. 6d. per cent. The interest allowed upon money at call by Messrs. Overend & Co. for twelve years, from January, 1843, to December, 1854, would average £2 10s. 10d. per cent. Upon bills, the rate allowed is usually half per cent. more, that is, £3 0s. 10d. per cent. £1,000,000 invested at £3 3s. 6d. would produce annually the sum of £31,750. At £3 0s. 10d. per cent. it would produce only £30,416 13s. 4d. This shows, that upon an *average of years* the funds are more productive than brokers' bills.

[The average Bank rate for the last fifty-four years, from 1826 to 1879 inclusive, has been about £3 18s. per cent., and as the brokers' rates for money at call are generally from 1¼ to 1½ under the Bank rate, this shows a large margin of yield in favour of consols.]

though in a state of perfect solvency, be compelled to stop payment from being unable to realize its investments.

Another advantage of a large investment in Government securities is, that the bank, by the publication of its balance-sheet, has always the means of showing to its depositors that a large portion of its deposits is at all times amply secured. The Bank of England state the amount of their "Government securities" distinct from the "other securities." It may so be that the "other securities" are as good as the Government securities, and perhaps more profitable, but the public do not know that to be the case; and were all the investments in "other securities," they might not feel the same degree of confidence as to the prompt repayment of their deposits. The same principle applies to other banks. And it may reasonably be supposed that between two banks in similar circumstances as to other respects, depositors would rather lodge their money in a bank which had a large amount of Government securities than in one which had none.

As we have referred in this section to some of the operations of the Stock Exchange, this may be a proper place to discuss the nature of these transactions, so far, at least, as concerns bankers.

The reader is of course aware that the "Stocks," or the "Funds," or by whatever other name they may be called, are debts due from the nation to those persons whose names are entered on the Bank books. The man who holds £100 consols is a creditor of the nation for £100, for which he receives £3 per annum; and the price of consols is the amount of the money for which he is willing to transfer this debt from himself to another person. Now, if this man knows another who is willing to give him, say £90 for this £100 consols, they can go to the Bank, and the seller being properly identified, will transfer this £100 consols into the name of the person to whom he has sold it. His account is then closed in the Bank books, and a new account is opened in the name of the buyer; for every holder of stock has an account in the Bank ledger, in the same way as bankers and merchants open ledger accounts for their customers. The seller of the stock will also give a receipt to the buyer for the money on a printed form issued by the Bank of England.

But parties do not usually treat with each other in this way. A broker is employed either to buy or to sell, as the case may be. The members of the Stock Exchange are an association consisting of over 2,200 persons, who meet together in a building in Capel Court, Bartholomew Lane, close to the Bank. Each member, before admission, must find three securities for £500 each, which sum is applied to meet any claims the other members of the "House" may have upon him during the first four years. The suretyship then ceases. The subscription paid by each member is twenty-one guineas per annum, and the entrance fee is one hundred and fifty guineas. The House is governed by a Committee of thirty persons chosen from the members.

Although all the "members of the House" are called stock-brokers by the public, yet within the House they are divided into two classes, brokers and jobbers. A broker, as the name implies, is an agent who buys or sells for his customers out of the House, and he charges them a commission upon the amount of the stock. A stock-jobber is a stock dealer; but he does not deal with the public: he deals only with the brokers; and he is at all times ready either to buy or to sell. The price at which he sells usually is $\tfrac{1}{8}$ more than the price at which he buys. If one broker has an order from his customer to buy £100 consols, and another broker has an order to sell £100 consols, these two brokers do not deal together, but both go to a jobber, who will "make him a price." One will sell his consols to the jobber, say at 90, and the other will buy his consols from the jobber at $90\frac{1}{8}$. Hence the difference between the buying and the selling price of consols is usually $\frac{1}{8}$, and thus in the newspapers the price is quoted in this way, 90 to $90\frac{1}{8}$.

A banker is, of course, one of the public, and when he wants to buy or to sell stock, he gives instructions to his broker, and the process is as we have now described.

Were there no jobbers, a broker would not easily find at all times another broker who had occasion to sell the same amount of stock which he wished to buy, and he would have a difficulty in buying or selling small amounts. But there is no difficulty with the jobbers. The jobbers will not only buy and sell stock on the same day, but they will buy stock on one day, and agree to sell it at a future day, or *vice versâ*. These future days are called the settling days, being the days on which the members of the House settle their accounts. They are fixed by the Committee of the Stock Exchange, and they now occur regularly once a month. Now, if a banker wants a sum of money for a short time, either to pay off a deposit, or to make an advance to a customer, he will direct his stock-broker to sell, say £50,000 consols "for money," and buy them "for time;" that is, against the next "settling day," or, as it is sometimes called, the next "account day." On the other hand, if a banker has money he wishes to employ for a short time, he will reverse the operation, and desire his broker to buy consols for money and sell them for time. He thus gets interest for his money, according to the difference of price between consols for time and consols for money.

Generally, the price for time is higher than the price for money; and the difference between these two prices is called the "Continuation." Supposing that the next settling day is a month distant, and the continuation is one-eighth per cent., that amounts to twelve-eighths, or one and a half per cent. per annum. The continuation will vary according to the near approach of the settling-day—according to the abundance of money, and the market rate of interest—and according to the abundance or scarcity of stock. The last cause is not so readily understood by the public, and we will therefore explain it. The stock-jobbers, as we have said, are stock dealers. Of course they are large holders of stock; it is their capital, on which they trade. But however large may be the sum they hold, they often agree to sell on the next settling day a much larger sum, expecting that in the mean time they shall buy a large sum, and thus be able to set off one against the other. But sometimes, as the settling day approaches, they find this is not the case, and they are consequently under an engagement to "deliver"—that is, sell—more stock than they hold. What can they do now? They will try to get stock from those who have it, by agreeing to buy it of them *now*, and selling it at the ensuing account day, a month hence, at the same price; thus abolishing "the continuation." When that is the case, a banker's broker will go to the banker and say, "If you like to lend your consols, you can get money for nothing till the next account day." The banker replies, "Well, I don't know that I can make much interest of the money just now; but as I can lose nothing, you may lend them." Thus the jobbers get their stock, and complete their engagements. But sometimes the jobbers are obliged to go farther, and even to offer a premium to parties who will lend their consols. This premium is called "Backwardation;" it is just the reverse of "Continuation," and implies that the time price of stock is less than the money price.

We have thus described the legitimate operations of the Stock Exchange, so far as it may be necessary to explain the transactions of bankers in the employment of their surplus funds.

SECTION XXI.

THE ADMINISTRATION OF A BANK DURING SEASONS OF PRESSURE.

A PRESSURE on the money market may be defined a difficulty of getting money in the London market, either by way of discounting bills, or of loans upon Government securities. This difficulty is usually accompanied by an unfavourable course of exchange, a contraction of the circulation of the Bank of England, and a high rate of interest. These three circumstances have the relation to each other of cause and effect. The unfavourable course of exchange induces the Bank of England to contract her circulation; and the contraction of the circulation, by rendering money more scarce, increases its value, and leads to an advanced rate of interest. The removal of the pressure is in the same order:—the foreign exchanges become favourable—the Bank of England then extends her circulation—money becomes more abundant, and the rate of interest falls. The degree to which the exchanges are unfavourable is indicated by the stock of gold in the Bank of England; and when this is at its lowest amount the pressure may be considered to have attained its extreme point; for as the amount of gold increases, the Bank will extend its circulation, and the pressure will subside.

If we take a review of all the recent pressures on the money market, we shall find they have always been preceded by the following circumstances:—First, by abundance of money; secondly, by a low rate of interest; thirdly, by some species of speculative investments. The principal pressures that have occurred of late years, have been those of 1825, 1836, 1839, 1847, 1857, 1866, 1875, and 1878.

The following is Mr. Horsley Palmer's opinion of the causes of the pressure of 1825, as stated to the Bank Committee of 1832:—

" Will you state to the committee what, in your opinion, was the nature and the march of the crisis in 1825 ?—I have always considered that the first step towards the excitement was the reduction of the interest upon the Government securities; the first movement in that respect was, I think, upon £135,000,000 of five per cents, which took place in 1823. In the subsequent year, 1824, followed the reduction of £80,000,000 of four per cents. I have always considered that reduction of interests, one-fifth in one case, and one-eighth in the other, to have created the feverish feeling in the minds of the public at large, which prompted almost everybody to entertain any proposition for investment, however absurd, which was tendered. The excitement of that period was further promoted by the acknowledgment of South American republics by this country, and the inducements held out for engaging in mining operations, and loans to those governments, in which all classes of the community in England seem to have partaken almost simultaneously. With those speculations arose general speculation in commercial produce, which had an effect of disturbing the relative values between this and other countries, and creating an unfavourable foreign exchange, which continued from October, 1824, to November, 1825, causing a very considerable export of bullion from the Bank—about seven millions and a half. Commercial speculations had induced some bankers, one particularly, to invest money in securities not strictly convertible, to a larger extent than was prudent; they were also largely connected with country bankers. I allude to the house of Messrs. Pole and Co.—a house originally possessed of very great property, in the persons of the partners, but which fell with the circumstances of the times. The failure of that banking-house was the first decisive check to commercial and banking credit, and brought at once a vast number of country bankers, which were in correspondence with it, into difficulties. That discredit was followed by a general discredit throughout London and the interior."—P. 47.

With regard to the pressure of 1836, there was in the beginning of that year no appearance of distress; but, on the contrary, every symptom of prosperity, attended by its usual concomitant, a readiness to engage in speculative undertakings.

The following description of this period is taken from the speech of Mr. Clay, on introducing his motion respecting Joint-Stock Banks, May 12, 1836 :—

"To what extent the operations of the joint-stock banks may have contributed to create the present state of excitement in the commercial world, must, of course, be mere matter of conjecture. That they have had some considerable influence is probable, from the fact that the excitement and rage for speculation is greatest in those parts of the kingdom where the operations of those establishments have been most active. London has been comparatively unmoved, but Liverpool and Manchester have witnessed a mushroom growth of schemes not exceeded by the memorable year 1825. I hold in my hand a list of seventy contemplated companies, for every species of undertaking, which have appeared in the Liverpool and Manchester papers within the last three months. This list was made a fortnight or three weeks since, and might probably now be considerably extended. It is impossible also, I think, not to suspect that the facility of credit, and consequent encouragement to speculation, to which I have alluded, cannot have been without its effect in producing the great increase of price in almost all the chief articles of consumption and raw materials of our manufactures. That increase has been enormous—not less than from twenty to fifty, and even one hundred per cent. in many of the chief articles of produce, of consumption, and materials of our manufactures."

These appearances continued with little alteration until the month of July, when the Bank of England raised the rate of discount to four-and-a-half per cent. It then became known that there had been a demand upon the Bank for gold from the preceding April, and this measure was adopted by the Bank as a means of rendering the foreign exchanges more favourable. This being found ineffectual, the Bank in September raised the rate of discount to five per cent. Besides raising the rate of interest, the Bank adopted other measures for increasing the value of money. A large amount of American bills upon first-rate houses had been offered for discount and rejected. A high degree of alarm was immediately spread throughout the community. The dread of a panic similar to that of 1825 almost universally prevailed. Those who had money were unwilling to part with it—trade became suddenly stagnant—the prices of all commodities fell considerably, and numbers of commercial houses, chiefly of the second class, suspended payment. Many railway and other projects now fell into oblivion.

The alarm that existed was kept up by the monthly accounts of the bullion in the Bank of England. The public returns showed a gradual decline from April, 1836, to February, 1837. It was therefore supposed that the Bank of England would be under the necessity, for its own safety, of still further contracting its issues, and thus increasing the existing pressure. This apprehension caused all persons who had money to retain it in their possession, and bankers and others withheld accommodation they would otherwise have been disposed to grant.

This state of alarm was considerably augmented by the publication of the Report of the Secret Committee of the House of Commons upon Joint-Stock Banks. This committee had been appointed on the motion of Mr. Clay, the Member for the Tower Hamlets, whose speech on the occasion might be termed a bill of indictment. The joint-stock banks had rapidly increased; they had issued small shares; they had large nominal capitals; they had circulated an excessive amount of notes; they had promoted speculation. These were the charges brought against them; and they had greater weight from being advanced by a member who was known to be friendly to joint-stock banking. The report of the committee appeared to sustain all Mr. Clay's accusations. This report was highly creditable to the talents and industry of the committee, but marked by a decided hostility of tone. While it enumerated all the actual or possible imperfections of the joint-stock banks, it ascribed to them scarcely a single excellence. At the same time, the committee deferred to the succeeding session the proposal of any measures for their improvement; thus the public were led to suppose that in the following session some stringent measures would be adopted with reference to joint-stock banks, but what they would be none could conjecture.

Had the report appeared at any other period it might possibly have done good; but as its appearance was contemporaneous with a pressure on the money market, and a high state of alarm, it unquestionably tended to weaken public confidence, at a time when it required to be strengthened. Persons who were unfriendly to joint-stock banks seized the opportunity of dispraising them, and believed, or pretended to believe, that the banks were unsound, and would certainly stop payment. Others, who were friendly, were apprehensive that the banks, being still in their infancy, would be found too weak to withstand the storm now raised against them. But though this alarm began with respect to joint-stock banks, it did not end there. It was soon foreseen that if a few joint-stock banks were to stop payment, the private banks in their neighbourhood would be put to a severe trial; and if the banks should even be compelled to withhold their usual advances to their customers, the credit of individuals must suffer. Hence the private bankers and the merchants, as well as the joint-stock banks, made preparations to meet any event that might occur, and by thus increasing the pressure on the London money market, occasioned still farther apprehensions.

The alarm was augmented by the stoppage of the Agricultural and Commercial Bank of Ireland, in the month of November, and the demand for gold which that stoppage occasioned in Ireland. The joint-stock banks of England now became subject to increased suspicion; the accommodation they had been accustomed to obtain by the rediscount of their bills in the London market was considerably restricted; and in the beginning of December, the Northern and Central Bank at Manchester, a bank having a paid-up capital of £800,000, with above 1,200 partners, and forty branches, applied for assistance to the Bank of England. This was afforded upon condition, in the first instance, that they should wind up all their branches, except that at Liverpool; and afterwards farther assistance was granted, upon condition they should discontinue business after February, 1837. Soon afterwards, the old and respectable London banking-house of Messrs. Esdaile and Co. received assistance upon similar terms.

The pressure which existed in England rapidly extended to America. A large amount of American securities, consisting chiefly of bonds of the respective States, had been remitted to the agency houses in England. This circumstance, in connection with the exportation of gold to America, attracted the notice of the Bank of England. A large amount of bills drawn from America upon first-rate London houses was rejected. In America the pressure became severe—money was wanted to remit to England to meet the drafts that had been drawn upon England, either upon credit or against securities that could not now be sold. The rate of discount at New York rose to two, and even to three per cent. per month.

From the pressure upon the money market, and from the great fall in the price of American produce, the cotton and other commodities sent from America to meet drafts upon the English agents could not be sold except at a ruinous loss. And other remittances not having arrived, several houses in the American trade, who were said to have given extensive credit to parties in America, applied for assistance to the Bank of England.

Such was the character of the pressure of 1836. We next proceed to the pressure of 1839. The pressure of 1836 may be said to have commenced from the month of May in that year. From that month the stock of gold in the Bank gradually and uniformly declined until February, 1837, when it reached its lowest point of depression. From this point it uniformly advanced: the lowest point of the circulation was in December, 1836, though even then it was not lower than it had been in the preceding January. The Bank raised the rate of interest from 4 to $4\frac{1}{2}$ per cent. in July, and to 5 per cent. in the following September.

During the whole of the year 1837 the amount of gold in the Bank of England continued to increase; the Bank extended its circulation, and after the payment of the July dividends, money became very abundant, and the market rate of interest experienced a considerable fall. The foreign exchanges continued to be favourable during the early part of 1838, and gold accumulated in the coffers of the Bank of England. In the spring of that year the directors of the Bank of England sent nearly a million of gold to America. Money became increasingly abundant, and the rate of interest fell. In February the Bank reduced their rate of discount to 4 per cent., and the interest on the loans granted during the shutting of the funds was reduced in March to $3\frac{1}{2}$ per cent. The low rate of interest caused large sums of money to be invested in American securities. Bonds of all kinds issued by the Bank of the United States, by the various States in the Union, and by numerous private undertakings, were poured upon the English market, and found eager purchasers. Several of the directors of the Bank of England, in their individual character as merchants, became agents for the distribution of these securities. About July the exchanges became unfavourable, and in the latter part of the year some symptoms of uneasiness were apparent in the money market; but as the stock of bullion in the Bank of England was considerable, and the directors granted their usual loans in December at $3\frac{1}{2}$ per cent., public confidence was not shaken. In the beginning of the year 1839 the exchanges became increasingly unfavourable, and the monthly returns of the Bank showed a gradual diminution in the stock of gold. The price of corn rose so high as to admit of foreign wheat at the lowest rate of duty. This occasioned a further demand for gold to be exported. The stock of gold in the Bank of England rapidly declined, until, in the month of October, it was no more than £2,525,000, while the liabilities of the Bank upon notes amounted to £17,612,000, and upon deposits to £6,734,000. The Bank directors were very anxious to stop this demand for gold. With this view, they raised the rate of interest on May 16th to 5 per cent., on June 20th to 5½ per cent., and on August 1st to 6 per cent.; and they charged the same rate upon their short loans. They are supposed to have sold large amounts of Government stock and exchequer bills, and on July 13th they announced that they were ready to receive proposals for the sale of the dead weight. None of the offers, however, met their approbation. Finding these measures not speedily effective, an arrangement was made with the Bank of France for a loan of £2,500,000. Messrs. Baring and Co. drew bills on account of the Bank of England upon houses in Paris for this amount, which the Bank of France undertook to discount. The directors also determined to refuse to discount any bills drawn or indorsed by any private or joint-stock bank of issue. Notwithstanding these measures, the stock of gold in the Bank continued to decrease until the 18th October, when it reached the lowest point of depression. From this point it continued to advance, and the pressure began gradually, but slowly, to subside.

It may be useful to notice the differences between the pressure of 1836 and that of 1839. If we measure the intensity of the pressure by the difference between the largest and the lowest stock of gold in the Bank of England, the former pressure will range from £7,801,000 to £4,032,000, and the latter from £10,126,000 to £2,525,000. In the pressure of 1836, one joint-stock bank, a London private bank, two country private banks, three large American agency houses, and a great many respectable merchants, stopped payment. In the pressure of 1839, there was scarcely a failure until the month of December, and then only among the second class of traders. In the pressure of 1836, the prices of nearly all commodities fell considerably, and almost immediately. In the pressure of 1839, the prices of most commodities remained for a length of time nearly the same. In 1836, the Bank of England did not raise their rate of interest above 5 per cent. In 1839, the rate of interest upon both discounts and loans was raised to 6 per cent. In 1839, the Bank gave notice that they were willing to sell the dead weight, and they made arrangements for borrowing £2,500,000 sterling from the Bank of France. In 1836, the Bank adopted neither of these measures. In 1836, the Bank of England rejected all bills drawn or indorsed by joint-stock banks of issue. In 1839, they rejected also all bills drawn and indorsed by private banks of issue.

It would appear that a season of pressure is always preceded by one of speculation; and hence it follows that a banker who wishes to be easy in a time of pressure must act wisely in the previous season of speculation. It requires no ordinary firmness to do this. To act wisely in a season of speculation is far more difficult than to act wisely in one of pressure. But unless a banker acts wisely in the previous time of speculation, his wisdom will probably be of little avail when the pressure arrives.

While, therefore, money is still abundant, the public funds high, and other bankers liberal in accommodation, he should be doubly cautious against taking bills of a doubtful character, or making advances upon irregular securities. He should not suffer the desire of employing his funds, or the fear of offending his customers, to induce him to deviate from sound banking principles. He should also take this opportunity of calling up all dead or doubtful loans, and of getting rid of all weak customers. He should also, under any circumstances, avoid making advances for any length of time, and investments in securities that are not at all times convertible, or the price of which is likely to sustain a great fall on the occurrence of a pressure. The discount of first-rate commercial bills having a short time to run, or short loans on stock or other undeniable security, however low the interest received, seem to be the most safe and advantageous transactions.

When the aspect of affairs seems to threaten that money will be in demand, and the failure of a number of merchants and traders may consequently be apprehended, it behoves him to prepare for approaching events by avoiding all discounts of bills of an inferior class, and by keeping his funds in an available state. With a view to these objects, he will review all his loan and discount accounts, call up his loans of long standing, where it can be done without injury to the interest or reputation of his bank, avoid all overdrawn accounts, and reduce the amount of discounts of the inferior class of accounts. In performing these operations, he will exercise due judgment and discretion, making proper distinctions between his customers, and reducing chiefly those bills which are not of a business character, or which are drawn upon doubtful people, or upon parties that he knows nothing about; he will also mark particularly those accounts which require large discounts, but keep no corresponding balance to the credit of their current accounts.

As the pressure advances, he will find that there are three demands upon his funds. First, his customers will reduce their balances, and keep less money in his hands. Money lodged at interest will be taken away, because the parties can make higher interest elsewhere, or they will be tempted by the low price of stock to invest it in Government securities. Secondly, he will have a greater demand for loans and discounts, not merely from weak people whom he might not care about refusing, but from persons of known wealth, whom it is his interest and his inclination to oblige. Thirdly, he will think it prudent to guard against sudden demands by keeping a larger amount of bank notes in his till. To meet all these demands he will be compelled to realize some of his securities, and he will realize those first on which he will sustain no loss.

If a banker has money lying at demand with a bill-broker, he will now have occasion to call it in. If he has money lent at short periods at the Stock Exchange, he will, as he has occasion, take in the money as the loans fall due. If he has discounted brokers' bills, he will receive the amounts when due, and discount no more. Should these operations not be sufficient to meet the demands upon his funds, he will then sell his stock or exchequer bills, or borrow on them in the money market. A country banker who has kept his reserve in bills of exchange will be anxious to re-discount them, and will think himself lucky if he can do so readily and at a moderate rate of interest.

It will be useless for a banker to attempt to call up dead loans, or to reduce his discounts, after the pressure has commenced. He should have thought of these matters in the previous season of abundance. As he cannot get in any outstanding advances, he had better not ask for them, but merely charge the parties an increased rate of interest. If he demand the money, he will not get it, and he may give rise to a surmise that he is short of funds. This season of pressure is, however, a good opportunity for calling up advances, or getting rid of connections that he would, on other grounds, like to be without. The "scarcity of money," the "pressure on the money market," are capital reasons to assign for refusing applications which, even otherwise, he would refuse, and for calling up loans which, under any circumstances, he would like to see repaid.

During a pressure, a banker will have to give a great many refusals, and some discretion will be necessary in the form of giving these refusals. Let him refuse in what way he may at such a season, he will be sure to give offence. And the party refused will possibly publish the refusal, and, from motives of ignorance or malignity, represent the refusal as having arisen from want of means, and possibly may circulate a report that the banker is about to stop payment. Hence rumours about banks are always rife in seasons of pressure, and they add to the general want of confidence which then prevails.

During a pressure, a banker will have offers of new accounts to be transferred from other bankers, provided he will consent to make certain advances. Some caution must be exercised in this matter. It is quite possible that some perfectly safe parties, having large accounts, may be disposed to remove in consequence of their present bankers not being equal to the supply of their wants. In this case, the banker will be regulated by the value of the proposed account and the extent of his own means. On the other hand, it is equally possible that weak people, to whom their present bank might not, in any case, have given advances, may use the "scarcity of money" as a pretext for making application to a new banker, stating their belief that their old banker was unable to meet their requirements. It behoves a banker to use much discretion in such a case, especially if it be a large account. If he errs at all, he should err on the side of caution.

It will rarely be wise for a banker in a season of pressure to attempt to get away the customers of other bankers by offering them greater accommodation. The best way of getting new connections is to treat well those that he has. It is better for a banker to employ his funds in supporting his old friends than in attempting to get new ones. If his funds are so ample that he can do both without inconvenience, very well. But caution is necessary in taking new accounts at this time, and he should be doubly cautious in making applications to parties. Unless he has the most ample and satisfactory information as to their circumstances, he had better wait until they apply to him. It would then devolve upon them to satisfy him that he would be justified in making the advances required.

During the pressure, a banker will find that some of his wealthier customers, who, when money was abundant, took their bills to be discounted by a bill-broker, because he would cash them at a lower rate, will come back, and expect to have discounts from their banker. This is no fault of the bill-brokers. People put money in their hands avowedly for temporary purposes. In seasons of abundance the bill-brokers are glutted with money. When the pressure commences this money is withdrawn. The consequence is, that in seasons of abundance the bill-brokers will discount at a lower rate than the bankers, and when money is scarce they discount at a higher rate, and in many cases will not discount at all. Sharp-sighted people, who are acquainted with the London money market, will, when money is abundant, take all their first-rate bills to a bill-broker, and send to their banker all their inferior bills, which a bill-broker would not take. Now, if a banker has occasion to curtail his advances in seasons of pressure, he should begin with people of this sort. But if he has ample means, and the parties are wealthy, he may deem it worth his while to take their bills, charging a high rate of interest, and gently reminding them of their former delinquencies. Exhortations to good behaviour have always a greater effect when administered in seasons of affliction. And reproof at this time to a party who has thus wandered may induce him to pursue in future a more righteous line of conduct.

During a pressure, a banker will find that some of his customers will get into difficulties, and will apply to him for assistance. He will often be at a loss to decide whether he should or should not grant the assistance required. This hesitation will arise from his doubts as to the extent to which he can prudently rely upon the calculations and anticipations of his customer. The party states that he must immediately stop payment unless he has assistance; but he has abundance of property, and his difficulties arise only from not being able to realize it. If he has a certain sum he can then go on comfortably. The banker grants him this sum. After a while, he comes again, and states he must now stop unless he has a farther sum. The banker hesitates, but ultimately gives him this farther sum. He comes a third time, and states he has not yet got enough; and not being able to get more, he then stops, leaving the banker at best with a large lock-up, and probably with an ultimate loss.

During a pressure, those banks that allow interest on deposits will be asked for a higher rate of interest.[1] It is quite right that those parties who have had deposits at the bank for some time, should receive a higher rate of interest, proportionate to the increased value of money. But it may be questioned whether it is worth while to re-

[1] The rate of interest allowed on deposits by the banks in London and throughout the country generally is regulated by the Bank of England rate for the time being, and is, as a rule, one per cent. below that rate. But in special instances, when money is scarce and the bank rate high, or plentiful and the bank rate low, one and a half per cent., and even more than that, below the bank rate, is frequently the rate allowed for deposits.

ceive farther lodgments, during a pressure, at a high rate of interest, unless they are lodged for a fixed period. For, should the pressure increase, these sums are sure to be withdrawn, or else applications will be made for a higher rate of interest than the banker can prudently give. Nor must it be forgotten that it is not wise for a banker to give, during a panic, an extravagant rate of interest. Should he do so, he will give rise to an opinion that he is short of funds, and this may cause more deposits to be withdrawn than he would obtain from his high rate of interest.

During a pressure, a banker will pay considerable attention to the published returns of the Bank of England. The increase or diminution of the gold and silver in the issuing department will show the progress of the pressure. As these increase, money will become less scarce, the rate of interest will fall, and the pressure will subside. In this department, it is the progress of increase or diminution, more than the actual amount, that should be the main object of attention. The banking department resembles any other bank. Its means are the paid-up capital—the real or surplus fund—the public deposits—the private deposits, and the seven-day bills. These means are employed in public securities, private securities, and cash in the till. Its ability to make advances, at any given time, depends on the amount of cash in the till. The diminution of this amount shows the increase of the pressure, and the banker will act accordingly.

As far as past experience goes, all panics or pressures have resulted in a subsequent abundance of money. It would be a grand thing for a banker if he could know beforehand at what precise point this change would take place. But this he cannot know, and he had better not speculate on the subject, but just follow the course of events as they occur. When, however, the point is fairly turned, he will act wisely in investing all his surplus funds in such convertible securities as are likely to advance in price, from the increasing low rate of interest. Exchequer bills are most likely to be the first affected, and then the public funds. He will, also, be more liberal in granting discounts, and other advances, and he will lower the rate of interest at which he takes deposits. At the same time, he will be cautious in the bills he discounts. For, though money may be abundant, yet trade may be depressed, and the effects of the previous panic may be the failure of a great number of persons in the middle class of society. The banker will therefore be cautious in extending his discounts, except on bills of an undoubted character.

We will observe, lastly, that, in a season of pressure, it is peculiarly necessary that a banker should pay regard to the state of his own health, and to the discipline of his own mind, so as to guard against any morbid or gloomy apprehensions with regard to the future. He should attempt to form a cool and dispassionate judgment as to the result of passing events; endeavouring so to arrange his own affairs as to be prepared for whatever may occur, but taking care not to increase the present evil by predicting greater calamities. If he suffer a feeling of despondency to get the mastery of his mind, he will be less able to cope with the difficulties of his position. He will then, probably, refuse reasonable assistance to even first-rate customers, realize securities unnecessarily at a heavy sacrifice, and keep in his till an amount of unemployed treasure excessively disproportionate to the extent of his liabilities. This will increase the pressure. Fear, too, is always contagious. A banker of this melancholy temperament will impart his apprehensions to others, and thus the panic will become more widely extended.

SECTION XXII.

THE ADMINISTRATION OF A BANK UNDER THE ACT OF 1844.

IT would not be consistent with the practical character of this work to discuss, at great length, any theory of the currency. But the Act of 1844, though founded on a theory, was a practical measure, and has so important a bearing on the administration of banking affairs, that our work would be regarded as incomplete were the subject altogether omitted.

"The Act of 1844" is the 7 & 8 Vict. cap. 32, and is entitled, "An Act to regulate the Issue of Bank Notes, and for giving to the Governor and Company of the Bank of England certain privileges for a limited period." It enacts that from and after the 31st August, 1844, the Issue department of the Bank of England shall be separated from the Banking department—that the issuing department may issue notes to the extent of £14,000,000 upon securities set apart for that purpose, of which the debt of £11,015,100 due from the Government to the bank shall form a part—that no amount of notes above £14,000,000 shall be issued, except against gold coin, or gold or silver bullion; and that the silver bullion shall not exceed one-fourth the amount of gold coin and bullion. Any person is entitled to demand notes from the issuing department, in exchange for gold bullion, at the rate of £3 17s. 9d. per ounce. Should any banker discontinue his issue of notes, the Bank of England may, upon application, be empowered by an Order of Council to increase its issue upon securities to the extent of two-thirds of the issue thus withdrawn; but all the profit of this increased issue must go to the Government.

The theory on which this Act was founded had, for several years previously, been brought before the public in pamphlets written by men of distinguished talent. Upon some of these pamphlets we wrote a critique, which appeared in the "Westminster Review" of January, 1841. That article was afterwards published separately, under the title of "Currency and Banking: a Review of some of the Principles and Plans that have recently engaged public attention, with reference to the administration of the Currency." In this review we made the following observations on the plan then proposed, and subsequently carried out in the Act of 1844:—

"*The plan of making the amount of the circulation fluctuate in exact correspondence with the amount of gold in the Bank of England.*

"This plan is open to the following objections:—

"Upon this plan there must be a perpetual increase and diminution in the stock of gold; consequently a perpetual increase and diminution in the amount of the currency. The increase in the amount of the currency would raise prices and stimulate speculation. The diminution in the amount of the currency would reduce prices and produce distress. And thus there must be a constant alteration from high prices to low prices, and again from low prices to high prices—from speculation to distress, and from distress to speculation.

"2. But depression of prices, and its attendant miseries, may not be experienced only when the foreign exchanges are unfavourable. Excessive caution, an apprehension of war, or political feeling, may cause a domestic demand for gold, and this would cause for a while a contraction of the currency as severe as that which would arise from an unfavourable exchange; and, as the bank directors would have no discretionary power, but would be required 'to adhere to principle,' by giving gold for notes, or notes for gold, they could do nothing to assuage these calamities. According to Mr. Loyd, a drain, from whatever cause it may arise, must be met by a contraction of the currency. Mr. Palmer, in laying down his rule, put in a saving clause —'except under special circumstances,' but Mr. Loyd[1] makes no exceptions.

"3. To carry this system into operation would require a separation of the issuing department from the other departments of the business of the bank, and this would cause still farther inconveniences. The management of the issuing department would be exceedingly simple. The office of the directors would be a complete sinecure, and, for anything they would have to do, their places might be as well supplied by four-and-twenty broomsticks. A few cashiers to exchange gold for notes, or notes for gold, would be all the establishment required; and could Mr. Babbage be induced to construct a 'self-acting' machine to perform these operations, the whole business of the currency department might be carried on without human agency. But the deposit department would require more attention. 'It is in the nature of banking business,' says Mr. Loyd, 'that the amount of its deposits should vary

---

[1] I wish I could have made this quotation without introducing the names. It would greatly assist our inquiries after truth, and lead to the formation of an independent judgment, if we could engage in discussions of this kind without any reference to those talented men who may have distinguished themselves as either the advocates or the opponents of the doctrines we investigate.

with a variety of circumstances; and, as the amount of deposits varies, the amount of that in which those deposits are invested (viz., the securities) must vary also. It is, therefore, quite absurd to talk of the bank, in its character of a banking concern, keeping the amount of its securities invariable.' As, therefore, the deposits might vary, the bank would be a buyer or a seller of Government securities; and as these variations are sometimes to a very large amount, the fluctuations in the price of the public funds, and of exchequer bills, would be very considerable. Thus the property of those who held these securities would be always changing in value. Again, the deposits would be withdrawn chiefly in seasons of pressure, and the bank would then be compelled to sell her securities. But suppose the scarcity of money should be so great that the securities would be unsaleable even at a reduced price, how then could the bank pay off her deposits?

"4. If the currency were administered upon this principle, the bank would be unable to grant assistance to the commercial and manufacturing classes in seasons of calamity.

"Mr. Loyd exclaims, 'Let not the borrowers of money, Government and Commerce, approach, with their dangerous and seductive influences, the creator of money.' But, with all deference to Mr. Loyd, we contend that it is the province of a bank to afford assistance to trade and commerce in seasons of pressure. Mr. Loyd, as a practical banker, would no doubt afford assistance to his own customers in such seasons; and if this be the province and duty of a private banker, the duty is more imperative on a public banking company, and more imperative still on a bank invested by the legislature with peculiar privileges for the public good. Mr. Loyd says, 'Let the bank afford this assistance out of her own funds.' But, under Mr. Loyd's system, she could grant assistance only by selling securities; and what relief would she afford by selling securities with one hand, and lending out the money with the other? Besides, is it certain that, under such a pressure as Mr. Loyd's system must occasionally produce, these securities would be saleable at even any price? 'But,' says Mr. Loyd, 'individuals may afford this assistance.' In seasons of pressure few individuals have more ample funds than what are necessary for the supply of their own wants.... When the distress is caused by a contraction of the currency, it can only be removed by an increased issue of notes. And there are many cases, such for instance as that of the Northern and Central Bank, in which assistance can only be effectually rendered in this manner.

"We consider that any system of administering the currency, which prohibits the banking institutions of the country from granting relief to the commercial and manufacturing classes, must be unsound. We should condemn such a system at once, even if we could not detect the fallacies on which it was founded. In political economy we can judge of principles only by their practical effects—and any system which produces these effects must be unsound. When seasons of calamity occur, it is not for the national bank to exclaim, *Sauve qui peut*. They ought to co-operate with the Government in attempting to relieve the distress, and to preserve the tranquillity of the country."

These remarks, written in the year 1841, might, if put into the past tense, almost serve for a history of the year 1847. The Act of 1844 was formed upon the principle which is here condemned; and the effects described have actually occurred. There have been great fluctuations in the amount of the circulation, in the rate of interest, and in the prices of the public securities. There have been great speculations, followed by great distress. The Government funds have in large amounts been unsaleable; and the bank has been unable to afford relief to the commercial classes. A severe pressure has taken place; and, in consequence of this severe pressure, the Act was suspended. It has been denied that this pressure was produced or increased by the Act. But, how stand the facts? The Act was passed, and, as predicted, a pressure came: the Act was continued, and the pressure increased: the Act was suspended, and the pressure went away. These are not opinions—they are facts.

At the meeting of Parliament in the latter end of 1847, committees were appointed by both the House of Lords and the House of Commons, to " inquire into the causes of the distress which has for some time prevailed among the commercial classes ; and how far it has been affected by the laws for regulating the issue of bank notes payable on demand." The following is an extract from the Report of the Lords' Committee as to the causes of the pressure :—

"A sudden and unexampled demand for foreign corn, produced by a failure in many descriptions of agricultural produce throughout the United Kingdom, coincided with the unprecedented extent of speculation produced by increased facilities of credit and a low rate of interest, and had for some time occasioned over-trading in many branches of commerce. This was more especially felt in railroads, for which calls to a large amount were daily becoming payable, without corresponding funds to meet them, except by the withdrawal of capital from other pursuits and investments. These causes account for much of the pressure under which many of the weaker commercial firms were doomed to sink, and which was felt even by the strongest. To these causes may be added a contemporaneous rise of price in cotton; and, with respect to houses connected with the East and West India trade, a sudden and extensive fall in the price of sugar, by which the value of their most readily available assets underwent great depreciation.

"Some of these causes are obviously beyond the reach of legislative control. But upon those which are connected with the extension of commercial speculation, encouraged or checked by the facility or the difficulty of obtaining credit by the advance of capital and the discount of bills, the powers and position of the Bank of England must at all times enable that corporation to exercise an important influence. The committee have consequently felt it to be their duty to inquire into the course pursued by the bank acting under the provisions of the 7 & 8 Vict. c. 32, and they have come to the conclusion that the recent panic was materially aggravated by the operation of that statute, and by the proceedings of the bank itself. This effect may be traced, directly, to the Act of 1844, in the legislative restriction imposed on the means of accommodation, whilst a large amount of bullion was held in the coffers of the bank, and during a time of favourable exchanges; and it may be traced to the same cause, indirectly, as a consequence of great fluctuations in the rate of discount, and of capital previously advanced at an unusually low rate of interest. This course the bank would hardly have felt itself justified in taking, had not an impression existed that, by the separation of the issue and the banking departments, one inflexible rule for regulating the bank issues had been substituted by law in place of the discretion formerly vested in the bank."

The nature and extent of the pressure is thus described

by the Governor and Deputy-Governor of the Bank of England:—

"The panic began by the failures in the corn trade. The price of wheat had risen to about 120*s*. Large arrivals of grain from the continent of Europe and from America, coupled with the prospect of an early and abundant harvest, caused a sudden fall in price to about 60*s*., with a corresponding decline in Indian corn. The failure of most of the corn speculators followed this great reduction in price, and their failure caused the stoppage of an eminent discount broker having a large country connection. This latter failure, by closing one of the principal channels of discount between the country and London, caused distrust to extend into the country. Credit became affected by these failures, and several London firms of high standing also failed. Then followed in rapid succession the failure of the Royal Bank of Liverpool, the Liverpool Banking Company, the North and South Wales Banking Company, some private country banks, and the Union Bank of Newcastle, followed by a tremendous run upon the Northumberland and Durham District Bank. To these disasters succeeded alarm, and an almost total prostration of credit. The London bankers and discount brokers refused to grant the usual accommodation to their customers, and necessarily obliged everyone requiring assistance to resort to the Bank of England. Money was hoarded to a considerable extent: so much so, that notwithstanding the notes and coin issued to the public, in October it exceeded by £4,000,000 or £5,000,000 the amount with the public in August; still the general complaint was of a scarcity of money. Credit was so entirely destroyed, that houses trading to distant countries, carrying on their business through the means of credit by a renewal of their acceptances as they became due, were no longer able to meet their engagements, and were forced to stop payment. This was the state of things previous to the issuing of the Government letter in October."[1]

The Committee of the House of Commons delivered a Report in favour of the continuance of the Bill without alteration—in opposition to the opinions of by far the majority of the witnesses who were examined.

Those witnesses who are friendly to the Act contend that it has secured the convertibility of the Bank of England note—that this convertibility was endangered in 1825, in 1837, and in 1839, and would have been endangered in 1847 but for this Act.[2]

By the phrase " securing the convertibility of the note," it is not meant that the issue department of the Bank of England held a sufficient amount of gold and silver to pay off all the notes it had issued. It is obvious that the gold and silver in hand must always be fourteen millions less than this amount, inasmuch as fourteen millions of notes are issued against securities. By " securing the convertibility of the note," is meant, that the issue department of the Bank of England were in a condition to pay off any amount of notes of which payment was likely to be demanded *for the purpose of exporting the gold*—the issue department was always in a condition to meet any *foreign* demand for gold. This is called, " securing the convertibility of the note."

It has been contended, that the Act has retained in the vaults of the Bank of England a larger amount of gold and silver than would otherwise have been retained. And as this amount is set apart for the express purpose of paying the notes, their payment is so far additionally

[1] Lords, No. 12.
[2] See the Evidence before the Committee of the House of Lords, Questions No. 1406 to 1409, and No. 3169.

secured. On the other hand, it has been maintained that, by thus reserving all the gold to pay the notes, we endangered the payment of the deposits. And had the banking department stopped payment, a domestic run would have taken place upon the issuing department, and thus the payment of the notes would still have been endangered.

The following is the evidence of a director of the Bank of Liverpool upon the subject:

"With regard to securing the convertibility of the notes, what is your opinion of the bill?

"I do not think it has secured the convertibility of the notes at all. The notes remained convertible up to the suspension of the Bill; but I believe that, if the Bill had not been suspended then, or some similar measure adopted, notes would have ceased to be convertible. Looking to the general state of things throughout the country, and to what I know to have been the state of things in London, and the position of trade generally—to the alarm that was spreading rapidly through the country, and to the fact that the power of the bank had been reduced to such a point, that if there had been any apprehension of the failure of the country banks, it could not farther support them, and that very little might have occasioned (I might perhaps go further, and say, would have occasioned) the failure of banks in large towns and in the country—believing that if one or two country banks of any magnitude had failed, alarm would have spread throughout the kingdom, or if one or two London banks had failed, consternation would have been general—seeing, also, the considerable amount of reserve in the hands of the country bankers and joint-stock banks, and the necessity that there would have been of having that reserve as early as possible converted into gold if the bank was obliged to stop—seeing that a reserve of £20,000 for each of 300 country banks would have taken six or seven millions, or of £15,000 each would have taken five millions—and that if the run for gold had once begun, it would probably have gone on till the treasury was drained—seeing all this, my firm opinion is, that the Bill of 1844 has not secured convertibility, and I state the grounds on which that opinion is formed."[1]

It seems useless at present to speculate upon such a state of things, as *we now* know that before the pressure arrived to such a height as to cause the banking department to stop payment, the Act would be suspended. But it seems fair to ask, whether the precautions of the Act are not disproportionate to the danger? We ought to consider not merely the greatness of the evil, but also the probability of its occurrence; and is it wise to inflict upon ourselves a vast number of serious evils merely to guard against a danger that may never occur? It may farther be asked, whether the stringent measures that were necessary to keep the banking department from stopping payment, would not have been equally effectual under the previous state of the law in preserving the convertibility of the notes?

It should be recollected, too, that previous to the passing of the Act of 1844, the bank had the power of rectifying the exchanges by means of foreign credits, as they did in the year 1839.[2] But the directors, being now relieved from all responsibility with regard to the issue department, have no inducement to engage in such an operation. Indeed, they might be censured for interfering with the principle of the Act, that the exchanges shall be rectified by a transmission of gold and silver.

[1] Commons, No. 94.
[2] Several of the witnesses made suggestions for rectifying this exchange by other means than the exportation of gold.—See Commons, 97, 2018, 2023, 2579, 2614, 2620.

It would appear from the evidence, that the SOLE advantage now claimed for the Act, is that it has secured the convertibility of the note. Other advantages, however, were expected to result. Those expectations are thus disposed of in the Report of the Lords' Committee:—

"It is true that to those who may have expected that the 7 & 8 Vict. c. 32, would effectually prevent a recurrence of cycles of commercial excitement and depression, the contrast between the years 1845 and 1847 must produce a grievous disappointment. To those who anticipated that the Act would put a check on improvident speculation the disappointment cannot be less, if reliance is to be placed (as the committee are confident it may) on the statement of the governor of the bank, and of other witnesses, that 'speculations were never carried to such an enormous extent as in 1846 and the beginning of 1847.' If the Act were relied on as a security against violent fluctuations in the value of money, the fallaciousness of such anticipation is conclusively proved by the fact, that whilst the difference between the highest and lowest rate of discount was in the calamitous years 1837 and 1839 but $2\frac{1}{4}$ to $2\frac{3}{4}$ per cent., the difference in 1847 rose to $6\frac{3}{4}$. If it was contemplated that the number and the extent of commercial failures would have been lessened, the deplorable narrative of the governor of the bank, recording the failure of thirty-three houses comparatively in large business, in London alone, to the amount of £8,129,000, is a conclusive reply. If the enormous extent to which railroad speculation has been carried be considered as an evil to which a sound system of banking could have applied a corrective, such a corrective has not been found in an Act, since the passing of which, during a period of three years, an increased railway capital of upwards of £221,000,000 has been authorized to be raised by Parliament; and when the enormous sum of

£76,390,000 is stated, on high financial authority, to have been actually expended on railways in two years and a half. If the power of obtaining banking accommodation on moderate terms were considered to be promoted by the Act of 1844, it cannot be said that this important object has been attained, since it appears in evidence that in 1847, in addition to an interest of 9 or 10 per cent., a commission was also frequently paid, raising the charge to 10, 20, or 30 per cent., according to the time which bills had to run."

The Report might have added, that if it was expected that the amount of notes in the hands of the public would fluctuate in exact correspondence with the fluctuations in the amount of gold in the Bank of England, that expectation has not been fulfilled. From the censure cast on the Bank of England before the Act was passed for not producing this correspondence, it may be inferred that such an expectation was entertained.[1]

Those who are opposed to the Act of 1844 bring against it the following accusations :—

First. The Act of 1844 is accused of having produced an abundance of money and a low rate of interest, and thus to have stimulated to excessive speculation. We showed, in the last section, that these are always the precursors of a pressure.

According to this Act, all persons are entitled to demand from the issue department of the Bank of England, Bank of England notes in exchange for gold bullion at the rate of £3 17s. 9d. per ounce of standard gold. When, therefore, the foreign exchanges are favourable to the importation of gold, this gold, consisting of gold bars and foreign gold coin, which could not be used as money in this country, is taken to the issue department, and instantly

[1] See the Evidence taken before the Committee on Banks of Issue, No. 2677—2713.

converted into Bank of England notes. The amount of notes is thus increased beyond what the transactions of the country require. Money becomes plentiful, the rate of interest falls, and the low rate of interest gives facilities to speculative undertakings.

It must be acknowledged that, previous to the passing of this Act, the bank directors had adopted the principle of purchasing all foreign gold that might be offered them at £3 17s. 9d. an ounce; and it formed a feature of their system of management, as explained before a committee of the House of Commons in the year 1832. When the advocates of the Act say that it is only during a season of pressure that the Act comes into operation,[1] they can mean only that it is during such a season that the system established by the Act differs from the system previously in existence. The Act is as much in operation when it gives out notes as when it gives out gold.

It must also be acknowledged that on the 31st August, 1844, when the Act came into operation, there was a large amount of gold in the bank, and a low rate of interest consequently prevailed. This gold had accumulated, not literally in consequence of the Act, but in consequence of the principle embodied in the Act. From the adoption of this principle, the gold in the vaults of the bank still farther increased after the passing of the Act.

It must be farther acknowledged, that although the Act requires the issue department at all times to issue notes against gold, it does not require that the Bank of England shall at all times issue £14,000,000 against securities. The Act merely requires that the amount *shall not exceed* £14,000,000. And a London banker who was examined as a witness before the Lords' Committee, said he expected that when the Act came into operation the bank would not

---

[1] Commons, 5121.

issue at first more than £11,000,000 against securities, and that the remaining £3,000,000 would not be issued until the rate of interest had advanced to 3½ or 4 per cent. But the Act did not require the Bank of England to adopt this course; and its adoption would probably have been considered by some parties as a departure from its principle. For it is a fundamental principle of the Act, that the amount of circulation shall jerk up and down in exact conformity to the importations or exportations of gold. And hence during a favourable course of exchange money must be abundant, and interest must be low.

It is alleged that the Act still farther reduced the rate of interest, and promoted speculative undertakings, by placing the Bank of England in a position in which the directors were led to adopt a new system of management.

In September, 1844, soon after the Act was passed, the directors, whose rate of interest had never previously been lower than 4 per cent., reduced it to 2½ per cent. The object of this reduction was to invest a larger portion of their funds in the discount of bills. It is stated that, to effect this object, the directors not only reduced their rate of discount, but also canvassed for business, and thus gave a stimulus to new transactions. They had been told that the banking department of the Bank of England was to be managed "like any other banking concern using Bank of England notes." And it is not an unusual thing for bankers, when they cannot employ their funds at so high a rate of interest as they wish to obtain, to employ them at a lower rate. Nor is it unusual for a banker to offer his surplus cash to bill-brokers and others, who are known to be in the habit of supplying bankers with bills. But however consistent the conduct of the directors may have been with banking principles, the reduction of the bank rate of discount immediately caused a reduction in the market rate, and in the rates charged by bankers throughout the country. For it must be observed, that when the bank lowers its rate of interest upon money in seasons of abundance, it has the necessary effect of reducing the market rate of interest still lower than the bank rate. Suppose, for instance, the bank discounts at 5 per cent. and the market rate of discount is 4 per cent., of course no bills are offered for discount to the bank. Then the bank, to get discounts, lowers its rate of interest to 4 per cent. A portion of bills that were previously discounted by private bankers and bill-brokers will then be taken to the bank; but the notes thus drawn from the bank make money still more plentiful, and the market rate falls to $3\frac{1}{2}$ or 3 per cent. Now, should the bank reduce its rate to 3 per cent. the same effects would again follow. For the additional notes thus drawn out would make money so abundant as to reduce the market rate of interest to $2\frac{1}{2}$ or 2 per cent., and so on.

But in seasons of scarcity, precisely the opposite effect follows. For when the bank raises the rate of discount, it has the effect of raising the market rate still higher. Thus, if the bank should be discounting at 5 per cent. and the market rate should be $5\frac{1}{2}$ per cent., let the bank raise her rate to 6 per cent. and the market rate will immediately become 7 or perhaps 8 per cent., or even higher upon inferior bills. For the bank rate of discount will be the market rate for only the first class of bills—such bills as could be discounted at the bank; and all bills of the second class will have to pay an advanced rate, and those of a still more inferior character will not be discountable at all.

In 1844 the rate of discount was lower than in any previous season of abundance of money. This low rate of interest was produced, in the first place, by the principle of the Act of 1844, which caused the issue of a large amount of notes against gold and silver bullion; and, secondly, by that provision of the Act which separated the two departments, and thus brought the banking department of the Bank of England into competition with other bankers and money dealers, as discounters of bills.[1] The directors of the bank seem to think that the spirit of the Act of 1844 required that the bank should employ its reserve.

"If we keep the notes in the reserve, instead of giving them out to the public, the effect that ought to be produced by gold coming into the country is counteracted; it induces a larger amount of capital to come into the country, because you do not allow that portion which has come in to be employed. If you do not put out the gold, or the representative of gold, you entirely prevent its having any effect upon the circulation. The exchange will be kept up, and gold will continue to come in."[2]

Thus it appears that, although there is no positive enactment in the Act respecting the management of the banking department, the directors so understand its spirit as to believe that when gold is going out of the country they ought to take measures to prevent its exit; and when gold is coming into the country, they ought to endeavour to drive it back again. The first object is attained by raising the rate of interest very high; the second, by reducing it very low. It must, however, be acknowledged that, apart from any efforts of the banking department, a large importation of gold will under the Act necessarily cause a low rate of interest.

Secondly. The next charge against the Act of 1844 is, that it does not admit of those occasional expansions of

---

[1] Commons, 2275, 5189, 5347—5350.   [2] Commons, 3009.

the amount of notes in circulation which are often required by the domestic transactions of the country.

It is alleged that one imperfection of the Act was strikingly manifested in the beginning of the year 1846. The Parliament required that all railway companies that intended to apply for an Act, should lodge 10 per cent. on their capital within fifteen days after the meeting of Parliament. It was impossible to say beforehand what amount of notes would be required to make these payments. It was variously estimated at from £12,000,000 to £25,000,000, while all the notes in the hands of the public amounted to only about £20,000,000. Ultimately the railway companies of Ireland and Scotland were allowed to make their payments in Dublin and Edinburgh, respectively; and the payments in London did not amount to more than £14,000,000.[1] This large sum was paid by means of the banking department of the Bank of England lending out the money as fast as it was received. Had the Act of 1844 not been in existence, the Bank of England (as in the case of the West India loan, and of previous loans) might have lent out the money before the time of payment arrived, and no apprehensions would have been entertained. The notes in circulation would have been largely increased for a few days, and then again have subsided to the former amount. As it was, the payment was not made through any virtue in the Act. And had it been required under different circumstances, or when the banking department had a smaller reserve, it could not have been made at all.[2]

It is farther alleged, that the Act of 1844 requires an immediate contraction in the amount of the notes whenever gold is exported for merely a temporary or specific purpose. Between March 13 and April 24, 1847,

[1] Lords, 1209, 1214.   [2] Lords, 1209.

£2,237,200 was exported in payments for corn. An equal amount of notes was of course cancelled by the issue department. The notes must have been taken out of the hands of the public, or from the banking department of the Bank of England. About the same time, the Government had occasion to borrow of the banking department about £3,500,000 to pay the April dividends. The banking department, consequently, for a while limited their discounts, and even refused to grant loans on exchequer bills. Great pressure was consequently felt, though it did not last for a long time. Now it is alleged, that if the Act of 1844 had not existed, the directors would have allowed the gold to be exported without *immediately* contracting the notes in circulation. They would have lent the money required by the Government, without refusing the loans and discounts to the public; and the contraction of the circulation, by being extended over one or two months, instead of a few weeks, might have produced no inconvenience.

By the Act of 1844, the circulation of the country banks was restricted to a certain amount. The average of the twelve weeks ending the 27th of April, 1844, was fixed for the maximum. During some months in the year the country requires more notes than this maximum; and, as the banks can issue no more notes of their own, they obtain Bank of England notes from London. In the year 1845 Acts of Parliament were passed for the regulation of the notes issued in Scotland and Ireland. Beyond certain fixed amounts, the banks in these countries are required to hold gold equal to the amount of notes in circulation. In both countries this circulation fluctuates. In Scotland, the highest amount is in November. In Ireland, the highest amount is in January or February. In these months they require more gold, and this gold they obtain from the issue department in exchange for Bank of England notes. Before the Act of 1844, the circulation of the country parts of England, of Scotland, and of Ireland, expanded or contracted as required by the wants of the public, without affecting the London circulation of the Bank of England; but under this Act, the expansion of the circulation of the country banks, the banks of Scotland, and of Ireland, are attended by a contraction of the circulation of Bank of England notes in London. This may not be a matter of much consequence in ordinary times, when the banking department of the Bank of England has a large reserve; but in seasons of pressure, such as occurred in 1847, this drain on the London circulation may be more severely felt.

It may be farther stated, that the withdrawal or discontinuance of a certain amount of bills of exchange, through loss of credit or otherwise, would render a larger amount of bank notes necessary to fill up the space formerly occupied by those bills of exchange. But for such a circumstance no provision is made by the Act.[1]

Thirdly. It is alleged that the Act of 1844 tends to produce and to aggravate pressure, and at the same time deprives the Bank of England of the power of granting adequate assistance, even when the pressure is most urgent, and when assistance can be rendered without any danger of affecting the foreign exchanges.

This objection assumes that a pressure is an evil. It assumes, that to advance the rate of interest to a rate which no profit can afford to pay—to deprive solvent houses of the means of meeting their legitimate engagements—to cause a universal reduction of prices, and thus to baffle the calculations of even the most prudent—to reduce wealthy merchants to the condition of paupers—to

[1] Lords, 232—235.

deprive manufacturers of the means of executing their orders, and thus to throw thousands of industrious people out of employment—to sell to foreigners large amounts of goods and manufactures at less than the prime cost, thus causing a great national loss—to paralyze the national industry—to stop the progress of useful works—and to destroy confidence and credit—the objection assumes, that a pressure which produces effects like these is a national evil. And such must be the opinion of those who suspended the Act, and of those who approve of that suspension; for it was to prevent or to remove evils like these that the Act was suspended.

It is alleged that the Act tends to produce such pressures. By issuing notes against all the importations of gold, it causes abundance of money, lowers the rate of interest, and stimulates to speculative undertaking (thus the low rate of interest in 1844 and 1845 stimulated the railway speculations), and then, speculation is always succeeded by pressure. If, therefore, similar causes produce similar effects, and if the future shall resemble the past, the operation of the Act of 1844 will tend to produce pressure.

It is farther alleged, that when a pressure occurs without being produced by the Act, then the Act tends to aggravate the pressure. An unfavourable course of the exchange may be produced by a large importation of corn. The Act requires that the exchange shall be rectified by an exportation of gold, and that this exportation of gold shall be attended by a contraction of the domestic circulation (according to the present meaning of the word circulation) to an equal amount. It is hardly necessary to show that these regulations must aggravate a pressure.

. It has been said, that the pressure of 1847 was produced by the railway speculations and the famine, and *therefore* it was not produced or increased by the Act of 1844. We do not perceive the soundness of this reasoning, and it seems to show a forgetfulness of the peculiar operation of the Act. The Act requires that the amount of notes in circulation shall fluctuate in exact accordance with the amount of bullion. Railway speculations, famine, foreign loans, or a hundred other things, may turn the foreign exchanges, and cause gold to be exported, but it is the Act which causes our circulation of notes to be contracted in proportion as the gold is withdrawn. So a hundred different circumstances may cause gold to be imported, but it is the Act which causes our circulation to be inflated in correspondence with this increased amount of gold. Herein, we think, is the injurious operation of the Act. When the exchanges are favourable, gold is imported. The gold is in bars and foreign coin, and could not pass as money. But the Act issues notes against this gold, thus increasing the circulation, lowering the rate of interest, and giving rise to speculations of all kinds. These speculations, co-operating possibly with other causes, turn the exchanges. Notes are then taken to the bank, and gold demanded, for the purpose of being exported. This contraction of the circulation of notes produces pressure, and the apprehension of farther pressure produces panic.

They who contend that the Act of 1844 has not "in the slightest degree tended either to create or to increase the pressure"[1] of 1847, seem to be inconsistent in contending, at the same time, that the Act has preserved the convertibility of the bank note. It was the pressure and the high rate of interest, and low prices consequent upon the pressure, that checked the efflux of gold, and turned the exchanges. Now, if the Act had no effect in producing or increasing that pressure, the convertibility of the note,

[1] Lords, 3106.

by whatever causes it was secured, was not secured by the Act. If the Act did not in the slightest degree either create or increase the pressure, in what way, we ask, could it preserve the convertibility of the note? It appears to us that those who contend that the Act preserved the convertibility of the note, are bound by consistency to admit that the Act produced or increased the pressure.

It is farther alleged that the Act aggravates a pressure by the "panic" which it creates. It is stated that, during the pressure of 1847, notes to the amount of £4,000,000 were hoarded under the influence of panic, and this hoarding was occasioned by the provisions of the Act. It must be acknowledged, however, that something of this kind has taken place in former pressures. We noticed this circumstance with reference to the pressure of 1836, and again with reference to the pressure of 1839.

A contraction of the circulation leads to a general apprehension of danger. Hence the bankers and others keep larger reserves of bank notes on hand, in order to be prepared for the worst, and thus the evils of the contraction are considerably increased. That portion of the notes of the Bank of England which is passing from hand to hand, may be called the active circulation. That portion which is hoarded, or kept in reserve to meet possible demands, may be called the dead circulation. Now, it is quite certain that the dead circulation, while it remains in that state, has no effect upon the prices of commodities—the spirit of speculation—or the foreign exchanges. These are affected only by the active circulation. In seasons of pressure the dead circulation is increased at the expense of the active circulation, because people hoard their money to meet contingencies. Hence we find the pressure is often more severe than the reduction of the bank circulation would seem to warrant. But the fact is, that the pressure is in proportion to the reduction of the active circulation, and not in proportion to the reduction of the whole circulation. On the other hand, in seasons of abundance, the dead circulation is diminished, the active circulation proportionably increased, and hence the stimulus given to trade and speculation is much greater than the returns of the Bank of England would warrant us to expect.

If this disposition to hoard—or, more properly, to make provision for future or contingent demands—existed in 1837 and 1839, when the Bank of England had the unrestricted power of issuing notes; when there was the most unbounded confidence in its ability to render assistance—and when every solvent person expected, if necessary, to receive that assistance—it is natural to suppose that this disposition would be stronger in 1847, when the Bank of England had become divided into two departments—one of which could issue no notes except against gold, and the other had barely notes enough to meet its own obligations. For this alteration in the condition of the Bank of England, and the consequent feelings it inspired, the Act of 1844 is clearly responsible.

It is said that this desire of "hoarding" arose from PANIC; and that the sum thus "hoarded" amounted to £4,000,000 of notes. It is difficult to state where prudence ends and panic begins. This hoarding was no doubt carried on by all the joint-stock and private bankers, who, having received from the public large sums of money payable on demand, deemed it prudent to put themselves in a condition to repay these sums in case they should be demanded. And, from the number of banking establishments that exist in London, and throughout the country, it is reasonable to suppose that the sums thus hoarded must have been considerable. Many private parties, too, from distrust of their bankers, probably kept their hoards in their own hands. No blame, however, can attach to the bankers; for, although this "hoarding" increases the pressure, yet, were they not to adopt this course, their banks might stop payment, and thus a heavier calamity would fall upon the public.

It is farther alleged that the Act of 1844 has deprived the Bank of England of the power of granting assistance by the issue of notes during a pressure, even when the pressure is most urgent, and the foreign exchanges are favourable. Before the passing of the Act, when there was no separation of departments, the bank directors restricted their issues when the exchanges were unfavourable, but extended them when the exchanges were favourable. Hence, during the pressure of 1837, they granted assistance by a farther issue of notes to the Northern and Central Bank, because the exchanges had become favourable. Between the periods of an efflux and an influx of gold there is always an interval of time. This interval is usually the highest point of the pressure; and heretofore the Bank of England would relieve the pressure by extending her issue of notes, in anticipation of the gold about to arrive. By this means solvent houses were prevented stopping. Confidence was restored, "hoarding" was diminished, and the pressure removed. But the Act of 1844 does not allow this. No additional notes can be issued until the gold has returned. The same course must be followed, whether the exchanges are favourable or unfavourable; and to anticipate the return of the gold by a farther issue of notes, under any circumstances, however urgent, would be a departure from the principle of the Act. That such a departure, however, may be made with immense advantage to the public, is obvious from the effects which immediately followed the suspension of the Act in October, 1847.[1]

[1] Commons, 5387—5389.

It is chiefly in this respect that the system established by the Act differs from the system previously in operation. And some of the witnesses, looking no farther than this, merely recommended that a power to suspend the Act in cases of severe pressure, should be lodged either with the Government or the Bank. We feel no regret that the legislature did not comply with this recommendation. It is this inflexibility of the Act which makes the commercial classes *feel* the unsoundness of its whole principle. Had a dispensing power been granted, we should merely have fallen back upon the previous system, with the additional disadvantage that the bank would never be able to adopt a better system, even if so disposed. The directors had for several years professed to govern the issue of notes by the foreign exchanges, but departed from that principle according to their discretion. The Act of 1844, by its inflexible enactment, put this principle to the test of experiment. The principle could not bear that test, and hence the Act was suspended. There is now a chance, at least, that we shall, ultimately, get a better system. The following is the language we addressed to the joint-stock banks at the time the Act was passed:—

"It must be acknowledged that the principle of regulating the currency by the stock of bullion in the Bank of England, as proposed by Sir Robert Peel, is one which the joint-stock banks, as well as the private banks, have strongly condemned. But since we cannot obtain the adoption of our own views, the question for our consideration is, Whether the existing system or that now proposed will best promote the interests of our establishments? And we shall probably determine that it is better to have a uniform law, the operations of which may be subjected to some degree of calculation, than unknown laws, which are applied or suspended according to the impulse of caprice.

"The proposed measure is an experiment; and so excellent is the machinery, that the experiment interferes as little as possible with existing interests. And the old machinery being retained by the continuance of the country issues, the return is easy to the former system, if necessary, before any serious injury can be inflicted on the country.

"As practical bankers, we contend that experience is the only test of the soundness of a theory. Let, then, 'the currency principle' be tried by this test. If it succeeds, the joint-stock bankers, in common with every other class of the community, will share the advantage. If it fails, then other principles will, perhaps, be tried; and, notwithstanding all the denunciations we have heard upon the subject, it may perhaps be ultimately found that the principle of 'competing issues,' as practised in Scotland, is the only effective principle by which the currency throughout the United Kingdom can be managed."

It is obvious that "the currency principle" has been tried and has failed. It seems now to be the proper time to try the antagonistic principle—that the amount of the domestic currency should be wholly unaffected by the importations or exportations of bullion. We doubt not that the talent and ingenuity which framed the Act of 1844 can construct a plan for bringing this principle also to the test of experiment. When this is done, we will judge of the soundness of the principle by its results. So far as it has hitherto been tried, it has never failed.

We have thus endeavoured to trace (impartially, as we believe) the practical operation of the Act of 1844. It is reasonable to suppose, that under similar circumstances it will produce similar effects. What will be its effects under other circumstances we have yet to learn.

We may be reminded that, should the Act work unfavourably under any circumstances, there is one remedy always at hand—the remedy which has already been applied—to suspend it. And no doubt, under any Government, men will be found who will have the courage to apply this remedy. But this will not remove the previous evil. The suspension, too, may be long delayed, and in the meantime much mischief may arise. In the next pressure the nation will be like "a cat in an air-pump." The animal will not be allowed to die, but at what precise period of exhaustion relief will be afforded will depend upon the views and theories of the philosophic statesmen who may at the time be performing the experiment.

It will not be safe for practical bankers to calculate with too much confidence upon the suspension of the Act. They should make their arrangements on the supposition that it will not be suspended. And it behoves them to inquire what are the principles upon which, under such circumstances, their establishments ought to be administered. This we shall now proceed to do.

We pointed out at the passing of the Act the course which we thought prudent bankers ought to pursue.

"In future, the amount of notes in circulation," we observed, "will be regulated by the foreign exchanges. When the exchanges are favourable, money will be abundant; when they are unfavourable, it will be scarce. The evils arising from a scarcity of money can only be avoided by following a prudent line of conduct when money is abundant. We, then, as prudent bankers, ought at present to check our desires of making large profits and declaring high dividends, and be content to employ our funds at a low rate of interest, rather than lock them up in hazardous or inconvertible securities. We should call up our old overdrafts, and our dead loans, and, if necessary, increase our capital, so as to place ourselves in the position most favourable for meeting an adverse state of the foreign exchanges. In cases of pressure on the money market, arising from an unfavourable course of exchange, the Bank of England will not be able, as heretofore, to relieve that pressure by a farther issue of notes, and, so far from granting assistance to other banks, she may, from the extent of her transactions, be more in need of assistance herself. We must, therefore, conduct our banks, individually, on a principle of self-dependence; we shall have to limit our overdrawn accounts, to avoid all advances on inconvertible securities, and to call up such an amount of capital as shall secure to us the means at all times of giving reasonable accommodation to our customers. On the recurrence of a pressure similar to that of 1839, the cry will be, *Sauve qui peut*—" Every one must take care of himself."

The knowledge we have acquired of the working of the Act will tend to give additional force to these recommendations. The attention of practical bankers will also be called to other points besides those which are here named.

It will become a question with them to what extent they should continue to allow interest on their deposits. Some of the joint-stock banks in London allow interest on the minimum balance of a current account. Others allow interest only on deposit receipts. But most London bankers, whether private or joint-stock, allow interest on the daily balance to their country connections.[1] In seasons of abundance, however, they usually limit the amount on

[1] Since 1877 all the leading London bankers have ceased to allow interest on current accounts, while continuing to allow it on deposit receipts or deposit accounts. The allowance of interest on the daily balances to country connections is now the exception rather than the rule.

which they allow interest, to prevent themselves being glutted with money from the country banks. But should the Act of 1844 produce those frequent alterations from abundance to pressure, and again from pressure to abundance, which we think it will produce, then it will become a matter of consideration how far the practice of allowing interest on deposits can be continued. It can never be worth a banker's while to allow interest on money which remains in his hands only so long as it cannot be employed, and is taken from him the moment it becomes valuable. During the year 1847 vast sums were withdrawn from both the London and the country bankers, not from any distrust of these bankers, but with a view to make more profitable investments. The rate of interest had been for some time previously very low. Consols had been at par; and when consols fell so low as to yield $3\frac{1}{2}$ per cent. interest, and the railway companies issued debentures bearing interest at 5 per cent., large sums were withdrawn from all the banks, as well as from the savings' banks, for the purpose of being invested in these securities. The bankers had no right to complain of this, as they were called upon only to fulfil their engagements; but they will probably be unwilling in future to allow interest on deposits of this description.

Another circumstance which the operation of the Act of 1844 will lead practical bankers to reconsider, will be the extent to which they should invest their surplus funds in Government securities. Many bankers have considered it as a sound principle to invest a certain portion of their funds in Government securities. We have laid before our readers extracts from evidence given before parliamentary committees, in favour of this principle, and we expressed our own convictions respecting the same doctrine. But we must acknowledge the operation of the Act is sufficient to show that this principle should be acted upon with caution, and should be limited in its application. The Act will cause money to be alternately abundant and scarce. When money is abundant, the funds are high; and when money is scarce, the funds are low. In seasons of abundance the banker will be full of deposits; in seasons of pressure his deposits will be withdrawn, and he will, moreover, be asked to assist his customers by farther advances. He will, therefore, always have occasion to sell out of the funds when the price is low, and thus he will sustain loss. It will, consequently, be his interest to employ his surplus funds in other investments, or even to keep his money unemployed in his till, rather than invest it in Government securities. His risk will be greater if the Act should be capriciously suspended. In October, 1847, several banks are said to have sold out of the funds only a few days before the appearance of the Government letter. After the issue of that letter the money was not wanted; but, as the funds immediately rose, the money could not be replaced but at considerable loss. The reports and proceedings of the joint-stock banks brought to light some transactions of this kind, and it is probable that the private banks sustained heavy losses by similar transactions.

Another lesson that will be more deeply impressed upon the minds of practical bankers, will be to conduct their establishments in such a way as to be self-dependent in seasons of pressure.

The events of the year 1847 are sufficient to show to what extent dependence can be placed on the Bank of England. Several of the directors complained that everybody looked for assistance to the Bank of England. No expectation could be more complimentary to the bank, nor show more strongly the confidence it had inspired under its previous government. In no preceding pressure had the bank refused assistance upon the ground that it was unable to grant it. But in former pressures there was no separation between the issuing and the banking departments. The bank's great strength lay in the power it possessed of expanding the circulation. That power was surrendered to the Act of 1844. The bank then became like "any other banking concern issuing Bank of England notes." Her locks are now shorn.[1]

The Bank of Liverpool had been one of the oldest and most respectable of the connections of the Bank of England. They had, from their commencement, never issued any but Bank of England notes, and had always a pretty large discount account with the branch at Liverpool. Yet, in the year 1847, their minute-book contains several entries similar to the following:—"The manager stated he had seen the agent of the branch bank this morning, and that he would not discount anything for us to-day." Even in the comparative light pressure of April, 1847, the bank suddenly restricted their discounts; and in October, 1847, they were quite unable to meet the public demand, although in some cases they lent consols instead of money. Indeed, it was because the means of the bank were unable to supply the demand for notes, that the Act of 1844 was suspended; yet the governor and all the other witnesses who supported the Act of 1844, stated their opinion that the pressure of 1847 was not so severe as some preceding pressures. How much sooner, then, would the means of the bank have been exhausted, if the pressure had equalled its predecessors in severity!

While bankers should not depend on the Bank of England, neither should they depend on the bill-brokers. A broker, as the name implies, is an intermediate party between the borrower and the lender. When money is

[1] Commons, 769, 3223-4, 3941-2, 4566, 5389.

abundant the bill-broker has large funds at his disposal, with which he will discount at a lower rate of interest than the bankers. When a pressure arrives, these funds are withdrawn, and his occupation is gone. Some bill-brokers have large capitals of their own, and take in deposits, repayable on demand; and to this extent they may be regarded as bankers. When money is abundant, sometimes cunning people, instead of going to their own bankers, will take their bills to the bill-brokers, who will discount them at a lower rate: and when the pressure arrives, and the brokers no longer discount, they think to return to their bankers. It is said that some country banks have occasionally adopted the same system. But it is clearly a bad system for any bank to adopt. A bank that is dependent on re-discount will most likely feel some inconvenience in a season of pressure, even when the bills are all undoubtedly good. But if the bank has, from a desire of making large profits, been induced in seasons of abundance to re-discount inferior bills, the results may be more serious. For in a season of pressure, a large portion of those bills will not be paid, and the bank will have to provide payments for its own indorsements, while its former channels of re-discount will be closed. All the joint-stock banks that stopped payment in 1847 had been accustomed to re-discount; and though some of them were unsound in other respects, yet the immediate cause of their stoppage was the inability to re-discount. We again refer to the proceedings of the Bank of Liverpool. "The manager stated that out of two small sums of £10,000 sent to London to the brokers only one had been done."— "We had then £100,000 at call with certain bill-brokers, who were unable, when applied to, to return us more than £25,000." The governor of the bank stated that the failure of the corn speculators caused the failure of an eminent discount-broker having a large country connection; and this failure, by closing one of the principal channels of discount between the country and London, caused distrust to extend into the country.

Banks should not only avoid depending on the Bank of England, or on bill-brokers: they should also avoid depending on other banks. Some banks in manufacturing districts are in the habit of discounting with banks in agricultural districts. A very good practice, as we think. But the banks requiring the discount should always recollect that when a pressure arrives, the discounting bank may have other ways of employing its funds. Country banks, too, should not rely too much on their London agents. Some London bankers have, no doubt, immense power. At the same time, in seasons of pressure, they have immense claims upon them.[1] If free from a run upon themselves, they will endeavour so to administer their funds as to afford reasonable assistance to all their connections. And no one connection should expect to receive more than this reasonable amount of assistance. But they may themselves be exposed to danger. The panic of 1847 was not a banking panic, but a commercial panic; and therefore the London bankers were comparatively free from molestation. The panic of 1825 commenced by the failure of a country bank. In such a case the London bankers could have rendered but little assistance to their country connections. It must be recollected that the Act of 1844 was suspended upon the application of the London bankers. The governor of the bank stated to the Committee of the House of Lords: " The London bankers and discount-brokers refused to grant the usual accommodation to their customers, and necessarily obliged every one requiring assistance to resort to the Bank of England."

[1] Commons, 2344-8.

The most effectual way of acquiring this self-dependence that we have been recommending, is to call up an adequate amount of capital. During a pressure, as we have already said, a banker has three additional claims on his funds. In the first place, a large amount of his deposits may be withdrawn. Secondly, many of his customers, and some probably of the wealthiest, will require additional assistance, in the way of loans and discounts. And, thirdly, he will think it prudent to keep a larger sum in his till, to meet contingent demands. On the other hand, the bills he holds will not all of them be regularly paid; the temporary loans he has granted will have to be renewed; and should he call up any of his permanent or dead loans, it will resemble calling spirits from the deep. In this case he will find the benefit of a large capital; and it is only by means of a large capital that all these operations can be performed with comfort to himself and satisfaction to his customers. But if we increase our capitals to the full extent that may be required in seasons of pressure, we must not expect to pay high dividends. It is obvious that with the same extent of business, a bank with a large capital must pay a lower dividend than a bank with a small capital. It seems therefore likely that the average rate of banking profits will be reduced.

The fluctuations in the value of money produced by attempting to regulate the currency by the foreign exchanges are injurious to both the London and the country bankers. In seasons when money is abundant, the bankers obtain but a low rate of interest on their loans and discounts—and they are tempted to make imprudent investments in order to employ their funds. And when, on the other hand, money is scarce, the amount of their lodgments is reduced—the rate of interest allowed on the permanent deposits is advanced—a larger sum is kept unemployed in the till—and there is more danger from losses, either by the failure of parties in debt to the bank, or by the necessity of realizing Government securities. Those country bankers who are in the habit of re-discounting their bills in London are induced, when money is abundant, to carry this system to a great extent, because they can obtain money at 2 or 3 per cent. in London, and lend it in the country at 4 or 5 per cent. But when money becomes scarce they have to pay an exorbitant interest or are denied discounts altogether, and they are then compelled to refuse their customers their usual accommodation, and then great distress is occasioned in the provinces. Except under peculiar circumstances, both the extremes of abundance and scarcity of money are unfavourable to large banking profits. A state in which money is easy without being abundant, and valuable without being scarce, is the most conducive to the prosperity of both the banking and the commercial interests of the country.

While, however, the profits of a banker from the ordinary operations of his business may be diminished, it is possible he may have opportunities of making other profits by those fluctuations in the prices of public securities which usually occur in the different periods of a circle of the currency. In the first period, immediately after a pressure, money is abundant without speculation; in the second period, money is abundant and speculations abound; in the third period, speculation begins to decline and money is in demand; in the fourth period, money is scarce and a pressure arrives. It is impossible to say how long each of these periods may last, as they will be influenced by political events—the abundance of the harvests—the direction which speculation may take—and the state of the public mind. Their approach or decline is generally indicated by the stock of gold in the Bank of England.

During the first period money will be abundant, because the importation of gold will cause an increased issue of bank notes; because, the import of commodities being diminished, there will be fewer bills drawn from abroad upon English houses, and offered for discount to the London bankers; and because trade will have become paralyzed at home, and prices will have fallen, so that less money will be required to carry it on. A banker, at this period, will have more money than he can employ. But at this period, the prices of the public funds and of other securities are low. The Act of 1844, by causing great fluctuations in prices, gives great advantage to prudent capitalists, at the expense of the less prudent or less wealthy classes of the community. "All fluctuations in trade," says Mr. Gurney, "are advantageous to the knowing man."[1] To those who are not "knowing men," these fluctuations are injurious. The abundance of the circulation produces a multiplication of contracts, and then the contraction of the circulation produces an inability to fulfil them.[2] And those who have stock or any other kind of saleable property, are obliged to realize in order to fulfil their engagements. Bankers may during this period make advantageous investments; and as they may calculate that another pressure will not arrive for two or three years, they may purchase a limited amount of securities that have six or twelve months to run. During the second period, money will be in demand, though there may be no great advance in the rate of interest. The securities purchased by the banker in the first period will now be falling due or advancing in price. But this will be the period of his greatest danger, and he must have a care not to let his desire of getting higher interest lead him to make undue advances upon the commodities or securities that may be

[1] Lords, 1324.   [2] Lords, 3845.

the subject of speculation. The third period will be the most profitable for the banker in his direct business. Money will be in full demand at a good rate of interest, and his deposits will hardly have begun to decline. He should now sell out stock and exchequer bills, or any other securities likely to be affected by the approaching pressure. He should make advances only by discounting short bills or making short loans. He should weed his accounts of such customers as have deeply engaged in the previous speculations—and put himself in a condition to support liberally through the pressure those who may be entitled to his assistance.

It seems, therefore, probable that bankers will, under the Act of 1844, endeavour to make up for diminished profits by investing more largely in securities. According to the evidence of Mr. Pease, the fluctuations in the currency have already produced similar effects in the departments of trade and commerce.

"I stated, as clearly as I was able to do, that the man who bought from hand to mouth, which is the common case, and did not watch those fluctuations of capital, so as to buy when things were unusually depressed, and to sell when things rose again, failed. The only man who succeeded in making money, succeeded in carrying on a speculative kind of business that has arisen from the want of regularity in the values of money and produce. The man who did not so speculate—buying largely at one time and selling very freely at another—did not succeed. It is of great importance that persons who do not desire to carry on a speculative business should have some assurance that it is moderately productive. That assurance they have lost, by being suddenly deprived by those fluctuations of that which they thought they had secured by their industry." [1]

[1] Commons, 4700, 4702.

Though we would not confound this kind of speculation with that which takes place by means of time bargains on the Stock Exchange, yet we do not think it desirable that banks should deal in the public securities merely with a view of making a profit from the fluctuations in price. Sometimes the banker will be out in his calculations, and, instead of selling at a profit, he will have to sell at a loss, or else submit to a lock-up of his funds. And at all times there is a danger that he will acquire a speculative feeling which will lead him to disregard the steady pursuit of his trade.

SECTION XXIII.

THE ADMINISTRATION OF THE BANKING DEPARTMENT OF THE BANK OF ENGLAND.

BY the Act of 1844, the banking department of the Bank of England was separated from its issuing department; and was to be managed like "any other banking concern issuing Bank of England notes." Taking this view of the banking department, we propose to inquire on what principles it ought to be administered. We shall do this, however, not so much with the view of bringing forward any notions of our own, as to lay before the reader some account of those principles which the bank directors have adopted for their government. This will lead us, peradventure, to discuss some principles of practical banking to which we have not hitherto had occasion to refer. We shall then trace the operations of this department for some years subsequent to the passing of the Act of 1844.

The Bank of England is governed by a court consisting of a governor and deputy-governor, and twenty-four directors. These are selected from the mercantile classes of London, virtually, by the other directors, who form what is called the House List. They recommend certain persons to be chosen as directors, and the proprietors almost invariably follow this recommendation. The court hold their meetings every Thursday, and they then receive a report of the position of the various bank accounts up to the preceding night. They also consider all proposals for discount accounts, or for exceptional advances, and generally all such business as the governors and the committee of daily waiting may not be empowered to determine on their own responsibility.

The executive administration in the meantime is in the hands of the governor and deputy-governor, who may be advised or assisted by the committee of treasury. This committee is composed of those directors who have held the office of governor, of the existing governor and deputy-governor, and of the director who is intended to be the next deputy-governor. A director is at first an ordinary director, and attends the weekly meetings of the court. In turn he becomes for one year a member of the committee of treasury, then deputy-governor for two years, then governor for two years, and afterwards a permanent member of the committee of treasury. This committee meets once a week, and at such other times as they may be called together specially by the governor. Sometimes they discuss the measures that are to be submitted to the next meeting of the court; but the court do not now so readily as formerly adopt their recommendations. The governor and deputy-governor for the time being make all loans and advances, and sometimes raise the rate of discount without waiting for the opinion of the court. They conduct all negotiations with the Government, and, subject to the sanction of the court, have the whole administration of the affairs of the bank. Each director must hold £2,000 bank stock, the deputy-governor £3,000, and the governor £4,000. It was the rule that every director should take his turn for becoming governor; but now it is the practice to place in that office the director whom the other directors shall, by ballot, think best qualified. Several suggestions were made before the parliamentary committees for improving the composition of the court of directors. It was proposed that all the directors should not be taken from the commercial classes, but that some should be selected from the banking and manufacturing interests. It was also asked, whether a permanent governor, either for life or for a number of years, would not be preferable to the present system.

The Act for separating the two departments came into operation on the 31st of August, 1844, and the following was the first return made under the Act, showing the condition of the banking department on the 7th of September, 1844:—

Account of the Liabilities and Assets of the Bank of England, for the week ending 7th September, 1844.

ISSUE DEPARTMENT.

Dr.			Cr.
Notes issued	£28,351,295	Government debt	£11,015,100
		Other securities	2,984,900
		Gold coin and bullion	12,657,208
		Silver bullion	1,694,087
	£28,351,295		£28,351,295

BANKING DEPARTMENT.

Proprietors' capital	£14,553,000	Government securities	£14,554,834
Rest	3,564,729	Other securities	7,835,616
Public deposits	3,630,809	Notes	8,175,025
Other deposits	8,644,348	Gold and silver coin	857,763
Seven-day and other bills	1,030,354		
	£31,423,240		£31,423,240

The following table will give a more detailed account of some of the items in the above return:—

7th September, 1844.

Dr.	£	£		Cr.	£	£
Circulation—				Public Securities—		
London	14,802,000			Advances on Exchequer Bills Deficiency	870,000	
Country	6,405,000	21,207,000		Other Exchequer Bills	311,000	
				Exchequer Bills Purchased	12,821,000	
Deposits, Public, viz.—				Stock and Annuities .		14,002,000
Exchequer Account . .	2,198,000					
For Payment of Dividends	315,000			Private Securities—		
Savings Banks, &c. . .	501,000			Bills discounted:		
Other Public Accounts .	617,000	3,631,000		London	113,000	
				Country	2,003,000	2,116,000
Deposits, Private, viz.—						
Railways	30,000			Exchequer Bills, Stock, &c.	661,000	
London Bankers . . .	963,000			East India Bonds	198,000	
East India Company .	636,000			City Bonds, &c. . .	3,357,000	
Bank of Ireland, Royal Bank of Scotland, &c. . . }	175,000			Mortgage	620,000	
Other Deposits . . .	5,631,000			Advances :—		
Deposits at Branches .	1,209,000	8,644,000		Bills of Exchange . .	883,000	5,719,000
						21,837,000
				Bullion		15,209,000
		£33,482,000				£37,046,000

It will be seen from the above, that the means or funds of the banking department for carrying on its business, consist of:—1. The Paid-up Capital—2. The Rest or surplus fund—3. The Public Deposits—4. The other Deposits—5. The seven-day and other Bills. These funds are invested in "Government securities" and in "other securities," and the remainder is kept as a reserve in the till.

1. Viewing this as the condition of a private and independent bank, the first thing that would strike the mind of a practical banker, would be the large amount of the PAID-UP CAPITAL. The capital is £14,553,000; while the total deposits are only £12,275,157. The object of a large capital is, in the first place, to secure the public confidence; then, to have the means of repaying the deposits whenever demanded; and also, of affording to the customers of the bank every reasonable accommodation in the way of loans or discounts. But after making due provision for these objects this amount of capital appears unnecessarily large. Were it only £7,000,000, that would be amply sufficient for carrying on the present extent of business, and the rate of dividends might then be increased. All above this amount could only be invested in Government securities, never likely to be required for banking purposes; and if required, could not be suddenly realized, or at least not within the period in which they are likely to be wanted.

2. The next thing that would appear remarkable for a private bank, is the large amount of the REST, or surplus fund.

The Rest, or surplus fund, or Guarantee Fund, as it is sometimes called, consists of the accumulation of surplus or remaining profits after the payment of the dividend. The amount of this fund should be regulated by the extent of the business, and the probable loss that might arise in conducting that business. If the fund is five or six times the amount of the deficiency that might possibly arise in making up the annual dividend, it would appear to be sufficient.[1] For if, after making up this deficiency for one, two, or three years, it should appear that the profits of the bank had become permanently diminished, then the course would be to reduce the dividend, until the surplus fund had recovered its former amount.

Banks that have made large profits have either increased the dividend, or distributed them among the shareholders in the form of bonuses, or have added them to the capital. The Bank of England has adopted all these plans. Yet, after all these distributions of increased dividends, bonuses, and additional capital, the bank had on the 7th of September, 1844, a rest, arising from surplus profits, of £3,564,729. No other "banking concern carrying on business with Bank of England notes," would think it necessary to keep such a rest. Neither the kind nor the extent of business carried on is ever likely to require anything like this amount to meet any occasional losses. The amount is altogether excessively disproportionate to the purposes for which a surplus fund is usually applied, and at the same time it tends to give an erroneous view of the profits of the bank. This rest is employed in the business, and yields profits, but it pays no dividends. The profits go to swell the dividend on the capital, and hence the capital appears to yield a profit of 7 per cent. But

---

[1] Since the text was written the transactions of the banks throughout the country have increased so much that the Rest, from being looked upon merely as a fund to equalize the dividends, is now regarded as a reserve to meet exceptional losses. Such a Rest now, therefore, cannot well be too great. The larger a bank's reserve fund is, the greater is the confidence inspired in the public mind.

the dividend of 7 per cent. is not made upon the capital alone, but on the capital and rest together, and hence upon the funds employed it amounts to only about $5\frac{3}{4}$ per cent.

3. THE DEPOSITS.

The Public Deposits are thus classified:—

	£
Exchequer account	2,198,000
For payment of Dividends	315,000
Savings Banks, &c.	501,000
Other public accounts.	617,000
	£3,631,000

The "Exchequer account" is the current account with the Government, and this account is credited with the amount of the taxes as they are lodged in the bank. In the beginning of January, April, July, and October, this account is debited for the amount necessary to pay the quarterly dividends, and the amount is carried to the credit of the account "for payment of dividends." The balance here standing to the credit of this account is the amount of the dividends that had not then been claimed. The next account is called "Savings Banks, &c." The trustees of the savings banks throughout the country are required to lodge the deposits in the Bank of England to the credit of the Commissioners for the reduction of the National Debt, who afterwards invest it in the public funds. We do not know what is meant by "&c.," nor yet by the "other public accounts." We believe there are certain accounts connected with the Court of Chancery that are required to be kept with the Bank of England; and by the last bankruptcy law, the effects of bankrupts' estates are required to be lodged in some one or other of the branches. These may form the "other public accounts."

The Private Deposits are thus classified:—

	£
Railways	30,000
London Bankers	963,000
East India Company	636,000
Bank of Ireland, Royal Bank of Scotland, &c.	175,000
Other Deposits	5,631,000
Deposits at Branches	1,209,000
	£8,644,000

With regard to both the public and the private deposits, a banker would inquire whether they were fluctuating or permanent; whether repayable at fixed periods, or liable to be suddenly withdrawn. He would thus ascertain what proportion could be profitably employed, and what amount should be kept in the till, to meet constant or occasional demands. He would observe, on inspection, that the balance of the "exchequer account" increases gradually during the quarter, from the receipt of the taxes, until the commencement of the next quarter, when it is largely reduced by the payment of dividends. He will, therefore, provide for these quarterly payments; but his provision will be less ample when informed, that, as the public deposits decline, the private deposits will increase, and more especially those of the London bankers. This is partly in consequence of the bankers holding powers of attorney to receive the dividends due to parties who reside in the country, and partly because the abundance of money caused by the payment of dividends increases their own deposits, and thus enables them to keep for a time larger balances in the Bank of England. We have already said that no rule can be given as to the amount of notes which any banker should keep in his till—the proper amount can be ascertained only by experience. But we should imagine that in ordinary times the deposits in the Bank of England are sufficiently steady to prevent any perplexity on the subject. We may be asked what we mean by "ordinary times," since now every year differs from its predecessor, and the steadiness and uniformity which heretofore characterized banking and commercial affairs are no longer known. We reply, that by "ordinary times" we mean those times that are the least affected by the foreign exchanges. For some years past it has been the practice to regulate the issue of bank notes by the foreign exchanges. When the foreign exchanges bring gold into the country, bank notes are issued against it, money becomes abundant, and the bank deposits increase. When the exchanges take out gold, the bank notes are diminished, and the bank deposits decline. This system has, in a great measure, been acted upon by the bank directors since the year 1832, and it is now rigidly enforced by the Act of 1844. These extraordinary seasons of great influx or great efflux of gold appear to be subject at present to no general rules. But at other times there seems to be no reason why the Bank of England should not profitably employ a large portion of her deposits. We may observe, however, that as the bank allows no interest on any of the deposits, it sustains no loss even when they are not employed; but were they to be employed the profits would be greater.

4. With regard to the INVESTMENTS, a banker would inquire first, Are they safe? secondly, Are they convertible?

There seems no ground to question their safety—their convertibility is not so obvious. The Government stock,

Exchequer bills, and East India bonds, must be considered in ordinary times, and to a reasonable amount, as strictly convertible. But this is not the case with the Government annuities. They could not be sold in the market; and even by private negotiation few buyers would be found, except the insurance offices. Even with them the negotiations would probably occupy considerable time. As to the city bonds, railway bonds, and mortgages, they would in a season of pressure be altogether useless. It may be said, that the bank's capital being so large, a portion may, without inconvenience, be locked up in dead securities. This observation is valid to a certain extent, but not to an indefinite extent, and after giving it due weight, the amount thus invested seems too large.

The annuities form a large portion of the amount of the "Stock and annuities." The first is an annuity of £585,740, usually called the "Dead Weight," which commenced on the 5th of April, 1823, and is to continue for forty-four years from that time. Other annuities arose out of the Bank Charter Act of 1833. The Government were to pay to the bank one-fourth of the permanent debit of £14,686,830, amounting to £3,671,700. At first it was arranged that the bank should receive in payment of this sum, £4,000,000 3 per cent. reduced annuities; but it was afterwards changed to an annuity for twenty-six years, to expire in 1860, at the same time as the "Long Annuity."[1]

The bills discounted, and the short loans called "Advances on bills of exchange, exchequer bills, stock, &c.," are most legitimate banking investments.

The plan of granting short loans was commenced in 1829, to obviate that tightness in the money market, which

[1] The "Long Annuity" and the "Dead Weight Annuity" expired respectively in 1860 and 1867.

was felt for a month or six weeks before the payment of the dividends, through the gathering in of the taxes into the exchequer. The rate of interest charged was usually about one per cent. less than the discount charged on bills. The loans were repayable to the bank at about the time that the dividends were paid to the public. Notices were issued, stating the rate of interest, and the kind of securities on which loans would be made, and the time of repayment. The first notice was issued on the 3rd of December, 1829, and the practice continued until after the passing of the Act of 1844.

Advances on deficiency bills are a kind of short loans made to the Government, whenever the taxes are less than sufficient to pay the public dividends. These advances seem to be very legitimate. The bank has one large customer. A customer who keeps large deposits will sometimes require large advances. These advances may peradventure be wanted at a time when it may not be exactly convenient for the banker to make them. All large accounts may at times be attended with some inconvenience. But if a banker takes such accounts, he must make his arrangements accordingly. In the present case, the bank has the advantage of knowing, by the progress of the lodgments on the "Exchequer account," whether such advance is likely to be required.

When the Government requires these advances, the bank must either make them out of her reserve in the till, or sell public securities to obtain bank notes, or restrict her advances to other parties. It is peculiarly unfortunate that the Government is more likely to require these advances in seasons of pressure, inasmuch as in those seasons the taxes are usually less productive and are less punctually paid. Hence the bank may be called upon to make advances to Government at the same time that similar advances are required by the commercial classes. In some cases the bank might not have the means of making advances to both parties. Had the Government required such advances in October, 1847, the commercial distress must have been considerably increased.

5. THE RESERVE.—A practical banker would, at first sight, consider this reserve as too large. From the amount and character of the deposits it would not appear that so large a reserve was necessary, and a portion might well be employed in earning interest instead of lying unproductive in the till. But, before we condemn the bank directors, we must give this matter farther consideration. We have already stated that, even before the passing of the Act of 1844, the directors had been in the habit of issuing their notes against gold and silver bullion; and when a large amount of notes had been thus issued, the deposits in the bank were increased. Now, when this Act came into operation—August 31st, 1844—the bank had in this way acquired a large amount of gold and silver bullion; indeed, it does not ever before appear to have had so large an amount in the whole course of its history. If we look to those years which preceded pressures (for in these years gold on hand is usually large), we shall find that in 1824 the amount was £13,810,080; in 1836, the highest quotation is £7,801,000; and in 1838, it is £10,126,000; but on the 7th of September, 1844, the amount returned in the issue department is, gold £12,657,208, and silver £1,694,087, while the sum of £9,032,790 was retained in the banking department. Notes of course had been issued against all this bullion, and the deposits in the bank had consequently increased. "Well," it may be said, "this will account for the increase of the deposits, but not for the increase of the reserve. Why were not the deposits invested?" We will explain this. There are some classes of investments which

the bank directors can make independently of other parties. For instance, they can purchase Government stock, exchequer bills, and railway bonds, just as they please. But, as we have stated, it is not prudent in a banker to invest the temporary increase of his deposits in this way, as, when the deposits are withdrawn, he may have to sell these securities at a lower price, and thus sustain loss. There are other classes of investments for which the bank is, to a certain extent, dependent on other parties; such, for example, as the discounting of bills and the granting of loans. The bank directors cannot invest their money in these ways unless there are parties willing to receive it. Now, while a portion of the notes issued against gold and silver bullion are lodged with the bank in the form of deposits, another portion, and sometimes the largest portion, do not go into the bank, but are circulated among the public, and soon find their way into the hands of bankers, bill-brokers, and money-dealers, who from the abundance of money, will discount bills and grant short loans at a lower rate of interest than the bank. The bank will, therefore, have no farther applications. When its bills and loans fall due, they will be paid, and the amount will go to increase the reserve. Thus it appears that the notes which, in a favourable course of the foreign exchanges, are issued against gold and silver bullion, will tend in two ways to increase the bank reserve; first, by increasing the deposits, and secondly, by diminishing the securities. This will account for the large amount of the reserve. The rule laid down by the directors is, that the reserve should be about one-third the amount of the deposits.

Having given these explanations, we shall now proceed to notice the operations of the banking department of the

Bank of England after its separation from the issuing department by the Act of 1844:—

I. The operations of the Banking Department, from the passing of the Act in 1844, to September 5, 1845.

The Act came into operation on the 31st of August, 1844, and almost immediately some important changes were introduced. Up to that date the bank had never discounted at a lower rate than 4 per cent. This rate, in ordinary times, had seldom varied, and all bills discounted at the same time were charged the same rate. But, on the 5th of September, the rate of discount on bills was reduced from 4 to $2\frac{1}{2}$ per cent., and on notes to 3 per cent. On the 18th of March, 1845, the bank introduced the principle of a *minimum* rate of discount; fixing $2\frac{1}{2}$ per cent. as the rate on first-rate bills, and charging a higher rate on other bills. The object of these changes was to employ a portion of the reserve in the discount of bills.

This line of conduct was by no means unwarranted by the practice of "other banking concerns." It is an established principle in practical banking, that a banker, when he cannot employ his surplus funds at so high a rate of interest as he wishes to obtain, should employ those funds at a lower rate, rather than keep them unemployed in his till. And it is also an established practice to charge different rates of discount on different bills, according to the class or character of the bills—the respectability of the parties—the time they have to run—and a variety of other circumstances. In adopting these regulations, therefore, the directors were only performing the work assigned to them, of conducting the banking department "like any other banking concern issuing Bank of England notes."

These changes gave rise, in the parliamentary committees of 1847, to some discussion upon the question as to whether the Bank of England governed the market-rate of interest; or the market-rate of interest governed the bank-rate? There can be but little difference of opinion upon this subject. The "market-rate" of interest is the rate which bankers and bill-brokers charge for discounting first-class bills to the public. When the foreign exchanges are bringing gold into the country, and notes are issued against this gold, the abundance of money in the hands of the bankers and bill-brokers causes the market-rate of discount to fall below the bank-rate. If during this season the bank charges a high rate, it gets but few bills. On the other hand, when gold is going out of the country, and money becomes scarce, the market-rate is higher than the bank-rate. If during this period the bank charges a low rate, it must soon limit its discounts, or the reserve will be exhausted. But, though the bank cannot change the course of the current, it can give it increased strength. Though it cannot make money dear when it is cheap, nor cheap when it is dear, yet when money is cheap it can make it cheaper, and when it is dear it can make it dearer. Hence, every alteration in the bank-rate has always an immediate influence on the market-rate.

Such was the case in September, 1844. The large importations of gold had reduced the market-rate of discount to $2\frac{1}{2}$ per cent. while the bank charged 4 per cent. But when the bank reduced its rate to $2\frac{1}{2}$ per cent. the market-rate went down to 2, and even to $1\frac{1}{2}$ per cent. To engage actively in discounting bills was a new feature in the bank management. In 1832 the then governor stated to the Committee of the House of Commons, that he thought the bank should be a bank of circulation and of deposit, and only *occasionally* a bank of discount. But the Act of 1844 placed the bank in a new position, and led to the adoption of new principles. Formerly the bank had invested its surplus funds in Government securities. But when it purchased, the price advanced; and when it sold, the price fell. This produced a fluctuation inconvenient to the public. Often, too, it purchased when the price was high, and sold when the price was low: and thus sustained loss. It was therefore deemed preferable to invest a portion of the reserve in the discount of bills. The sums thus invested would return as the bills fell due, and the reserve could at any time be strengthened by checking the discounts.

The directors having determined to invest a portion of their funds in discounts, it became necessary to reduce their rate of interest to nearly the market-rate, or they would have got no bills.

An eminent London banker, distinguished by his support of the Act of 1844, says: "If the bank is to continue as a large discounting body (of the expediency of which I entertain considerable doubts), I think it very desirable that its rate of interest should conform to the real market-value of money."[1] The directors seemed to think it necessary that they should in some way employ their reserve, in order to prevent the too great accumulation of bank notes in the issue department.[2] We here give no opinion as to the best way of employing the bank's reserve, but we are quite ready to admit, as the governor admits in reply to a question, that "the true principles of banking are, first, that a bank shall never place itself in such a position as that it shall be unable to meet its liabilities; and next, that it shall employ the whole of its resources at the greatest profit that it can with reference to prudence, looking to its reserve."[3]

In thus coming into competition with the money-dealers,

[1] Lords, 1632.   [2] Commons, 3009.   [3] Commons, 3722.

reducing the rate of interest, exciting a feverish state of feeling in the public mind, and giving facilities to the formation of companies for speculative purposes, the bank directors are accused of having violated their public duties as the bank of the Government, and thus sacrificed the interests of the nation to the interests of their proprietors. We shall not meddle with this question. We have here nothing to do with the PUBLIC duties of the bank directors. We are considering the banking department as "any other banking concern." Generally speaking, Providence has so constituted human society that all banking companies, and all individuals too, will most effectually promote the public interests when by honourable means they promote their own. If this is not the case with the Bank of England, it must have arisen from the acts of the Legislature; and the fact—if it be a fact—is presumptive evidence against the wisdom and the justice of those laws by which the bank was placed in that position.

At the close of this period we find that the London discounts had increased from £113,000 to £2,365,000, and the "City Bonds, &c." had increased from £3,357,000 to £4,009,000, owing, it is presumed, to the purchase of railway debentures. The circulation of the issuing department had increased from £28,351,295 to £28,953,300, and the minimum rate of interest charged by the bank was $2\frac{1}{2}$ per cent.

II. The Administration of the Banking Department from September 6, 1845, to September 5, 1846.

During this period there were three alterations in the minimum rate of interest. On October 16, 1845, it was raised from $2\frac{1}{2}$ to 3 per cent.; on November 6, to $3\frac{1}{2}$ per cent.; and on August 17, 1846, it was again reduced to 3 per cent. In fixing the rate of discount, the directors took into account the amount of bullion in the issue department, the reserve in the banking department, and the amount of the discounts. The amount of bullion virtually regulated the other two; and thus the interest was governed by the foreign exchanges. At the same time, the directors, as practical bankers, would pay the greatest attention to their reserve, as it was only from this source that any advances could be made. Hence, sometimes, one object of raising the rate of discount was to diminish the number of applications. It was thought better to protect the reserve by raising the rate than by positively refusing to discount.

In the beginning of 1846 a circumstance occurred which increased both the deposits and the discounts of the bank, and added greatly to its profits. The railway companies who were desirous of obtaining Acts of Parliament to authorize the construction of their lines, were required to pay into the Bank of England, within fourteen days after the meeting of Parliament, 10 per cent. on the estimated amount of their capital—to be returned when the company had obtained the Act, or when the application had been rejected. Everybody wondered beforehand how so large a sum could be paid out of the amount of notes then in circulation. But the bank acted with the railway deposits as she had been accustomed to act with the public deposits previous to the payment of dividends. As fast as the money came in, it was lent out, and thus a transaction of large magnitude was effected without much difficulty. This shows the importance of a Government bank. Had the deposits been required to be lodged in the exchequer, and there to remain until reclaimed by the railway companies, the operation could not have been effected. The bank could have performed it with greater facility previous to the passing of the Act of 1844. She could then have lent out her notes *before* the lodgments were required to be made; there would have been no previous apprehensions, nor any tightness during the operation.

III. The Administration of the Banking Department from September 5, 1846, to September 4, 1847.

In September, 1846, the minimum rate of discount was 3 per cent. On January the 14th, 1847, it was raised to 3½ per cent., and on the 20th of the same month to 4 per cent. On April the 8th to 5 per cent., and on the 5th of August to 5½ per cent.

During the whole of this period the foreign exchanges were unfavourable, and the circulation of the issuing department declined from £29,760,870 to £22,396,845.[1] This was attended by a decline in the reserve of the banking department, and an increase in the amount of loans and discounts.

The bank directors did not raise their rate of discount above 3 per cent. until the month of January, 1847. For this they have been severely censured by parties who have had the advantage of not being compelled to form any opinion until after the result was known. The month of April was an important month. From the deficiency of the harvest, large importations of corn took place. These imports were paid for in gold, which was suddenly withdrawn from the issue department, for exportation.

Contemporaneous with this export of gold, the Government required to borrow £3,500,000 upon deficiency bills in order to pay the dividends. Under the old system this might not have been a matter of much importance, but the case was different under the Act of 1844. The banking department was rather in danger of getting into what the Americans call "a fix." To avoid this "fix," the directors raised the rate of discount to 5 per cent.; they refused to

---

[1] By deducting £14,000,000 from this sum, we see the amount of gold and silver bullion on hand in the issue department.

lend money even upon exchequer bills; they limited their discounts; and they borrowed £1,275,000 on consols. These measures caused a severe pressure on the money market, but it soon subsided. From this period the foreign exchanges were favourable to this country.

The operations of this month of April, 1847, have given rise to much discussion.

The advocates of the Act of 1844 have pointed to the transactions of this month to prove that the management of the issue department cannot be safely entrusted to the bank directors. They say that if the bank had advanced its rate of interest it might have prevented the unfavourable course of exchange, and consequently have avoided the pressure which then occurred. On the other hand, it has been stated that the bank ought to be guided in its rates of interest by the amount of its reserve—that from November, 1846, to April, 1847, the reserve was above one-third of its deposits, a greater reserve than any other bank would think it necessary to keep—that the demand for gold was so sudden, and for so large an amount, that no ordinary rules could have prevented it; and even had it been prevented, it might have been injurious to the country, as it would have checked the importation of corn, which was then required in consequence of the deficiency in the harvest. There can be no doubt that, under the Act of 1844, a sudden exportation of gold must cause a sudden contraction of the amount of notes in circulation. This "self-acting machine" acts by jerks, like a steam-engine without a fly-wheel; and its advocates look to the banking department to supply the fly-wheel, and to cause the machine to move smoothly and equably. It may be doubted whether the banking department has the power of doing this. But when this is not done the advocates of the Act throw the blame upon that department. They resemble the court preceptor, who, when the royal pupil did anything wrong, inflicted the beating on his fellow-student. If on this occasion the bank did wrong, it may be feared that it was its court connection which led it astray. The Government were then negotiating a loan of eight millions for the relief of Ireland. And "there was a feeling in the court that, in the face of the Government negotiating a loan, it would be an act of want of courtesy to put up the rate of interest immediately."[1] In the secret history of the Bank of England we may possibly find other instances of similar faults. But if on the present occasion it was influenced by such considerations, it did not act "like any other banking concern."

The events of April, 1847, also lead us to remark that the London bankers never vary their rate of discount with a view to regulate the foreign exchanges. If it behoves the banking department to do this, it has certainly to perform duties which are not considered to belong to "any other banking concern." Nor do the London bankers suddenly and abruptly stop discounting for those customers in whom they have confidence. The frequent occurrence of such suspension of loans and discounts as occurred in April, 1847, would form an insuperable barrier to the banking department ever acquiring that kind of business which is carried on by the London bankers. No merchant would like to depend on such a bank for the means of making his daily payments. We believe, however, that most mercantile firms that have a discount account with the Bank of England have another banking account elsewhere, and some have also accounts with the large bill-brokers.

The pressure that existed in April, 1847, has been attributed to the publication of the amount of the bank's reserve. It was said, and said truly, that the bank might

[1] Commons, No. 3001.

very prudently reduce its reserve for a few days below the average amount, knowing that by bills falling due, or by other means, it would soon receive a sum that would replenish its coffers. But the public, seeing only the amount of the reserve, and knowing nothing of the sums about to be received, might become unnecessarily alarmed, and hence, a panic might ensue. Upon this ground, some parties questioned the policy of publishing the bank accounts in their present form. But the remedy for this is not to suppress the returns, but to circulate throughout the community such an amount of knowledge as shall enable them to judge accurately respecting banking affairs. Other parties, of a higher class than those we denominate the public, have fallen into erroneous opinions by a literal adhesion to these returns. Almost up to the time of the suspension of the Act of 1844, it was contended by some who "sit in high places" that there could be no pressure on the commercial classes, since there were THEN more notes in the hands of the public than in former seasons when no pressure existed. And before the Parliamentary Committees of 1847 it was stated by the governor and deputy-governor, that it could make no difference to the public whether the bank advanced three millions, or any other sum, to the Government on deficiency bills, or advanced the same sum in loans and discounts to the commercial classes, inasmuch as the returns would show that the amount of notes in circulation would be the same. The events that followed the suspension of the Act showed the fallacy of these opinions. It was shown that the amount of notes in the hands of the public is not of itself a certain criterion by which to judge of the amount of banking facilities enjoyed by the commercial classes.

IV. The Administration of the Banking Department from September, 1847, to September, 1848.

During this period the minimum rate of interest was advanced from 5½ to 6 per cent. on the 23rd of September; to 8 per cent., by authority of the Government letter, on the 25th of October. It was reduced to 7 per cent. on the 22nd of November; to 6 per cent. on the 2nd of December; to 5 per cent. on the 23rd of December; to 4 per cent. on the 27th of January, 1848; and to 3½ per cent. on the 16th of June.

At the commencement of this period a great number of commercial houses failed, not only in London, but also in Liverpool and Glasgow, and other large places. The following is the account given by the Governor of the bank to the Committee of the House of Lords:—

"An unprecedented large importation of food, caused by a deficient harvest, required in payment the export of a large amount of bullion, to the extent of about £7,500,000, from the coffers of the bank, and probably not less than £1,500,000 from other sources—together £9,000,000. From this great reduction in the available capital of the country, in addition to the still larger amount invested in railway expenditure, acting suddenly upon a previous high state of credit and excessive speculation, arose the pressure in the money market. There was an abstraction of £7,500,000 from the bullion held by the bank, and consequently a diminution in the notes to that extent."[1]

During this period the bank acted with great liberality. The following is a list of the advances made between the 15th of September and the 15th of November:—

"1. The Bank of England being applied to by a very large firm in London, who had at that time liabilities to the extent of several millions sterling, advanced £150,000 on the security of debentures to that amount of the Go-

[1] Lords, 12.

vernor and Company of the Copper Miners in England, and thereby prevented them from stopping payment; it was distinctly understood that the operation was for that purpose. 2. The bank advanced £50,000 to a country banker on the security of real property. 3. On the urgent representations of several parties of the first importance in the city of London, the bank advanced £120,000 to the Governor and Company of the Copper Miners, on the guarantee of approved names, taking at the same time a mortgage on the Company's property for £270,000 to cover this sum, and the amount of £150,000 debentures before advanced upon; it was stated that the stoppage of this company would have thrown 10,000 people out of employment. 4. The bank advanced £300,000 to the Royal Bank of Liverpool, on the security of bills of exchange, over and above their usual discounts to this bank; this advance unfortunately proved inadequate, and the Royal Bank, having no more security to offer, stopped payment. 5. The bank assisted another joint-stock bank in the country with £100,000, on the security of bills of exchange, over and above usual discounts. 6. The bank advanced £130,000 on real property to a large mercantile house in London. 7. The bank advanced £50,000 to another mercantile house on the guarantee of approved names. 8. The bank advanced £50,000 to a joint-stock issuing bank on bills of exchange, and agreed to open a discount account with the said bank, on condition that it should withdraw its issues, but the joint-stock bank stopped payment before the arrangement could be completed. 9. The bank advanced £15,000 on real property to a large establishment in London. 10. The bank assisted, and prevented from failing, a large establishment in Liverpool, by forbearing to enforce payment of upwards of £100,000, of their acceptances, and engaging to give further aid if required. 11. The bank assisted a very large joint-stock bank in the country with advances on loans on bills of exchange to the extent of £800,000 over and above usual discounts. 12. The bank advanced £100,000 to a country banker on real property. 13. The bank advanced a joint-stock bank in the country £200,000 on the security of local bills, besides discounting £60,000 of London bills. 14. The bank assisted another joint-stock bank in the country with an advance of £100,000 on local and London bills. 15. The bank advanced £100,000 to a large mercantile house in London, on approved personal security. 16. The bank assisted a large house at Manchester to resume payment, by an advance of £40,000 on approved personal security. 17. The bank advanced £30,000 to a country bank on real property. 18. The bank assisted many other houses, both in town and country, by advances of smaller sums on securities not admitted by the bank under ordinary circumstances; nor did the bank, during the period in question, reject at their London establishment any one bill offered for discount, except on the ground of insufficient security." [1]

Some of these advances were not made till after the appearance of the Government letter on the 25th of October. Up to that date the efforts of the bank were inadequate to allay the pressure, while they largely reduced the bank's reserve. On Saturday, the 23rd of October, a deputation from the London bankers waited on the Government, who then determined to suspend the Act of 1844; and on the same day gave intimation of their intention to the Bank of England. On Monday morning a letter appeared from Lord John Russell and the Chancellor of the Exchequer, authorizing the directors of the Bank of England to enlarge

[1] Commons, 2645.

their discounts and advances, and promising that if by so doing the existing law should be infringed, the Government would apply to the Legislature for a bill of indemnity. The letter suggested that these advances should not be made at a lower interest than 8 per cent. The effect of this letter was immediate. Confidence was restored, the hoarded notes were brought into circulation, and discounts were everywhere readily obtained. From these causes no infringement of the Act took place.

The state of the bank reserve at the date of the suspension of this Act occupied the attention of the Parliamentary Committees. On Saturday, the 23rd of October, the notes on hand amounted to £1,547,270, and the coin to £447,246. This, it should be remembered, was the amount at the London office and at the thirteen branches put together. At the same time the public deposits were £4,766,000, and the private deposits £8,581,000, of which £1,615,000 belonged to the London bankers. The questions put to the governor on this subject seemed designed to show that the bank, so far from being able to assist others, was not in a condition to meet its own engagements. But the governor contended that the amount of the reserve should have been taken on the Friday night, before they were acquainted with the intention of the Government to issue their letter. The reserve then was £2,376,000. The directors had from £2,000,000 to £2,500,000 of stock which they could have sold, and a large amount of the bills they held fell due in the following week. From these sources they would easily have increased their reserve. On the other hand, some of the witnesses declared that no large amount of stock could have been sold, and that, had a run taken place on the London bankers, such as that which had taken place on the banks at Newcastle, the bankers' deposits must have been withdrawn, and the Bank of England itself might have been placed in jeopardy.

As we have considered in a previous Section the operation of the Act of 1844, it is not necessary to pursue this subject any farther. After the Government letter was issued, the bank still continued to make advances with caution, and, with the view of not infringing the Act, they borrowed money on the Stock Exchange at 7 per cent., though they had the unlimited power of issuing notes.

Soon afterwards the gold began to return, and money became abundant. From the high rate of interest, the amount imported was large; and from trade having been paralyzed by the pressure, the demand for it was very small. As the gold increased, the bank rate of interest was reduced. By September 2nd, 1848, the circulation of the currency department amounted to £26,883,505, and the bank reserve to £9,410,952.

To show the further progress of the bank since September, 1848, we have added the Returns for the week ending the 2nd of February, 1849, premising that since the year 1849 the administration of the Bank of England has been influenced by the importations of gold from California and Australia. We shall here merely state the amounts of gold and silver on hand in the first week in September, in the years that have transpired since 1848, and the minimum rates of interest charged by the Bank of England at those respective periods.

Date.	Gold.	Silver.	Rate of Interest.
	£	£	
8 Sept. 1849	13,631,153	277,077	3
7 Sept. 1850	15,880,617	219,958	$2\frac{1}{2}$
6 Sept. 1851	13,674,190	33,375	3
4 Sept. 1852	21,334,921	19,154	2
10 Sept. 1853	15,866,770	nil.	$3\frac{1}{2}$
9 Sept. 1854	12,630,110	nil.	5
8 Sept. 1855	14,368,010	nil.	$3\frac{1}{2}$

The following is a copy of the Official Returns for the four years that have passed under review :—

BANK OF ENGLAND WEEKLY RETURNS.

Account, pursuant to the Act 7th and 8th of Victoria, cap. 32, for the weeks ending as follows:—

ISSUE DEPARTMENT.

	1844. September 7th.	1845. September 6th.	1846. September 5th.	1847. September 4th.	1848. September 2nd.	1849. February 2nd.
	£	£	£	£	£	£
Notes issued	28,351,295	28,953,300	29,760,870	22,396,845	26,883,505	28,330,845
Government Debt . .	11,015,100	11,015,000	11,015,100	11,015,100	11,015,100	11,015,100
Other Securities . .	2,984,900	2,984,900	2,984,900	2,984,900	2,984,900	2,984,900
Gold Coin and Bullion	12,657,208	12,982,591	13,057,997	7,373,815	12,177,567	13,828,773
Silver Bullion . . .	1,694,087	1,970,709	2,702,873	1,023,030	705,938	502,072
	£28,351,295	£28,953,300	£29,760,870	£22,396,845	£26,883,505	£28,330,845

BANKING DEPARTMENT.

	1844. September 7th.	1845. September 6th.	1846. September 5th.	1847. September 4th.	1848. September 2nd.	1849. February 2nd.
	£	£	£	£	£	£
Proprietors' Capital	14,553,000	14,553,000	14,553,000	14,553,000	14,553,000	14,553,000
Rest	3,564,729	3,608,180	3,864,479	3,986,593	3,826,382	3,576,625
Public Deposits (including Exchequer, Savings' Banks, Commissioners of National Debt, and Dividend Accounts)	3,630,809	6,474,705	7,318,919	7,722,704	5,021,591	3,922,307
Other Deposits	8,644,348	8,507,213	8,557,109	6,791,373	8,824,607	11,328,544
Seven-day and other Bills	1,030,354	1,921,689	935,830	842,711	1,016,921	1,144,824
	£31,423,240	£34,164,787	£35,229,337	£33,896,381	£33,242,501	£34,525,300
Government Securities (including Dead Weight Annuity)	14,554,834	13,468,643	12,961,735	11,636,340	12,462,735	13,882,267
Other Securities	7,835,616	11,967,081	12,523,550	17,508,119	11,368,814	10,314,654
Notes	8,175,025	8,255,505	9,231,095	4,189,830	8,784,795	9,553,460
Gold and Silver Coin	857,765	473,558	512,937	562,092	626,157	774,919
	£31,423,240	£34,164,787	£35,229,337	£33,896,381	£33,242,501	£34,525,300

We have thus taken a review of the first four years of the proceedings of the Banking Department of the Bank of England. Whatever may be the future operations of that department, this portion of its history will always be interesting. This period is remarkable also as containing one of those monetary cycles to which we must always be liable as long as our currency is regulated by the Act of 1844. Each year has a peculiar character. The first commenced at a period of full currency—money was abundant and cheap, the minimum of the bank rate being 2½ per cent. In the second year the exchanges fluctuated, and the rate of interest fluctuated also. During the whole of the third, the exchanges were unfavourable—gold was exported, and the rate of interest advanced. At the commencement of the fourth year came the pressure: then a favourable course of exchange brought back the gold, the rate of interest was reduced, and again money became abundant.

This period is moreover important as an indication of the principles on which the banking department will hereafter be governed. The governor and deputy-governor were examined before the parliamentary committees in March, 1848. They stated that they approved of the reduction of interest in September, 1844; but they expressed regret that the bank had not advanced the rate of interest in November, 1846, and that they suffered the reserve to fall so low in October, 1847. Should these sentiments be acted upon in future, we may expect that the "banking department" will reduce its rate of interest as heretofore; but when money becomes scarce, it will advance its rate at an earlier period, and be less liberal in making advances.

The following question was put to the governor by a member of the Committee of the House of Commons:—
"You have described as part of the operation of the Act

of 1844, that you were during the year 1847 obliged to lend consols instead of notes, on account of the limit prescribed by the Act,—that you borrowed on consols in April,—that you were obliged to raise the rate of interest to 9 per cent.,—that you refused loans on exchequer bills,—that there was a pressure in April, and a panic in October,—and that Government were obliged to interpose by a letter, in order to protect the public from the restrictive effects of the Act—Do you call that a satisfactory history of any system?"[1]

We must, however, distinguish between "the system" as established by the Act of Parliament, and the administration of the banking department in consequence of the establishment of that system. We have given in the preceding section our opinion of the system. But the administration of the Banking Department of the Bank of England under the system, has, in our sober judgment, been distinguished by a high degree of both wisdom and liberality.

The administration of the banking department since September, 1848, does not call for any particular remark. We had the usual indications of the first stage after a panic. The bullion in the issue department increased from £12,883,505 to £14,330,845 ; the notes in reserve from £8,784,795 to £9,553,460. Money had been abundant, and the rate of interest low. On the 2nd of November, 1848, the bank reduced the minimum rate of discount to 3 per cent. This would probably have been done at an earlier period but for the political aspect of the Continent. The same reason possibly induced the Directors to maintain the same interest to February, 1849, although this appears to be an abandonment of the principle adopted in the year 1844.

[1] Commons, 3450.

SECTION XXIV.

THE ADMINISTRATION OF JOINT-STOCK BANKS, WITH AN INQUIRY INTO THE CAUSES OF THEIR FAILURES.

THE chief points in which a joint-stock bank differs from a private bank are,—the number of its partners—the permanency of its capital—and the form of its government. A private bank formerly could not have more than six partners; a joint-stock bank may have any number of partners. If a partner in a private bank die, or become insolvent, his capital is withdrawn from the bank; in the case of a partner in a joint-stock bank, his shares are transferred, and the capital of the bank remains the same. In a private bank all the partners may attend to its administration: a joint-stock bank is governed by a board of directors. The business principles on which these two kinds of banks are administered are the same, and the observations of the preceding sections will equally apply to both. The topics, therefore, to which we shall in this section more particularly direct our attention will be those that have a special reference to the constitution of joint-stock banks. After the 6th of May, 1844, it was not lawful for any new company of more than six persons to carry on the trade or business of bankers *in England*, unless by virtue of letters patent to be granted by her Majesty according to the provisions of that Act.

I. All joint-stock banks have a certain amount of paid-up capital.

The payment of a certain portion of the capital before

the commencement of business, is a pledge that the project is not a mere bubble, and this is especially necessary when the proprietors have no further liability. But even with unlimited liability a certain amount appears to be necessary. The employment of capital judiciously is sometimes a means of acquiring business; and in case of loss there should always be a sufficient capital to fall back upon without recurring to the shareholders.

There is an evil in a bank having too small a capital. In this case, the bank will be but a small bank; the number of proprietors will be few, and the number of persons eligible to be chosen directors will be few; hence there will not be the same guarantee for good management. If a bank with a small capital have also a very small business, it had much better cease as an independent establishment, and become the branch of a larger bank. If, on the other hand, it has a large business, with a large circulation, large deposits, and large loans or discounts, its losses will sometimes be large, and hence the whole capital may be swept away. It is true, that while it avoids losses the shareholders will receive large dividends; but these large profits had much better be left in the bank as an addition to its capital than shared among the proprietors in the form of dividends. There is danger too that the high premium on those shares may induce many shareholders to sell out and form other, and perhaps rival establishments.

On the other hand, there is an evil in a bank having too large a capital. In this case, as the capital cannot be employed in the business, the directors are under the temptation of investing it in dead or hazardous securities for the sake of obtaining a higher rate of interest; perhaps too they may speculate in the funds, and sustain loss. Hence it is much better that a bank should commence business with a small capital, and increase the amount as the business may require.

It is difficult to state in all cases what proportion a capital ought to bear to the liabilities of a bank. Perhaps the best criterion we can have is the rate of dividends, provided that dividend be paid out of the business profits of the company. When we hear of a bank paying from 15 to 20 per cent. dividend, we may be assured that the capital is too small for the business. The liabilities of the bank, either in notes or deposits, must far exceed the amount of its capital. As a general maxim, the greater the capital the less the dividend. Let the whole capital be employed at any given rate of interest, say 3 per cent., then the capital raised by notes or deposit, produces, after paying all expenses, a certain sum as profit. Now, it is evident that if this amount of profit be distributed over a large capital, it will yield a less rate per cent. than when distributed over a small capital. Sometimes, however, a large capital may have increased the rate of dividend, in consequence of having been the means of acquiring a large increase of business. It may have done this in consequence of inspiring the public with confidence in the bank, and thus inducing them to make lodgments or circulate its notes; or it may have enabled the bank to make large advances, and thus gained the support of wealthy and influential customers.

Although the proportion which the capital of a bank should bear to its liabilities may vary with different banks, perhaps we should not go far astray in saying it should never be less than one-third of its liabilities.[1] I would

---

[1] This view was no doubt a very reasonable one at the time the text was written, when joint-stock banking in England was in its infancy; but, as experience has proved that public confidence has in no way been impaired by the very large increase of banking liabilities, without a

exclude, however, from this comparison all liabilities except those arising from notes and deposits. If the notes and deposits together amount to more than three times the amount of the paid-up capital, the bank should call up more capital. It may be said, that the bank is liable also for its drafts upon its London agents, and for the payment of those bills which it has endorsed and re-issued:—admitted; but in both these cases, the public have other securities besides that of the bank.

Presuming that banks are to commence with a moderate amount of capital, and to increase that amount as the business increases, the question is suggested, what is the best way of increasing the capital? The English banks have followed two ways of doing this: one, by a further issue of shares; and the other, by further calls upon the existing shareholders. The capital of all the joint-stock banks in England is divided into certain portions, called shares; each proprietor holds a certain number of these shares, and pays a certain sum upon them. If he wishes to transfer a portion of his capital he cannot transfer a half share or a quarter share, but must transfer a whole share, or a certain number of shares. Thus, if the capital of a bank be £500,000, it may be divided into 5,000 shares of £100 each, or 50,000 shares of £10 each, and a certain proportion of the amount of each share will be paid up; and this proportion is called the real or the paid-up capital. Thus, if one-tenth of the above capital

corresponding increase of capital, since that period, it may now be regarded as quite untenable. Were the view of the proper proportion of capital to liabilities here propounded generally adopted, bank dividends, at the present average rates of profit, would in many cases entirely vanish, and in no case would the return be at all commensurate with the risk. As a matter of fact the capital of no bank in the kingdom bears anything like so high a relation to its liabilities as the proportion here considered proper.

is paid up, then £50,000 will be the real or paid-up capital, and £500,000 will be called the nominal capital. In the chartered banks, on the other hand, there is usually no nominal capital, and the real capital is not divided into shares or portions, but any fractional sum may be transferred.[1] The capital is then called stock. When there is no nominal capital, nor any way of increasing the amount of the real capital, this is the best way. But, in the other case, it is more convenient to have the capital divided into shares.

Some persons have objected altogether to a nominal capital; but their objections have been directed more to the misrepresentations that may attend it, than to the thing itself. They say, "a bank announces that it has a capital of £500,000, whereas few shares are issued, and but a small sum is paid on each share; hence people are misled, and the bank acquires a confidence which it does not deserve." The objection here is against representing the nominal capital to be paid-up capital; it does not bear upon the principle of a nominal capital. In fact, we are misled by words. What is called nominal capital is nothing more than a further sum, which the directors have the power of calling up. If this sum had not been called capital, it would not be objected to, as it could lead to no misapprehension. But the inquiry simply is, ought the directors to have the power of calling upon the shareholders for a further amount of capital beyond that already paid up? Were they not to have the power, the bank would at its commencement probably have too large a capital, and after its business had advanced would have too small a capital. And if the bank by any unforeseen

---

[1] The Colonial chartered banks are an exception to this rule. The capital of such banks has invariably been raised by shares (not stock), with usually a liability thereon of double the amount.

occurrence became involved, and should have occasion for further sums to extricate itself from its difficulties, it could not make any further call upon its shareholders, although a very small advance might prevent its utter ruin. In case of a very large capital, such as two or three millions, a nominal capital may not be necessary, as so large a sum is likely to be in all cases amply sufficient. But in banks of a second class, it will always be best to give the directors the power of making further calls upon the shareholders.

The second way of increasing the capital of a bank, is by the issue of new shares. The whole amount of shares to be issued is fixed in the first instance, and the bank commences as soon as a certain proportion has been issued. If the bank was not allowed to commence business until the whole of the shares were taken, a small amount would be fixed upon, and the bank would be proportionably weaker. But by beginning with a small number of shares you have capital enough for your business, and you acquire more as you proceed. Many persons will join a bank after it is established who would not take shares at the commencement. Some shares are therefore reserved for persons of this description; and as the shares are more valuable when the success of the undertaking is no longer doubtful, they are often given out at a premium, and always a greater degree of caution is exercised as to the persons to whom they are distributed.

Some members of the parliamentary committee of 1836 appear to have an objection to shares of a small amount; they apprehend that these shares are taken by an inferior class of persons; and hence the body of proprietors are less respectable. But it would appear from the returns, that the general effect of small shares is, that each shareholder takes a greater number. Thus in the banks of

£100 shares each proprietor has taken upon an average twenty-eight shares, on which he has paid the sum of £444. In the banks of £20 shares, each proprietor has taken forty-three shares, and paid £359. In the banks of £10 shares, each proprietor has taken fifty-two shares, and paid £400. While in the only bank of £5 shares, each proprietor has taken 117 shares, and paid £585. It appears to me that the chief objection to which small shares are liable is, that they do not admit of a large amount of nominal capital. The banks of £5 and £10 shares have usually the whole capital paid up, and hence in case of necessity the directors have no power to call for a further amount.

II. Joint-stock banks are governed by a board of directors.

" The directors are chosen from among the shareholders at a general meeting—the pecuniary qualification being that they hold a stipulated number of shares in the company.

" There are several points of view in which a man becomes eligible as a director of a bank, independent of his qualification as the holder of the required number of shares. Indeed, his qualification as a shareholder, merely, must not be taken into the account.

" 1. He ought, in the first place, to be a man enjoying public confidence. Unless he is a man whom the community contemplate as deserving of their confidence and esteem, it is not presumable he can be of much service to the bank, either by his influence or character. The public are not likely to deposit their money in an establishment where they cannot place the fullest reliance upon the directors; and, for the same reason, parties of respectability will not readily be induced to open accounts with the bank.

"2. He ought to be a man possessing a knowledge of commercial business. It is a matter of great importance to the satisfactory and efficient management of a bank, that those to whom is entrusted the direction of its affairs, be in some measure conversant with the ordinary affairs of trade. Men who are retired from business are unquestionably the most eligible, not merely from their business knowledge, but because they are not apt to be contemplated with that suspicion, jealousy, and distrust, which tradesmen will sometimes exercise towards such directors of a bank as are likewise engaged in trade. But retired men of business are not readily to be had as directors of a bank, nor are they in most cases disposed to accept of such an office. Where such is the case, men of high standing and character, engaged in trade, should be sought for.

"3. A bank director should be a man of strict integrity and uprightness. This is a qualification perfectly indispensable to the welfare of the bank. He must be above all trafficking in the stock of the company, or taking any undue advantage over the other shareholders through his intimate knowledge of the state of their affairs as regards the bank. He must never for a moment forget, that while he is a partner in the concern, and as an honest man is bound to conduct it in as faithful and diligent a manner as he would his own private affairs, that he is at the same time appointed to a solemn trust, in having the interests of numerous others, equally interested with himself, under his management and control. In fact, unless the director of a bank is a man of strict integrity, he is placed in a position calculated to be productive of great mischief. He is invested with power to ruin the fortunes of others, and to inflict much commercial evil upon the community. Where there is a want of integrity, there is a want of principle, and the bank must necessarily be mismanaged.

"4. A bank director should be a man of influence and respectability. He ought to be a man well known and respected in the district. Such a man is desirable in a variety of ways. He adds his own personal respectability to the establishment, and he influences the favour and support of his friends and acquaintances. His standing in society gives the public confidence in the establishment with which he is connected—and they bring their money and business to its support; the paper of the bank becomes more readily current in the district, and the weight of his influence destroys any suspicion of its stability.

"5. A bank director should be in good pecuniary circumstances. It would be a most wholesome regulation, were it stipulated in all deeds of settlement that no bank director should be privileged to overdraw his account. The great facilities which directors enjoyed of raising money from overdrawing their bank accounts, have, in some instances, resulted in extensive commercial disasters, and in the total wreck of large establishments. The temptation to speculations of all descriptions which such facilities hold out, necessarily increases the risk of the bank, and induces a less rigid inspection of the accommodation afforded to other customers. Where those who are entrusted with the management of the bank forget the extent and importance of the trust reposed in them, and begin to enter into unwarrantable speculations with the funds committed to their care, it is not supposable that they will be particularly scrupulous as to the general management of the affairs of others.

"6. A bank director should be one who can bestow some attention upon the affairs of the establishment. It has appeared in evidence that gentlemen have been appointed, and have accepted the office of directors of banks, who gave little or no attention to the affairs: who, in fact, appear to have considered that the office of director was conferred on and accepted by them more for the purpose of complying with the letter of the deed of settlement, which enjoined the appointment of a certain number of directors, than from any idea of their being expected, or of its being necessary for them to know anything regarding the management. The consequence of this has been, that the duties which devolved upon the directors, perhaps six individuals, were confined to two, or possibly only one, and the others approving, without suitable knowledge or proper inquiry, of all their acts, the mass of shareholders, as well as an extensive commercial circle, have been involved in the disastrous results of mismanagement. It is altogether an anomaly that any man, or body of men, should have the credit, honour, and distinction, of being managers and directors of a bank, and yet not exercise any of the active functions and important duties that relate thereto. Upon what principle can they undertake, as by accepting the office they unquestionably do, to discharge a solemn trust, in faithfully administering the affairs of a bank, into which they make it no part of their business to look? Were the fact not very well known, it would seem absurd; yet it is not the less absurd that it is known."[1]

Mr. Taylor, in his "Statesman," makes the following observations upon the *age* of members of public boards:—

"Boards, or other co-operative bodies, should be so formed that youthfulness and elderliness may meet in due

---

[1] These observations are taken from the "Philosophy of Joint-Stock Banking," by G. M. Bell (Longman). I recommend the perusal of this little work to all directors and managers of joint-stock banks.

proportion in their counsels. If any such body be wholly composed of elderly men, it will commonly be found to be ineffective, so far as invention of new courses, and intrepidity of purpose is required; and perhaps, also, unequal to any unusual amount of spontaneous activity. If, on the other hand, it be composed wholly of young men, its operations will probably be wanting in circumspection; and the foresight by which it will be guided will be too keenly directed to the objects of a sanguine expectation—too dully to prospects of evil and counteraction. The respective positions in life of the young and the old operate to these results not less than their temperaments; for the young have their way to make—a reputation to earn—and it is for their interest to be enterprising, as well as in their nature; the old have ascertained their place in life, and they have, perhaps, a reputation to lose."

III. Joint-stock banks have a principal officer, called a manager.

"The prudent and satisfactory management of a Joint-stock bank very materially depends upon the upright and consistent discharge of those social duties and reciprocal interchanges of confidence which ought to characterize the directors and manager.

"The manager, from his experience, and the importance of the office he fills, is entitled to the kind consideration and entire confidence of the directors. He is selected by them to occupy an arduous and highly responsible situation, and ought to be rewarded not merely with an adequate pecuniary remuneration, but with the respect and friendship of the directors, by whom he should be considered in every respect, so far as regards the bank, at least upon an equally elevated footing. Without the confidence and friendship of the directors, he can neither take his place at their meetings free from restraint, discuss with them matters relating to the welfare of the establishment with composure, nor appear before the customers with that satisfaction and independence which is required to the proper discharge of his duties. Having placed him in the position of manager of the bank, it is their duty always to contemplate him in that light, to respect and confide in his opinions and conduct, which in many cases have been formed by long years of active and arduous employment in the profession; and to speak well of him among their friends and acquaintances. In the degree in which the manager is respected, and well spoken of by the directors, will respect and confidence be extended to him, and consequently to the establishment, by the public, and a good opinion entertained of their judgment and discernment in his selection.

"The conduct of the manager ought to be characterized by great circumspection and uprightness. He ought, unquestionably, in every instance, to be chosen for his business qualifications, and not because he is a rich man, a gentleman, a man of fashion, or a man with an extensive circle of friends. To choose him on account of any one of these qualifications, and not principally from his practical experience of banking, would be similar to appointing a man to the care and management of a steam-engine, who knew nothing of its mechanism, nor the nature of its operation, but was recommended solely because he had a taste for travelling; or it would be like placing a man at the helm to pilot a vessel over quicksands, and through a reef of rocks, who knew nothing of a seafaring life, but was fond of contemplating the grandeur of the elements. The manager of a joint-stock bank ought to be chosen exclusively for his experience in banking; other qualifications are well enough in their own place, but ought never to be taken into consideration in choosing a person to act as manager of a bank. In this way a stimulus is given to persons of talent, who may be looking forward to the reward of a life of toil and drudgery; and thus merit is patronized and protected. In a well-regulated office no one will be promoted over the head of another, but a prudent selection being made at the outset, a system of regular promotion should be uniformly practised.

"The manager of a bank may be contemplated in three important points—in his intercourse with the customers and the public; with the directors; and with the subordinate officers of a bank. In each of these departments he has important duties to perform. He must be scrupulously diligent in his attention to the affairs of the bank, courteous in his interviews with the public, affable and unreserved in his communications with the directors, and kind and conciliating towards the subordinates of the bank, treating them as those who may be one day placed in a similar situation with himself. The days are now gone past when a man of business was considered in the light of a machine—a mere automaton for the purpose of forming figures and casting up accounts; but it is still necessary, enlarged as our views of the powers and capabilities of the human mind are, in order to the proper management of any business, that it be carefully attended to. The manager of a joint-stock bank, being allowed a competent salary, cannot be justified in occupying his time with any other employment which may occasion his absence from the duties of the bank. But it is not intended to insinuate that he must be a man of one idea, and restrained from turning his mental acquirements to his own amusement or profit. This would be as absurd as it would be unreasonable. Nor is it meant that a man of business may not be also a man of great erudition, and it may happen, of literary and scientific eminence. On the contrary, it cannot be denied that, in the present day, this is often the case. What is contended for is, that the bank is entitled to, and ought to have, his close and chief attention.

"As it is obvious that he cannot manage any other trade or profession, without sacrificing or delegating more or less the duties he owes to the bank; it seems also very doubtful whether he can be justified in taking a prominent part in public or political affairs. There are two arguments against his being a public character: the first is, that he may be drawn away during the hours of business; the second, that, by becoming a partisan, he is certain of being more or less obnoxious to a portion of the inhabitants, and, it may be, of the bank's customers. A man whose mind is occupied in framing political speeches, in promoting political schemes, and whose time is partially given to political, magisterial, or other meetings, cannot possibly, from the exciting nature of such subjects, give that cool, deliberate, and uniform attention to the duties of the bank which they necessarily require.

"The customers ought always to be treated with civility and kindness, their business transacted promptly and cheerfully, and every inquiry regarding their accounts, or any matter of business, readily and satisfactorily explained. When an accommodation is to be declined, it ought to be done in as polite and inoffensive a manner as possible—the manner of a refusal being of paramount moment to the character of a manager.

"The shareholders, being, in other words, the proprietors of the bank, are to be received with that freedom and confidence which is due to their character as such, but without compromising or revealing to them either the business and accounts of each other, or of the customers of the bank.

"Next to being secret and cautious, a manager ought to be prompt and decided in all his measures, free from party influence, and firm in his purpose. A habit of promptitude and decision is very essential to the proper regulation of the business of a bank, and acquired by forethought and circumspection. It is, perhaps, a constitutional virtue which cannot be enjoyed by everyone in the same degree, but it is nevertheless a virtue which everyone may acquire by proper attention. Nothing makes a manager look more silly and contemptible than a hesitating, dubious, and capricious manner. His answer ought to be prompt and satisfactory; he should be sufficiently acquainted with business to say, at once, whether an act can be done or not, and should appear free from restraint, and not disposed to alter an opinion when once formed."[1]

IV. In joint-stock banks the administrative functions are usually distributed between the directors and the manager.

With reference to both private and joint-stock banks, the distribution of the administrative functions is a most important topic of inquiry. By what parties ought these functions to be exercised?—We have spoken of "the banker," as though a bank consisted of only one person, and this one person administered all the powers and functions of the bank. But few banks consist of only one person. One class of banks consists of two, three, four, five, six, or more persons, some or all of whom attend to the practical administration of the bank. Another class of banks consists of a great many, it may be of several hundred persons, who appoint some dozen or score of their own number to administer the bank on their behalf.

But how many soever the number of partners may be in a bank, the administrative functions are in fact practically

[1] Bell's "Philosophy of Joint-stock Banking."

exercised by a small number of persons. A private bank may consist of as many as six or more partners, but it is rarely, we believe, that so many as six are actually engaged in the business. When more than one are thus employed their duties may be distributed according to their seniority or other circumstances. In ordinary matters there may be a division of labour, and each partner may preside over a distinct department of the business. But in all important cases there is usually one leading partner who practically guides the others. When a bank has risen speedily to eminence, it has generally been through the talents of some one man. It does not follow that this one man did not receive great assistance from the advice or suggestions of his partners. It is the part of a wise man to avail himself of the knowledge and wisdom of others; and he will often gather much useful information from men far below himself in general talents. There is, perhaps, more uniformity, consistency, and energy in the proceedings of a bank managed by a few partners than by many. On the other hand, banks have sometimes been ruined by placing too much power in the hands of one or two of the partners.

In a joint-stock bank, though the number of directors may be large, the daily exercise of the administrative power is practically in the hands of a few persons. In some banks this power is vested solely in the manager; sometimes in one or two managing directors; sometimes in a permanent committee of two directors and the manager; and in other cases, in a changeable committee, on which each member of the board takes his rota of service for two or three weeks in succession. In all cases, however, the board of directors lay down the general principles on which the bank is to be administered; reports are made to them at their weekly meeting of the actual condition of the bank in all its departments, and all very important matters are reserved for their special consideration.

V. Some joint-stock banks have many branches.

When the law existed in England that no bank should have more than six partners, the branch system scarcely existed. In some cases, a bank had a branch or two a few miles distant, but no instance occurred of a bank extending itself throughout a county or a district. But with joint-stock banking arose the branch system—the head office was placed in the county town, and branches were opened in the principal towns and villages around. The credit of the bank being firmly established, its notes circulated freely throughout the whole district. The chief advantages of this system are the following:—

There is greater security to the public. The security of the whole bank is attached to the transactions of every branch; hence there is greater safety to the public than could be afforded by a number of separate private banks, or even so many independent joint-stock banks. These banks could have but a small number of partners—the paid-up capital and the private property of the partners must be comparatively small; hence the holder of a note issued by one of the independent joint-stock banks could have a claim only on that bank: but if that bank, instead of being independent, were a branch of a large establishment, the holder of a note would have the security of that large establishment; hence the branch system unites together a greater number of persons, and affords a more ample guarantee.

The branch system provides greater facilities for the transmission of money. The sending of money from one town to another is greatly facilitated if a branch of the same bank be established in each of those towns, for all the branches grant letters of credit upon each other. Otherwise you have to ask the banker in the town from which the money is sent to give you a bill upon London, which is transmitted by post; or you request him to advise his London agent to pay the money to the London agent of the banker who resides in the town to which the money is remitted. This takes up more time, and is attended with more expense. A facility of transmitting money between two places usually facilitates the trade between those places.

The branch system extends the benefits of banking to small places where independent banks could not be supported. An independent bank must have an independent board of directors, who in most cases will be better paid—the manager must have a higher salary, because he has a heavier responsibility, and a large amount of cash must be kept unemployed in the till, because there is no neighbouring resource in case of a run. There must be a paid-up capital, upon which good dividends are expected; a large proportion of the funds must be invested in exchequer bills, or other Government securities, at a low interest, in order that the bank may be prepared to meet sudden calls; and the charge for agencies will also be more. On the other hand, a branch has seldom need of a board of directors, one or two being quite sufficient—the manager is not so well paid: there is no necessity for a large sum in the till, because in case of necessity the branch has recourse to the head office, or to the neighbouring branches; nor is a large portion of its funds invested in Government securities that yield but little interest, as the head office takes charge of this, and can manage it at a less proportional expense. Besides, at some branches, the manager attends only on market days, or once or twice a week. The business done on those days would not bear the expense of an independent establishment.

PRACTICE OF BANKING. 415

The branch system provides the means of a due distribution of capital. Some banks raise more capital than they can employ, that is, their notes and deposits amount to more than their loans and discounts. Others employ more capital than they raise, that is, their loans and discounts amount to more than their notes and deposits. Banks that have a surplus capital usually send it to London to be employed by the bill-brokers. The banks that want capital must either restrict their business, or send their bills to London to be rediscounted. Now, if two banks, one having too much, and the other too little capital, be situated in the same county, they will have no direct intercourse, and will consequently be of no assistance to each other; but if a district bank be established, and these two banks become branches, then the surplus capital of one branch will be sent to be employed at the other—thus the whole wealth of the district is employed within the district, and the practice of rediscounting bills in London will be proportionately diminished.

The branch system secures a better system of management. The only way to secure good management is to prevent the formation of small banks. When banks are large, the directors are men of more wealth and respectability—they can give large salaries to their officers, and hence can command first-rate talent—there will be a more numerous proprietary; and in a large number there will be always some active spirits who will be watchful of the conduct of the directors and the manager; besides, in a numerous proprietary there is a greater number of persons eligible to be directors, and consequently there is a wider choice. In populous cities, such as London or Manchester, a large bank may be formed without branches; but in smaller places there is no way of forming a large bank but by giving it branches throughout the district. A branch bank in a small town will probably be better managed than an independent bank in the same place. The directors and manager of the branch will be appointed by the directors at the head office, assisted by the general manager, who are very competent to judge what qualifications are necessary for these offices, and who would not be biased by local partialities. But the directors of the independent bank would most likely be self-appointed, or chosen by the proprietors, because no others could be obtained, and these directors would appoint some friend of their own to be manager. The manager of the branch, besides the superintendence of the directors, which he has in common with the manager of the independent bank, will be subject to visits from the general manager or the inspector; and he must send weekly statements of his accounts to the head office. The consciousness of responsibility will thus secure a more anxious attention to his duties; and, besides, he will probably be looking forward for promotion to a higher branch as a reward for his successful management. These circumstances seem to insure a higher degree of good management to the branch.

At the same time, it must be admitted that banks with numerous branches require a proportionate paid-up capital, and that the capital be kept in a disposable form; it also requires vigilant and constant inspection, and a rigid system of discipline.

A proportionate paid-up capital is necessary, because, in case of a run, there are a greater number of points of attack: hence the funds must be divided to meet all these possible attacks; for if one branch be overpowered, the whole bank is immediately exposed to suspicion.

Another danger arises from the incompetency or negligence of the managers of branches. Among a number of men, it is not likely that all are clever, and all prudent;

and one case of neglect on the part of one manager may, in times of alarm, throw discredit on the whole establishment. Besides, there is sometimes danger even from the zeal of the branch managers. Each manager is naturally anxious to increase the business of his own branch; and he will perhaps find that the most easy way of doing this is to extend his loans and discounts. Hence each manager tries to employ as much capital as he can; and the urgent remonstrances he receives from head-quarters, requiring him to restrict his discounts, are either evaded or delayed. Thus the bank proceeds until some heavy demand for money arises at head-quarters, and it is then found that all the capital of the bank has been absorbed by the branches. These advances cannot be suddenly recalled, and thus the bank is ruined.

What number of branches a bank ought to have, and what distance they ought to be from the head office, have been the subject of much discussion. No general rules can be given. The subject may very safely be left to the discretion of the banks themselves. The banks in Scotland have from twenty up to one hundred and thirty branches. The Provincial Bank of Ireland, and the National Bank, whose head offices are in London, have branches spread all over Ireland. I am not aware that in these cases any danger or inconvenience has been experienced. When branches are found troublesome or unprofitable, they will very soon be discontinued. In some instances, even in Scotland, the branches of the larger banks have been withdrawn, in consequence of being unable to sustain a competition with the local banks of the district.

Had the Act of 1826 permitted joint-stock banks of issue to be established in London, we should probably by this time have had ten or a dozen banks having their head-quarters in London, and extending their branches throughout the country. But as the law prohibited joint-stock banks of issue being established within sixty-five miles of London, it necessarily gave rise to banks occupying particular districts in the country. The advantages which are alleged to belong to the district system are the following:—That the bank will be better adapted to the wants and habits of the people—that a local feeling will be excited in its favour: hence the inhabitants of the district will take shares, and the occurrence of runs upon the bank will be less probable—that a better system of management may be expected, as it can more easily be governed, and will be more under control—that a panic in the district will not affect the other parts of the country, and hence supplies may be more easily obtained—that banks will be of a moderate size, and hence will be attended with the advantages arising from numerous banks acting as checks upon each other, instead of a few large banks who may combine for objects injurious to the nation; and that as each bank will have an agent in London, the bills they draw will thus have two parties as securities, and the public will have a pledge that there is no excessive issue in the form of kites or accommodation bills. On the other hand, it may be contended, that in Scotland the large metropolitan banks, which have branches extended throughout the country, have generally been more successful than the provincial or district banks—that there is a greater security to the public for the notes or deposits—that advances are not so likely to be made to speculative parties merely on account of their local influence—that the capital raised in one part of the country can be employed in another—that the transmission of money from one part of the country to another is more rapid and direct—that the establishment of the bank being on a larger scale, you have a superior class of directors, and can demand the services of higher talents in those who are employed as officers.

It does not appear that these two systems are necessarily at variance with each other. County or district banks have no doubt many advantages, but they do not seem to supersede banks on a larger scale.

VI. Joint-stock banks have half-yearly meetings of shareholders, to whom is usually exhibited a balance-sheet showing the assets and liabilities of the bank.

All banks do not exhibit a balance-sheet. The practice is said to be open to the following objections:—

1. That it is not a fair criterion by which you can form any judgment of the real condition of the bank. You might see that the bank had a certain amount of securities, or had advanced a certain sum upon loans; but whether those securities were available, or whether those loans could suddenly be called up, are points upon which the balance-sheet could give no information.

2. It lays the bank open to attacks from its rivals or opponents. The balance-sheet will show in what way the funds of the bank are employed, but it will not state the reasons why they are so employed. The opponents of the bank may attack every item of the balance-sheet, and the directors may not be able to repel those attacks without a breach of confidence that would be injurious to the establishment. Suppose, for instance, the balance-sheet should show that the bank had advanced a few thousand pounds upon mortgage. This might be justly considered as a departure from the sound principles of banking; yet it might in this case be justified by some peculiar circumstances, which, nevertheless, the directors could not publish without serious injury to the parties concerned. The production of a balance-sheet is advocated upon the ground that it would enable the shareholders to judge of

the ability and prudence of the directors. But how can they do this without knowing the reasons by which the directors are influenced in their decisions?

3. It causes a great deal of speculation in the shares. The shareholders and the public would form their opinions of the bank from the statements in the balance-sheet; and according to these opinions the price of the shares would fluctuate in the market. Suppose it were seen that the bank had invested a large portion of its funds in Government securities, and it was known that during the year the price of those securities had experienced a considerable fall, would not the bank shares immediately fall too? Again, suppose at the end of a year like 1836, it should appear that the bank held a considerable amount of overdue bills, the apprehension of loss would cause the bank shares to fall; soon afterwards these bills might be paid, and then the shares would rise again.—Thus, the publication of balance-sheets would keep the prices of shares in perpetual fluctuation, and furnish a most fruitful source of speculation and gambling.

4. It is perfectly inefficient as a protection against fraud. The balance-sheet, it seems, is to be a check upon the directors, and yet the directors themselves are to prepare the balance-sheet. They must be stupid knaves indeed, if they produce such a balance-sheet as shall expose their own knavery. Besides, the balance-sheet merely shows the state of the bank on one day in the year. Would it not be easy to put the bank on that day in such a condition as would give satisfaction to the shareholders?

VII. At the annual, or the half-yearly meeting, the directors announce the amount of the profits and the mode of their distribution.

The first appropriation of the profits is to pay to the shareholders a dividend on the capital. But all the profits are not usually thus appropriated; a certain portion is generally retained as a rest, or surplus fund, or, as it is sometimes called, a guarantee fund. This last title has led to an erroneous impression with regard to the nature and purposes of this fund. It is not designed as a guarantee to the depositors for the amount of their deposits—these are guaranteed by the paid-up capital and the liability of the shareholders—but as a guarantee to the shareholders for the uniformity of their dividends.[1] Should the profits in any one year fall below the sum necessary to pay the usual dividend, the deficiency may then be taken from the surplus or guarantee fund. The amount of this fund, therefore, will be regulated by the amount of the transactions, and the consequent danger of loss. But it sometimes happens that, after paying a liberal dividend, the surplus fund accumulates far beyond the sum necessary for the above purpose. In this case a portion of the fund may be employed either in still farther increasing the dividend, or it may be distributed to the shareholders in the form of bonuses, or it may be added to the capital. The course to be adopted must depend upon circumstances. When the capital is small, it will probably be best to make an addition from the surplus fund; but when the capital is sufficiently large, the best way will be to give an occasional bonus to the proprietors. This is usually better than increasing the dividend. For if the dividend be once increased, the same rate of dividend will always be expected. And it is better not to make any advance, unless there is good reason to believe that the same rate will always be maintained.

Those persons are under a mistake who object to a reserved or surplus fund on the ground that it takes away the profits from the existing shareholders, and gives them to the future shareholders. This is not the fact. An existing shareholder who keeps his shares until the fund

[1] See note on page 370.

is in some way distributed, receives of course his portion of the fund. But an existing shareholder who sells out his shares before the fund is distributed receives the value of his portion of the fund in the price of his shares. The amount of the surplus fund will influence the market value of the shares.

We consider it of high importance that a bank should maintain an ample surplus fund. Without such a fund the dividends will fluctuate very widely, and sometimes there may be no dividend at all, even though upon a series of years the bank may have been very successful. Even if it is known that a bank has met with losses, its credit is not so much affected when it has an ample reserved fund to fall back upon. And besides the ordinary losses in the way of business, a bank will sometimes, in a season of pressure, be called upon to sustain loss by the realization of securities; and it is very convenient to have a surplus fund sufficiently ample to bear all these contingencies. Such a fund too has a moral effect in strengthening the reputation of the bank in public estimation. It is regarded as an indication that its affairs are governed by a wise and prudent administration.

It will assist us in forming a correct judgment as to the principles on which joint-stock banks ought to be administered, if we take a view of those banks that have fallen, and notice the causes to which their failure may be assigned. In investigating these causes, we shall find that the disasters which have befallen joint-stock banks have arisen not from any unsoundness in the principles of joint-stock banking, but purely from mal-administration. It was predicted by their opponents that they would be ruined by the excessive issue of their notes; but the banks that have failed have been chiefly those that did not issue notes. It was stated they would be ruined by carrying on an extensive business with a small capital; but among the banks that have stopped have been some of the largest capital. It was supposed they would be ruined by unprincipled men getting to be directors, who, having no property of their own, would care little about squandering the property of others. But the fallen banks are chiefly those which were governed by honourable men; and the greatest sufferers have been the directors. Nor can it be said that the joint-stock banks have made their losses by engaging in speculations unconnected with banking. Private bankers have done so. But joint-stock banks are confined by their deeds of settlement to the business of banking. Nor has it appeared—except, perhaps, in the Isle of Man Bank—that they have violated their deeds in this respect. To what, then, must we ascribe the failure of so many joint-stock banks? We reply, To mal-administration; or, in other words, to bad management. And this leads us to inquire, In what way has this mal-administration been exemplified? What are those erroneous principles that have led to these fatal results? Without attempting to enumerate them all, we will endeavour to specify a few of the most prominent.

I. Taking the unsound business of other banks.

One cause of the rapid extension of joint-stock banks in 1836, was the "merging" of numerous private banks. It appears that 138 private banking establishments merged in joint-stock banks. Some of the private banks sold their business after the joint-stock banks had come into operation. Others formed a joint-stock bank upon the private bank, the senior partner often becoming a director, and the junior partner the manager, of the new bank.

In by far the majority of cases, these unions, or "merges," were advantageous to both parties. The private bankers obtained the value of the business they had surrendered, and an interest in the future prosperity of the bank they had joined. On the other hand, the new joint-stock bank acquired a business already formed, and also obtained the advantage of the practical knowledge and superintendence of experienced bankers.

But in some instances the bargain was a disastrous one for the joint-stock bank. The bad and overdrawn accounts were taken without due examination, and soon afterwards occasioned considerable loss. The loss of the purchase-money was generally by far the smaller loss of the two. A joint-stock bank in the west of England purchased a private bank in a country town for a large sum, and took the overdrawn accounts without a guarantee. These accounts were considered good at the time, but a few years afterwards the parties failed, and the joint-stock bank lost considerably. A joint-stock bank gave to the Northern and Central Bank the sum of £6,500 for their business at Leeds, after they had stopped. The accounts they took over were afterwards the occasion of great loss. The Isle of Wight Joint-stock Bank was formed upon a private bank, but a few months only had elapsed when they found they were insolvent from the losses that would arise from the bad accounts they had accepted. They immediately determined to wind up, and transfer their business to the National Provincial Bank of England. Other instances might be adduced of joint-stock banks having been founded on private banks which are now supposed to have been, at the time, in a state of insolvency.

II. Some banks have sustained losses by making advances on dead security.

Instead of the word "some," we think we might use the word "all." For among the banks that have failed we doubt if we could find one that had not sinned in this respect. But the greatest sinners were those banks that were established in places of the greatest trade. All the banks at Newcastle advanced money on collieries, and also on other public works. The banks of Manchester made advances on mills and manufactories, as did also some of the banks at Leeds. These advances were attended with several evil effects. In the first place, there was a lock-up of capital, which restrained the operations of the bank. To relieve themselves from this restriction, they took bills for their loans, and rediscounted them in the London money market. The facilities thus obtained induced them to extend this system of advance. Bills were perpetually renewed, and perpetually rediscounted. At last a pressure came, and the renewed bills could not be rediscounted. The bank could not take up the old bills that were returned, and consequently stopped payment. Sometimes, too, the bank tried to relieve itself from this pressure by increasing its drafts on its London agent. It was for a long time the practice in Lancashire to pay for cotton with a three months' banker's bill. Banks in difficulties availed themselves of this practice to make all their advances by drafts on London, instead of cash. The Bank of Manchester had at one time an enormous circulation of this kind.

Another effect was that, however good the security might be at the time the advance was made, when a change took place in the state of trade, its value fell much below the amount of the advance, and in some cases it could not be sold at any price. But the evil did not stop here. As the property given as security would have been worth nothing if not worked, the bank was induced to make farther advances, to carry on the works on their own account. A colliery, if not kept in operation, soon gets out of order; and it will then require a considerable sum to set it at work again. Hence some of the collieries at Newcastle were worked by the banks; and mills in the neighbourhood of Manchester were carried on in the same way. The plan, however, does not often succeed. It is generally throwing good money after bad. The ultimate loss is usually increased. We may just observe in passing, that the banks in the East Indies get involved in the same way, through making advances on indigo works. These works are of no value except when kept in operation; and hence it has occurred that a bank which has made an advance, is compelled to carry on the works to keep up the value of its security. To show that a bank governed by the strictest rules may sometimes be drawn into transactions of this kind, it may be observed that an iron concern in Wales was said to have been carried on by the Bank of England. It belonged to the Governor and Company of the Mines Royal. The bank made an advance on mortgage to this corporation during the pressure of 1847, and took the profits of the works. Some joint-stock banks have made advances upon buildings. This has occurred chiefly in places where there has been an increasing population. A few years ago a joint-stock bank in a town of fashionable resort advanced large sums to builders upon the security of the houses they were erecting. The houses did not let—they could not be sold for anything like the cost price—the builders were ruined—and the loss fell upon the bank. The bank had recourse to the expedient of rediscounting the builder's bills; but after a while it was compelled to stop payment. In agricultural districts banks have sometimes made considerable advances to farmers and graziers. Indeed, it is almost a universal practice to do so at some seasons of the year. These advances are not individually of large amount, and are not usually attended with much loss—not with anything like the losses incurred by advances on collieries, mills, and houses. But it is a lock-up of capital until the year comes round.

III. Some banks have lost large amounts through advances made by way of loan or discounts to men engaged in speculative undertakings.

Two of the banks that stopped at Newcastle-upon-Tyne sustained great losses through advances to corn-merchants. Speculations in corn are usually carried on more by bills than by loan. A merchant buys a quantity of corn, and places it in the hands of a factor, and draws bills for something under the market value, leaving the factor a margin to guard against loss. He gets these bills discounted, buys more corn, which he also places in the hands of his factor, and then draws fresh bills. This second batch of bills he also gets discounted, and buys more corn; and thus he goes on in the same course. Now if he thinks the market will rise (as all speculators do), he will not allow his factor to sell the corn; but when the first bills fall due he will renew them, and with the produce of the new bills, when discounted, he will pay the old ones. It is thus that a large speculation may be carried on with a small amount of capital (and that may be borrowed from the bank), and all the speculation is kept afloat by bills. These bills are always for large amounts, and when the parties fail the losses are usually heavy. The failures in the corn trade in 1847 fell heavily on the banking and monied interests. It was the stoppage of Messrs. Lesley, Alexander, and Co., the corn-factors, that caused the stoppage of Messrs. Sanderson and Co., the bill-brokers.

Wool is another "heavy article," as it is called; that is, it costs a great deal of money, and the bills are usually for large amounts. Occasionally there is much speculation in this article.

Builders are generally a speculative class. Banks that advance money to parties engaged in this trade have usually to take possession of the buildings. We have already noticed an instance of this in the conduct of a joint-stock bank.

People who speculate in railway and other companies are dangerous customers to a bank.

It may be remarked, that it is generally bad policy in a bank to make a very large permanent advance to any one customer. The word "large" is a relative term, and must be understood with reference to the extent of business that the customer is carrying on, and to the means of the bank. It is not the business of bankers to supply their customers with capital to carry on their trade. But it is their business to make temporary advances, and these advances may sometimes be large. In such cases, the banker should have a kind of security, that shall not only secure the debt, but shall prevent its becoming permanent. Almost every bank that has failed can point to some one, two, or three large accounts, to which it mainly ascribes its failure.

But the worst form of illegitimate advance is that which is made by a bank to one of its own directors.

A bank that is known to act imprudently in making large advances will occasion a suspicion that its smaller advances are made with, at least, equal imprudence. A large number of imprudent small transactions may be as fatal to a bank as a smaller number of a larger amount. A sum which appears small as a loan will appear large as a loss. A manager who accustoms himself to examine all the circumstances connected with the small bills he discounts, will acquire a habit of investigation that will guide him with safety in dealing with large transactions. But if he get into a laxity of manner in regard to small amounts, he will ultimately deal less carefully with large sums, and be in danger of making great losses. In every case the rules of sound banking should be strictly applied.

IV. Some banks have become involved in difficulties

through a general want of system and discipline in conducting its affairs. This laxity usually shows itself in two ways—the absence of a good system of book-keeping, and the want of a proper control over its branches.

We could not adduce a more striking illustration of this observation than has been furnished in the history of the Agricultural and Commercial Bank of Ireland, as related before a Committee of the House of Commons in the year 1837. The following are extracts from this evidence:—
" The books at the head office had not been posted for four months. There were no stock books, showing the amount each shareholder had paid on his share. There were no books showing the amount of the circulation." An auditor states:—" They showed us no general account—their books were in a perfect chaos. They had no account at the head office by which they could check any transaction at the branches. Bills were sent away to be rediscounted without any entry of them being made in the bank books. At the branches there was no regular system of accounts. At no one branch was there a system of accounts that formed an adequate check upon the amount of notes in circulation. From one branch we were told that returns had not been made to the head office for fourteen months, and from another for six weeks, and there was no question about it from the head office."

We will not intimate that anything like this has ever existed in a joint-stock bank in England. We never heard that any one has had any difficulty in making out a statement of its affairs. With some banks, however, there has been a laxity in regard to the government of their branches. The system of inspection was not well understood—the returns from the branch were not so ample as they should have been—and the orders of the head office were not rigorously enforced. We could mention the names of several fallen banks that lost very considerably by their branches. In some cases the banks had opened branches in towns that required an amount of capital disproportionate to the means of the bank, and their administration had been entrusted to parties who had neither banking nor local knowledge.

A good system of book-keeping cannot be too highly valued. Its object is not merely to secure accuracy of accounts between the bank and its customers. A farther object is to classify and arrange all the transactions in such a way as easily to produce a weekly balance-sheet, showing the actual condition of the bank. Nor must it be supposed that such abstracts or balance-sheets are intended merely for the use of the directors. They are of the utmost use to the manager, and should be the subject of his constant study. A manager who, day after day, attends only to individual transactions, and that, too, possibly in a state of mental excitement, may involve his bank in difficulty, even though each transaction may, upon its own ground, be perfectly justifiable, unless he attends to those summaries and classifications of his transactions which are presented in the weekly balance-sheet. He will there see on one side the means of the bank, and on the other the way in which his funds are employed. He will notice if his loans, or over-drawn accounts, or past-due bills, are unduly increased. If a good system of book-keeping does not prevent a manager from going wrong, it will prevent his going wrong without knowing it. If he act unwisely, his balance-sheet will stare him in the face and remind him of his faults.

It is a great defect not to take an accurate estimate of the losses every half-year before striking the balance of profit and loss. It is clear that common sense and common honesty require that the loss should be taken into account as well as the profit. Yet some of the banks that failed went on, year after year, exhibiting a balance-sheet to their shareholders showing a respectable profit, which enabled the directors to declare a fair dividend, and to make an addition to the reserved fund. While the annual balance-sheets thus showed a steady increase of profit, the bad debts had actually eaten up the whole of the capital.

Another defect is, not to have an account in the general ledger showing the amount of bills reissued or rediscounted. The amount of these bills not due should appear on both sides of the account—on one side as a liability, and on the other as an asset. For want of doing so, some banks have not been able to ascertain easily what amount of bills they have under rediscount. But it is important to know this. For it may be expected that, during a season of pressure, no small portion of these bills will be returned unpaid, and the bank must find funds to take up its endorsements. If they fail to do this, it amounts to a stoppage of payment. In fact, the amount of such bills suddenly returned has in some cases been the *immediate* cause of a bank stopping payment.

We have no horror of numerous branches. When we see that the largest and most prosperous banks have each a large number of branches, we are led to believe that branches are not attended with any dangers which cannot be overcome by wise administration. At the same time, we are ready to admit that numerous branches require a peculiar mode of government, and a rigid system of discipline. The chief officer of such a bank should be a good banker, and something more. He must be a good administrator; that is, skilled in the administrative department of good government.

In the first place, each branch must have a good system of book-keeping, and the system must be uniform at every branch. Secondly, Care should be taken to appoint efficient officers. Thirdly, A code of laws should be drawn up, and the branch manager should be distinctly informed as to the extent to which he may exercise his discretion, and what cases must be referred for the consideration of the directors. Fourthly, Weekly returns must be made to the head office of all the transactions, and a half-yearly balance-sheet, attended with full supplementary details. Fifthly, Special reports should be occasionally required, as special circumstances may occur, either with reference to the branches generally, or with reference to a branch individually. Sixthly, An inspector should be appointed for the purpose of visiting the branches. His duties will be to explain the instructions of the directors, and to see that they are properly observed—to maintain a uniform system of transacting business at all the branches—to instruct the officers of the branch in their duties when necessary, and to communicate the knowledge he has acquired in visiting the other branches—to answer any difficult or knotty questions that may be proposed to him by the manager, and to consult with the manager as to the best means of promoting the interests of the branch—to observe the talents and capabilities of the several officers, and to recommend for promotion any who seem to have qualities that might be usefully employed in a higher department in the bank. In large banks there are usually several inspectors.

Branches should always be kept in strict subordination to the head office. Prompt obedience to orders is a duty that must be rigidly enforced. The chairman of the Northern and Central Bank stated to the Parliamentary Committee, that at some of the branches where the heaviest losses had occurred, the managers had not obeyed the orders they had received from the directors. Similar accusations were made against some of the branch managers of the Commercial Bank of England. It is quite impossible for any bank to be well administered as a whole, if every branch is allowed to exercise an independent authority. Upon this ground some parties object altogether to the appointment of local directors at the branches. A local board, consisting of the branch directors and the manager, are more likely than the manager alone to assume independent authority—to postpone carrying out the directions they may receive from head-quarters—and to take upon themselves the responsibility of acting somewhat at variance with the strict letter of their instructions. And although local directors may sometimes be useful in extending the connections of the bank, or in aiding the managers with information or advice, yet, for the above or other reasons, they are now in England but very seldom appointed. The branch is under the sole care of a manager. The general manager of the bank is not merely the manager of the head office, but has authority also over all the branches. Whenever necessary or expedient, he issues circular letters of instruction to the branch managers, and these instructions the branch managers are expected to obey.

V. Some banks have been unfortunate in consequence of having made no provision to meet contingencies.

This class of banks has not fallen into any of the practices that we have enumerated. They have not, on the whole, been badly managed, but they have traded to the full amount of their means, and have kept no reserve, either in Government stock, exchequer bills, or bills of exchange, to meet those contingencies to which all banks are liable. One bank of this class had, during the railway speculation, received from some of these companies a large amount of deposits. A portion of these deposits was lodged, as its agent, with another bank. That bank stopped. This bank was, consequently, unable to pay back the deposits to the railway companies. From this circumstance, and the known connection between the two banks having damaged its credit, it also was compelled to stop payment. Another bank had but a small capital, but for a number of years it was exceedingly well managed. In 1847 it had discounted, and again re-discounted, a large amount of bills on a first-rate London house that failed. The London house afterwards paid 20*s*. in the pound. But the directors concluded from this circumstance, that a bank with a small capital was not in a condition to bear a large loss, and they resolved to wind up the concern. After sustaining the losses and expenses of winding up (and in such a case some losses necessarily occur), the bank realized nearly the whole of its paid-up capital. We doubt not that some of the other banks that have wound up their affairs have done so from causes similar to those we have described.

We consider that this head of our inquiry is not less instructive than the four by which it was preceded. *They will teach us the vices we ought to avoid—this will teach us the virtues we ought to cultivate.* The lessons we here gather are, that we ought not only to avoid all mismanagement, but we ought also to provide for those contingencies to which, even with good management, we are exposed. We ought to raise our capital in proportion to our business, or else keep down our business to a level with our capital—we ought to have a surplus fund adequate to meet any unforeseen loss—we ought to have a reserve of convertible securities ready to meet contingent evils; and, finally, we ought always to keep our bank in such a condition that, even if not successful, we shall still be in a condition to wind up our affairs without inconvenience to the public.

VI. We may observe, that these erroneous principles of administration have sometimes been the result of a defect in the constitution of the bank—of the appointment of incompetent persons—or of an unwise distribution of the administrative functions.

Joint-stock banking did not grow up gradually in England as in Scotland. On the introduction of this system into England, the directors were necessarily unacquainted with the practical operations of banking.[1] For all the practice and experience were confined to the private bankers, whom the new system was intended to subvert. In some places there was a prejudice against directors who were in business. Hence officers in the army, barristers, solicitors, medical men, retired tradesmen, and country gentlemen, were considered as the most eligible directors. These boards of directors, all of whom were unacquainted with banking, and some of whom were destitute of business habits, had to encounter difficulties which would have tried the most experienced bankers.

The want of experience in a board of directors did not, however, produce any dangerous consequences when they appointed an efficient manager. He prudently advised and instructed them. They gradually increased their knowledge, adopted his principles, and were guided by his counsels. By their daily intercourse with him, by their own reflections, by the direction given to their thoughts, and by the experience they acquired, they became in a few

---

[1] The Chairman of the Northern and Central Bank gave the following answers to a Committee of the House of Commons:—

"Is there any one of your colleagues in the direction of the bank that had previous experience in banking business?—I do not think there was one.

"Had any of the directors of the joint-stock banks about you previous banking experience?—I do not recollect one."—*Committee on Joint-Stock Banks*, 1837.

years as conversant with their duties as the manager himself. We believe this was almost uniformly the case with those joint-stock banks that were formed within five or six years after they were allowed to be established in England.

But, after joint-stock banks were started as matters of speculation, they increased more rapidly than efficient managers could be found. The new banks naturally enough looked to Scotland. But the Scotch banks had the sagacity to raise the salaries of their principal officers, to prevent their emigration to England. In some cases, those Scotchmen who were appointed managers of English banks had never held office in a bank before, or else it was an office so inferior that all they knew about banking was merely the routine of the office. Wherever efficient managers were appointed, whether English or Scotch, the same effects were produced as in the former cases. The inexperienced directors acquired the knowledge and experience necessary to the discharge of their duties, and the banks prospered. But sometimes the case was reversed. The manager was inefficient, and the directors inexperienced, and then the effects were disastrous.

In some cases the manager laboured under an inconvenience from being taken from a lower social position. Not a few of the managers were previously bankers' clerks; and the appointment to the office of bank manager did not, in England (as it does in Scotland and in Ireland), raise him to the same social position as a banker. This was injurious to the bank in several ways. It lessened his influence with his directors. From the days of Solomon to the present time, the degree of deference paid to even good advice has depended upon the social rank of the party who offered it: "Wisdom is better than strength; nevertheless the poor man's wisdom is despised, and his words are not heard." [1] The public, too, had been so long accustomed to private banking, that, seeing the manager paid by a salary, they could not bring their minds to view him as *the* banker, but considered him as holding an office analogous to that of chief clerk in a private bank. It may be feared, that in some banks the directors took the same view, and thought that the influence and the salaries of the two offices ought to correspond. These impressions have now passed away.

In some cases the manager was superseded in his functions by the appointment of managing directors. The manager was a man of banking knowledge and experience, but he had placed over him a couple of managing directors, who had neither knowledge nor experience. Consequently, his voice was never heard in the board-room, and, with the name of manager, he acted only in the capacity of a chief clerk. The manager was thus deprived of the opportunity of discharging the most important of his functions—that of giving advice to the directors—and was required to confine his attention to the more easy duty of obedience.

In other cases the managing directors and the manager formed a secret committee, who alone were acquainted with the actual condition of the bank. The directors of the Bank of Manchester stated, in their first report, that "two of their body, who are out of business, alone have access to the accounts, and are authorized to advise with the manager, when requisite, on the current transactions of the bank. At the same time, each of the other directors engaged, individually, to refrain entirely from inspecting any of the customers' bills or accounts; thus combining all the secrecy of a private bank with the advantages of a public institution." The Bank of Manchester had at that

[1] Eccles. viii. 16.

time the largest paid-up capital of any joint-stock bank in England. Three of its directors were examined before the bank Charter Committee, in the year 1832, they presented to the committee a list of twenty-three joint-stock banks then formed, and strongly urged that measures should be adopted to require from them an adequate amount of paid-up capital. It is somewhat remarkable that, out of these twenty-three banks, the only one that has stopped payment is the Bank of Manchester. Another has ceased to exist, but it was by a transfer of its business.

In some cases a bank has been ruined by its manager; in others, by the manager and the managing directors conjointly; in others, by the managing directors without the manager; and in others, by one, two, or three directors, who, though not formally appointed managing directors, have, by their influence with the board, virtually monopolized that office, and discharged its functions. It may be questioned whether any case has occurred in England of a bank being ruined by the acts of its whole board, where all the directors were honest and intelligent men, and each was accustomed to think and judge for himself.

VII. We may observe, that sometimes joint-stock banks have been led into erroneous principles of administration by the proceedings of the proprietors.

The constitution of joint-stock banks appears theoretically absurd. The manager— the banker—who is presumed to have some knowledge and experience in banking, is placed under the command of a board of directors, whose knowledge and experience are supposed to be inferior to his own. These directors are again placed under the control and instruction of a body of proprietors, whose knowledge of banking is much less than that of the directors. Practically, however, the system works well. But when an attempt is made to carry out the theory, the effects are injurious; and some joint-stock banks have fallen into danger through the operations being too much regulated by the proceedings of the proprietors.

Sometimes the directors have been influenced by the applauses of the shareholders.

It is natural to all shareholders to wish for large dividends upon the capital they have invested. Hence they applaud most loudly those directors who contrive to declare the highest dividends, to make the largest bonuses, to keep up the shares at the highest premiums in the market, and then to distribute more shares at par. The directors, knowing these to be the feelings of the shareholders, very naturally attempt to gratify them. But those transactions that yield a large immediate profit are either attended with a risk of loss, or a lock-up of capital. But the profit is immediate: the danger is remote. With the applauses of the shareholders ringing in their ears, the directors become too giddy for reflection, and recklessly engage in a course of action that ends in ruin. This evil is increased when there are two joint-stock banks of about equal strength in the same place. The spirit of rivalry is natural to man. The competition between the two boards of directors is not which bank shall be governed with the greatest prudence, and with the strictest regard to sound banking principles, but which shall produce the most glowing reports—which shall declare the longest dividends —and which shall keep up its shares at the highest price in the market. A strong competition is carried on, which ends in the destruction of one or both of the rival banks. Such feelings are said to have prevailed at Manchester; and at that place several boards of directors were presented with services of plate, by their respective shareholders, within a short time of the stoppage of their banks.

Sometimes directors are induced to act unwisely from the censures of their shareholders.

Every one who knows anything of banking must know that it cannot be carried on without occasional losses. A bank that is so conducted as never to make a loss, will seldom make much profit. And sometimes these losses will be so great as to absorb a large portion of the profits of the year. The object of having a surplus fund is to provide for these contingencies, so that the usual dividend may be maintained. But when an occasion arises for making use of a portion of this fund, there is often what is called "a stormy meeting," and the shareholders walk away sulky and dissatisfied. This produces a bad effect on the minds of the directors. It is a great mistake to suppose that boards of directors are indifferent to the applauses or censures of their shareholders. As a general rule, the fact is lamentably the reverse. In some cases they have had so much dread of "the general meeting" that they could not muster courage enough to make honest reports. Had they done so in the first instance, their banks might have been saved from destruction.

Sometimes directors are in danger of being led astray by the admonitions and instructions of their shareholders.

A very prudent class of proprietors exhort the directors to practise the strictest economy. When rightly understood, this exhortation is worthy of the rounds of applause with which it is usually attended. But it is liable to be misunderstood. In banking, as in housewifery, the lowest priced article is not always the cheapest. The largest portion of the expenditure of a bank consists of salaries. Hence an exhortation to economy amounts to—"Keep down the salaries of your officers;" and as the manager has the largest salary, he will most likely be the heaviest sufferer.

A more mischievous recommendation, when thus understood, can hardly be conceived. Next to having a dishonest manager, the greatest evil is to have one that is badly paid. If he is known to be poor, his advice will have less weight in the board-room; the directors individually will treat him with less respect, his wealthy customers will not disclose to him their private affairs; the needy class, when refused discount, will insult him by threatening to complain to the directors, and his inferior officers will be less prompt in their obedience. But worse than all this will be the effect produced upon his own mind. He will not be, and he cannot be, so efficient a manager when badly paid, as he would be if he received a liberal remuneration. It is the besetting sin of men of business, that they never pay attention to MIND, though among no class are mental phenomena more strikingly exhibited. The amount of his salary is the only tangible means by which a manager can judge how far his character and his services are appreciated. It is not the money alone, but the feelings, of which the money is an indication, that produces an effect on the mind. It is a law of our nature, that the kindness, liberality, and generosity of others will produce corresponding feelings in ourselves. And it is another law of our nature, that when the mind is under the influence of such feelings, it is capable of intellectual efforts of a higher order. But we forget;—we were writing about pounds, shillings, and pence, and our pen has darted off into philosophy. We will now return.

Sometimes the shareholders fly at higher game, and canvass the salaries of the directors. Such discussions are always unpleasant, as they are carried on in the presence of the parties interested. Among all the charges brought against the directors and managers of banks that have failed, we have never met with the accusation that they received excessive salaries. We are tempted to fancy that, had their salaries been higher, the banks might not have failed. As far as salary is concerned, they certainly would have had a greater interest in preventing the failure. In some banks, however, directors have paid themselves for their services in ways far more costly to the bank. Take the following instance:—

"The qualification for directors of the Northern and Central Bank was 100 shares. It was, however, ascertained that each of the original directors took 1,000 shares, and that besides these, other shares were, at later dates, distributed among the directors and their near connections. Instead of paying the calls to the bank, the directors and their nominees were severally debited with the amount in a private ledger, locked up, and the key deposited with the chief accountant. In addition to this, each director had a current account with the bank, and many of them had overdrawn their accounts to a very large amount. Nor was this all, for it further appeared that many of them were also indebted in large sums of money on notes of hand, which being placed to the account of securities, did not appear in the books as a debt against the directors. Upon combining these several items of debt, it was ascertained that there was no less than £290,000 due by the directors, and that there was near £14,000 due by the managers and clerks."

It is not creditable to any bank to receive the services of its directors as a matter of charity. Nor is it wise. A director who is paid for his services may justly be called to account for neglect of duty. In this case, too, he cannot expect payment in any other way. In his transactions with the bank he is then on the same footing as any other customer. It has been said, that the directors are such honourable men that they will attend to their duty as strictly if badly paid as if liberally paid. If so, they ought to be liberally paid, as it is very desirable that such honourable men should be most closely attached to the bank. But we doubt the fact. In matters of almsgiving, men will give only what they can conveniently spare. If a director is to give his time for nothing, he will give only that portion of his time which he cannot more profitably or more agreeably employ elsewhere. In matters of business, men will apportion their services according to the return they receive for them. There is no way of securing constant punctuality of attendance on the part of directors, but by paying them liberally for that attendance. In some cases where payment has not been given, or given only to the managing directors, it is said that the government of the bank has fallen into the hands of a few persons, whose punctuality of attendance has been almost their only banking virtue. But the main advantage of liberal payment is its effect upon the *minds* of the directors. Every honourable man will attend to his duty with alacrity and energy, and will even make extra exertions for the benefit of the bank, when he finds that his services are handsomely and liberally appreciated.

We need hardly say, that the faults we have pointed out in the administration or constitution of joint-stock banks are by no means inherent in the system. They are accidental circumstances, arising from its establishment in a new country, by parties who had no previous opportunity of understanding its principles. The system is no longer new—its principles are now well understood—and it may reasonably be expected that the calamities of the past will never recur.

END OF VOL. I.

CHISWICK PRESS:—C. WHITTINGHAM AND CO., TOOKS COURT,
CHANCERY LANE.

COMPLETE CATALOGUE

OF

BOHN'S LIBRARIES,

CONTAINING

STANDARD WORKS OF EUROPEAN LITERATURE IN THE ENGLISH LANGUAGE, ON HISTORY, BIOGRAPHY, TOPOGRAPHY, ARCHÆOLOGY, THEOLOGY, ANTIQUITIES, SCIENCE, PHILOSOPHY, NATURAL HISTORY, POETRY, ART, FICTION, WITH DICTIONARIES, AND OTHER BOOKS OF REFERENCE. THE SERIES COMPRISES TRANSLATIONS FROM THE FRENCH, GERMAN, ITALIAN, SPANISH, SCANDINAVIAN, ANGLO-SAXON, LATIN, AND GREEK. PRICE 3s. 6d. OR 5s. PER VOLUME (WITH EXCEPTIONS). A COMPLETE SET IN 627 VOLUMES, PRICE £140 2s.

Catalogues sent Post-free on Application.

LONDON:
GEORGE BELL AND SONS, YORK STREET,
COVENT GARDEN.
1881.

May, 1881.

COMPLETE CATALOGUE
OF
BOHN'S LIBRARIES.

STANDARD LIBRARY.

A SERIES OF THE BEST ENGLISH AND FOREIGN AUTHORS, PRINTED IN POST 8VO.

269 *Vols. at 3s. 6d. each, excepting those marked otherwise.*

Addison's Works. With the Notes of Bishop HURD, much additional matter, and upwards of 100 Unpublished Letters. Edited by H. G. BOHN. *Portrait and 8 Engravings on Steel.* In 6 vols.

Alfieri's Tragedies, including those published posthumously. Translated into English Verse, and edited with Notes and Introduction, by EDGAR A. BOWRING, C.B. 2 vols.

Bacon's Essays, Apophthegms, Wisdom of the Ancients, New Atlantis, and Henry VII., with Introduction and Notes. *Portrait.*

Ballads and Songs of the Peasantry of England. Edited by ROBERT BELL.

Beaumont and Fletcher, a popular Selection from. By LEIGH HUNT.

Beckmann's History of Inventions, Discoveries, and Origins. Revised and enlarged. *Portraits.* In 2 vols.

Bremer's (Miss) Works. Translated by MARY HOWITT. *Portrait.* In 4 vols.

Vol. 1. The Neighbours and other Tales.
Vol. 2. The President's Daughter.
Vol. 3. The Home, and Strife and Peace.
Vol. 4. A Diary, the H—— Family, &c.

British Poets, from Milton to Kirke WHITE. Cabinet Edition. In 4 vols.

Browne's (Sir Thomas) Works. Edited by SIMON WILKIN. In 3 vols.

Burke's Works. In 6 Volumes.

Vol. 1. Vindication of Natural Society, On the Sublime and Beautiful, and Political Miscellanies.
Vol. 2. French Revolution, &c.
Vol. 3. Appeal from the New to the Old Whigs; the Catholic Claims, &c.
Vol. 4. On the Affairs of India, and Charge against Warren Hastings.

Burke's Works—*continued.*

Vol. 5. Conclusion of Charge against Hastings; on a Regicide Peace, &c.
Vol. 6. Miscellaneous Speeches, &c. With a General Index.

Burke's Speeches on Warren Hastings; and Letters. With Index. In 2 vols. (forming vols. 7 and 8 of the works).

—— **Life.** By PRIOR. New and revised Edition. *Portrait.*

Butler's (Bp.) Analogy of Religion, and Sermons, with Notes. *Portrait.*

Camoëns' Lusiad, Mickle's Translation. Edited by E. R. HODGES.

Cary's Translation of Dante's Heaven, Hell, and Purgatory. Copyright edition, being the only one containing Cary's last corrections and additions.

Carafas (The) of Maddaloni: and Naples under Spanish Dominion. Translated from the German of Alfred de Reumont.

Carrel's Counter Revolution in England. Fox's History, and Lonsdale's Memoir of James II. *Portrait.*

Cellini (Benvenuto), Memoirs of. Translated by ROSCOE. *Portrait.*

Cervantes' Galatea. Translated by GORDON GYLL.

Chaucer's Works. Edited by ROBERT BELL. New Edition, improved. With Introduction by W. W. SKEAT. 4 vols.

Coleridge's (S. T.) Friend. A Series of Essays on Morals, Politics, and Religion.

—— **(S. T.) Biographia Literaria,** and two Lay Sermons.

Commines. (*See Philip de Commines.*)

Condé's Dominion of the Arabs in Spain. Translated by Mrs. FOSTER. In 3 vols.

Cowper's Complete Works. Edited, with Memoir of the Author, by SOUTHEY. *Illustrated with 50 Engravings.* In 8 vols.

  Vols. 1 to 4. Memoir and Correspondence.
  Vols. 5 and 6. Poetical Works. *Plates.*
  Vol. 7. Homer's Iliad. *Plates.*
  Vol. 8. Homer's Odyssey. *Plates.*

Coxe's Memoirs of the Duke of Marlborough. *Portraits.* In 3 vols.
  *** An Atlas of the plans of Marlborough's campaigns, 4to. 10s. 6d.

────── **History of the House of Austria.** *Portraits.* In 4 vols.

Cunningham's Lives of Eminent British Painters. New Edition by Mrs. HEATON. 3 vols.

Defoe's Works. Edited by Sir WALTER SCOTT. In 7 vols.

De Lolme on the Constitution of England. Edited, with Notes, by JOHN MACGREGOR.

Emerson's Works. 2 vols.

Foster's (John) Life and Correspondence. Edited by J. E. RYLAND. In 2 vols.

────── **Lectures at Broadmead Chapel.** Edited by J. E. RYLAND. In 2 vols.

Foster's (John) Critical Essays. Edited by J. E. RYLAND. In 2 vols.

────── **Essays—On Decision of Character, &c. &c.**

────── **Essays—On the Evils of Popular Ignorance, &c.**

────── **Fosteriana:** Thoughts, Reflections, and Criticisms of the late JOHN FOSTER, selected from periodical papers, and Edited by HENRY G. BOHN (nearly 600 pages). 5s.

Fuller's (Andrew) Principal Works. With Memoir. *Portrait.*

Gibbon's Roman Empire. Complete and Unabridged, with Notes; including, in addition to the Author's own, those of Guizot, Wenck, Niebuhr, Hugo, Neander, and other foreign scholars; and an elaborate Index. Edited by an English Churchman. In 7 vols.

Goethe's Works, Translated into English. In 8 vols.
  Vols. 1. and 2. Autobiography, 20 Books; and Travels in Italy, France, and Switzerland. *Portrait.*
  Vol. 3. Faust. Two Parts. By Miss SWANWICK.

Goethe's Works—*continued.*
  Vol. 4. Novels and Tales.
  Vol. 5. Wilhelm Meister's Apprenticeship.
  Vol. 6. Conversations with Eckermann and Soret. Translated by JOHN OXENFORD.
  Vol. 7. Poems and Ballads, including Hermann and Dorothea. Translated by E. A. BOWRING, C.B.
  Vol. 8. Götz von Berlichingen, Torquato Tasso, Egmont, Iphigenia, Clavigo, Wayward Lover, and Fellow Culprits. By Sir WALTER SCOTT, Miss SWANWICK, and E. A. BOWRING, C.B. *With Engraving.*

────── **Correspondence with Schiller.** *See Schiller.*

Greene, Marlowe, and Ben Jonson, Poems of. Edited by ROBERT BELL. With Biographies. In 1 vol.

Gregory's (Dr.) Evidences, Doctrines, and Duties of the Christian Religion.

Guizot's Representative Government. Translated by A. R. SCOBLE.

────── **History of the English Revolution of 1640.** Translated by WILLIAM HAZLITT. *Portrait.*

────── **History of Civilization.** Translated by WILLIAM HAZLITT. In 3 vols. *Portrait.*

Hazlitt's Table Talk. A New Edition in one volume.

────── **Lectures on the Comic Writers, and on the English Poets.**

────── **Lectures on the Literature** of the Age of Elizabeth, and on Characters of Shakespear's Plays.

────── **Plain Speaker.**

────── **Round Table;** the Conversations of JAMES NORTHCOTE, R.A.; Characteristics, &c.

────── **Sketches and Essays,** and Winterslow (Essays Written there). New Edition.

Hall's (Rev. Robert) Miscellaneous Works and Remains, with Memoir by Dr. GREGORY, and an Essay on his Character by JOHN FOSTER. *Portrait.*

Hawthorne's Tales. In 2 vols.
  Vol. 1. Twice Told Tales, and the Snow Image.
  Vol. 2. Scarlet Letter, and the House with the seven Gables.

Heine's Poems, complete, from the German, by E. A. BOWRING, C.B. 5s.

Hungary: its History and Revolutions; with a Memoir of Kossuth from new and authentic sources. *Portrait.*

Hutchinson (Colonel), Memoirs of, with the Siege of Latham House.

Irving's (Washington) Life and Letters. By his Nephew, PIERRE E. IRVING. In 2 vols.
—— **Complete Works.** In 15 vols.
  Vol. 1. Salmagundi and Knickerbocker *Portrait of the Author.*
  Vol. 2. Sketch Book and Life of Goldsmith.
  Vol. 3. Bracebridge Hall and Abbotsford and Newstead.
  Vol. 4. Tales of a Traveller and the Alhambra.
  Vol. 5. Conquest of Granada and Conquest of Spain.
  Vols. 6 and 7. Life of Columbus and Companions of Columbus, with a new Index. *Fine Portrait.*
  Vol. 8. Astoria and Tour in the Prairies.
  Vol. 9. Mahomet and his Successors.
  Vol. 10. Wolfert's Roost and Adventures of Captain Bonneville.
  Vol. 11. Biographies and Miscellanies.
  Vols. 12-15. Life of Washington. *Portrait.*
  For separate Works, see Cheap Series.

James's (G. P. R.) Richard Cœur-de-Lion, King of England. *Portraits.* 2 vols.
—— **Louis XIV.** *Portraits.* 2 vols.

Jameson's Shakespeare's Heroines: Characteristics of Women. Moral, Poetical, and Historical.

Junius's Letters, with Notes, Additions, and an Index. In 2 vols.

Lamartine's History of the Girondists. *Portraits.* In 3 vols.
—— **Restoration of the Monarchy,** with Index. *Portraits.* In 4 vols.
—— **French Revolution of 1848,** with a fine *Frontispiece.*

Lamb's (Charles) Elia and Eliana. Complete Edition.
—— **Dramatic Poets of the Time** of Elizabeth; including his Selections from the Garrick Plays.

Lanzi's History of Painting. Translated by ROSCOE. *Portraits.* In 3 vols.

Lappenberg's Anglo-Saxon Kings. 2 vols.

Lessing's Dramatic Works. Complete, with Memoir by HELEN ZIMMERN. *Portrait.* 2 vols.
—— **Laokoon.** (By BEASLEY) Hamburg Dramatic Notes, Representation of Death (by Miss ZIMMERN), Frontispiece.

Locke's Philosophical Works, containing an Essay on the Human Understanding, &c., with Notes and Index by J. A. ST. JOHN. *Portrait.* In 2 vols.
—— **Life and Letters,** with Extracts from his Common-Place Books, by Lord KING.

Luther's Table Talk. Translated by WILLIAM HAZLITT. *Portrait.*

Machiavelli's History of Florence, The Prince, and other Works *Portrait.*

Martineau's, Harriet, History of England, from 1800-15.
—— **History of the Peace,** from 1815-1846. 4 vols.

Menzel's History of Germany. *Portraits.* In 3 vols.

Michelet's Life of Luther. Translated by WILLIAM HAZLITT.
—— **Roman Republic.** Translated by WILLIAM HAZLITT.
—— **French Revolution,** with Index. *Frontispiece.*

Mignet's French Revolution from 1789 to 1814. *Portrait.*

Milton's Prose Works, with Index. *Portraits.* In 5 vols.

Mitford's (Mary R.) Our Village. Improved Ed., complete. *Illustrated.* 2 vols.

Molière's Dramatic Works. Translated by C. H. WALL. In 3 vols. *Portrait.*

Montesquieu's Spirit of the Laws. A new Edition revised and corrected. 2 vols. *Portrait.*

Neander's Church History. Translated: with General Index. In 10 vols.
—— **Life of Christ.** Translated.
—— **First Planting of Christianity, and Antignostikus.** Translated. In 2 vols.
—— **History of Christian Dogmas.** Translated. In 2 vols.
—— **Christian Life in the Early and Middle Ages,** including his 'Light in Dark Places.' Translated.

Ockley's History of the Saracens Revised and completed. *Portrait.*

Percy's Reliques of Ancient English Poetry. Reprinted from the Original Edition, and Edited by J. V. PRICHARD. In 2 vols.

Philip de Commines, Memoirs of, containing the Histories of Louis XI. and Charles VIII., and of Charles the Bold, Duke of Burgundy. To which is added, The Scandalous Chronicle, or Secret History of Louis XI. *Portraits.* In 2 vols.

Plutarch's Lives. By G. LONG and A. STEWART. Vols. 1 and 2 *ready.*

Poetry of America. Selections from 100 American Poets, from 1776—1876. Edited by W. J. LINTON. *Portrait.*

Ranke's History of the Popes. Translated by E. FOSTER. In 3 vols.

Ranke's Servia and the Servian Revolution.

Reynolds' (Sir Joshua) Literary Works. *Portrait.* In 2 vols.

Richter (Jean Paul Fr.) Levana and Autobiography. With Memoir.

——— Flower, Fruit, and Thorn Pieces. A Novel.

Roscoe's Life and Pontificate of Leo X., with the Copyright Notes, and an Index. *Portraits.* In 2 vols.

——— Life of Lorenzo de Medici, with the Copyright Notes, &c. *Portrait.*

Russia, History of, by WALTER K. KELLY. *Portraits.* In 2 vols.

Schiller's Works. Translated into English. In 6 vols.
  Vol. 1. Thirty Years' War, and Revolt of the Netherlands.
  Vol. 2. *Continuation of the Revolt of the Netherlands;* Wallenstein's Camp; the Piccolomini; the Death of Wallenstein; and William Tell.
  Vol. 3. Don Carlos, Mary Stuart, Maid of Orleans, and Bride of Messina.
  Vol. 4. The Robbers, Fiesco, Love and Intrigue, and the Ghost-Seer.
  Vol. 5. Poems. Translated by EDGAR BOWRING, C.B.
  Vol. 6. Philosophical Letters and Æsthetical Essays.

——— Correspondence with Goethe, translated by L. DORA SCHMITZ. 2 vols.

Schlegel's Philosophy of Life and of Language, translated by A. J. W. MORRISON.

——— History of Literature, Ancient and Modern. Now first completely translated, with General Index.

——— Philosophy of History. Translated by J. B. ROBERTSON. *Portrait.*

Schlegel's Dramatic Literature. Translated. *Portrait.*

——— Modern History.

——— Æsthetic and Miscellaneous Works.

Sheridan's Dramatic Works and Life. *Portrait.*

Sismondi's Literature of the South of Europe. Translated by Roscoe. *Portraits.* In 2 vols.

Smith's (Adam) Theory of the Moral Sentiments; with his Essay on the First Formation of Languages.

Smyth's (Professor) Lectures on Modern History. In 2 vols.

——— Lectures on the French Revolution. In 2 vols.

Sturm's Morning Communings with God, or Devotional Meditations for Every Day in the Year.

Sully, Memoirs of the Duke of, Prime Minister to Henry the Great. *Portraits.* In 4 vols.

Taylor's (Bishop Jeremy) Holy Living and Dying. *Portrait.*

Thierry's Conquest of England by the Normans. Translated by WILLIAM HAZLITT. *Portrait.* In 2 vols.

Ulrici (Dr.) Shakespeare's Dramatic Art. Translated by L. D. Schmitz. 2 vols.

Vasari's Lives of the Painters, Sculptors, and Architects. Translated by Mrs. FOSTER. 5 vols.

Wesley's (John) Life. By ROBERT SOUTHEY. New and Complete Edition. Double volume. *With Portrait.* 5s.

Wheatley on the Book of Common Prayer. *Frontispiece.*

HISTORICAL LIBRARY.

21 *Vols. at 5s. each.*

Evelyn's Diary and Correspondence. *Illustrated with numerous Portraits, &c.* In 4 vols.

Pepys' Diary and Correspondence. Edited by Lord BRAYBROOKE. With Notes. Important Additions, including numerous Letters. *Illustrated with many Portraits.* In 4 vols.

Jesse's Memoirs of the Reign of the Stuarts, including the Protectorate. With General Index. *Upwards of 40 Portraits.* In 3 vols.

Jesse's Memoirs of the Pretenders and their Adherents. 6 *Portraits.*

Nugent's (Lord) Memorials of Hampden, his Party, and Times. 12 *Portraits.*

Strickland's (Agnes) Lives of the Queens of England, from the Norman Conquest. From official records and authentic documents, private and public. Revised Edition. In 6 vols.

——— Life of Mary Queen of Scots. 2 vols.

COLLEGIATE SERIES.

6 Vols. at 5s. each.

Donaldson's Theatre of the Greeks. Illustrated with Lithographs and numerous Woodcuts.

Keightley's Classical Mythology. New. Edition. Revised by. Dr. L. SCHMITZ. With 12 plates.

Herodotus, Turner's (Dawson W.) Notes to. With Map, &c.

Herodotus, Wheeler's Analysis and Summary of.

Thucydides, Wheeler's Analysis of.

New Testament (The) in Greek. Griesbach's Text, with the readings of Mill and Scholz, Parallel References, a Critical Introduction and Chronological Tables. *Two fac-similes of Greek MSS.* 3s. 6d.; or with Lexicon, 5s. Lexicon Separately. 2s.

PHILOSOPHICAL LIBRARY.

11 Vols. at 5s. each, excepting those marked otherwise.

Comte's Philosophy of the Sciences. By G. H. LEWES.

Draper (J. W.) A History of the Intellectual Development of Europe. By JOHN WILLIAM DRAPER, M.D., LL.D. A New Edition, thoroughly Revised by the Author. In 2 vols.

Hegel's Lectures on the Philosophy of History. Translated by J. SIBREE, M.A.

Kant's Critique of Pure Reason. Translated by J. M. D. MEIKLEJOHN.

Logic; or, the Science of Inference. A Popular Manual. By J. DEVEY.

Miller's (Professor) History Philosophically considered. In 4 vols. 3s. 6d. each.

Tennemann's Manual of the History of Philosophy. Continued by J. R. MORELL.

ECCLESIASTICAL AND THEOLOGICAL LIBRARY.

15 Vols. at 5s. each, excepting those marked otherwise.

Bleek (F.) An Introduction to the Old Testament, by FRIEDRICH BLEEK. Edited by JOHANN BLEEK and ADOLF KAMPHAUSEN. Translated from the German by G. H. VENABLES, under the supervision of the Rev. E. VENABLES, Canon of Lincoln. New Edition. In 2 vols.

Chillingworth's Religion of Protestants. 3s. 6d.

Eusebius' Ecclesiastical History. With Notes.

Hardwick's History of the Articles of Religion. To which is added a Series of Documents from A.D. 1536 to A.D. 1615. Together with Illustrations from Contemporary Sources. New Edition, revised by Rev. F. PROCTER.

Henry's (Matthew) Commentary on the Psalms. *Numerous Illustrations.*

Pearson on the Creed. New Edition. With Analysis and Notes.

Philo Judæus, Works of; the contemporary of Josephus. Translated by C. D. Yonge. In 4 vols.

Socrates' Ecclesiastical History, in continuation of Eusebius. With the Notes of Valesius.

Sozomen's Ecclesiastical History, from A.D. 324-440: and the Ecclesiastical History of Philostorgius.

Theodoret and Evagrius. Ecclesiastical Histories, from A.D. 332 to A.D. 427 and from A.D. 431 to A.D. 544.

Wieseler's Chronological Synopsis of the Four Gospels. Translated by CANON VENABLES. New Edition, revised.

ANTIQUARIAN LIBRARY.

35 Vols. at 5s. each.

Bede's Ecclesiastical History, and the Anglo-Saxon Chronicle.

Boethius's Consolation of Philosophy. In Anglo-Saxon, with the A. S. Metres, and an English Translation, by the Rev. S. Fox.

Brand's Popular Antiquities of England, Scotland, and Ireland. By Sir HENRY ELLIS. In 3 vols.

Chronicles of the Crusaders. Richard of Devizes, Geoffrey de Vinsauf, Lord de Joinville.

Dyer's British Popular Customs, Present and Past. An Account of the various Games and Customs associated with different days of the year. By the Rev. T. F. THISELTON DYER, M.A. With Index.

Early Travels in Palestine. Willibald, Sæwulf, Benjamin of Tudela, Mandeville, La Brocquière, and Maundrell; all unabridged. Edited by THOMAS WRIGHT.

Ellis's Early English Metrical Romances. Revised by J. O. HALLIWELL.

Florence of Worcester's Chronicle, with the Two Continuations: comprising Annals of English History to the Reign of Edward I.

Gesta Romanorum. Edited by WYNNARD HOOPER, B.A.

Giraldus Cambrensis' Historical Works: Topography of Ireland; History of the Conquest of Ireland; Itinerary through Wales; and Description of Wales. With Index. Edited by THOS. WRIGHT.

Henry of Huntingdon's History of the English, from the Roman Invasion to Henry II.; with the Acts of King Stephen, &c.

Ingulph's Chronicle of the Abbey of Croyland, with the Continuations by Peter of Blois and other Writers. By H. T. RILEY.

Keightley's Fairy Mythology. *Frontispiece by Cruikshank.*

Lepsius's Letters from Egypt, Ethiopia, and the Peninsula of Sinai.

Mallet's Northern Antiquities. By Bishop PERCY. With an Abstract of the Eyrbiggia Saga, by Sir WALTER SCOTT. Edited by J. A. BLACKWELL.

Marco Polo's Travels. The Translation of Marsden. Edited by THOMAS WRIGHT.

Matthew Paris's Chronicle. In 5 vols.
FIRST SECTION: Roger of Wendover's Flowers of English History, from the Descent of the Saxons to A.D. 1235. Translated by Dr. GILES. In 2 vols.
SECOND SECTION: From 1235 to 1273. With Index to the entire Work. In 3 vols.

Matthew of Westminster's Flowers of History, especially such as relate to the affairs of Britain; to A.D. 1307. Translated by C. D. YONGE. In 2 vols.

Ordericus Vitalis' Ecclesiastical History of England and Normandy. Translated with Notes, by T. FORESTER, M.A. In 4 vols.

Pauli's (Dr. R.) Life of Alfred the Great. Translated from the German. To which is appended Alfred's Anglo-Saxon version of Orosius, with a literal Translation, and an Anglo-Saxon Grammar and Glossary.

Roger De Hoveden's Annals of English History; from A.D. 732 to A.D. 1201. Edited by H. T. RILEY. In 2 vols.

Six Old English Chronicles, viz.:— Asser's Life of Alfred, and the Chronicles of Ethelwerd, Gildas, Nennius, Geoffrey of Monmouth, and Richard of Cirencester.

William of Malmesbury's Chronicle of the Kings of England. Translated by SHARPE.

Yule-Tide Stories. A Collection of Scandinavian Tales and Traditions. Edited by B. THORPE.

ILLUSTRATED LIBRARY.

84 Vols. at 5s. each, excepting those marked otherwise.

Allen's Battles of the British Navy. Revised and enlarged. *Numerous fine Portraits.* In 2 vols.

Andersen's Danish Legends and Fairy Tales. With many Tales not in any other edition. Translated by CAROLINE PEACHEY. 120 *Wood Engravings.*

Ariosto's Orlando Furioso. In English Verse. By W. S. ROSE. *Twelve fine Engravings.* In 2 vols.

Bechstein's Cage and Chamber Birds. Including Sweet's Warblers. Enlarged edition. *Numerous plates.*
*** All other editions are abridged.
With the plates coloured. 7s. 6d.

Bonomi's Nineveh and its Palaces. New Edition, revised and considerably enlarged, both in matter and Plates. *Upwards of 300 Engravings*

Butler's Hudibras. With Variorum Notes, a Biography, and a General Index. Edited by HENRY G. BOHN. *Thirty beautiful Illustrations.*

———; or, *further illustrated with* 62 *Outline Portraits.* In 2 vols. 10s.

Cattermole's Evenings at Haddon Hall. 24 *exquisite Engravings on Steel, from designs by himself* the Letterpress by the BARONESS DE CARABELLA.

China, Pictorial, Descriptive, and Historical, with some Account of Ava and the Burmese, Siam, and Anam. *Nearly 100 Illustrations.*

Craik's (G. L.) Pursuit of Knowledge under Difficulties, illustrated by Anecdotes and Memoirs. Revised Edition. *With numerous Portraits.*

Cruikshank's Three Courses and a Dessert. A Series of Tales, *with 50 humorous Illustrations by Cruikshank*

Cruikshank's Punch and Judy. With 24 Illustrations. 5s.

Dante. Translated by I. C. WRIGHT, M.A. New Edition, carefully revised. *Portrait and 34 Illustrations on Steel, after Flaxman.*

Didron's History of Christian Art in the Middle Ages. From the French. *Upwards of 150 outline Engravings.*

Dyer (T. H.) The History of Pompeii; its Buildings and Antiquities. An account of the City, with a full description of the Remains, and an Itinerary for Visitors. Edited by T. H. DYER, LL.D. *Illustrated with nearly 300 Wood Engravings, a large Map, and a Plan of the Forum.* A New Edition, revised and brought down to 1874. 7s. 6d.

Gil Blas, The Adventures of. 24 *Engravings on Steel, after Smirke, and* 10 *Etchings by George Cruikshank.* 6s.

Grimm's Gammer Grethel; or, German Fairy Tales and Popular Stories. Translated by EDGAR TAYLOR. *Numerous Woodcuts by Cruikshank.* 3s. 6d.

Holbein's Dance of Death, and Bible Cuts. *Upwards of* 150 *subjects, beautifully engraved in fac-simile,* with Introduction and Descriptions by the late FRANCIS DOUCE and Dr. T. F. DIBDIN. 2 vols. in 1. 7s. 6d.

Howitt's (Mary) Pictorial Calendar of the Seasons. Embodying the whole of Aiken's Calendar of Nature. *Upwards of* 100 *Engravings.*

——— **(Mary and William) Stories** of English and Foreign Life. *Twenty beautiful Engravings.*

India, Pictorial, Descriptive, and Historical, from the Earliest Times. *Upwards of* 100 *fine Engravings on Wood, and a Map.*

Jesse's Anecdotes of Dogs. New Edition, with large additions. *Numerous fine Woodcuts after Harvey, Bewick, and others.*

———; or, *with the addition of* 34 *highly-finished Steel Engravings.* 7s. 6d.

King's Natural History of Precious Stones, and of the Precious Metals. *With numerous Illustrations.* Price 6s.

——— **Natural History of Gems** or Decorative Stones. *Finely Illustrated.* 6s.

——— **Handbook of Engraved Gems.** *Finely Illustrated.* 6s.

Kitto's Scripture Lands and Biblical Atlas. 24 *Maps, beautifully engraved on Steel,* with a Consulting Index.

———; *with the maps coloured,* 7s. 6d.

Krummacher's Parables. Translated from the German. *Forty Illustrations by Clayton, engraved by Dalziel.*

Lindsay's (Lord) Letters on Egypt, Edom, and the Holy Land. New Edition, enlarged. *Thirty-six beautiful Engravings, and* 2 *Maps.*

Lodge's Portraits of Illustrious Personages of Great Britain, with Memoirs. *Two Hundred and Forty Portraits, engraved on Steel.* 8 vols.

Longfellow's Poetical Works. *Twenty-four page Engravings, by Birket Foster and others, and a Portrait.*

———; or, *without illustrations,* 3s. 6d.

——— **Prose Works.** 16 *page Engravings by Birket Foster, &c.*

London's (Mrs.) Entertaining Naturalist. Revised by W. S. DALLAS, F.L.S. *With nearly* 500 *Woodcuts.*

Marryat's Masterman Ready; or, The Wreck of the Pacific. 93 *Woodcuts.* 3s. 6d.

——— **Poor Jack.** *With* 16 *Illustrations, after Designs by C. Stanfield, R.A.* 3s. 6d.

——— **Mission; or, Scenes in Africa.** (Written for Young People.) *Illustrated by Gilbert and Dalziel.* 3s. 6d.

——— **Pirate; and Three Cutters.** New Edition, with a Memoir of the Author. *With* 8 *Steel Engravings, from Drawings by C. Stanfield, R.A.* 3s. 6d.

——— **Privateers - Man One Hundred Years Ago.** *Eight Engravings on Steel, after Stothard.* 3s. 6d.

——— **Settlers in Canada.** New Edition. *Ten fine Engravings by Gilbert and Dalziel.* 3s. 6d.

Maxwell's Victories of Wellington and the British Armies. *Steel Engravings.*

Michael Angelo and Raphael, their Lives and Works. By DUPPA and QUATREMÈRE DE QUINCY. *With 13 Engravings on Steel.*

Miller's History of the Anglo-Saxons. Written in a popular style, on the basis of Sharon Turner. *Portrait of Alfred, Map of Saxon Britain, and 12 elaborate Engravings on Steel.*

Milton's Poetical Works. With a Memoir by JAMES MONTGOMERY, TODD'S Verbal Index to all the Poems, and Explanatory Notes. *With 120 Engravings by Thompson and others, from Drawings by W. Harvey.* 2 vols.
   Vol. 1. Paradise Lost, complete, with Memoir, Notes, and Index.
   Vol. 2. Paradise Regained, and other Poems, with Verbal Index to all the Poems.

Mudie's British Birds. Revised by W. C. L. MARTIN. *Fifty-two Figures and 7 Plates of Eggs.* In 2 vols.
———; or, *with the plates coloured*, 7s. 6d. per vol.

Naval and Military Heroes of Great Britain; or, Calendar of Victory. Being a Record of British Valour and Conquest by Sea and Land, on every day in the year, from the time of William the Conqueror to the Battle of Inkermann. By Major JOHNS, R.M., and Lieutenant P. H. NICOLAS, R.M. *Twenty-four Portraits.* 6s.

Nicolini's History of the Jesuits: their Origin, Progress, Doctrines, and Designs. *Fine Portraits of Loyola, Lainez, Xavier, Borgia, Acquaviva, Père la Chaise, and Pope Ganganelli.*

Petrarch's Sonnets, and other Poems. Translated into English Verse. By various hands. With a Life of the Poet, by THOMAS CAMPBELL. *With 16 Engravings.*

Pickering's History of the Races of Man, with an Analytical Synopsis of the Natural History of Man. By Dr. HALL. *Illustrated by numerous Portraits.*
———; or, *with the plates coloured* 7s. 6d.
   *** An excellent Edition of a work originally published at 3l. 3s. by the American Government.

Pictorial Handbook of Modern Geography, on a Popular Plan. 3s. 6d. *Illustrated by 150 Engravings and 51 Maps.* 6s.
———; or, *with the maps coloured*, 7s. 6d.

Pope's Poetical Works. Edited by ROBERT CARRUTHERS. *Numerous Engravings.* 2 vols.

Pope's Homer's Iliad. With Introduction and Notes by J. S. WATSON, M.A. *Illustrated by the entire Series of Flaxman's Designs, beautifully engraved by Moses (in the full 8vo. size).*

———— **Homer's Odyssey, Hymns,** &c., by other translators, including Chapman, and Introduction and Notes by J. S. WATSON, M.A. *Flaxman's Designs beautifully engraved by Moses.*

———— **Life.** Including many of his Letters. By ROBERT CARRUTHERS. New Edition, revised and enlarged. *Illustrations.* The preceding 5 vols. make a complete and elegant edition of Pope's Poetical Works and Translations for 25s.

Pottery and Porcelain, and other Objects of Vertu (a Guide to the Knowledge of). To which is added an Engraved List of Marks and Monograms. By HENRY G. BOHN. *Numerous Engravings.*
———; or, *coloured.* 10s. 6d.

Prout's (Father) Reliques. Revised Edition. *Twenty-one spirited Etchings by Maclise.* 5s.

Recreations in Shooting. By "CRAVEN." New Edition, revised and enlarged. *62 Engravings on Wood, after Harvey, and 9 Engravings on Steel, chiefly after A. Cooper, R.A.*

Redding's History and Descriptions of Wines, Ancient and Modern. *Twenty beautiful Woodcuts.*

Rennie's Insect Architecture. New Edition. Revised by the Rev. J. G. WOOD, M.A.

Robinson Crusoe. With Illustrations by STOTHARD and HARVEY. *Twelve beautiful Engravings on Steel, and 74 on Wood.*
———; or, *without the Steel illustrations,* 3s. 6d.

Rome in the Nineteenth Century. New Edition. Revised by the Author. *Illustrated by 34 Steel Engravings.* 2 vols.

Sharpe's History of Egypt, from the Earliest Times till the Conquest by the Arabs, A.D. 640. By SAMUEL SHARPE. With 2 Maps and upwards of 400 Illustrative Woodcuts. Sixth and Cheaper Edition. 2 vols.

Southey's Life of Nelson. With Additional Notes. *Illustrated with 64 Engravings.*

Starling's (Miss) Noble Deeds of Women; or, Examples of Female Courage, Fortitude, and Virtue. *Fourteen Illustrations.*

Stuart and Revett's Antiquities of Athens, and other Monuments of Greece. *Illustrated in 71 Steel Plates, and numerous Woodcuts.*

Tales of the Genii; or, the Delightful Lessons of Horam. *Numerous Woodcuts, and 8 Steel Engravings, after Stothard.*

Tasso's Jerusalem Delivered. Translated into English Spenserian Verse, with a Life of the Author. By J. H. WIFFEN. *Eight Engravings on Steel, and 24 on Wood, by Thurston.*

Walker's Manly Exercises. Containing Skating, Riding, Driving, Hunting, Shooting, Sailing, Rowing, Swimming, &c. New Edition, revised by "CRAVEN." *Forty-four Steel Plates, and numerous Woodcuts.*

Walton's Complete Angler. Edited by EDWARD JESSE, Esq. *Upwards of 203 Engravings.*

———; or, *with 26 additional page Illustrations on Steel,* 7s. 6d.

Wellington, Life of. From the materials of Maxwell. *Eighteen Engravings.*

Westropp's Handbook of Archæology New Edition, revised. *Numerous Illustrations.* 7s. 6d.

White's Natural History of Selborne. With Notes by Sir WILLIAM JARDINE and EDWARD JESSE, Esq. *Illustrated by 40 Engravings.*

———; or, *with the plates coloured.* 7s. 6d.

Young, The, Lady's Book. A Manual of Elegant Recreations, Arts, Sciences, and Accomplishments. *Twelve Hundred Woodcut Illustrations, and several Engravings on Steel.* 7s. 6d.

———; or, *cloth gilt, gilt edges,* 9s.

CLASSICAL LIBRARY.

93 Vols. at 5s. each, excepting those marked otherwise.

Æschylus translated into English Verse by A. SWANWICK.

———, Literally Translated into English Prose by an Oxonian. 3s. 6d.

———, Appendix to. Containing the Readings given in Hermann's posthumous Edition of Æschylus. By GEORGE BURGES, M.A. 3s. 6d.

Ammianus Marcellinus. History of Rome from Constantius to Valens. Translated by C. D. YONGE, B.A. Dble. vol., 7s. 6d.

Antoninus. The Thoughts of the Emperor Marcus Aurelius. Translated by GEO. LONG, M.A. 3s. 6d.

Apuleius, the Golden Ass; Death of Socrates; Florida; and Discourse on Magic. To which is added a Metrical Version of Cupid and Psyche; and Mrs. Tighe's Psyche. *Frontispiece.*

Aristophanes' Comedies. Literally Translated, with Notes and Extracts from Frere's and other Metrical Versions, by W. J. HICKIE. 2 vols.
   Vol. 1. Acharnians, Knights, Clouds, Wasps, Peace, and Birds.
   Vol. 2. Lysistrata, Thesmophoriazusæ, Frogs, Ecclesiazusæ, and Plutus.

Aristotle's Ethics. Literally Translated by Archdeacon BROWNE, late Classical Professor of King's College.

——— Politics and Economics. Translated by E. WALFORD, M.A.

——— Metaphysics. Literally Translated, with Notes, Analysis, Examination Questions, and Index, by the Rev. JOHN H. M'MAHON, M.A., and Gold Medallist in Metaphysics, T.C.D.

Aristotle's History of Animals. In Ten Books. Translated, with Notes and Index, by RICHARD CRESSWELL, M.A.

——— Organon; or, Logical Treatises. With Notes, &c. By O. F. OWEN, M.A. 2 vols., 3s. 6d. each.

——— Rhetoric and Poetics. Literally Translated, with Examination Questions and Notes, by an Oxonian.

Athenæus. The Deipnosophists; or, the Banquet of the Learned. Translated by C. D. YONGE, B.A. 3 vols.

Cæsar. Complete, with the Alexandrian, African, and Spanish Wars. Literally Translated, with Notes.

Catullus, Tibullus, and the Vigil of Venus. A Literal Prose Translation. To which are added Metrical Versions by LAMB, GRAINGER, and others. *Frontispiece.*

Cicero's Orations. Literally Translated by C. D. YONGE, B.A. In 4 vols.
   Vol. 1. Contains the Orations against Verres, &c. *Portrait.*
   Vol. 2. Catiline, Archias, Agrarian Law, Rabirius, Murena, Sylla, &c.
   Vol. 3. Orations for his House, Plancius, Sextius, Coelius, Milo, Ligarius, &c.
   Vol. 4. Miscellaneous Orations, and Rhetorical Works; with General Index to the four volumes.

——— on the Nature of the Gods, Divination, Fate, Laws, a Republic, &c. Translated by C. D. YONGE, B.A., and F. BARHAM.

Cicero's **Academics, De Finibus, and** Tusculan Questions. By C. D. YONGE, B.A. With Sketch of the Greek Philosopher.

——— **Offices, Old Age, Friendship,** Scipio's Dream, Paradoxes, &c. Literally Translated, by R. EDMONDS. 3s. 6d.

——— **on Oratory and Orators.** By J. S. WATSON, M.A.

Demosthenes' Orations. Translated, with Notes, by C. RANN KENNEDY. In 5 volumes.
Vol. 1. The Olynthiac, Philippic, and other Public Orations. 3s. 6d.
Vol. 2. On the Crown and on the Embassy.
Vol. 3. Against Leptines, Midias, Androtrion, and Aristocrates.
Vol. 4. Private and other Orations.
Vol. 5. Miscellaneous Orations.

Dictionary of Latin Quotations. Including Proverbs, Maxims, Mottoes, Law Terms, and Phrases; and a Collection of above 500 Greek Quotations. With all the quantities marked, & English Translations.

———, with Index Verborum. 6s. Index Verborum only. 1s.

Diogenes Laertius. Lives and Opinions of the Ancient Philosophers. Translated, with Notes, by C. D. YONGE.

Epictetus. Discourses, with Encheiridion and Fragments. Translated with Notes, by GEORGE LONG, M.A.

Euripides. Literally Translated. 2 vols.
Vol. 1. Hecuba, Orestes, Medea, Hippolytus, Alcestis, Bacchae, Heraclidae, Iphigenia in Aulide, and Iphigenia in Tauris.
Vol. 2. Hercules Furens, Troades, Ion, Andromache, Suppliants, Helen, Electra, Cyclops, Rhesus.

Greek Anthology. Literally Translated. With Metrical Versions by various Authors.

——— **Romances of Heliodorus,** Longus, and Achilles Tatius.

Herodotus. A New and Literal Translation, by HENRY CARY, M.A., of Worcester College, Oxford.

Hesiod, Callimachus, and Theognis. Literally Translated, with Notes, by J. BANKS, M.A.

Homer's Iliad. Literally Translated

——— **Odyssey, Hymns, &c.** Literally Translated.

Horace. Literally Translated, by SMART. Carefully revised by an OXONIAN. 3s. 6d.

Justin, Cornelius Nepos, and Eutropius. Literally Translated, with Notes and Index, by J. S. WATSON, M.A.

Juvenal, Persius, Sulpicia, and Lucilius. By L. EVANS, M.A. With the Metrical Version by Gifford. *Frontispiece*

Livy. A new and Literal Translation. By Dr. SPILLAN and others. In 4 vols.
Vol. 1. Contains Books 1—8.
Vol. 2. Books 9—26.
Vol. 3. Books 27—36.
Vol. 4. Books 37 to the end; and Index.

Lucan's Pharsalia. Translated, with Notes, by H. T. RILEY.

Lucretius. Literally Translated, with Notes, by the Rev. J. S. WATSON, M.A. And the Metrical Version by J. M. GOOD.

Martial's Epigrams, complete. Literally Translated. Each accompanied by one or more Verse Translations selected from the Works of English Poets, and other sources. With a copious Index. Double volume (660 pages). 7s. 6d.

Ovid's Works, complete. Literally Translated. 3 vols.
Vol. 1. Fasti, Tristia, Epistles, &c.
Vol. 2. Metamorphoses.
Vol. 3. Heroides, Art of Love, &c.

Pindar. Literally Translated, by DAWSON W. TURNER, and the Metrical Version by ABRAHAM MOORE.

Plato's Works. Translated by the Rev. H. CARY and others. In 6 vols.
Vol. 1. The Apology of Socrates, Crito, Phaedo, Gorgias, Protagoras, Phaedrus, Theaetetus, Euthyphron, Lysis.
Vol. 2. The Republic, Timaeus, & Critias.
Vol. 3. Meno, Euthydemus, The Sophist, Statesman, Cratylus, Parmenides, and the Banquet.
Vol. 4. Philebus, Charmides, Laches, The Two Alcibiades, and Ten other Dialogues.
Vol. 5. The Laws.
Vol. 6. The Doubtful Works. With General Index.

——— **Dialogues,** an Analysis and Index to. With References to the Translation in Bohn's Classical Library. By Dr DAY.

Plautus's Comedies. Literally Translated, with Notes, by H. T. RILEY, B.A. In 2 vols.

Pliny's Natural History. Translated, with Copious Notes, by the late JOHN BOSTOCK, M.D., F.R.S., and H. T. RILEY, B.A. In 6 vols.

Pliny the Younger, The Letters of. MELMOTH's Translation revised. By the Rev. F. C. T. BOSANQUET, M.A.

Propertius, Petronius, and Johannes Secundus, and Aristaenetus. Literally Translated, and accompanied by Poetical Versions, from various sources.

Quintilian's Institutes of Oratory.
Literally Translated, with Notes, &c., by J. S. WATSON, M.A. In 2 vols.

Sallust, Florus, and Velleius Paterculus. With Copious Notes, Biographical Notices, and Index, by J. S. WATSON.

Sophocles. The Oxford Translation revised.

Standard Library Atlas of Classical Geography. *Twenty-two large coloured Maps according to the latest authorities.* With a complete Index (accentuated), giving the latitude and longitude of every place named in the Maps. Imp. 8vo. 7s. 6d.

Strabo's Geography. Translated, with Copious Notes, by W. FALCONER, M.A., and H. C. HAMILTON, Esq. With Index, giving the Ancient and Modern Names. In 3 vols.;

Suetonius' Lives of the Twelve Cæsars, and other Works. Thomson's Translation, revised, with Notes, by T. FORESTER.

Tacitus. Literally Translated, with Notes. In 2 vols.
Vol. 1. The Annals.
Vol. 2. The History, Germania, Agricola, &c. With Index.

Terence and Phædrus. By H. T. RILEY, B.A.

Theocritus, Bion, Moschus, and Tyrtæus. By J. BANKS, M.A. With the Metrical Versions of Chapman.

Thucydides. Literally Translated by Rev. H. DALE. In 2 vols. 3s. 6d. each.

Virgil. Literally Translated by DAVIDSON. New Edition, carefully revised. 3s. 6d.

Xenophon's Works. In 3 Vols.
Vol. 1. The Anabasis and Memorabilia. Translated, with Notes, by J. S. WATSON, M.A. And a Geographical Commentary, by W. F. AINSWORTH, F.S.A., F.R.G.S., &c.
Vol. 2. Cyropædia and Hellenica. By J. S. WATSON, M.A., and the Rev. H. DALE.
Vol. 3. The Minor Works. By J. S. WATSON, M.A.

SCIENTIFIC LIBRARY.

57 Vols. at 5s. each, excepting those marked otherwise.

Agassiz and Gould's Comparative Physiology. Enlarged by Dr. WRIGHT. *Upwards of 400 Engravings.*

Bacon's Novum Organum and Advancement of Learning. Complete, with Notes, by J. DEVEY, M.A.

Bolley's Manual of Technical Analysis. A Guide for the Testing of Natural and Artificial Substances. By B. H. PAUL. 100 *Wood Engravings.*

BRIDGEWATER TREATISES.—

——— **Bell on the Hand.** Its Mechanism and Vital Endowments as evincing Design. *Seventh Edition Revised.*

——— **Kirby on the History, Habits,** and Instincts of Animals. Edited, with Notes, by T. RYMER JONES. *Numerous Engravings, many of which are additional.* In 2 vols.

——— **Kidd on the Adaptation of** External Nature to the Physical Condition of Man. 3s. 6d.

——— **Whewell's Astronomy and** General Physics, considered with reference to Natural Theology. 3s. 6d.

——— **Chalmers on the Adaptation** of External Nature to the Moral and Intellectual Constitution of Man.

BRIDGEWATER TREATISES—*cont.*

——— **Prout's Treatise on Chemistry,** Meteorology, and Digestion. Edited by Dr. J. W. GRIFFITH.

——— **Buckland's Geology and** Mineralogy. 2 vols. 15s.

——— **Roget's Animal and Vegetable Physiology.** *Illustrated.* In 2 vols. 6s. each.

Carpenter's (Dr. W. B.) Zoology. A Systematic View of the Structure, Habits, Instincts, and Uses, of the principal Families of the Animal Kingdom, and of the chief forms of Fossil Remains. Revised by W. S. DALLAS, F.L.S. *Illustrated with many hundred Wood Engravings.* In 2 vols. 6s. each.

——— **Mechanical Philosophy, Astronomy,** and Horology. A Popular Exposition. 183 *Illustrations.*

——— **Vegetable Physiology and** Systematic Botany. A complete Introduction to the Knowledge of Plants. Revised, under arrangement with the Author, by E. LANKESTER, M.D., &c. *Several hundred Illustrations on Wood.* 6s.

——— **Animal Physiology.** In part re-written by the Author. *Upwards of 300 capital Illustrations.* 6s.

Chevreul on Colour. Containing the Principles of Harmony and Contract of Colours, and their application to the Arts. Translated from the French by CHARLES MARTEL. Only complete Edition. *Several Plates.* Or, with an additional series of 16 Plates in Colours. 7s. 6d.

Ennemoser's History of Magic. Translated by WILLIAM HOWITT. With an Appendix of the most remarkable and best authenticated Stories of Apparitions, Dreams, Table-Turning, and Spirit-Rapping, &c. In 2 vols.

Hogg's (Jabez) Elements of Experimental and Natural Philosophy. Containing Mechanics, Pneumatics, Hydrostatics, Hydraulics, Acoustics, Optics, Caloric, Electricity, Voltaism, and Magnetism. New Edition, enlarged. *Upwards of 400 Woodcuts.*

Hind's Introduction to Astronomy. With a Vocabulary, containing an Explanation of all the Terms in present use. New Edition, enlarged. *Numerous Engravings.* 3s. 6d.

Humboldt's Cosmos; or, Sketch of a Physical Description of the Universe. Translated by E. C. OTTÉ and W. S. DALLAS, F.L.S. *Fine Portrait.* In five vols. 3s. 6d. each; excepting Vol. V., 5s.

*** In this edition the notes are placed beneath the text, Humboldt's analytical Summaries and the passages hitherto suppressed are included, and new and comprehensive Indices are added.

——— **Travels in America.** In 3 vols.

——— **Views of Nature; or, Contemplations of the Sublime Phenomena of Creation.** Translated by E. C. OTTÉ and H. G. BOHN. With a complete Index.

Hunt's (Robert) Poetry of Science; or, Studies of the Physical Phenomena of Nature. By Professor HUNT. New Edition, enlarged.

Joyce's Scientific Dialogues. By Dr. GRIFFITH. *Numerous Woodcuts.*

——— **Introduction to the Arts and Sciences.** With Examination Questions. 3s. 6d.

Knight's (Chas.) Knowledge is Power. A Popular Manual of Political Economy.

Lectures on Painting. By the Royal Academicians. With Introductory Essay, and Notes by R. WORNUM, Esq. *Portraits.*

Lilly's Introduction to Astrology. With numerous Emendations, by ZADKIEL.

Mantell's (Dr.) Geological Excursions through the Isle of Wight and Dorsetshire. New Edition, by T. RUPERT JONES, Esq. *Numerous beautifully executed Woodcuts, and a Geological Map.*

——— **Medals of Creation;** or, First Lessons in Geology and the Study of Organic Remains; including Geological Excursions. New Edition, revised. *Coloured Plates, and several hundred beautiful Woodcuts.* In 2 vols., 7s. 6d. each.

——— **Petrifactions and their Teachings.** An Illustrated Handbook to the Organic Remains in the British Museum. *Numerous Engravings.* 6s.

——— **Wonders of Geology; or, a Familiar Exposition of Geological Phenomena.** New Edition, augmented by T. RUPERT JONES, F.G.S. *Coloured Geological Map of England, Plates, and nearly 200 beautiful Woodcuts.* In 2 vols., 7s. 6d. each.

Morphy's Games of Chess. Being the Matches and best Games played by the American Champion, with Explanatory and Analytical Notes, by J. LÖWENTHAL. *Portrait and Memoir.*

It contains by far the largest collection of games played by Mr. Morphy extant in any form, and has received his endorsement and co-operation.

Richardson's Geology, including Mineralogy and Palæontology. Revised and enlarged, by Dr. T. WRIGHT. *Upwards of 400 Illustrations.*

Schouw's Earth, Plants, and Man; and Kobell's Sketches from the Mineral Kingdom. Translated by A. HENFREY, F.R.S. *Coloured Map of the Geography of Plants.*

Smith's (Pye) Geology and Scripture; or, The Relation between the Holy Scriptures and Geological Science.

Stanley's Classified Synopsis of the Principal Painters of the Dutch and Flemish Schools.

Staunton's Chess-player's Handbook. *Numerous Diagrams.*

——— **Chess Praxis.** A Supplement to the Chess-player's Handbook. Containing all the most important modern improvements in the Openings, illustrated by actual Games; a revised Code of Chess Laws; and a Selection of Mr. Morphy's Games in England and France. 5s.

Staunton's Chess-player's Companion. Comprising a new Treatise on Odds, Collection of Match Games, and a Selection of Original Problems.

———— **Chess Tournament of 1851.** *Numerous Illustrations.*

Stockhardt's Principles of Chemistry, exemplified in a series of simple experiments. Based upon the German work of Professor STOCKHARDT, and Edited by C. W. HEATON, Professor of Chemistry at Charing Cross Hospital. *Upwards of* 270 *Illustrations.*

Ure's (Dr. A.) Cotton Manufacture of Great Britain, systematically investigated; with an introductory view of its comparative state in Foreign Countries. New Edition, revised by P. L. SIMMONDS. *One hundred and fifty Illustrations.* In 2 vols.

———— **Philosophy of Manufactures;** or, An Exposition of the Factory System of Great Britain. Continued by P. L. SIMMONDS. 7s. 6d.

REFERENCE LIBRARY.

25 Vols. at various prices.

Blair's Chronological Tables, Revised and Enlarged. Comprehending the Chronology and History of the World, from the earliest times. By J. WILLOUGHBY ROSSE. Double Volume. 10s.; or, half-bound, 10s. 6d.

Clark's (Hugh) Introduction to Heraldry. *With nearly* 1000 *Illustrations.* 18*th Edition.* Revised and enlarged by J. R. PLANCHÉ, Rouge Croix. 5s. Or, with all the Illustrations coloured, 15s.

Chronicles of the Tombs. A Collection of Remarkable Epitaphs. By T. J. PETTIGREW, F.R.S., F.S.A. 5s.

Handbook of Domestic Medicine. Popularly arranged. By Dr. HENRY DAVIES. 700 pages. With complete Index. 5s.

———— **Games.** By various Amateurs and Professors. Comprising treatises on all the principal Games of chance, skill, and manual dexterity. In all, above 40 games (the Whist, Draughts, and Billiards being especially comprehensive). Edited by H. G. BOHN. *Illustrated by numerous Diagrams.* 5s.

———— **Proverbs.** Comprising all Ray's English Proverbs, with additions; his Foreign Proverbs; and an Alphabetical Index. 5s.

Humphrey's Coin Collector's Manual. A popular Introduction to the Study of Coins. *Highly finished Engravings.* In 2 vols. 10s.

Index of Dates. Comprehending the principal Facts in the Chronology and History of the World, from the earliest time, alphabetically arranged. By J. W. ROSSE. Double volume, 10s.; or, half-bound, 10s. 6d.

Lowndes' Bibliographer's Manual of English Literature. New Edition, enlarged, by H. G. BOHN. Parts I. to X. (A to Z). 3s. 6d. each. Part XI. (the Appendix Volume). 5s. Or the 11 parts in 4 vols. half morocco, 2l. 2s.

Polyglot of Foreign Proverbs. With English Translations, and a General Index, bringing the whole into parallels, by H. G. BOHN. 5s.

Political Cyclopædia. In 4 vols. 3s. 6d. each.

———— Also in 2 vols. bound. 15s.

Smith's (Archdeacon) Complete Collection of Synonyms and Antonyms. 5s.

The Epigrammatists. Selections from the Epigrammatic Literature of Ancient, Mediæval, and Modern Times. With Notes, Observations, Illustrations, and an Introduction. By the Rev. HENRY PHILIP DODD, M.A., of Pembroke College, Oxford. Second Edition, revised and considerably enlarged; containing many new Epigrams, principally of an amusing character. 6s.

Wheeler's (W. A., M.A.) Dictionary of Noted Names of Fictitious Persons and Places. 5s.

Wright's (T.) Dictionary of Obsolete and Provincial English. In 2 vols. 5s. each; or half-bound in 1 vol., 10s. 6d.

www.ingramcontent.com/pod-product-compliance
Lightning Source LLC
Chambersburg PA
CBHW021423300426
44114CB00010B/612